Britain and the Greek Economic Crisis
1944–1947

BRITAIN AND THE GREEK ECONOMIC CRISIS 1944–1947

FROM LIBERATION TO THE
TRUMAN DOCTRINE

Athanasios Lykogiannis

UNIVERSITY OF MISSOURI PRESS
COLUMBIA AND LONDON

Library of Congress Cataloging-in-Publication Data

Lykogiannis, Athanasios.
  Britain and the Greek economic crisis, 1944–1947 : from liberation to the Truman
  Doctrine / Athanasios Lykogiannis.
    p.   cm.
  Originally presented as the author's thesis (doctoral)—London School of Economics,
  1999.
  Includes bibliographical references and index.
  ISBN 0-8262-1422-3
    1. Greece—Economic conditions—1918–1974.   2. Greece—Economic policy—1918–
1974.   3. Greece—Politics and government—1935–1967.   4. Greece—Foreign economic
relations—Great Britain.   5. Great Britain—Foreign economic relations—Greece.
I. Title.
HC295 .L95 2002
330.9495'074—dc21

                                                                          2002028796

⊗™ This paper meets the requirements of the
American National Standard for Permanence of Paper
for Printed Library Materials, Z39.48, 1984.

DESIGNER: KRISTIE LEE
TYPESETTER: BOOKCOMP, INC.
PRINTER AND BINDER: THOMSON-SHORE, INC.
TYPEFACE: MINION

For my parents

A N D

for Robert Boyce and Simon Niziol,
who furnished immense help

CONTENTS

ACKNOWLEDGMENTS

In preparing this book, originally a doctoral dissertation defended at the London School of Economics (LSE) on July 12, 1999, I received support from a number of individuals and institutions. Financial assistance came from several sources. These included the Scholarships Office of the LSE, the Royal Historical Society, the Hellenic Foundation, and Crafoordska Stiftelsen. I would also like to acknowledge the assistance of the staffs of the National Archives and Records Administration in Washington, D.C., the Bank of England Archive, the Public Record Office at Kew, the British Library of Political and Economic Science, the Imperial War Museum in London, the National Museum of Labour History in Manchester, the Library of the Bank of Greece, the Photographic Archive of the Benaki Museum, the Hellenic Literary and Historical Archive, the Historical Archive of the National Bank of Greece, and the British Embassy in Athens. They made available to me a mass of unpublished documents and published materials, and their helpfulness made working with them a pleasure.

Parts of this work have appeared elsewhere in different forms. A segment was read before an international conference at King's College London (KCL) that focused on "Domestic and International Aspects of the Greek Civil War," to be published in a volume edited by the organizers, Dr. Philip Carabott of KCL and Dr. Thanasis Sfikas of the University of Central Lancashire. To both I express my gratitude. Another part was presented at the MGSA (Modern Greek Studies Association) 30th Anniversary Symposium at Princeton University. Finally, I am grateful to Professor Susan Buck Sutton and the Johns Hopkins University Press for permission to reprint here my article published previously in the *Journal of Modern Greek Studies.*

A special word of thanks is due to Professor Alan Milward of the European University Institute, without whose initial encouragement and critical insight during my first year of study at the LSE this work would never have been conceived. Others who read all or parts of the manuscript and made countless helpful suggestions include Professor Richard Clogg of Oxford University, Professor John O. Iatrides of Southern Connecticut State University, Professor Forrest Capie of City University, Dr. George Petrochilos of Coventry University, and Professor Nicos Mouzelis, Dr. Max-Stephan Schulze, and Dr. Spyros Economides of the LSE. I also wish to thank Dr. Rena Zafiriou for hours of stimulating discussion and helpful suggestions, and whose generosity made possible part of my stay in Washington, D.C. I am grateful to her, as I am to Mr. Kostas Papachrysanthou, Mr. David Kessler, and Mr. James C. Warren, Jr.

Above all, I am deeply indebted to Dr. Robert Boyce of the LSE, who graciously read the manuscript several times and furnished the close and critical reading that can come only from a perceptive supervisor. I would also like to express my deep gratitude to a former colleague from the LSE, Dr. Simon Niziol, for furnishing superb editorial guidance and answering numerous inquiries by phone, by mail, and by personal conversations. Last but not least I must thank my parents, without whose encouragement, understanding, patience, and financial support this work would never have seen the light of day. I alone, of course, am responsible for any shortcomings or errors in the text.

ABBREVIATIONS

ACO	Autonomous Currant Organization
AFHQ	Allied Forces Headquarters
AGIS	Anglo-Greek Information Service
AMAG	American Mission for Aid to Greece
BE	Bank of England
BEM	British Economic Mission
BMA	British Military Authority
CAB	Cabinet
DRF	Drachma Reconstruction Fund
DSR	Department of State Records
EAC	Economic Advisory Committee
EAM	National Liberation Front
EDES	National Democratic Hellenic League
ELAS	National People's Liberation Army
EKKA	National and Social Liberation
ERP	European Recovery Program
ESC	Economic and Supply Committee
Ex-Im Bank	Export-Import Bank
FAO	Food and Agriculture Organization
FEA	Foreign Economic Administration
FO	Foreign Office
FRBNY	Federal Reserve Bank of New York
FRUS	Foreign Relations of the United States

FTA	Foreign Trade Administration
GCC	Greek Commercial Cooperation
GRCC	Greek Reconstruction Claims Committee
HANBG	Historical Archive of the National Bank of Greece
IBRD	International Bank for Reconstruction and Development
IFC	International Financial Commission
IMF	International Monetary Fund
JCC	Joint Coordinating Committee
JPC	Joint Policy Committee
KEPES	Central Committee for the Protection of Domestic Wheat Production
KKE	Communist Party of Greece
KVA	Kyriakos Varvaressos Archive
LBG	Library of the Bank of Greece
MESC	Middle East Supply Center
ML	Military Liaison
MLHQ	Military Liaison Headquarters
NARA	National Archives and Records Administration
NBG	National Bank of Greece
PEEA	Political Committee of National Liberation
PRO	Public Record Office
SACMED	Supreme Allied Command in the Mediterranean
T	Treasury
UNRRA	United Nations Relief and Rehabilitation Administration
WO	War Office

TABLES

ILLUSTRATIONS

Frontispiece: Crowds assembled to hear the prime minister's first major speech after liberation in Syntagma Square, Athens, October 18, 1944 (Photograph courtesy of the Imperial War Museum, London).

P. 5. Galloping inflation. Five hundred million drachmae for an egg, November 9, 1944 (Photograph courtesy of the Imperial War Museum, London).

P. 49. Prime Minister Papandreou and the EAM ministers of his National Unity Government, September 2, 1944. From left: Elias Tsirimokos, minister of national economy; Angelos Angelopoulos, deputy minister of finance; Papandreou; Miltiadis Porfyrogenis, minister of labor; Ioannis Zevgos, minister of agriculture; Nikolaos Askoutsis, minister of communications (Photograph courtesy of the Hellenic Literary and Historical Archive, Athens).

P. 50. A British sniper fires on ELAS positions from the Acropolis, December 10, 1944 (Photograph courtesy of the Imperial War Museum, London).

P. 52. George II, King of the Hellenes, September 1946 (Photographic Archive of the Benaki Museum, Athens. Photo: Dimitrios Charisiadis).

P. 55. Three Red Cross ships bringing aid to Greece, November 2, 1944 (Photograph courtesy of the Imperial War Museum, London).

P. 56. Signing the UNRRA Agreement. After the ceremony, on the steps of the Palace, March 1, 1945. From left to right: R. G. A. Jackson, Lincoln MacVeagh, Ioannis Sophianopoulos, General Plastiras, R. F. Hendrickson, Reginald Leeper, M. Bellen (Photograph courtesy of the Imperial War Museum, London).

P. 63. Prime Minister Papandreou helps to load the first sack of flour into a truck brought in by ML, while Lieutenant General Scobie looks on, October 21, 1944 (Photograph courtesy of the Imperial War Museum, London).

P. 66. Sir Reginald Leeper, British ambassador to Greece, 1943–1946 (Photograph courtesy of the British Embassy, Athens).

P. 67. Sir Clifford Norton, British ambassador to Greece, 1946–1951 (Photograph courtesy of the British Embassy, Athens).

Britain and the Greek Economic Crisis 1944–1947

INTRODUCTION

In October 1944, after Greece's liberation from the German occupiers, the National Unity Government took power. It faced an inflationary crisis of a magnitude sufficient to tax the competence of any government. Although it could count on considerable assistance and advice from its Allies, much depended on Greece's own actions and its determination to restore economic normality. Success was meager, and by the time the British pulled out in the spring of 1947, economic stability remained elusive despite all the aid and advice. In the Greek case, political factors played a crucial role in shaping the attempts to stabilize the drachma and create a basis for long-term recovery, offering an excellent example that although hyperinflation and stabilization are essentially economic issues, political realities need to be appreciated in order to understand the particular course that both processes can take.

This book does not attempt to offer a definitive account of Greek history between 1944 and 1947, but seeks to contribute to a better understanding of this complex and troubled period by concentrating on Anglo-Greek interaction on economic matters. A vast body of literature has already dealt with the Greek crisis, most of which has concentrated solely on political developments. Such works, frequently reflecting the political stance of their authors, usually have sought to explain the course of events in terms of political motives and actions alone, with little emphasis on the dynamics of economic problems. Economic issues have thus tended to be pushed into the background. This book is a work of political history combining elements of economic history and international relations, and seeks to highlight economic issues by addressing four major questions. First, it places the developments of 1944–1947, particularly the hyperinflation and the failed stabilization attempts, within the proper context of Greek economic history, as yet another episode of destitution and foreign tutelage in an underdeveloped country with chronic budgetary and balance of payments deficits. Second, it analyzes the interplay of economic and political factors that aggravated and prolonged the crisis: the extensive polarization of Greek society, and the weakness, timidity, and ineptitude of the country's governments. Third, it assesses British involvement in the episode: the quality of measures recommended to the Greeks, the constraints facing British advisers in the country, and the reasons for the ultimate failure of British intervention. Fourth, it seeks to contrast and compare the two periods of western tutelage of Greece: that of the

British from 1944 to 1947, and of the Americans from 1947 to 1948. The book aims to address these questions in a dispassionate manner, by treating economic issues on their own merits rather than as moral choices dictated by any particular political outlook.

The Structure of the Book

Chapter 1 introduces concepts crucial for assessing the performance of the key players in the Greek economic crisis. A brief description of the causes and features of hyperinflation, together with a summary of the measures normally used to restore currency stability, offers a yardstick with which to judge the effectiveness of Greek government actions and the foreign advice proffered. To make sense of the underlying themes of British advice, the chapter concludes with a section on the British wartime experience of economic management at home and elsewhere.

Chapter 2 seeks to identify the long-term trends, attitudes, and developments, especially the broad patterns of Greek economic and political life prior to 1944, that were to influence the course of events after liberation. Many of the decisive features of the 1944–1947 period had their roots in past experience. The chapter also describes the factors influencing British attitudes toward Greece and the methods the British employed to achieve a changing set of objectives, with special reference to the political and financial dilemmas involved.

Chapter 3 describes the events following the end of the Nazi occupation. Despite its euphoric public reception, the new government in Athens was soon overwhelmed by the sheer scale of the crisis, and the British were forced to take a much more involved approach to economic issues. The chapter concentrates on the policy choices and performance of successive post-liberation governments, and the implementation and outcome of the first stabilization scheme of November 1944.

Chapter 4 considers the course of the so-called Varvaressos Experiment. Kyriakos Varvaressos, the governor of the Bank of Greece, had spent the war in London and was well versed in the British approach to inflation. The British were thus keen to see him given a chance to direct the Greek government's efforts to restore economic stability after the disappointing showing of the first months following liberation. After lengthy pressure from the British, Varvaressos entered the government and immediately launched a series of reforms containing several orthodox anti-inflationary measures. Within months, widespread hostility to the package left Varvaressos completely isolated, and few of his reforms survived his resignation.

Chapter 5 describes the gradual British realization that a more comprehensive approach was called for, a process culminating in the London Agreement of January 1946, which created the framework for Anglo-Greek interaction until the British pulled out in the spring of 1947. The problems encountered by two institutions arising out of the London Agreement—the British Economic Mission and the Currency Committee—underlined the weakness of the entire British involvement in Greece: the lack of resources to tackle problems or encourage cooperation, and the lack of power to enforce compliance with British advice.

Chapter 6 deals with the American stance toward Greece. The British consistently sought American backing for their Greek policy, while Greek officials were anxious to secure extensive financial assistance from Washington. In both cases, the United States was reluctant to become more actively involved. This position changed radically once Washington became convinced of the threat of communist expansionism. The Americans took over the British role in Greece in the summer of 1947 and immediately encountered the same problems that had thwarted the British for so long. Despite material resources and powers far beyond those of their British predecessors, American advisers were to find that stability remained elusive.

As each chapter contains its own lengthy conclusions in which many points are explored in depth, the concluding chapter merely gathers together the main lessons of the Greek economic crisis of 1944–1947.

A Note on Sources

The subject is examined principally in the light of British and American archival sources. The originality of this book lies in the focus rather than the deployment of large amounts of new information. Many of the British official documents consulted, particularly those of the Foreign Office, have already been used extensively by historians primarily concerned with the political aspects of the Anglo-Greek relations. Nevertheless, a huge number of Foreign Office papers hitherto ignored by the majority of previous researchers have been examined, together with Treasury, Cabinet, and War Office documents in the Public Record Office at Kew, the Bank of England Archive, and internal Labour Party records held in the National Museum of Labour History in Manchester. In the United States, considerable use was made of State Department records deposited in the National Archives and Records Administration in Washington, D.C. These have been supplemented by published collections of U.S. diplomatic papers. Use has also been made of doctoral dissertations by American participants in the events after 1944—Gardner Patterson and Charles Coombs. Both have been almost entirely ignored by previous researchers.

For records held in Greece, the book has been one of the first to consult the Kyriakos Varvaressos Archive at the Bank of Greece. The author was also able to contact surviving participants, including Dr. Rena Zafiriou, onetime assistant to Varvaressos, and Mr. David Kessler, former member of the British Economic Mission in Greece. Both provided useful comments, as did Mr. James Warren, Jr., who served as chief, Import Program Office, the Marshall Plan Mission to Greece from 1950 to 1954. In addition to the primary sources, the book has made use of a huge amount of secondary literature on the Greek crisis as well as several historical and theoretical works on the causes, course, and control of hyperinflation.

1

HYPERINFLATION AND STABILIZATION

One of the main problems facing the National Unity Government after liberation from German occupation was the dramatic depreciation of the drachma. Whereas the note circulation had averaged 7.6 billion drachmae during the period from September 1, 1938, to August 31, 1939, by November 10, 1944, it had increased 826,308,303 times and reached a figure of 6,280 quadrillion drachmae

Galloping inflation. Five hundred million drachmae for an egg, November 9, 1944. Photograph courtesy of the Imperial War Museum, London.

(Table 2.4). In order to appreciate the gravity of the crisis, it is necessary to understand the concept of hyperinflation, while the preoccupations of the British economic and financial advisers can be explained only with reference to the anti-inflationary policies of the British at home and abroad. The first section of this chapter therefore offers a brief theoretical description and historical survey of hyperinflation and stabilization. The second section describes the British wartime experience of combating inflation at home and in the Middle East.

Inflation, Hyperinflation, and Stabilization

In basic terms, inflation is a fall in the value of money, which occurs when purchasing power persistently runs ahead of the output of goods and services available to the public, resulting in a spiral of price and wage rises. In cost-push inflation, rising wages are the main influence, while in the demand-pull variety, a decrease in the availability of consumer goods is the chief cause. While a modest degree of "creeping" inflation has been the norm for most countries in recent times, there have been several occurrences of "runaway" or "galloping" inflation, otherwise known as hyperinflation, where the fall in the value of money has reached extreme proportions. Hyperinflation is a severely disruptive phenomenon, creating chaos and uncertainty in everyday life, and impoverishing those with savings or fixed incomes.

Economists have never agreed upon a single definition of hyperinflation expressed in terms of the rate of price rises, but Cagan's classic yardstick of 50 percent per month remains the most widely accepted standard. Other definitions involving annual rates of 1,000 percent would eliminate all but one example in history, although a recent survey by Capie suggests the term "very rapid inflation" be used to cover any case where prices rise by 100 percent in any single year. The most famous cases of hyperinflation occurred after the two world wars, with Poland, Germany, Austria, Hungary, and Russia between 1919 and 1925, and Greece, China, and Hungary in the 1940s. The Hungarian situation after World War II produced the highest rate of inflation ever recorded, with prices rising by 3×10^{25} between July 1945 and August 1946. Capie's definition allows the inclusion of three pre–twentieth century cases: the United States during the War of Independence, Revolutionary France, and the Confederacy during the American Civil War. Hyperinflation is not a solely historical phenomenon, as the number of cases continues to grow, with new occurrences in Latin America and elsewhere.[1]

1. F. H. Capie, "Conditions in Which Very Rapid Inflation Has Appeared," 4, 9–27, 35–50.

Capie's historical survey shows that despite gaps in the statistical data available, two features were apparent in all cases: the enormous growth of the money supply in the form of an unbacked paper currency, and persistent and substantial budget deficits. The two are clearly interrelated: the governments concerned had sought to overcome a shortfall in revenue by printing money. Moreover, a qualitative approach finds that severe political or social unrest was present in all but one of the historical examples, while even in recent times hyperinflation has usually developed in countries with social unrest or at least relatively weak government. However, even if political and social instability have invariably accompanied rapid inflation, they cannot be regarded as sufficient causes in themselves. As Capie points out, social unrest and even revolution have not automatically led to rapid inflation. After 1918, Czechoslovakia and Latvia faced problems similar to those which accompanied hyperinflation elsewhere in Europe, but were able to prevent serious disruption by implementing strict fiscal policies. The absence of decisive action to restrain inflationary tendencies seems to be crucial—hyperinflation usually follows when disruptive factors are allowed to run unchecked for "quite a while" without appropriate countermeasures.[2]

Whatever the implications of the qualitative similarities between past occurrences of hyperinflation, the invariable presence of large budget deficits and rapid growth of the money supply makes it clear what the priorities of any stabilization package should be. Thus although stabilization schemes have often contained a wide range of measures, restricting monetary growth—refusing to print more money—is crucial if hyperinflation is to be overcome. This is far from straightforward, as the monetary expansion that fuels hyperinflation is itself a consequence of the government's dependence on new issues of paper money, and the revenue involved may be difficult to replace. In such circumstances, only a considerable effort to reduce budget deficits can remove the necessity for further recourse to the printing press. This would normally require increases in tax and other revenues, as well as stricter controls over expenditure. Neither may be easy to achieve, particularly if the government is faced with urgent expenditure needs or if the taxation system is inefficient.

Dornbusch et al. stress the need for a thorough reform of the taxation system aimed at creating a broad tax base with moderate rates, and emphasize that the law must be enforced. Moreover, tax rates need to be fully indexed to inflation, so that the value of tax revenue is not eroded during the inevitable lags in collection. They

---

2. Ibid., 16, 36, 44; R. Dornbusch, F. Sturzenegger, and H. Wolf, "Extreme Inflation: Dynamics and Stabilization," 3.

cite the example of Mexico, where fiscal stability was restored following the careful auditing of higher-income groups. Another important consideration is whether the government possesses the political will to impose strict fiscal policies. It is clear that any "government that is unwilling to balance the budget is hardly likely to do so." One possible restraint on money creation is the presence of a central bank with the powers to refuse limitless loans to the government. Nevertheless, such an institution can be circumvented. Evasions of central bank restrictions can often take bizarre forms, such as the Polish case in 1925 when the Treasury continued to create money by exercising its right to mint coins.[3] As the Greek case will demonstrate, discipline is nonexistent when the central bank does not act independently.

Several other measures to end hyperinflation have proved useful but not essential. These include foreign loans either to underwrite budget deficits until public finances can be restored to equilibrium or to prevent a depletion of foreign currency reserves. Such external support can play the important role of lending credibility to the stabilization package. The creation of a new means of exchange to replace the former discredited currency can provide the psychological advantage of a new start and gives the government control over the size of the initial post-stabilization money stock, but may have only symbolic value if other problems remain unaddressed.

More controversial measures include controls over prices and wages. Efficient price controls could suppress inflation during periods of commodity shortages, while wage ceilings could prevent excessive pay demands from adding to pressure on prices. Controls over prices have been attacked as a device merely postponing rather than overcoming inflation, requiring a vast bureaucracy to implement and likely to encourage evasion and the growth of a black market. Nevertheless, such controls can be effective if properly administered against a backdrop of popular support for the government's actions, as demonstrated by the British and American experience during World War II. It has been emphasized that all such control measures are not a solution in themselves, but would have to supplement the main tasks of monetary restraint and fiscal reform.[4]

Apart from individual measures, all stabilization schemes are ultimately dependent on "credibility," the ability to convince the public that the government is totally

3. Dornbusch et al., "Extreme Inflation," 11, 55–56; R. Dornbusch and S. Fischer, "Stopping Hyperinflations Past and Present," 20.

4. H. Rockoff, "Price and Wage Controls in Four Wartime Periods," 382; H. Rockoff, *Drastic Measures: A History of Wage and Price Controls in the United States*, 246. For a summary of effective controls over prices and wages, see J. Butterworth, *The Theory of Price Control and Black Markets*, 11–16.

TABLE 1.1. Summary of Stabilization Measures

Measures	Importance/Conditions for Success
Budget Reforms	Crucial Political will to reduce budget deficits Improvements to taxation system Restraint over expenditure Examples: (G) Budget balanced after a few months (P1) Temporary improvement (P2) Surplus achieved (A) Deficit reduced
Central Bank	Power and willingness to refuse money creation Examples: (G, P2, A) Restrictions on new issues to government (P1) Restrictions on new issues but Treasury still allowed to mint coins
Foreign Loans	Useful but not essential Examples: (G) Dawes loan in 1924 (P1) Loan granted (P2, A) Loans accompanied by foreign supervision
New Currency	Symbolic but not essential Examples: (G, P1) New currency issued (A) New currency issued later (P2) New currency not issued
Price Controls	Controversial - importance under question Popular compliance or proper enforcement Efficient administration Control over supply and distribution Examples: no controls imposed
Wage Controls	Controversial - importance under question Popular compliance Examples: no controls imposed

Summarized from Dornbusch and Fischer, "Stopping Hyperinflations Past and Present," 41, Table 17.

Key: (G) = Germany 1923   (P1) = Poland 1924 (unsuccessful)
(A) = Austria 1922   (P2) = Poland 1926/27

committed to ending the conditions causing or prolonging hyperinflation, and that all necessary steps will be taken to achieve that goal. As already stated, foreign support or the symbolic introduction of a new currency can play an important role in this, but the creation of sufficient popular optimism will largely depend on the prevailing political circumstances.

Successful stabilizations in the past have contained varying permutations of these features. Almost every successful stabilization saw substantial reductions or the elimination of budget deficits. In most cases, legal restrictions on new note issues, enforced by either a central bank or an external authority, were a significant factor in imposing the necessary discipline on governments. Actual or promised foreign loans were a feature of all the pre-1939 episodes, though they were not always necessary. Loans were usually linked with an element of foreign supervision. Apart from the famous German case of 1923, currency reform was rarely employed. Neither price nor wage controls were a part of the prewar packages, but were attempted during several stabilizations in the 1980s.[5]

The British Experience at Home and Abroad

The effectiveness of the British approach to managing scarcity and controlling inflation during World War II is generally acknowledged. The British experience, not only at home but also through international institutions such as the Middle East Supply Center (MESC), is worth recounting in greater detail, as it provided a ready-made set of potential remedies once British officials were faced with the daunting task of proposing solutions for the Greek economic crisis of 1944–1947.

The sole priority for Britain was to win the war by fully mobilizing its resources for military purposes: by absorbing a large proportion of the population into the armed forces or war-related industries, and by restricting the output of consumer goods in order to concentrate on armament production. As Milward points out, warfare and inflation have been inseparable in modern history. The British case was no exception, with policies creating two ideal preconditions for inflation: rising money incomes due to both the expansion of the labor force and the lengthening of hours of work, and reduced quantities of purchasable goods.[6]

These dangers had not been sufficiently dealt with during World War I, resulting in an unprecedented degree of inflation (roughly 100 percent between July 1914 and 1918) which lasted until 1920. The price rises contributed to extensive labor unrest, disrupting industrial production and raising social tensions. With Nazi Germany posing a far greater threat after 1939, it was clear that all the problems of the previous war would be vastly magnified during the current conflict, and that far more extensive action was required from the government. The initial response was fairly leisurely. An Excess Profits Tax, designed to capture 60 percent of the increased profits of armament manufacturers, was introduced soon after the declaration of war, but income tax was left unchanged until the budget of April 1940. Although this raised the rate of the Excess Profits Tax to 100 percent and the standard rate of

5. Dornbusch and Fischer, "Stopping Hyperinflations Past and Present," 40–44; T. J. Sargent, "The Ends of Four Big Inflations," 41–97.

6. P. Howlett, "The Wartime Economy, 1939–1945," vol. 3, 6, 10–11; A. S. Milward, *War, Economy and Society, 1939–1945*, 105.

income tax from 27.5 to 42.5 percent, yields from direct taxes still increased more slowly than those of indirect taxes until 1941.[7]

The turning point came in 1941, with the adoption of the Keynesian concepts of national income accounting and the twin-pronged attack on inflation. In the previous year, Keynes had underlined the inevitability of an "inflationary gap" between aggregate demand and aggregate supply in an economy mobilized for war production. Without government intervention, this gap would only be closed by an inflationary rise in prices. Hitherto, the Treasury had been unable to solve this problem, preoccupied as it was with the notion of "what the tax-payer could bear." Instead, Keynes suggested that the Treasury should calculate national income and the level of revenue the government required in order to close the inflationary gap. Excess demand would have to be absorbed by extra taxation and forced savings. Keynes went to work in the Treasury in the summer of 1940, and his ideas were adopted in the budget of April 1941.[8]

This was the first budget to offer a survey of the economy rather than a simple balance sheet of government finances. It was also the first to be conceived in national income terms, and employed two sets of measures to counter the twin causes of the inflationary gap. Increased taxation and forced savings were used to combat demand-pull inflation, while cost-of-living subsidies were introduced to reduce the likelihood of cost-push inflation. Forced savings were achieved mainly by restricting various investment opportunities and creating sufficient attractive government bonds. At the same time, all forms of taxation were increased. The standard rate of income tax was raised to 50 percent, while personal allowances were reduced. Surtax for the highest earners was raised to a huge 19s. 6d. in the pound, an increase of 97.5 percent. Purchase tax was also expanded as a means of further restricting consumption. Along with new forms and levels of taxation, the tax-gathering machinery was also improved considerably. In September 1943 the Pay As You Earn (PAYE) scheme was introduced, greatly simplifying the collection of income tax.[9]

The new approach produced impressive results. Income tax yields more than trebled by the end of the war, while the Excess Profits Tax delivered an average 450 million pounds per annum between 1943 and 1945. Accordingly, direct taxes as a proportion of ordinary revenue increased from 52 percent in 1939 to nearly 63

7. P. Dewey, *War and Progress: Britain 1914–1945*, 31, 40–41, 284–285.

8. J. M. Keynes, *How to Pay for the War: A Radical Plan for the Chancellor of the Exchequer;* Howlett, "Wartime Economy, 1939–1945," vol. 3, 14–15.

9. Howlett, "Wartime Economy, 1939–1945," vol. 3, 15–16; G. C. Peden, *British Economic and Social Policy: Lloyd George to Margaret Thatcher*, 134.

percent in 1945, and financed 55 percent of the government's enormous wartime expenditure. This reduced the need to create huge levels of internal and external debt, and virtually eliminated the dangers of money creation to pay for the war. In fact, only 2.7 percent of government spending was financed by resorting to the printing press.[10]

The immediate inflationary threat was also reduced—or rather replaced by disguised inflation—thanks to an extensive program of subsidies affecting foodstuffs, rent, fuel, and certain services. Some temporary food subsidies had been introduced in December 1939, but it was the 1941 budget that advocated the widespread use of subsidies to stabilize the cost of living by controlling the prices of key commodities in the official basket. This measure proved expensive, with costs rising from 47 million pounds in 1939 to 302 million pounds in 1945—but it produced the desired effect. While the admittedly imperfect Board of Trade cost-of-living index rose from 100 in 1938 to 128 by 1941, it remained stable thereafter, rising to only 130 in 1945. Although the more reliable wholesale price index showed an increase of 67 percent in the same period, demonstrating that the threat of cost-push inflation had been merely deferred rather than overcome, the problem had at least been minimized for the duration of the war.[11]

While many prices were held down by means of subsidies, physical controls were also employed for this purpose. As early as November 1939 the Price of Goods Act froze prices of certain household goods and items of clothing. During the same period, the Rent and Mortgage Interest Restrictions Act froze rents at prewar levels for all properties below a specified rateable value. The next major legislation came with the 1941 Goods and Services (Price Control) Act, which contained provisions to restrict price rises. Unlike subsidies, which did not directly affect returns to sellers, formal price controls required enforcement and compliance. The former was applied by price regulation committees, and strengthened by the threat of punishment (up to three months imprisonment for a first offense) for noncompliance. The effectiveness of price controls was bolstered by command over supply and distribution, demonstrated by an elaborate though efficient rationing system, which came to embrace a large range of goods. Some authors assert that it was the rationing system which allowed the whole control package to work so well. Shortly after the war, one study suggested that popular compliance or the "will to co-operate" was the main determinant of success, but subsequent historians point

10. Howlett, "Wartime Economy, 1939–1945," vol. 3, 16–17; Dewey, *War and Progress*, 284–86.

11. Dewey, *War and Progress*, 286–87; Howlett, "Wartime Economy, 1939–1945," vol. 3, 17; F. H. Capie and G. E. Wood, "The Anatomy of a Wartime Inflation: Britain, 1939–1945," 31.

to the complete integration of control measures, amounting to a considerable degree of regimentation of the entire economy, as the crucial factor.[12]

Apart from control measures enacted at home, the British also assumed a large degree of control over the coordination of commodity supply and demand for other countries. The most notable of the formal arrangements was the MESC, established in the spring of 1941. This was a response to the closure of the Mediterranean following Italy's entry into the war. As early as November 1940, reduced imports and considerable purchases of local goods by British forces led to severe shortages of civilian commodities in Egypt, creating the threat of economic chaos, inflation, and ultimate civil unrest. With the entire region likely to face similar problems, the strategic implications were enormous. The British thus expanded their responsibility for Egypt into a collaborative program overseeing procurement and shipping allocations for the whole eastern Mediterranean and the Middle East. At different periods the MESC covered a range of territories of varying status, including British colonies, dependencies and mandates, Allies such as Yugoslavia and Greece, and independent neutrals such as Turkey and Iran.

The main task of the MESC was to minimize the risk of catastrophic food shortages arising from curtailed peacetime trade. With all supplies from outside the region having to be diverted around the Cape, pressures on scarce shipping ensured that food imports would fall far below prewar levels. In addition, the demands of the armed forces further reduced the quantity of goods available for civilian purposes. To avert famine, the MESC promoted the reorganization of agriculture throughout the region to increase food production, encouraged greater reliance on interregional trade, and coordinated import programs and the maintenance and allocation of reserve stocks.

Apart from the strategic planning involved with such an undertaking, implementing the MESC programs entailed applying a series of practical control measures over the supply and distribution of foodstuffs. Food was collected directly from producers and passed on to consumers via rationing schemes, with both the purchase and sale taking place at fixed prices. Although statistics on the degree of reduced consumption are patchy, no serious famine occurred in the region, but occasional bread riots did take place in Persia and Syria. Infant mortality statistics for Egypt, Cyprus, and Palestine demonstrate that apart from a major crisis in 1942,

12. Capie and Wood, "Anatomy of a Wartime Inflation," 31, 35; L. Robbins, *The Economic Problem in Peace and War,* 45; G. Mills and H. Rockoff, "Compliance with Price Controls in the United States and the United Kingdom during World War II," 212–13.

figures for 1941–1945 were below the prewar average, suggesting that the MESC's management of food and agriculture was clearly successful in helping to prevent a potential disaster.

Although the MESC initially had been concerned with achieving sufficient levels of military and civilian supplies, it soon became involved in combating inflation, the inevitable consequence of commodity shortages combined with high levels of military expenditure. As Table 1.2 shows, prices had risen by at least 50 percent above prewar levels by the end of 1941. The only countries to escape inflation were those without paper money—Saudi Arabia, Ethiopia, and Yemen.

The British response was to organize a series of conferences to establish a package of measures to combat inflation. These included the familiar policies already implemented in Britain—rationing, price controls, and tax increases. All were applied to varying degrees, depending partly on the individual circumstance of each country and partly on the efficiency of the respective administrations. The British felt generally satisfied with the results achieved. As Table 1.2 demonstrates, between 1941 and 1944 not one of the countries concerned experienced an uncontrollable degree of inflation. In Egypt, Sudan, and Palestine wholesale prices kept well below corresponding increases in money circulation, and they did not run too far ahead in the other three countries.

A final measure to combat inflation, recounted here in some detail because of the later British experience in Greece, was the sale of gold to the public. This was intended to mop up surplus purchasing power, thus reducing the pressure on scarce commodities; to acquire local currency for military expenditure, thereby slowing down the growth of circulation; and to bring down the price of gold throughout the region in the hope of generating a fall in the prices of other goods. The move was not undertaken without considerable resistance, particularly from within the Bank of England. Some officials felt that the sale of gold would undermine confidence in local paper currencies and even sterling, and that if governments in the Middle East demanded payments in gold for all purposes, the gold reserves of the sterling area

TABLE 1.2. Wholesale Prices and Money Supply in the Middle East, 1941-1944 (1939=100)

	Wholesale Prices		Money in Circulation	
	1941	1944	1941	1944
Egypt	150	273	183	452
Sudan	149	202	169	231
Palestine	184	297	153	496
Cyprus	266	473	165	468
Syria/Lebanon	361	812	183	733
Persia	143	500	192	468

Source: Lloyd, *Food and Inflation in the Middle East*, 179-87.

would soon prove inadequate. Others feared no such repercussions, believing that gold sales were unlikely to have any significant effect on prices. During 1943–1944, some 1.2 million ounces (equivalent to 5.1 million gold sovereigns) worth about 17 million pounds were sold. The British felt the measure to have been a success, contributing to a slow-down in the rate of inflation of all the countries concerned. They believed that the amount sold was little more than 10 percent of the total gold already in private hands throughout the region, and that there had been no undermining of local currencies.[13]

The British experience of combating inflation at home and abroad was reasonably successful given the difficult circumstances. At home, the combination of financial and physical controls went a long way toward allowing Britain to survive a ruinous war without severe inflation or large-scale social unrest provoked by commodity shortages. Even in the Middle East, British efforts enabled a degree of normality to be maintained. With many measures remaining in force throughout most of 1944–1947, and with the success of others fresh in the memory, it was hardly surprising that British authorities viewed the Greek economic crisis largely through the prism of their own experience and promoted similar policies as appropriate solutions to the country's problems.

13. This analysis is based on E. M. H. Lloyd, *Food and Inflation in the Middle East 1940–45*, 3, 74–82, 179–87, 208–44, 321–29. For more on the MESC, see P. W. T. Kingston, *Britain and the Politics of Modernization in the Middle East, 1945–1958*; M. W. Wilmington, "The Middle East Supply Center: A Reappraisal," 144–66.

2

POLITICAL AND
ECONOMIC BACKGROUND

To explain the phenomenon of Greek hyperinflation, it is sufficient to recount the developments of 1941–1944, when Greece was occupied by the Axis powers. At liberation, the returning Greek government inherited an economic disaster arising out of deliberate exploitation and mismanagement. However, a full explanation of the protracted return to normality requires an understanding of many features of Greek economic and political life from the nineteenth century onwards. The first section of this chapter seeks to identify the long-term trends, attitudes, and developments that were to influence the course of events after liberation. The second section concentrates specifically on the period after 1941, with particular emphasis on the economic, political, and psychological legacy of the occupation. The third section describes the factors influencing British attitudes toward Greece and the methods the British employed to achieve a changing set of objectives, with special reference to the political and economic dilemmas involved. The aim is not to produce an exhaustive study of any of the topics considered, but to throw light on the Greek response to the economic crisis of 1944–1947.

Economic and Political Trends up to World War II

The Nature of Greek Politics

In 1844, after barely a decade of independence, Greece adopted the institutions of parliamentary democracy. Twenty years later universal male suffrage was introduced. Despite the early adoption of a Western-style parliament, political life conspicuously failed to evolve along Western lines during the subsequent century.

Greek politics owed far more to rivalries between competing networks of personal allegiances than to disagreements over ideas, with the acquisition of power as an end in itself rather than as a means to pursue policies. While such relationships were commonplace in premodern states, they proved sufficiently adaptable in Greece to endure long after they had been superseded by broad-based mass politics in Western Europe. Instead of parties in the modern sense, the country possessed fluid configurations of coteries centered around notable individuals, held together by patronage rather than by any common cause. The absence of nonclientelistic parties allowed considerable scope for political horse-trading between individuals, cliques, and vested interests. With frequent shifts of allegiance and no party discipline, most governments were unstable and relatively short-lived. The need both to dispense and secure patronage proved an obstacle to formulating coherent policies, since it consumed a considerable portion of both the time and the energies of participants in the political game. Patronage politics ensured a system unresponsive to important changes both within and outside the country.

In a political world largely devoid of debates over issues, only two questions aroused any degree of passion. The first of these was the "Great Idea" (*Megali Idea*), which became virtually the dominant ideology of the newly emergent state. This advocated the creation of a "Greater Greece" embracing the whole nation. At first, the "Great Idea" was directed entirely toward the Ottoman Empire, and mutual distrust often erupted into open warfare. As the empire declined, the emergence of rival nationalisms with their own irredentist aspirations led to bloody struggles between the successor states. Although the preoccupation with the "Great Idea" yielded some concrete results in that Greece expanded from its original area of 48,000 square kilometers to 127,000 square kilometers by 1922, most of the territorial acquisitions were the result of Great Power bargaining at conference tables rather than feats of arms by the Greeks themselves. The "Great Idea" had many unfortunate consequences in that it diverted attention away from pressing internal issues and absorbed an inordinate proportion of the country's material and financial resources. Moreover, the intensification of local rivalries opened the door to Great Power intrigues within the region. A "Greater Greece" seemed close to fulfillment in 1920 with the territorial gains confirmed by the Treaty of Sèvres, but it collapsed in ruins two years later when a resurgent Turkey ejected Greek forces from the disputed areas. Although the military defeat was a profound shock that burdened Greece with more than a million refugees from Asia Minor, it also allowed the country to refocus on long-neglected domestic issues.

Apart from the "Great Idea," the most burning issue within Greek political life was the question of the powers of the monarchy. In 1864, resistance to the extension of royal power led to the deposition of the Bavarian king Otho. Thereafter, the matter lost its urgency but resurfaced with a vengeance during World War I, leading to the "National Schism" (*Ethnikos Dichasmos*), which was to poison Greek politics for decades to come. In 1914, conflicting views between Prime Minister Eleftherios Venizelos and King Constantine I over the choice of military alliances split the country and led to virtual civil war, culminating in the exile of the king. The republican victory was short-lived, as electoral defeat in 1920 led to the restoration of the monarchy. With the bitterness aroused by the schism proving ever more divisive, the republicans took advantage of the shock of 1922 to seize power once again. Two years later, the king was deposed and a republic was proclaimed.

As with the "Great Idea," the schism was to prove a dangerous and futile distraction obscuring all other issues. The role of the king succeeded in dividing the Greek political establishment into two hostile camps, formed around the Liberal and the Populist parties. Despite the intensity of the mutual hatred, the policy differences were far less fundamental than the depth of the division would suggest. Although the Liberals were largely republican, moderate, and advocates of modernization while the Populists were broadly royalist and generally right-wing, the dividing line was far from clear. Neither grouping could be said to derive from any coherent ideological position. The fluidity of the schism allowed ample scope for opportunism, notably on the part of several army officers able to switch sides as the occasion demanded. Despite the futility of the endless debates over the constitutional issue, the matter was never allowed to drop. Following political deadlock after 1932, a series of unsuccessful republican coups led to a counter-coup from royalist army officers, who suppressed the republic and restored the king yet again.

Thus by the mid-1930s, Greek politics had become trapped in a pointless cycle of recriminations and counter-recriminations from aging personalities increasingly out of touch with the demands posed by a changing world and a changing society. When several of the old protagonists passed away within months of each other, it seemed possible that a younger generation of politicians might lay aside the old quarrels to tackle more pressing problems. Given the growing disillusionment with traditional parties and democratic forms, as well as the apparent success of totalitarian regimes elsewhere in Europe, more radical solutions began to gain appeal.

The experience of the Communist Party of Greece (KKE) largely mirrored that of its counterparts in eastern and southeastern Europe. Originally formed as a socialist party in 1918, it affiliated with the Comintern and accepted the Leninist program. Comintern direction inevitably led to factionalism and internal squabbles, from which the party did not recover until the early 1930s. Despite official persecution, the KKE benefited from social unrest to win 5 percent of the vote at the general election of September 1932 and 6 percent at that of January 1936. It also performed credibly at the municipal elections of February 1934. Highly centralized, well organized, and intolerant of internal debate, the Communists were qualitatively different from any other party in Greece, and seemed to pose a formidable new challenge to traditional Greek politics. Although Communist support was relatively small and KKE membership reached only fifteen thousand at its height in 1936, anticommunism became a major feature of interwar Greek politics and was espoused by both main parties. In 1927 royalist politicians castigated the Liberal government for its complacency toward the Left. The Liberals responded by launching a series of oppressive anti-Communist measures, culminating in the so-called *Idionymon* law of 1929. This outlawed public meetings held by Communists or other "subversive elements" and even criminalized the discussion of communistic ideas. The bill was supplemented by additional measures increasing the powers of the police and allowing suspects to be sent into exile without trial. By 1932 more than eleven thousand arrests had been made under the *Idionymon,* with more than two thousand convictions. Throughout this period the Communist threat was a convenient scapegoat for traditional politicians, who were able to blame social unrest on Communist agitation rather than the shortcomings of government policies.[1]

Anticommunism served as the main pretext for the last major development in prewar Greek politics—the imposition of the Metaxas dictatorship in August 1936. Metaxas suspended the parliament and declared himself to be above party factionalism, while his regime announced its intention of establishing a corporatist state modeled on fascist and quasi-fascist regimes elsewhere in Europe. More authoritarian than radical, it sought to transform Greece through a combination of incessant rhetoric and increased oppression, but it was unable to solve any of the country's underlying problems. The dictatorship proved to be short-lived, being swept away by the German invasion of 1941, but it lasted long enough to create a fresh legacy of bitterness and alienation.

Greece passed under Nazi occupation after a turbulent decade that saw the final bankruptcy of its parliamentary system, the discrediting of its political elites, and an unpleasant experiment in authoritarian rule. During the subsequent vacuum, old divisions began to resurface, but with one important addition: the arrival of the Communists as a major force. The confrontation between the vigorous resistance movement controlled by the KKE and the remnants of the traditional parties would play a decisive role in shaping later events.

1. D. H. Close, *The Origins of the Greek Civil War,* 15–27; M. Mazower, "Policing the Anti-Communist State in Greece, 1922–1974," 137–41.

The Hydrocephalous State

A direct consequence of the nature of Greek politics was the emergence of a hydrocephalous state. As elsewhere in the Balkans, the machinery of the Greek state expanded far more rapidly than its actual functions. By the later nineteenth century, the proportion of civil servants to total population was seven times higher in Greece than in Britain.[2] Unlike the industrialized Western democracies, where such expansion was a response to the growing needs of an increasingly complex and dynamic society, the growth of the Greek state owed little to economic or social factors. It provided few services and offered its citizens very little. Its overmanning was not so much a response to any legitimate need but rather a result of the widespread practice of granting employment as a form of political patronage.

Patronage politics concentrated decision-making in the hands of a small number of individuals. Ministers were far more important than their ministries. They enjoyed the right to appoint senior officials and exercised power from above. In the absence of permanent administrative heads of departments, continuity of policy was difficult to achieve, particularly during times of political instability, when ministers could succeed each other with monotonous regularity. The presence of political appointees ensured that ministers had little access to impartial advice. In a system where power was rarely delegated, ministers personally handled all matters down to the most trivial and spent much of their time besieged by crowds of suppliants. Such practices were hardly conducive to devising coherent policies. The overcentralization of the system ensured that its inertia was transmitted to the provinces. All meaningful decisions were taken in Athens, where all senior appointments were made. Local government was rudimentary, with its tasks limited to the provision of the most basic public amenities. This stifled initiative throughout the country, as few officials were willing to take action or assume any responsibility without prior instructions from the central authorities.[3]

For the politicians, control over the civil service was not only a source of power but also an important channel of patronage. In a largely rural economy where the state was a major employer, jobs within the civil service were highly prized. The disposing of posts as a form of patronage had serious consequences, both in terms of efficiency and quality of intake. Although minimum levels of education were a

---

2. N. P. Mouzelis, *Modern Greece: Facets of Underdevelopment*, 17.
3. H. R. Gallagher, "Administrative Reorganization in the Greek Crisis," 250–58; W. G. Colman, "Civil Service Reform in Greece," 86–93; FO371/67101 R2377, Interim Report of the British Economic Mission to Greece, January 31, 1947, 8–19; DSR 868.50/4–347, Tentative Report of the American Economic Mission to Greece, April 1, 1947, chap. 4.

condition of entry, there was little apparent reward for honesty and hard work. In the lower grades, promotion was virtually automatic after the completion of specified periods of service. In the higher grades, both appointments and promotions were dependent on personal connections rather than aptitude. Practically all officials enjoyed total security of tenure. As British observers later noted, civil servants were "rarely dismissed for anything short of murder." Even if purged for political reasons, they could invariably return to work if the political merry-go-round swung back in their favor. Thus any individual joining the ranks of the civil service was virtually guaranteed employment until retirement and a generous pension thereafter. In these circumstances, it seems hardly surprising that the civil service never developed a strong sense of professional pride or adequate standards.[4]

Some belated attempts to address the shortcomings of the machinery of the state were made by the Metaxas dictatorship. By introducing training for several branches of the public service and by strengthening discipline, the regime improved both the morale and the efficiency of the bureaucracy.[5] Nevertheless, the problems of the civil service were too deep-seated to be overcome within such a short period. In any case, both efficiency and morale would soon collapse completely during the Axis occupation, with grave consequences after liberation.

Greek Economic Development, 1830–1940

At independence, Greece possessed a backward agriculture and little manufacturing industry. Although Greek merchants had long established a predominant position in the regional trade of the Balkans and the eastern Mediterranean, few of them lived in the new state. Even those who did rarely invested their healthy profits in other sectors. Greek economic history thus combines painfully slow growth in agriculture and industry, occurring almost in isolation from the country's main area of comparative advantage.[6]

Agriculture remained the predominant sector within the Greek economy until well into the twentieth century. Prior to the acquisition of Thessaly and Macedonia, the main crops cultivated were olives, citrus fruits, grapes, and currants. With the addition of the fertile northern plains, Greece gained a considerable area suitable for wheat and tobacco. Greek agriculture, however, was never able to overcome

4. Ibid.
5. D. H. Close, *The Character of the Metaxas Dictatorship: An International Perspective*, 13.
6. I. Pepelasis Minoglou, "Political Factors Shaping the Role of Foreign Finance: The Case of Greece, 1832–1932," 252.

backwardness, escape overreliance on a limited range of crops, or generate any impetus for growth elsewhere in the economy. In many areas, peasant farming relied exclusively on traditional methods and rarely rose above subsistence level. Geography and climate were partly to blame for this state of affairs. Most of the land was barren, and fertile soil was always in short supply. As late as 1929, only 18 percent of the total area was under cultivation.[7] Any stimulus to modernize was further stifled by the large number of small family freeholds. Despite the high degree of urbanization, transportation difficulties severely limited peasant access to most urban markets, which found it easier to trade with other coastal areas in the eastern Mediterranean than with their own hinterland. Furthermore, interest rates ranging from 20 to 24 percent on mortgages and 36 to 50 percent on personal loans ensured high indebtedness and discouraged investment.[8]

Nevertheless, several opportunities materialized for Greek farmers. The first came with the expansion of European demand for currants during the second half of the nineteenth century. As early as 1821, 6,000 tons of currants were exported, mainly to Britain. With the acquisition of new markets in France, Italy, and elsewhere on the continent, exports rose to 43,000 tons in 1861 and to 81,000 tons in 1871. A further stimulus was created by the French phylloxera crop epidemic, which pushed world prices to unprecedented heights. Average annual currant output in Greece reached 163,000 tons from 1890 to 1894, of which 98 percent was exported. Profits, however, were invested not in better methods, but in an expansion of the area under cultivation. By 1900 more than a quarter of all cultivated land and a third of the agricultural labor force was given over to currants. Unfortunately, the boom proved to be transient. As French production gradually recovered, world prices returned to previous levels and annual Greek exports fell by an average 27 percent from 1905 to 1914. Despite the drop in revenue, producers were reluctant to switch to other crops, and total output remained steady until World War I. Growing poverty in the currant-producing regions ushered in a wave of emigration to the New World. The government intervened by buying up surplus currants for alcohol production and setting up a special bank to provide subsidized credit to growers. Before long even this proved inadequate, and the government was forced to accept currants in lieu of land taxes. Although prices rose again during World War I, and British demand increased briefly after 1918, the trend was clearly unfavorable. Following the onset of another crisis in the mid-1920s, the government responded by

7. This compared with contemporary figures of 39 percent for Bulgaria, 49 percent for Rumania and 63 percent for Hungary; Royal Institute of International Affairs, *South-Eastern Europe: A Political and Economic Survey*, 158.

8. L. S. Stavrianos, *The Balkans since 1453*, 296–98.

establishing a new entity to subsidize and administer production, the Autonomous Currant Organization (ACO). For a while, this provided a degree of stability, but by the end of the decade the ACO faced bankruptcy. A more farsighted approach to the long-term decline of currant production was obviously necessary, but it never materialized.[9]

As prospects for currant growers declined, a new export opportunity opened up in the 1920s. Tobacco had long been a specialty of the areas acquired after the Balkan wars. With international demand buoyant after World War I, Greek producers responded accordingly, and average harvests from 1923 to 1926 doubled those of 1919 to 1922. As with currants, profits were invested in the expansion of the area under cultivation. By 1926, nearly 10 percent of agricultural land was given over to tobacco, which accounted for half of total export earnings. Such rich pickings could not last indefinitely. Exports became heavily dependent on the German market and suffered once German demand began to decline after 1926. However, Greek producers continued to expand output, with the cultivated area doubling between 1926 and 1929. Unsurprisingly, tobacco prices fell by 45 percent during these years. Although some areas subsequently switched to other crops, it was clear that tobacco was encountering the same major difficulties that had long confronted currant growers, and that it was unlikely to provide a long-term solution to the severe structural problems of Greek agriculture.[10]

With both export staples in trouble, the need to diversify became magnified. Cereal cultivation received particular emphasis. Greece had always been heavily dependent on wheat imports, a fact painfully borne out by the Allied blockade during World War I. The resulting hardship led to calls to promote domestic grain production. This was finally translated into government action in 1927, with the introduction of tariff protection and legislation to oblige mill owners to process a stipulated percentage of domestically produced wheat. In the following year state intervention was enhanced by creating an organization (KEPES) at the ministry of agriculture specifically to protect the interests of cereal producers. Some obvious progress was achieved. From 1933 to 1937 the average cultivated area given over to wheat rose by 43 percent over the average for the years from 1928 to 1932. Yields per hectare also rose by 46 percent, partly due to the use of new, more productive strains, and as a result harvests increased by 109 percent during this period. To a smaller extent, cotton cultivation was another beneficiary of the state-sponsored

9. M. Mazower, *Greece and the Inter-War Economic Crisis,* 81–86; Stavrianos, *Balkans since 1453,* 298, 477–78; A. F. Freris, *The Greek Economy in the Twentieth Century,* 23–24.

10. Mazower, *Greece and the Inter-War Economic Crisis,* 86–88.

autarky drive. With tariffs newly imposed on raw cotton imports, the cultivated area given over to cotton doubled between 1928–1932 and 1933–1937. By 1937, the cotton crop was five times higher than the average for 1929–1931. The growth in output satisfied an increasing percentage of home demand, despite the considerable expansion of the textile industry during the same period.[11]

The early industrial development of Greece reflected the country's position as a backward agricultural economy with limited natural resources. Manufacturing gained little benefit from the prosperity of the country's merchants, as the clear preference for short-term gains from trade led to a reluctance to invest in industry. This hesitancy was shared by the banking sector, dominated by the National Bank of Greece (NBG), which rarely went beyond short-term loans to finance trade. As late as the nineteenth century, banks were involved with no more than a dozen industrial firms. In such circumstances, industrial development was slow. Manufacturing remained traditional in methods and organization, usually involving the small-scale processing of domestically produced crops such as olive oil and grapes. Other industries had been swept away by technological change occurring elsewhere. The handicraft production of cotton thread collapsed in the face of British competition, while the once-vigorous shipbuilding industry went into prolonged decline with the gradual transition to steamships. The decades prior to World War I saw the first flows of foreign capital into mining ventures, together with the emergence of successful Greek industrialists involved in the large-scale production of commodities such as cement, soap, and artificial fertilizers. However, large modern plants remained the exception in a sector dominated by traditional producers.[12]

During the quarter of a century after 1914, industry at last became firmly established within Greece, although confined to the areas around Athens and Thessaloniki. World War I proved largely beneficial to firms geared toward military demand, particularly textile producers. However, the real spurt came in the 1920s, when the average annual growth of manufacturing was estimated at 6.8 percent. This was the result of several factors. The influx of refugees following the Asia Minor disaster created a huge pool of cheap labor. Tax concessions and tariff increases in 1926 also provided a large stimulus to further growth, as did the credit policies of the NBG, which had finally shed its inhibitions toward investing in industry. The

11. Ibid., 88–91, 239, 243, 251, 253; Royal Institute of International Affairs, *South-Eastern Europe*, 156, 159–60.

12. M. Dritsas, "Bank-Industry Relations in Inter-War Greece: The Case of the National Bank of Greece," 203–17; M. Mazower, "Banking and Economic Development in Interwar Greece," 206–31; Mazower, *Greece and the Inter-War Economic Crisis*, 53–55; Stavrianos, *Balkans since 1453*, 298–99; G. Harlaftis, *A History of Greek-Owned Shipping: The Making of an International Tramp Fleet, 1830 to the Present Day*, 115–17.

industrial labor force, which stood at 154,633 in 1920, reached 278,855 in 1930. Nevertheless, such expansion did not amount to economic development in the fuller sense. Manufacturing remained limited to light industries geared almost entirely to domestic consumption, enjoying a measure of protection behind tariff walls. Moreover, the growth years of the 1920s saw no great structural changes within industry, which continued to consist of a handful of large enterprises coexisting with a mass of tiny firms. In 1930, firms with five workers or less employed 42 percent of the total labor force. By contrast, firms with twenty-five workers or more employed 39 percent. As the average ratio of workers per firm had actually fallen during the decade, it appears that it was the explosion of small firms that had made the major contribution to recent growth, rather than large-scale modern enterprises.[13]

Individual industries continued to flourish during the 1930s, largely in response to the government's autarky drive. The emphasis on import substitution, encouraged by import quotas and higher tariffs, enabled producers to expand output for the domestic market. For many manufacturers, however, the enjoyment of a virtual monopoly allowed healthy profits without the need for continuous investment to stave off foreign competition. Within such a hothouse atmosphere, several industries (notably cotton, textiles, and chemicals) proved immensely profitable. Unsurprisingly, this had adverse effects. Official reluctance to release foreign exchange for capital goods imports acted as a further disincentive to the replacement of capital stock. Yet within their protected markets, manufacturers continued to reap handsome profits from increasingly obsolete equipment. A 1936 survey of the cotton industry suggested that more than a third of the machinery was in need of immediate replacement. The trend away from competition toward monopolies was encouraged by the operations of the NBG, which heavily favored large firms and actively promoted the takeover of weaker companies and the establishment of cartels. The ever-decreasing emphasis on competitiveness boded ill for the future. With firms able to abuse monopoly power to the detriment of the rest of the economy, it was clear that much of Greek industry would simply be swept away if tariffs were reduced.[14]

The only sector to attain and maintain international significance and competitiveness was shipping. As early as 1838, the merchant fleet possessed more than a thousand sailing ships of thirty net tons or more, and by 1870 it had a net tonnage

---

13. Mazower, *Greece and the Inter-War Economic Crisis,* 55–57, 91–95; Dritsas, "Bank-Industry Relations in Inter-War Greece," 203–17; Mazower, "Banking and Economic Development in Interwar Greece," 206–31.

14. Mazower, *Greece and the Inter-War Economic Crisis,* 210–24, 250–56; Dritsas, "Bank-Industry Relations in Inter-War Greece," 203–17; Mazower, "Banking and Economic Development in Interwar Greece," 206–31.

of 268,000. Following a period of decline caused by the rise of the steamship, the fleet recovered toward the end of the nineteenth century, thanks mainly to purchases of second-hand vessels. By 1902, steamship tonnage (181,000) exceeded that of sailing ships (176,000) for the first time. By 1914 the fleet had grown to 592,000 net registered tonnage (NRT), with sailing ships being gradually phased out. Although World War I saw substantial losses (147 ships of 366,000 gross registered tonnage [GRT]), huge profits were made from the higher freight charges that were to continue until the end of 1920. The fleet grew throughout the interwar period, to 1.9 million GRT in 1937, making it the ninth largest in the world. In its specialty, dry cargo tramps, its tonnage was second only to that of Britain.[15]

By the onset of World War II, the long-term problems of the Greek economy were still far from resolved. Agriculture remained too fixated on export staples, of which one was in terminal decline and the other dangerously overreliant on German demand. The productivity gains in wheat were the only positive trend, as for the first time the efforts of growers were partly directed at improving the quality of cultivation rather than the simple expansion of cultivated area. Nevertheless, agriculture was still backward, and offered little stimulus to other sectors of the economy. Industry similarly made little advance, despite the expansion of the interwar years, which was more the result of the availability of cheap labor and tariff protection than any real improvement in productivity or technology. This offered a poor basis for future growth. The profitability of the merchant marine, Greece's one international success, was also potentially counterproductive in that it diverted investment away from agriculture and industry. Given the prevailing backwardness, the Greek economy was hardly equipped to stand up to the trials it was to face after 1940.

The Laissez-Faire State

Few of the positive developments within the Greek economy owed much to the intervention of the state, which was rarely able to escape from an obsession with politics, be it internal squabbles or the "Great Idea." Preoccupation with the past glories of classical Greece or Byzantium obscured any vision of the future, and few governments appreciated the need to create a climate conducive to economic development. Two examples of this confused thinking were highlighted by Pepelasis. The first was the failure to provide an education system tailored to the needs of the modern world. As late as 1938, vocational education was neglected in favor of classical subjects. In that year, only 0.6 percent of secondary-school pupils received

15. Harlaftis, *History of Greek-Owned Shipping*, 108–9, 187–94, 365.

any form of practical instruction. Technical education was consistently regarded as inferior and enjoyed little state support. Even in agriculture, less than 1 percent of new entrants into farming received any vocational training. The second major failure was the adoption of a legal system combining diverse elements such as modern French and medieval Byzantine law, which coexisted with regional codes already in operation. The resulting legal mosaic created endless uncertainties, particularly in commercial transactions, and hindered the development of more advanced forms of business organization.[16]

As late as 1922, little was done to protect local manufacturing. Greece entered the twentieth century with a laissez-faire tradition never seriously challenged by its political establishment. Even if attention was refocused after the military defeat in Asia Minor, there was confusion as to the best way forward. Governments sought and obtained foreign loans to finance public works, aimed chiefly at land reclamation and infrastructural improvements. At the same time, much official thinking was less enthusiastic toward some aspects of modernity. Although the decade witnessed an unprecedented degree of industrial expansion, partly due to a favorable tariff regime, politicians from both sides of the schism seemed to doubt the desirability of further industrialization in Greece. In 1927 the finance minister announced his complete indifference to industry, which he claimed was depriving the state of customs revenue by reducing the volume of imports. Others warned that industry was a dangerous distraction, and that the long-term solutions to the country's economic problems were to be found in developing commerce and resuming emigration.[17]

Such views, firmly rooted within a preindustrial past, seemed even more out of touch following the arrival of the worldwide economic slump in the late 1920s. Until hopes of securing further foreign capital were dashed, Greek politicians failed to appreciate the seriousness of the situation. After 1928 the government had expanded its public works program, and remained confident of obtaining further loans from abroad. These hopes evaporated with the onset of the international financial crisis. Following costly but unsuccessful attempts to remain on the gold standard, the government was forced to devalue the drachma and ultimately to default on its foreign debts in 1932. No longer able to turn to foreign capital, Greece was for the first time thrown entirely onto its own resources. In response to the new situation, some degree of state economic direction was adopted, though this fell far short of a decisive break with laissez-faire. The immediate reaction was to impose controls over

16. A. A. Pepelasis, "The Image of the Past and Economic Backwardness," 20–25.
17. Mazower, *Greece and the Inter-War Economic Crisis,* 94–99, 258.

imports in order to stem the outflow of foreign exchange. Quotas were announced for a wide range of goods, later to be replaced by a licensing system. However, the main thrust of official policy was directed toward an autarky drive intended to reduce Greece's vulnerability to developments elsewhere. Greece was hardly unique in espousing autarky, which had temporarily gained widespread support throughout Europe after 1918 and revived after the collapse in international trade. What was characteristic of the Greek case was the ambivalence and lack of clarity with which the aim was pursued. There was no clear sense of priority as to how the savings resulting from the suspension of debt repayments ought to be spent, and despite endless debates, no comprehensive economic plan was produced.[18]

Even when proposals were mooted, a major constraint on government actions was the need to placate powerful vested interests opposed to any measure that could affect their position. The arguments of interest groups, although couched in terms of liberalism and antibolshevism, were more about self-interest than principles. In 1932 a plan to impose state control over certain imports was abandoned following protests from importers. An attempt to resurrect the plan in the following year foundered for the same reason. Merchants attacked the measure as amounting to a "sovietisation of the market." Industrialists voiced similar accusations of "unprecedented bolshevism" in 1935, in response to a government proposal to curb excess profits. Within a year textile producers, who enjoyed the highest profits of all, were calling for higher tariffs to discourage French "dumping" in Greek markets and complaining about the state's indifference to industrial problems. Clashes between and within interest groups were common: industrialists and importers invariably disagreed about tariffs and import policies, grain merchants and growers could unite to oppose the activities of KEPES, and industrialists could complain about the restrictive credit policies of the commercial banks while uniting among themselves to restrict competition. Such jealous guarding of privileged positions was not limited to manufacturing. The commercial banks led by the NBG resented the establishment of a central bank—the Bank of Greece—in 1928, not only refusing at first to recognize its authority but also deliberately undermining its actions. The power of vested interests to place severe limitations on both the effectiveness and the actions of other groups within the economy was a problem that was never satisfactorily resolved.[19]

The results of the autarky drive were mixed. In agriculture, higher yields per hectare were achieved, but almost nothing was done to raise general soil fertility or to improve the cultivation of any other crop. For manufacturing, the out-

18. Ibid., chaps 6, 7, 8, 9, 10, 11.
19. Ibid., chaps 3, 4, 5, 6, 8, 9.

come was even more limited. With increased tariff protection creating a hothouse atmosphere, firms were able to increase profits without investing in productivity improvements. The true cost of the policy was borne by consumers forced to pay higher prices for monopoly products. The cautious flirtation with *étatisme* had produced deeply unsatisfactory compromises rather than meaningful solutions to Greece's underlying problems.

The emphasis on the role of the state increased dramatically with the coming of the Metaxas dictatorship. The regime's avowed aim of creating a corporate state underlined the need to generate prosperity by encouraging agriculture, launching a program of public works, and laying the foundations of a welfare system. A start was made on several fronts, but the achievements were far less impressive than the rhetoric suggested. Some of the measures owed much to previous governments, while others existed mainly on paper. Although international developments prematurely terminated its initiatives, the regime already displayed a marked tendency to "mistake word for deed."[20]

The overall contribution of the Greek state to economic development was thus hardly inspiring. Most politicians remained wedded to laissez-faire attitudes that were becoming increasingly inadequate in the face of the complex needs of a modern economy, particularly within the changing international climate. Few had any long-term vision regarding the future, and many preferred to look back to a preindustrial past. In 1936 the British ambassador Sydney Waterlow noted the extreme difficulty of combining a "managed economy" with a political system "inherited from the age of laissez faire" and warned that the problem might prove "insoluble."[21] Even when governments did act, political motives usually dictated policies of doubtful economic utility, such as the extensive support for currant growers in the face of a collapse in international demand, or the tariff protection for owners of immediately profitable but technologically stagnant factories. Laissez-faire was supplanted as the prevailing doctrine only in the last years before World War II, with the imposition of a quasi-fascist regime. But the last experiment was too short-lived to generate any fundamental changes in attitudes.

The Insolvent State

After Greece became independent, both its budget and balance of payments were almost always on shaky foundations. In both cases, the lackluster performance of

20. Close, *Character of the Metaxas Dictatorship*, 5; J. V. Kofas, *Authoritarianism in Greece: The Metaxas Regime*, 64–76.

21. FO371/20389 R2033, Waterlow to Eden, March 1, 1936.

the economy was largely to blame. However, the problems were also complicated by the general attitudes of the political establishment, in that few governments were ever seriously concerned with the pursuit of policies of sound finance. The chronic deficits inevitably perpetuated dependence on foreign capital.

As Table 2.1 indicates, the balance of commodity trade was always unfavorable. Greece was unable to escape from an overdependence on a narrow range of export staples. The substantial profits from the currant and tobacco booms failed to stimulate diversification. Even as late as 1938, it is clear that little had been done to promote a more sophisticated range of exports. In that year, tobacco still accounted for 50.4 percent of all exports by value, while currants and raisins contributed 14.4 percent. By contrast, industry's major export earner was textiles and fibers, with a share of 1.4 percent. Thus Greece's prime export goods were semi-luxuries for high-income markets such as Germany, the United States, and Britain.[22] The high elasticity of demand for such products left Greece particularly vulnerable to any disruption of the international environment.

The single positive feature of the Greek balance of payments in the interwar period was the steady growth in invisible earnings. This was the result of the increasing size and success of the merchant fleet, as well as the gradual rise of Greece as an international tourist destination. A further source of revenue was emigrant remittances, largely a welcome by-product of the wave of emigration prior to 1914. In 1939, invisible earnings totaled more than $31 million ($17.1 million from remit-

TABLE 2.1. Value of Exports as Percentage of Imports

Period	Percentage
1861–1865	52.0
1866–1870	53.5
1871–1875	65.2
1876–1880	60.0
1881–1885	62.3
1886–1890	78.7
1891–1895	74.6
1896–1900	69.3
1901–1905	62.6
1906–1910	80.0
1911–1913	80.1
1923–1930	48.5
1931–1938	60.9

Source: Mazower, *Greece and the Inter-War Economic Crisis*, 312; Jackson and Lampe, *Balkan Economic History*, 165.

22. United Nations Relief and Rehabilitation Administration, *Foreign Trade in Greece*, 4–6.

tances, $8.7 million from shipping and $5.5 million from tourism), amounting to 26 percent of all receipts.[23]

Given the chronic balance of payments deficits, a modicum of stability was achieved only through periodical inflows of foreign capital in the form of loans or direct investment. The availability of such funds allowed occasional respite, but any interruption of the flow created immediate problems, as will be seen. When debts needed to be serviced or repaid, the usual response was either to seek further loans or to default. The modest improvement of the balance of payments position achieved by the end of 1930s (with total receipts of $119.3 million almost able to offset payments of $120.4 million)[24] had been the result of the short-term expediency of the self-proclaimed debt moratorium and the associated autarky drive. This simply alienated foreign lenders without creating any significant basis for Greece to overcome its balance of payments problems using its own resources. The onset of World War II thus found Greece in a vulnerable position and ensured that whatever the outcome, its bargaining power with the rest of the world would be weak.

Reliance upon foreign capital was also a consequence of the attitudes of successive Greek governments toward public finances. As Table 2.2 indicates, budgets remained chronically in deficit. Expenditure consistently exceeded revenue from taxation. Sizable increases in expenditure, invariably for military purposes, were usually met by foreign loans, or by the use of inflation as a financing instrument (in other words, by printing money). The latter practice led to frequent suspensions of drachma convertibility, although the desire to return to a fixed-rate regime, seen as a means of facilitating access to international capital markets, dictated some prudence after such episodes.[25]

Given the recurring problems of financing increases in public spending, the lethargic approach to revenue collection displayed by most Greek governments seems somewhat puzzling. Direct taxes on land and property were assessed according to ad hoc criteria rather than the property owner's ability to pay. Little was done either to standardize rates or to raise the efficiency of tax collection. As Table 2.3 indicates, in a surprising contrast with trends in industrialized countries, especially Britain, the Greek government's reliance on direct taxation declined steadily between 1833 and 1914. Pepelasis Minoglou interprets this as a consequence of the

23. Ibid., 6.
24. Ibid.
25. S. Lazaretou, "Monetary and Fiscal Policies in Greece: 1833–1914," 285–311; S. Lazaretou, "Government Spending, Monetary Policies, and Exchange Rate Regime Switches: The Drachma in the Gold Standard Period," 28–50.

TABLE 2.2. Government Expenditure as Percentage of Total Tax Revenues

Period	Percentage
1833-1847	144.6
1848	118.3
1849-1868	124.0
1869-1870	126.1
1871-1876	109.5
1877-1884	163.1
1885	206.8
1886-1897	135.8
1898-1909	119.3
1910-1914	166.7
1915-1919	223.6
1920-1927	168.8
1928-1936	118.1

Source: Lazaretou, "Government Spending, Monetary Policies, and Exchange Rate Regime Switches," 31; Lazaretou, "Macroeconomic Policies and Nominal Exchange Rate Regimes," 650.

TABLE 2.3. Direct Tax as Percentage of Total Tax Revenues

Period	Percentage
1833-1840	57.89
1841-1850	52.58
1851-1860	48.54
1861-1870	39.36
1871-1880	30.66
1881-1890	20.52
1891-1900	19.04
1901-1910	17.18
1911-1914	17.44
1915-1919	21.00
1920-1927	17.60
1928-1936	16.60

Source: Lazaretou, "Monetary and Fiscal Policies in Greece," 31; Lazaretou, "Macroeconomic Policies and Nominal Exchange Rate Regimes," 650.

prevailing social contract whereby the Greek state sought "political stability and social cohesion" rather than the maximization of revenue and economic efficiency. In practical terms, this meant the undertaxation of both the rich and the peasantry. The latter, engaged mainly in subsistence farming and barter trade, were relatively unaffected by indirect taxes. Although the rich were subject to an inheritance tax from 1898, the first form of income tax was not introduced until 1910. Even then, evasion was commonplace.[26]

26. Lazaretou, "Government Spending, Monetary Policies, and Exchange Rate Regime Switches," 31–32; Pepelasis Minoglou, "Political Factors Shaping the Role of Foreign Finance," 262–63.

The established pattern did not alter dramatically with the growth of wartime expenditure after 1914. The government was forced to increase its indebtedness both at home and abroad, but the extra spending was financed mainly by the use of the printing press. Although some attempts were made to increase direct taxation, particularly by capturing a share of the "exceptional profits" of industries such as shipping, the immediate returns were not spectacular. The most radical move came in 1922, when the government authorized a forced loan to help cover the spiraling deficits. Despite the political upheavals of the period between the defeat in Asia Minor and the Italian invasion in 1940, the tax structure saw no fundamental adjustments toward a greater reliance on direct taxation. After 1922 the republican government introduced new taxes on export earnings and property and raised import duties. Further tariff increases followed in subsequent years, particularly in 1926 and in the early 1930s. A second forced loan was carried out in 1926. Even the coming of the Metaxas dictatorship brought little change. Thus during the entire interwar period Greece underwent a shift similar to that of the nineteenth century, and entirely contrary to that occurring elsewhere. As Table 2.3 indicates, direct taxes, which had comprised 21 percent of total tax revenue in 1915–1919, saw their share slide during subsequent decades, falling to 17.6 percent in 1920–1927 and to 16.6 percent in 1928–1936.[27]

Greece had thus survived more than a century of independent existence with a tax structure unable to satisfy the needs of a modern state. The perennial difficulties of fulfilling even current obligations left successive governments overdependent on foreign capital when seeking to invest in public works, or—more often—to ride out periods of crisis. The only satisfactory long-term solution was to overhaul the entire taxation system. The failure to create proper machinery to assess and collect direct taxes proved costly on several occasions. By undertaxing potential windfalls, such as the huge profits earned from currants, tobacco, shipping, or most of industry in the 1930s, governments deprived themselves of much-needed revenue and were obliged to fall back on less reliable methods such as loans from abroad, or unpopular measures such as forced loans and tariff increases. The introduction of a modern taxation system as practiced in more advanced economies would have given Greek governments far more room to maneuver. Chronic insolvency had a destabilizing effect on domestic politics and increased the danger of foreign interference.

27. S. Lazaretou, "Macroeconomic Policies and Nominal Exchange Rate Regimes: Greece in the Interwar Period," 647–70; Mazower, *Greece and the Inter-War Economic Crisis,* 56, 60–65, 90, 96, 207, 212; Harlaftis, *History of Greek-Owned Shipping,* 185–86.

The Price of Insolvency

Greece's economic problems had an adverse effect on the country's external relations, particularly its special relationship with Britain, France, and Russia. The excessive reliance on foreign capital and the poor subsequent record on debt repayment made for a century of uncomfortable interaction between the Greek state and its foreign creditors. Many of the conflicts could have been avoided had the sums been put to efficient use. Unfortunately, foreign loans were often used to cover current deficits rather than to lay the basis for future prosperity. The cycle usually began with reckless spending, problems with repayment and servicing, culminating in ultimate default. On some occasions the unilateral suspension of debt obligations was allowed to pass unpunished, but on others it led to a significant loss of economic sovereignty and political face.[28]

This cycle had begun even before Greece achieved independence. As early as 1821, the financial plight of the insurgent government forced it to seek loans from abroad. Following unsuccessful attempts to negotiate loans in Spain and various Italian and German states, the Greeks turned their attention to London. In 1824, eight hundred thousand pounds were secured on usurious terms. Unfortunately, the money was not used for its intended purpose, being largely squandered in factional fighting. Similar misuse befell a second loan of £1.1 million raised in London in 1825. Independence failed to bring financial stability, and in 1832 an international loan worth 60 million francs (£2.4 million), guaranteed by the three Protecting Powers (Britain, France, and Russia), was contracted with the banking house of the Rothschild Brothers in Paris. The loan coincided with the imposition of Prince Otho and largely helped to finance the expenses of the new monarch, as did further loans from Bavaria in 1835 and 1836.[29]

As early as the 1830s, the Greek government failed to pay any interest charges on their loans, and only sporadic payments were made thereafter. By the mid-1840s the failure to meet debt obligations had aroused the anger of the three Protecting Powers, especially Britain. Negotiations dragged on fruitlessly, leading to several heated incidents, including a British blockade of the port of Piraeus in 1850 and partial Anglo-French occupation during the Crimean War. Following Greek complaints of inability to pay, an International Financial Commission of Inquiry was set up in 1857 to investigate Greece's public finances and to suggest reform measures

28. For a detailed treatment of the subject see, J. V. Kofas, *Financial Relations of Greece and the Great Powers, 1832–1862;* J. A. Levandis, *The Greek Foreign Debt and the Great Powers, 1821–1898.*
29. Kofas, *Financial Relations of Greece,* chaps 1, 2; Levandis, *Greek Foreign Debt,* chaps 1, 2.

to be adopted by the government in Athens. Foreign interference in Greek affairs continued to escalate, and by 1862 it was being suggested that the Powers should assume control over the country's customs revenue in order to liquidate the debt. The move was postponed only because of the political unrest that deposed King Otho later in the year. A compromise was finally reached in 1864, by which one-third of the customs revenues of the port of Syra were put aside for debt repayment.[30]

The 1864 agreement brought a partial resolution to the debt crisis. By the end of the 1870s, however, developments both within Greece and in Paris ushered in a new wave of borrowing. The Athens government sought funds in order to cope with rising military expenditures and to undertake a public works program. Meanwhile, the international unwillingness to consider any further loans to Greece was changed in 1879, when French political motives proved decisive in allowing the flotation of new loans on the Bourse. With the reopening of European credit markets, the following twelve years witnessed an "orgy of directionless borrowing."[31] The Greek government received a net total of 459 million francs, but the sums were "hastily contracted and aimlessly applied." There was no subsequent explosion of productive investment. Only 7 to 8 percent of the sums went to finance railway construction. Instead, military expenditure absorbed at least a quarter of the total, with the servicing of the previous loans taking up most of the residue. Belated attempts to improve government finances by increasing taxes and imposing spending cuts proved largely abortive. By the early 1890s debt servicing was swallowing up a third of public revenue. In 1893, when the raising of further loans proved impossible, the government defaulted once more.[32]

At first, the foreign response was muted. Despite protests from investors, no serious action was taken against the Greeks, who doggedly refused to grant any concessions to the creditors. Negotiations over the repayment of the debt dragged on for four years, until Greece initiated a disastrous war with Turkey over Crete. With the Sultan's armies advancing unhindered, the Athens government was able to secure foreign support to impose an armistice only by agreeing to hand over control of certain revenues to an International Financial Commission (IFC). Under the supervision of this body, receipts from the Piraeus customs, state monopolies, and stamp and tobacco duties were to be diverted into a sinking fund to pay off out-

30. Kofas, *Financial Relations of Greece*, chaps 2, 4; Levandis, *Greek Foreign Debt*, chaps 1, 2.

31. R. E. Cameron, *France and the Economic Development of Europe 1800–1914: Conquests of Peace and Seeds of War*, 496–97.

32. Levandis, *Greek Foreign Debt*, chap. 3; Pepelasis, "Image of the Past and Economic Backwardness," 26.

standing debts. The agreement also placed restrictions on government actions on internal borrowing and the size of note circulation.[33]

The interwar period witnessed a repetition of the previous pattern. At first, foreign capital flows were unavailable as a result of the failure to achieve a settlement of Greek war debts to Britain and the United States, which remained unresolved until 1927. However, a £12.3 million loan sponsored by the League of Nations was granted in 1924 to help assimilate the refugees from Asia Minor. This soon proved insufficient, and before long further credits were being sought. In early 1928 another loan worth £9 million was approved in London, to be repaid out of IFC revenues. In total, loans with a nominal value of £38 million were contracted from 1924 to 1931. In addition, direct foreign investment began to flow into Greece after 1924.[34]

This new wave of borrowing soon generated problems identical to those that had proved so troublesome ever since the 1820s. By 1930, 36 percent of government expenditure was being allocated to the servicing of public debt (both internal and external), a percentage exceeded only by Britain and Belgium.[35] Such a burden could not be sustained indefinitely. In 1932 the Athens government sought to reschedule repayment, and when the talks dragged on it took the unilateral decision to impose a debt moratorium. Occasional interest payments were made thereafter, particularly after the establishment of the Metaxas dictatorship, but Greece entered World War II in a state of default. Although some temporary relief had been achieved, the country was no nearer to resolving its chronic reliance on foreign capital to paper over deficiencies in the balance of payments.[36]

Thus the pattern of foreign loans and insolvency was set within decades after independence and was to recur all too often in the future. If the initial loans were essential to win the war of secession, subsequent loans served merely to finance the extravagant expansion of the machinery of state and from time to time to pursue hostilities against the Turks. From the very beginning, little attention was paid to the need to put borrowed money to the best possible use, with insufficient emphasis on the need to create a basis for future economic prosperity. Having once defaulted, the Greek negotiators did not help matters by maintaining an inflexible stance with

---

33. Levandis, *Greek Foreign Debt*, chaps 3, 4; H. Feis, *Europe the World's Banker 1870–1914: An Account of European Foreign Investment and the Connection of World Finance with Diplomacy before the War*, 289–91.

34. A. Orde, *British Policy and European Reconstruction after the First World War*, 284–88, 297–98; Mazower, *Greece and the Inter-War Economic Crisis*, 102–4, 106; G. J. Andreopoulos, "The International Financial Commission and Anglo-Greek Relations (1928–1933)," 343.

35. G. Politakis, *Greek Policies of Recovery and Reconstruction, 1944–1952*, 23–25.

36. Mazower, *Greece and the Inter-War Economic Crisis*, 189–98.

the representatives of the Powers. In the long run, Greece's failure to honor international agreements to which it had been a signatory increased the likelihood of foreign meddling in the country's affairs.

For their part, Britain, France, and Russia were hardly blameless. While the early loans had been extended on understandably stiff terms, several British individuals had been guilty of misappropriating parts of the funds. Moreover, by imposing Otho on the Greeks, the Powers bore much responsibility for subsequent developments. Once Greece defaulted, each of the Powers sought to gain influence within the country at the expense of the others.[37] It would be naive to assume that each was not motivated as much by political self-interest as by a determination to recover the sums advanced. In any case, the pressure put on Greece was only moderately successful, in that a compromise took two decades to achieve.

The imposition of the IFC created considerable resentment within Greece, but the arrangement was far from unique. In fact, it was fairly typical of relations between defaulting and creditor states at that time. The Greek experience was largely mirrored by that of its Balkan neighbors. In 1895, Serbia avoided bankruptcy only by handing over the management of certain revenues to an international financial commission representing foreign bondholders. In 1902, Bulgaria staved off financial disaster by accepting a control commissioner appointed by the Banque de Paris et des Pays Bas with the cooperation of the French government. As with Greece, both countries had borrowed heavily on international markets, and invested more in military than productive purposes. Existing borrowing patterns were simply resumed once new credits became available with the establishment of external supervision.[38]

Unwelcome as these arrangements were, economic mismanagement could have led to far more embarrassing consequences. Despite the irksome aspects of foreign interference, the Balkan countries were spared the earlier fate of Egypt, where catastrophic financial ineptitude and subsequent bankruptcy resulted in a virtual loss of independence, with real power passing to the British consul general in 1883. As a result of British administration, Egyptian finances improved considerably over the following three decades, allowing both extensive investment in infrastructure and a reduction of individual tax burdens, thereby raising the general standard of living.[39] Such progress resulted from sound financial management achieved only

37. Kofas, *Financial Relations of Greece,* chap. 1.

38. Cameron, *France and the Economic Development of Europe,* 500–501; Feis, *Europe the World's Banker,* chap. 12.

39. J. Foreman-Peck, *A History of the World Economy: International Economic Relations since 1850,* 132.

by politically drastic arrangements, which would have proved unacceptable to the Balkan states. To a certain extent, the Balkan governments may well have had some justification in seeing themselves as partial victims of Great Power rivalry, which could both impose unsuitable borders and exacerbate regional tensions. Nevertheless, it is also fair to say that chronic financial ineptitude and a blatant disregard for sound economic principles played a major part in the crises, thus leading to the imposition of foreign supervision.

The IFC was designed solely to protect the interests of Greece's foreign creditors, and ensured that the latter fared reasonably well in comparison with others who had invested in the Balkans. However, despite the hostility of both government and public opinion in Greece, the agreement was not without some benefit for the country's economy. Revenues collected by the IFC increased gradually up to 1914, allowing an initial reduction of the foreign debt burden, and reopened access to international capital markets. If the benefits to the Greek economy fell far short of what they could have been, this was not the fault of the foreign representatives. The increases in revenue derived almost entirely from the management of the Piraeus customs, while little was achieved in augmenting receipts from the other sources. Despite its formal powers, the IFC found itself unable to transform "established ways and practices," and frequently complained that its suggestions for reforms had been largely ignored. Popular resentment of the institution often necessitated extra pressure from the Powers. In any case, potential gains were more than neutralized by the huge cost of the two Balkan Wars (400 million drachmae).[40] Greece's ability to withstand such outlays had derived mainly from the unprecedented degree of financial stability and the renewed access to credit, both consequences of the IFC's presence. Foreign capital had thus allowed the country to pursue military adventures to the detriment of its economic development.

During the interwar period, most elements of the familiar cycle were repeated. Sizable amounts of foreign capital were absorbed after 1924. As with the IFC, the conditions imposed by foreign lenders made a positive contribution to long-term Greek stability. At the insistence of the League of Nations, the loans were made conditional upon the creation of a central bank—the Bank of Greece. Although many within Greece resented the imposition, the new institution performed a useful role during the subsequent crisis.[41] The loans of the 1920s had been contracted on the implicit assumption that the flows would never cease. Once it became clear that

---

40. Feis, *Europe the World's Banker*, 291–92; Mazower, *Greece and the Inter-War Economic Crisis*, 60–65.

41. Mazower, *Greece and the Inter-War Economic Crisis*, 104–6; Mazower, "Banking and Economic Development in Interwar Greece," 215–26.

no more loans would be forthcoming, the cost of servicing and repaying previous debts became excessive. While the IFC continued to exercise some influence, both it and the international community as a whole were powerless to take any meaningful action once the Greeks chose to default again in 1932. The suspension of payments allowed a degree of temporary relief without solving the perennial problem of budget and balance of payments deficits and the consequent overreliance on foreign capital. In such circumstances, defiance was clearly counterproductive. Had history not taken the course it did in the late 1930s, some eventual accommodation with the foreign creditors would have been inevitable. However, the actual course of events ensured that within a short space of time, Greece would become more than ever dependent on foreign help, albeit in circumstances no one could have envisaged.

The Legacy of the War

Occupation and Inflation

Although the human and material losses suffered by Greece during the occupation have never been ascertained with satisfactory accuracy, they were undeniably massive. Approximately 520,000 people perished. Both agricultural and industrial output declined dramatically, while the Greek merchant fleet, once fundamental to the country's balance of payments, lost 1.3 million GRT, 72 percent of its total tonnage. The transport infrastructure, inadequate even before the war, suffered further as a result of the almost total destruction of locomotives and rolling stock, road and rail bridges and tunnels, together with damage to ports and canals.[42]

Several factors contributed to the extent of the losses. Even before the abortive Italian invasion of October 1940, the disruption of world trade patterns had a particularly ruinous effect on the Greek balance of payments. The Axis occupation and the resulting Allied blockade separated Greece from important international markets, leading to the loss of both export revenue and food imports. This created serious problems for a country that normally imported more than a third of staple foodstuffs and led to catastrophic food shortages. Moreover, by forcing Greece to pay for not only its military occupation but also the expenses of strategic projects in the eastern Mediterranean, the Axis ensured that an already underdeveloped

---

42. G. Patterson, *The Financial Experiences of Greece from Liberation to the Truman Doctrine (October 1944–March 1947)*, chap. 1; Harlaftis, *History of Greek-Owned Shipping*, 226–27.

country with little current revenue was obliged to transfer a considerable portion of its national wealth to support the Nazi war effort. As Ritter shows, German policy toward Greece was primarily designed to finance Wehrmacht operations from local resources, and followed three distinct phases: a) initial detachment, leaving the Italians to shoulder the main burden of the country's problems; b) direct intervention in conjunction with Italy in October 1942, when the drachma faced collapse just as the military situation in the Mediterranean began to swing against the Axis; and c) the assumption of total control over the Greek economy following the Italian withdrawal, in a desperate attempt to prevent civil unrest from erupting into widespread partisan warfare.[43]

The immediate result of the military defeat in April 1941 was partition among the Axis powers. Apart from the northeastern provinces absorbed by Bulgaria, the Wehrmacht retained only areas of particular military importance, with the rest placed under Italian administration. After the fall of Mussolini, the Germans assumed direct control over the Italian zone. The relative fortunes of the various zones were mixed: while the Bulgarians ruthlessly exploited the areas under their control, Italian occupation was relatively benign. The partition had two serious consequences. First, the creation of new boundaries cut across long-established internal trade patterns, further disrupting economic life. Second, the isolation of the main agricultural areas of Macedonia and Thrace from the major centers of population, together with the elimination of food imports, led to severe scarcities in the other zones, culminating in widespread starvation during the first winter of the occupation. Although the final death toll from hunger is uncertain, it was estimated that food shortages claimed three hundred thousand lives between 1941 and 1944.[44] The death toll would have been considerably higher had the Red Cross not sponsored a huge relief effort from the summer of 1942 onward. This prevented a recurrence of the starvation of 1941–1942, but throughout the occupation, hunger and malnutrition remained a permanent feature of Greek life.

Apart from individual tragedies, the chronic scarcity of goods had disastrous implications for economic and social stability, as it coincided with the inevitable problem of wartime budget deficits. The two factors came together to produce runaway inflation, which assumed terrifying proportions by the end of the occupation. The finances of the puppet regime were destroyed by a combination of massive expenditure increases accompanied by a collapse of revenue. While the sums Greece was

43. H. Ritter, "German Policy in Occupied Greece and its Economic Impact, 1941–1944," 173–74.

44. M. Mazower, *Inside Hitler's Greece: The Experience of Occupation 1941–44*, 41.

forced to pay for its own occupation cannot be calculated with any precision, they were undoubtedly huge: in 1941–1942, the levy was estimated as the equivalent of 113.7 percent of the country's national income. The second major burden on public finances was the trebling of the state payroll between 1941 and 1944, as the government was forced to take on the financing of both local authorities and numerous public institutions that had gone bankrupt.[45]

In the face of such demands, the puppet regime was able to deploy only meager resources. The gold reserves of the Bank of Greece had followed the government into exile and remained in South Africa for the rest of the war. In addition, the tax-collecting machinery had been severely damaged by both the disruption of normal economic life and deliberate evasion, and budget deficits rose to horrific levels: from only 4 percent in 1938–1939 to 71 percent in 1941–1942, 82 percent in 1942–1943, and 94 percent in 1943–1944.[46] The puppet regime had little choice but to fall into the dangerous habit of printing drachmae to meet its current expenditure. As Table 2.4 demonstrates, the note circulation grew alarmingly, with the rate of increase accelerating wildly as the war progressed.

The consequences were soon apparent. With a continuous flood of new banknotes during a time of chronic scarcity, the value of the drachma plunged as note circulation rocketed out of control. As the drachma depreciated, the public rapidly lost confidence in paper currency. While the poorest sections of society often resorted to barter, sizable transactions were settled in gold sovereigns, the only stable means of exchange and store of value. The drachma-sovereign rate of exchange is shown in Table 2.4. The so-called sovereign rate became the most reliable barometer not only of inflation, but also of public confidence in the economy and the government, a role it would retain long after Greece was liberated.

One of the main causes of price rises was the growing scarcity of food. In the beginning of the occupation the puppet regime introduced a rationing scheme, and price ceilings, and attempted to control the collection and distribution of agricultural produce. The efforts were severely undermined by Greek farmers, who had been antagonized by Axis looting in 1941 and failed to respond to government demands to deliver crops at prices lower than those of the free market. Most produce was either hoarded or sold on the black market. Despite appeals to farmers and the

45. G. Etmektsoglou-Koehn, *Axis Exploitation of Wartime Greece, 1941–1943*, 466; FO371/48334 R14106, Economic and Financial Developments in Greece November 1944–June 1945, C. A. Coombs, August 1, 1945, 4–5.

46. Bank of Greece, *The Economic Situation in Greece and the Bank of Greece in 1946: Report for the Years 1941, 1944, 1945 and 1946*, 8–10; Patterson, *Financial Experiences of Greece*, 13.

TABLE 2.4. Note Circulation and Sovereign Rate, 1939-1944

End of Month	Drachmae	Sovereign
August 1939	(a) 9,980,613,000	961
October 1940	12,598,979,600	1,063
June 1941	24,075,484,400	7,400
July	23,960,159,300	8,000
August	29,058,920,250	11,220
September	33,842,143,550	12,130
October	39,067,186,950	20,800
November	43,528,194,100	28,650
December	48,794,900,550	21,130
January 1942	53,013,793,350	21,500
February	58,489,884,700	21,500
March	67,865,385,400	37,250
April	79,143,708,500	50,500
May	92,183,523,400	59,030
June	109,845,947,100	58,830
July	132,344,589,900	130,500
August	155,108,028,100	196,210
September	185,587,421,700	217,530
October	238,324,853,900	352,870
November	289,671,447,700	273,000
December	335,081,365,550	151,720
January 1943	367,793,525,000	144,350
February	401,898,186,300	134,710
March	465,663,180,000	161,320
April	560,224,889,500	170,500
May	622,774,636,000	239,625
June	712,666,711,000	307,175
July	869,344,534,400	322,240
August	1,062,125,368,100	355,230
September	1,301,726,501,150	419,120
October	1,734,712,486,350	762,400
November	2,303,915,762,050	1,253,080
December	3,199,235,134,300	1,562,890
January 1944	3,989,646,308,000	3,112,000
February	5,167,762,000,000	5,520,000
March	7,722,165,101,000	14,720,000
April	16,838,986,498,000	35,700,000
May	31,237,735,492,000	102,964,000
June	61,133,096,791,000	126,260,870
July	131,192,927,932,000	364,230,769
August	552,851,854,046,000	2,390,846,153
September	7,305,500,000,000,000	18,528,000,000
October	694,570,820,000,000,000	2,583,111,000,000
10 November 1944	6,279,943,102,000,000,000	(c) 43,166,600,000,000
(b) 11 November 1944	125,598,800	2,100

Source: Delivanis and Cleveland, *Greek Monetary Developments*, Statistical Appendix.

(a) Average circulation for period September 1, 1938, to August 31, 1939, 7,600 million drachmae.
(b) After currency reform 1 new drachma=50,000,000,000 old drachmae
(c) Average of rates for first ten days

introduction of taxes in kind, actual deliveries fell far short of requirements and the rationing program was never honored in full. Meat and dairy products disappeared within months, and only bread remained available in meaningful quantities. With so little food available through official rationing schemes, pressure on black market supplies pushed prices far beyond the means of the average citizen. All price ceilings failed with the exception of the moratorium on rents. Spiraling prices led to inevitable pressure on wages, which were frequently readjusted and supplemented with additional food allowances and payments in kind for certain groups of workers. By the end of the occupation, wages were revalued every five days, but real wages had fallen to an estimated 6 percent of their prewar levels by July 1944.[47]

At first the Germans did little to alleviate the growing economic chaos, apart from agreeing to receive the Red Cross relief shipments. No major action was taken until the first crisis of the drachma in the summer of 1942, when an Axis economic mission under Hermann Neubacher was sent to Athens in an attempt to solve Greece's economic predicament. Neubacher was motivated solely by a desire to preserve social and political stability by rescuing the drachma as a means of exchange, rather than promoting broader economic recovery, and his measures failed to address the root causes of the crisis. He reduced the occupation levy and abolished rationing and price controls. A credit squeeze was imposed in an attempt to compel speculators to part with hoarded stocks. Plans were also announced that substantial quantities of foodstuffs would be imported from elsewhere in the Balkans as well as manufactured commodities from Germany. The combination of measures was initially successful. Hoarded goods flooded the markets, leading to price decreases of up to 80 percent for some commodities, while wages and prices kept in balance for more than four months.[48]

But the respite was short-lived. Within months, the course of the war forced the Germans to give increasing priority to the transport of military supplies and personnel rather than consumer goods. By the spring of 1943 the occupation levy was increased again. Following a rise in partisan activity, the growing economic chaos threatened to erupt into widespread civil unrest. Neubacher attempted to relieve upward pressure on the drachma by a policy of controlled gold sales. A million gold sovereigns were brought in between February and September, and sold after

47. Etmektsoglou-Koehn, *Axis Exploitation of Wartime Greece,* 408–26; WO204/3562, The Greek Hyperinflation 1943–1944; S. Agapitides, "The Inflation of the Cost of Living and Wages in Greece during the German Occupation," 648–49.

48. H. R. Ritter, *Hermann Neubacher and the German Occupation of the Balkans, 1940–1945,* chap. 4; Ritter, "German Policy in Occupied Greece," 164–69; Etmektsoglou-Koehn, *Axis Exploitation of Wartime Greece,* 525–29.

November 1943. Once again, this proved effective for a limited period, briefly reducing the sovereign rate and slowing down inflation, but could only delay rather than prevent the total collapse of the economy. By May 1944, with the German military position deteriorating rapidly, inflation spiraled out of control.[49] Thereafter, with the onset of hyperinflation, the drachma rapidly lost touch with reality. In October 1944 the Germans withdrew from Greece, leaving behind them a disaster of their own making. The colossal task of overcoming years of deliberate exploitation and mismanagement was left to the returning Greek government and its Allies.

The psychological legacy of the occupation was as serious as the physical damage inflicted on the country. The chronic scarcity and the subsequent inflation had a devastating effect on social cohesion, as it was clearly perceived that the suffering had not been distributed equitably. Shortages created almost universal impoverishment, as the cost of a normal diet soared beyond the reach of most of the population, particularly in the urban centers. As Thomadakis demonstrates, recourse to the black market was hardly feasible for ordinary wage earners. In most cases, it required liquidating tangible wealth, personal property from household possessions to real estate. It would be simplistic to assume that the privations were borne equally, or that the occupiers were the sole beneficiaries. While contact with the black market was a painful but unavoidable necessity for survival, it was also a source of considerable gain for those few in a position to sell food. Thus alongside the general misery, vast fortunes were made from the black market. A contemporary observer remarked that many Greeks had "got rich on the blood of their brothers." As Mazower notes, access to goods and power offered unique opportunities for enrichment. Popular perceptions helped create the myth that a new class of war profiteers had emerged, displacing the old elites. The brisk trade in urban housing and rural holdings—more than 350,000 urban properties and rural estates were sold during the occupation—indicates that even formerly prosperous individuals were not immune to the general impoverishment. However, although the topic has not been fully researched, it is likely that the true picture was much more complex. While many individuals undeniably joined the ranks of the rich before liberation, many of the prewar elites were equally successful in maintaining or even increasing

49. Ritter, "German Policy in Occupied Greece," 170–73; Ritter, *Hermann Neubacher and the German Occupation of the Balkans,* 134–36; M. Palairet, *The Four Ends of the Greek Hyperinflation of 1941–1946,* 36–37. Drachma obtained from gold sales furnished between 16 percent and 72 percent of the Werhmacht's monthly expenditures during this period; Etmektsoglou-Koehn, *Axis Exploitation of Wartime Greece,* 544.

their wealth by using their connections to exploit the new realities.[50] The black market proved socially divisive, and the resulting legacy of bitterness would continue to haunt Greece long after liberation.

To a large degree, the massive redistribution of wealth within Greece was reinforced by the deliberate policy of using gold sales as the sole weapon in a futile effort to arrest inflation. This allowed those who profited from the occupation to protect their assets, as belief in the sovereign remained unshaken. The increased possibility of investing in gold was also an unfortunate consequence of the similar British practice of using gold coins to finance the various resistance movements. By such means, more than two million sovereigns entered Greece, double the amount sold by the German occupiers.[51] The easy availability of gold strengthened its role as the only reliable form of tender and store of value. This contrasted sharply with the demise of the drachma. Hyperinflation destroyed confidence in paper money, creating distrust that even the liberation could not eradicate. With the total ascendancy of the gold mentality, subsequent efforts to establish confidence in a new drachma bore little fruit for several years.

Another consequence of the occupation with serious implications for the post-liberation period was the effect on the size and quality of the state administration. With successive puppet governments offering employment and pensions as a form of welfare, the state payroll grew alarmingly. Thus by November 1944 the number of state employees and pensioners had grown to 72,000 and 117,000 respectively (the corresponding figures for 1938–1939 were 53,000 and 87,000). The government also assumed responsibility for thousands of individuals from bankrupt institutions and enterprises who would otherwise have been reduced to starvation, thereby adding 80,000 employees and 55,000 pensioners to the state payroll. The total number of individuals directly supported by the state thus rose from 141,000 before the war to 324,000 by the liberation.[52] As will be seen, the implications for public finances were to prove terrifying.

While the civil service grew in numbers, its quality was further undermined. Little attention was paid to qualifications or competence. Furthermore, the hard-

50. S. Thomadakis, "Black Markets, Inflation, and Force in the Economy of Occupied Greece," 71–75; Mazower, *Inside Hitler's Greece*, 53–64; C. Hadziiossif, "Economic Stabilization and Political Unrest: Greece 1944–1947," 32–33.

51. C. A. Coombs, *Financial Policy in Greece during 1947–1948*, 181.

52. FO371/48334 R14106, Economic and Financial Developments in Greece November 1944–June 1945, C. A. Coombs, August 1, 1945, 4–5.

ships of everyday life rapidly eroded both the morale and the efficiency of the bureaucracy. Of all wage earners, civil servants were among the hardest hit by inflation. The fight to maintain a minimum standard of living inevitably involved neglect of official duties and all too often corruption. Matters were not helped by the inevitable accusations of collaboration and the active harassment by resistance forces.[53]

As a result, the state of the Greek civil service after liberation was worse than at any time in the past. Given the huge numbers on the government payroll, most employees had nothing to do and turned up only to collect their wages. For those who had something to do, work practices were less than strenuous. As late as July 1947 the average working week was twenty-five hours. This allowed several bad practices picked up during the occupation period to flourish unhindered. Thus many employees used all means to boost their meager wages, including doing other jobs during office hours and abusing overtime and other sources of special payments. One particularly lucrative activity was participation in specially constituted committees. As each attendance was paid, there was little incentive for swift decision-making, as action could always be postponed until the next session. Even worse, the catastrophic overmanning within departments was further compounded by the reappearance of traditional patterns of political patronage after liberation. In each of the numerous governments, ministers gave jobs to associates and supporters. As dismissals were still rare, apart from the occasional purge for political reasons, the numbers continued to swell.[54] As will be seen, the problems of the civil service were to have a decisive bearing on the course of the struggle against inflation after 1944.

Political Developments, 1941–1947

While the Greek economy moved ever more rapidly toward complete breakdown, political developments both within and outside Greece ensured that those responsible for restoring economic stability after liberation would have to contend with a new set of difficulties. The weakening of the traditional parties, the resumption of the old constitutional squabbles, and above all the new challenge of the organized Left—all occurring under the watchful eyes of the British—came to monopolize the attention of Greek politicians after 1944, diverting energies away from the crucial search for economic normality.

53. LBG/KVA/B5, Memorandum on the Greek Economic Situation, K. Varvaressos, August 2, 1946, 42–44.
54. Gallagher, "Administrative Reorganization in the Greek Crisis," 250–58; Colman, "Civil Service Reform in Greece," 86–93.

The swift collapse of Greek and British resistance in the face of the German onslaught in April 1941 marked the abrupt end of the dictatorship founded by Metaxas. Within weeks the king and his government, together with remnants of the armed forces, were forced to pass into exile in Egypt, then to London in September 1941 and back to Cairo in March 1943. The government-in-exile was headed by Emmanuel Tsouderos, a former governor of the Bank of Greece rather than a career politician, who remained in the post until the spring of 1944. In the beginning, the government contained a large number of survivors from the Metaxas regime, and could hardly claim to enjoy a substantial following within Greece. Eventually, after British pressure to disassociate itself from the dictatorship, the government dismissed ministers who had served under Metaxas, announced the restoration of the civil liberties suspended in 1936, and coopted several representatives of the traditional parties who had been able to escape from occupied Greece.

At first the Tsouderos government concentrated its efforts on the pursuit of territorial claims, but increasingly focused its attention on the long-running controversy over the future of the monarchy. Old antagonisms had been revived by the king's dubious actions in helping to establish the Metaxas dictatorship, and few Greek politicians of any hue were enthusiastic about the king returning after liberation without some form of prior referendum. Stronger action was prevented by British insistence on supporting the king, although they eventually agreed to the referendum proposal.

In the meantime, developments within Greece itself led to a new polarization of political opinion far more fundamental than that resulting from the schism. The hardships endured under the occupation and the emergence of a strong resistance movement inevitably radicalized the population, which led to a strengthening of the Left, grouped around the KKE. The traditional parties, bereft of proper organizational structures and discredited by their acquiescence in the Metaxas regime, proved utterly unable to mobilize popular support. The highly disciplined Communists, with long experience of clandestine activity behind them, were able to create a genuine mass movement. Active resistance was undertaken almost solely by EAM and its military wing ELAS, in which the Communists were joined by representatives of the moderate Left and Center. Although EAM was controlled by the KKE, it drew support from most sections of society and many of its rank and file were not committed Communists.

The huge success of EAM in harnessing the popular mood frightened not only the German occupiers but also the traditional parties, the government-in-exile, and the British. Its establishment of an alternative government (PEEA) in the mountains was a direct challenge not only to the Germans but also to the authority and legitimacy of the government-in-exile. The traditional parties belatedly attempted to create an alternative resistance movement, with limited results. The largest grouping (EDES) failed either to achieve wider significance or to entice individuals away from EAM. The uneasy relationship between EDES and ELAS eventually deteriorated into a virtual civil war, particularly after negotiations to broker a wider coalition agreement ended in failure in the autumn of 1943. The most vigorous response to EAM-ELAS came with the creation of the SS-sponsored Security Battalions, consisting of anticommunist Greek collaborators who fought alongside the SS in major anti-ELAS operations marked by extreme brutality on both sides.

Tsouderos resigned following a Communist mutiny within the exiled Greek armed forces and was succeeded briefly by Sophocles Venizelos, who was himself replaced by Georgios Papandreou in April 1944. During the next month an effective compromise was achieved with EAM, which accepted minority participation in the National Unity Government and agreed to place its forces under the coalition's control. The uneasy alliance was reached partly as a result of pressure from the British, who dispatched troops to convey the Papandreou government to Athens after the German withdrawal in October 1944.

The compromise proved short-lived. The plans to absorb all military formations into a unified national army—thus effectively disarming ELAS and EDES—exacerbated tensions between the coalition partners. In early December 1944, less than seven weeks after liberation, the fragile unity collapsed when police opened fire on an EAM-sponsored demonstration. EAM withdrew from the government, and ELAS forces launched an attack against several police stations in Athens. The fighting escalated into a virtual civil war in the capital, ending with the total defeat of ELAS following the deployment of British troops backed by armor and air support. The British brokered an uneasy peace in February 1945. Under the terms of the so-called Varkiza Agreement, ELAS was to be disarmed but an amnesty was extended to its members. All civil liberties were to be restored and enforced, while the civil service and security organs were to be purged of supporters of the Metaxas dictatorship and wartime collaborators. The agreement set the agenda for future political developments by stipulating that parliamentary elections and a referendum on the future of the monarchy were to be held as soon as possible. The temporary status of the king had already been settled back in December 1944, when Archbishop Damaskinos of Athens and All Greece was appointed as regent.

The events of December 1944 had a tremendous impact on subsequent political developments and attitudes. The Left was severely weakened as a result of its military setback, and the brutality of its methods led to a considerable loss of popular

Prime Minister Papandreou and the EAM ministers of his National Unity Government, September 2, 1944. Left to right: Elias Tsirimokos, minister of national economy; Angelos Angelopoulos, deputy minister of finance; Alexandros Svolos, minister of finance; Papandreou; Miltiadis Porfyrogenis, minister of labor; Ioannis Zevgos, minister of agriculture; Nikolaos Askoutsis, minister of communications. The Hellenic Literary and Historical Archive, Athens.

support. The main beneficiaries were the royalist Right, which needed no excuse to resume its own vendetta against the Communists and their sympathizers. The Varkiza Agreement's emphasis on civil liberties and the fair treatment of political opponents was never likely to be respected given the resurgence of the extreme Right. The Greek political establishment was able to subvert the spirit of Varkiza by using its provisions to further weaken the Left. In a return to the traditional

A British sniper fires on ELAS positions from the Acropolis, December 10, 1944.
Photograph courtesy of the Imperial War Museum, London.

practice of purging opponents, EAM supporters were removed from the civil service, security forces, and universities. The increasing confidence and ferocity of the
Right allowed wartime collaborators to be exonerated as fighters against communism rather than denounced as pro-Nazi traitors. Former members of the Security
Battalions were recruited into the police and military, and former supporters of the
puppet governments gained political office. As Papastratis claims, the Greek record
of prosecuting collaborators was "lamentable." Although eighteen thousand individual charges had been made by mid-1945, the vast majority were never brought
to justice. The reluctance of successive governments in Athens to punish collabora-

tors contrasted strikingly with the trend elsewhere in Europe. The leniency shown toward those who had cooperated with the Nazis was not extended to the Left. By the end of 1945 nearly forty-nine thousand EAM supporters had been imprisoned, and more than twelve hundred had been murdered by the National Guard or unofficial paramilitary units. This so-called White Terror enjoyed the support of much of the Greek political establishment, and continued despite the protests of the embarrassed British.[55]

All this was happening at a time when power was theoretically being exercised not by the Right but by the republican Center. British insistence on steering a middle course ensured a succession of cabinets run by a mixture of moderates, often not career politicians. Cabinets succeeded one another with monotonous rapidity, each one proving itself to be fragile. General Nikolaos Plastiras, who replaced Papandreou in January 1945, was soon followed by Admiral Petros Voulgaris in April. Voulgaris' resignation in October 1945 created a prolonged political crisis, during which the regent himself assumed the premiership for a brief period. A government under Panayotis Kannelopoulos collapsed within weeks, leading in November 1945 to the appointment of Themistoklis Sophoulis, who remained in office until the first postwar elections in March 1946. As the frequent change of governments indicates, the coalitions of moderates wielded little real power. Although implacably opposed to EAM, they were also opposed to the restoration of the monarchy. However, throughout 1945–1946 they not only found themselves powerless to restrain the right-wing terror but also allowed the political agenda to pass firmly to the royalist Right.

The ascendancy of the Right was confirmed by the first postwar elections. Helped by the strategic blunder of the left-wing parties, which abstained, the Populists won an overwhelming victory. The royalist triumph was complete in September 1946 when the referendum on the future of the monarchy produced a majority in favor of the king's return. With the Right now secure in power, the brutality of the anti-Communist struggle was given official blessing. With the escalation of both the White Terror and armed resistance from the Communists, the country drifted inexorably toward civil war. The armed struggle that followed brought more misery to a devastated country. In the fighting between 1946 and 1950 at least 34,000 people died, with another 50,000 ending up in government prisons and 140,000 leaving for exile, most never to return.[56]

55. Mazower, "Policing the Anti-Communist State in Greece," 129–50; M. Mazower, "The Cold War and the Appropriation of Memory: Greece after Liberation," 272–94; P. Papastratis, "The Purge of the Greek Civil Service on the Eve of the Civil War," 46–47.
56. Close, *Origins of the Greek Civil War,* 219–20.

George II, King of the Hellenes, September 1946. Photographic Archive
of the Benaki Museum, Athens. Photo by Dimitrios Charisiadis.

In 1944 Greece emerged from the most tragic episode in its history. The Axis occupation had left an indelible mark on the national psyche. Before long, many came
to believe that the country had escaped from one brutal totalitarian empire only
to be threatened with absorption into another. This increased the political polarization and encouraged extremism, leading to civil war rather than reconciliation.
Despite the apparent gravity of the new challenges, a ruthless anti-Communist tradition had long existed within both major strands of Greek politics. The polarization between Left and Right was a new form of schism marked by an unprecedented
degree of brutality. From the point of view of the economic crisis, the challenge was

to pursue the restoration of stability as the first priority, leaving political divisions to be shelved until the country had recovered. Such an approach found few enthusiasts within Greece.

The International Relief Effort

The rigors Greece endured during the Axis occupation also gave rise to another phenomenon: the common belief that the country had played a vital role in the war and that its sufferings had been far greater than those borne by any other participant. Such arguments were usually supported by reference to expressions of international admiration for Greece's courageous stand against the Italians in 1940–1941 and the Germans thereafter. By claiming that the Greek army's heroic resistance had disrupted the timetable for Operation Barbarossa, which ultimately led to the Axis' defeat, the proponents of this line of thinking could present Greece as the de facto savior of the free world.[57]

Such claims or beliefs only added to Greece's difficulty in addressing its postwar problems. Greek politicians became excessively inward-looking, continuously emphasizing Greece's losses to the exclusion of any other consideration. Once Greece was liberated, its politicians showed little interest in the subsequent course of the war and little appreciation of the continuing problems elsewhere. Equally damaging was the expectation that if reparations could not cover the full cost of Greek reconstruction, the Western Allies would be morally obliged to foot the bill. While the Allies fully acknowledged that Greece had the right to expect both compensation and international support, they deplored the implication that the "world owed Greece a living"—in other words, that the country would not have to mobilize its own resources in the task of recovery.[58] This fundamental divergence of attitudes was to prove harmful during the prolonged economic crisis of 1944–1947.

57. F. A. Spencer, *War and Postwar Greece: An Analysis Based on Greek Writings*, 12–18, 20, 26–27, 41; DSR 868.50/4–446, Greek Reconstruction Claims Committee: Statement, March 1946. The belief in the fatal delay to Operation Barbarossa has persisted in Greece to this day. In a recent study, Richter noted that it had become an "integral part of the national mythology," but pointed out there was little basis in fact; H. Richter, *Η Ιταλο-Γερμανική Επίθεση εναντίον της Ελλάδος* (The Italo-German Attack on Greece), 635–58. Another historian totally refuted the idea as based on "sloppy scholarship" and "wishful thinking"; M. Van Creveld, "The German Attack on the USSR: The Destruction of a Legend," 85. The fact that the defense of Greece did not influence the invasion of Russia should in no way undermine the heroism of the defenders.

58. DSR 868.51/8–1944, Shantz to the Secretary of State, August 19, 1944 (Enclosure: Memorandum by H.A. Hill); DSR 868.50/4–345, MacVeagh to the Secretary of State, April 23, 1945 (Enclosure: Memorandum by H. A. Hill, April 21, 1945); DSR 868.50/4–446, Rankin to the Secretary of State, April 4, 1946; DSR 868.50/6–1946, Rankin to the Secretary of State, June 19, 1946.

Greek hopes for favorable treatment from the Allies were largely successful, as the country became a major beneficiary of the postwar international relief effort and received large amounts of additional aid from the British and American governments. Greece had already been unique in receiving a considerable quantity of supplies while still under occupation. In late 1941 the growing realization of the extent of hunger within Greece led to calls for relief supplies. This required the consent of not only the occupying forces but also the British, who had to agree to a temporary relaxation of their blockade of the Greek coast. This proved far from straightforward. The British saw the feeding of occupied Europe as the responsibility of the occupiers themselves and were reluctant to allow the Axis to escape their obligations. Such attitudes attracted fierce resentment, and in the face of escalating pressure from various quarters the Foreign Office devised a plan by which food could be shipped to Greece from Turkey. Up to nineteen thousand tons of foodstuffs were supplied by August 1942,[59] before the scheme was dropped owing to growing shortages in Turkey. The amounts were in any case small compared to Greece's needs, and achieved little. More substantial shipments became possible only with the initiative of the Canadian government, which promised a monthly quota of fifteen thousand tons of wheat. Originally meant to form the basis of an international relief pool after liberation, the whole amount was made available to Greece for immediate use. In addition, the American government donated large quantities of pulses, powdered milk, and medical supplies. The goods were shipped in Swedish vessels and distributed under the aegis of Red Cross officials from Sweden and Switzerland. Despite considerable difficulties—several vessels were sunk either by mines or by aircraft from both sides—611,000 tons of supplies were delivered up to March 1945. Although neither the total costs nor the full value of the deliveries have been calculated, the scheme had cost about $41 million up to the end of March 1944.[60]

Despite the immediate importance of this effort for the population of occupied Greece, most attention was focused on the far greater task of postwar reconstruction. The first attempt to quantify the likely needs of liberated countries came with the creation of the Inter-Allied Bureau of Post-War Requirements in late 1941. This British-sponsored organization was in no position to furnish anything like the sums demanded and soon lost significance once the United States entered the

59. Several conflicting figures have been quoted: from 14,000 tons in G. A. Kazamias, "Turks, Swedes and Famished Greeks: Some Aspects of Famine Relief in Occupied Greece, 1941–44," 296; to 19,000 in Etmektsoglou-Koehn, *Axis Exploitation of Wartime Greece*, 448.

60. Kazamias, "Turks, Swedes and Famished Greeks," 293–307; Etmektsoglou-Koehn, *Axis Exploitation of Wartime Greece*, 445–56.

Three Red Cross ships bringing aid to Greece, November 2, 1944. Photograph courtesy of the Imperial War Museum, London.

war. The Americans set up their own body—the Foreign Economic Administration (FEA)—to deal with such issues, but with the growing understanding of the enormity of the task, a special agency was established under the auspices of the United Nations in 1943. This was the United Nations Relief and Rehabilitation Administration (UNRRA), which was to coordinate the international relief effort until its winding down at the end of 1946. Its first major task was to ascertain the likely needs of each recipient country. Inevitably, this led to lengthy exchanges, as each recipient country sought to obtain recognition for the largest possible claim. For the Greek side, negotiations were conducted by Kyriakos Varvaressos, the governor of the Bank of Greece, who succeeded in winning the acceptance of the Greek government's estimates in the face of mistrust from the Americans and the British, who regarded them as suspiciously high. Two major points of disagreement emerged. The Americans, who bore almost sole responsibility for financing UNRRA, were adamant that relief shipments would have to reflect the logistical possibilities of supply rather than actual demand. A second point arose from American concern that each recipient country should make the most efficient use of its own resources rather than rely solely on UNRRA aid. With the preservation of its gold and foreign exchange reserves, Greece was in a uniquely privileged position compared to

Signing the UNRRA Agreement. After the ceremony, on the steps of the palace, March 1, 1945. From left to right: R. G. A. Jackson, Lincoln MacVeagh, Ioannis Sophianopoulos, General Plastiras, R. F. Hendrickson, Reginald Leeper, M. Bellen. Photograph courtesy of the Imperial War Museum, London.

other occupied countries. Initially, UNRRA wished to offer relief supplies free of charge only to countries not in possession of foreign exchange, requiring that the rest should at least offer part payment. Varvaressos argued that given the exceptional degree of destruction in Greece, the foreign reserves would be essential to supplement reconstruction in areas not covered by UNRRA. His argument was accepted in late 1944, and Greece was released from the obligation to pay for relief supplies.[61]

Until UNRRA commenced operations in Greece in April 1945, the relief effort was carried out under the Military Liaison (ML) program, financed by the American, Canadian, and British governments and executed by British forces. Under the ML program, goods worth $27.7 million were shipped to Greece, including 336,000 tons of food, several thousand tons of industrial raw materials and agri-

61. Politakis, *Greek Policies of Recovery and Reconstruction*, 68–80; LBG/KVA/B/1, Η Δράσις μου εις την Διοίκησιν της Τραπέζης της Ελλάδος (My Years in the Bank of Greece), K. Varvaressos, 1953, 14–21.

cultural seeds, and a thousand vehicles and medical supplies. In addition, ML undertook repair work on bridges and public utilities and distributed huge quantities of footwear and clothing donated by the Red Cross. All items under ML were also furnished free of charge.[62]

Greece was one of the biggest beneficiaries of UNRRA's activities. As Table 2.5 shows, Greece (including the Dodecanese islands, formally incorporated in 1948) received goods worth $351 million, equivalent to 12.2 percent of the entire UNRRA program. The shipments included 1,056,000 tons of grain and grain products, 106,000 tons of dairy products, 57,000 tons of sugar, 177,000 tons of fertilizer, 51,000 tons of livestock, 520,000 tons of fuel and lubricants, 76,500 tons of raw materials, and 12,700 tons of farm machinery and tools. This compared very favorably with the totals for other countries, partly reflecting Greece's position as a net importer of food. Greece, with much the smallest population of any of the major recipients of UNRRA aid, received a greater value of food than either China or the Ukraine.[63]

The American and British governments also provided various forms of assistance. The British waived the £46-million 1940–1941 war loan, financed the Greek armed forces, which cost about £30 million during 1944–1947 alone, and extended a series of credits, of which the most important was the £10-million stabilization loan of January 1946. From the United States, Greece received credits worth $115 million during the same period: the Export-Import Bank loan of $25 million, $45 million for the purchase of American surplus war materiel in Europe, and another $45 million to finance the acquisition of one hundred Liberty ships to replace Greek merchant shipping lost during the war. In addition, various organizations in the United States and Britain raised more than $13 million for relief purposes in Greece.[64]

In addition to the assistance it was receiving from the Allies, Greece had expected to secure huge sums in compensation from the former occupying countries. In late 1945 Greek representatives at the Paris Conference on Reparations submitted claims amounting to $15.7 billion at 1938 prices. Under various settlements, Greece was eventually awarded $2.7 million from Germany, $105 million from Italy, and $45 million from Bulgaria, all to be paid in kind. The size of the awards caused considerable resentment within Greece, where it was felt that the extent of the wartime

62. Patterson, *Financial Experiences of Greece,* 157–58; FO371/48333 R12094, Report on Economic Conditions in Greece, May 31, 1945, 30–31.

63. G. Woodbridge et al., *The History of the United Nations Relief and Rehabilitation Administration,* vol. 3, 429 (Table 16); vol. 2, 462–65 (Tables 49, 50, 51, 52).

64. Patterson, *Financial Experiences of Greece,* 632–36; R. Frazier, *Anglo-American Relations with Greece: The Coming of the Cold War 1942–47,* 108; DSR 868.50/4–347, Tentative Report of the American Economic Mission to Greece, April 1, 1947, chap.10.

TABLE 2.5. Major Recipients of UNRRA Aid

Country	Total ($million)	Percentage of UNRRA total
China	517.8	18.03
Poland	477.9	16.64
Italy	418.2	14.56
Yugoslavia	415.6	14.47
Greece (a)	351.0	12.23
Czechoslovakia	261.3	9.10
Ukraine	188.2	6.55

Source: Woodbridge et al., *History of the United Nations Relief and Rehabilitation Administration*, vol. 3, 428 (Table 15).

(a) Including the Dodecanese Islands

TABLE 2.6. Major Components of UNRRA Aid to Greece (a)

Heading	Value ($million)	Percentage of UNRRA Total
Food	181.5	14.75
Grain Products	80.5	
Dairy Products	30.3	
Meat Products	12.2	
Clothing, Textiles & Footwear	33.7	8.04
Finished Clothing	10.0	
Raw Wool	5.0	
Raw Cotton	4.2	
Agricultural Rehabilitation	43.4	13.54
Livestock	9.6	
Machinery & Tools	6.3	
Seeds	5.9	
Industrial Rehabilitation	38.6	5.7
Fuels	8.7	

Source: Woodbridge et al., *History of the United Nations Relief and Rehabilitation Administration*, vol. 2, 450–53 (Tables 37, 38, 39, 40); 462–65 (Tables 49, 50, 51, 52); vol. 3, 428 (Table 15).

(a) Including the Dodecanese Islands

losses had not been acknowledged, and that Greek interests had been sacrificed to those of the former Axis powers. Such beliefs were to persist for decades.[65]

Apart from the reparations issue, however, Greece was relatively fortunate in obtaining international assistance on favorable terms. It received a much more generous share of UNRRA supplies than many far larger countries, while Allied governments were also providing various forms of subsidy and credit. In addition, Greece had its wartime debts waived and was able to receive relief supplies free of charge, despite having retained its prewar gold and foreign exchange reserves. In per capita

65. Patterson, *Financial Experiences of Greece*, 629–31. The issue of reparations still rages in the Greek press; for an example, see *Τὸ Βῆμα* (To Vema), November 8, 1998.

terms, it obtained more international aid than Britain—and in the Greek case almost the entire sum was in the form of grants, in stark contrast to what Britain had received.[66] Nevertheless, as subsequent chapters will demonstrate, the foreign assistance was to prove much less decisive than the donors had hoped. Greek politicians persistently complained about the inadequacy of Allied assistance and pressed for further credits and concessions, resisting all calls to mobilize their own resources for reconstruction. Much of the aid was put to poor use or even wasted, and did little more than allow successive governments in Athens to avoid uncomfortable decisions, unnecessarily prolonging ultimate economic recovery.

Aspects of British Involvement in Greece, 1940–1947

Prior to the mid-1930s British interests in Greece had been negligible, and owed as much to economic as to political considerations. This was to change when international tension escalated following Mussolini's invasion of Abyssinia. For Britain, Greece had little significance in itself, but its geographical location was important for Imperial communications and defense. Anxious to preserve this outpost, the British strove to reestablish a democratic and economically solvent Greece that would remain friendly to British interests and safe from the encroachment of the Soviet Union and its allies. To this end they were prepared not only to offer a large degree of moral support and some practical assistance but also to interfere in Greek political life, first by promoting the king, and then by seeking to build up a strong Center in order to neutralize the Far Left. As both internal divisions and the economic crisis became more acute, the British agonized over the measures necessary to secure their aims, fearing the need to assume an almost colonial degree of responsibility to ensure stability. This escalation of involvement became increasingly problematic as Britain lurched toward its own economic crisis, and by early 1947 London decided to scale down an effort that had yielded so few tangible results.

A Vital Imperial Problem

From the Greek point of view, the link with Britain had been of vital importance ever since independence. Britain was both Greece's main creditor and the principal guarantor of the country's territorial integrity. However, the view from London was very different. The British relationship with Greece was the result of

66. A. S. Milward, *The Reconstruction of Western Europe 1945–51*, 69.

two interrelated factors: Britain's role as a leading member of the Concert of Europe, anxious to prevent any major shift in the balance of power, and its economic predominance, which made it the world's biggest capital market. The intervention of the Great Powers, which helped secure Greek independence and led to the guarantee of 1832, was motivated mainly by the desire to prevent Greece from falling under the domination of any single power. In essence, the guarantee (which was not formally abolished until 1923) was similar to that extended to Belgium later in the decade. British concern over Greece was closely correlated to Great Power rivalry in the region, and became a major consideration only when events threatened to upset the balance of power in the Balkans or the eastern Mediterranean.

For Britain, Greece was neither an important market for industrial exports nor a significant source of raw materials, and remained a minor trading partner. However, Britain's role as the world's banker and pivot of the international economy created a long-standing interest in Greece because of the country's frequent refusal to honor its foreign debts. As previously recounted, Britain was always in the forefront of international efforts to secure a satisfactory settlement, playing a major role in the confrontation after 1843, the setting up of the IFC, and during the interwar loan negotiations.

Thus British involvement in Greek affairs derived from neither philanthropy nor even any great affection for a country that Hector McNeil, the undersecretary of state for foreign affairs, could dismiss as "backward, extravagant and irresponsible." As another official bluntly reminded his colleagues, the British were helping the Greeks solely out of "self interest."[67] For the British, it was the geographical proximity to the eastern Mediterranean and the Middle East that gave Greece special importance, and they were anxious to prevent it from coming under the domination of any third party. While the financial aspect gradually lost significance, the political dimensions assumed unprecedented importance following the international crisis arising out of Mussolini's invasion of Abyssinia. For Whitehall, the sole motive was to strengthen its ties with potential allies in the Mediterranean to counter the growing threat from Fascist Italy. Greece was thus merely one card in a larger British game varying between appeasement and containment of Italy. This vacillation toward Mussolini, together with the perceived impossibility of resisting any land attack on Greece, discouraged the British from seeking any formal alliance with Athens. Once a more sinister threat—from Hitler's Germany—emerged in early 1941, British attention focused on using Greece to build a wider Balkan coali-

---

67. FO371/58678 R3496, Minute by McNeil, March 29, 1946; FO371/48452 R20925, Lascelles to Hayter, November 11, 1945.

tion to resist Nazi expansion. The failure of such plans left Greece as Britain's "last card" in the region, an outcome that London had never intended, and one that spelt doom for British influence in southeastern Europe for the foreseeable future.[68]

Following the swift defeat of Greece by the Wehrmacht, British policy concentrated on maintaining close links with those Greek institutions that had successfully fled the country and ensuring that British influence would be restored once the Axis powers were defeated. To that end, the king and the government were transferred to exile in the British-controlled Middle East, while the armed forces served under the British High Command. Initially, the international aspect of Anglo-Greek relations became less important than the problem of the growing political polarization between the Greeks themselves, particularly the increasing importance of EAM-ELAS. The seriousness of the internal divisions within Greece was readily apparent once it became obvious that the Soviet Union—the natural ally of the Communist-led Left—would inevitably become a major player in southeastern Europe following its successes against the Wehrmacht. By May 1944 it was clear that the restoration of Greece as a "British sphere of influence" also necessitated the prevention of "Russian domination" of the country. A series of meetings with Soviet officials sought to obtain Moscow's recognition of British predominance in post-liberation Greece, a task given greater urgency by the Red Army's occupation of Bulgaria. The aim was finally achieved in October 1944, when without the knowledge of the Greeks, Churchill and Stalin signed the notorious percentages agreement, amounting to a partition of the Balkans into respective spheres of influence.[69]

Shortly afterwards, the British acted to safeguard what they came to regard as their "outpost in South-Eastern Europe." They established a physical presence in Greece soon after the German withdrawal in the form of an expeditionary force of ten thousand troops sent in with the National Unity Government in order to forestall any attempt to establish a Communist regime. Although the War Office spoke of the assumption that an entry into Greece would be "solely for the purpose of relief," it is hard to believe that other considerations played no part. Even if the presence of a disciplined military contingent was necessary for the efficient distribution of relief supplies, its commander—Lieutenant General Ronald Scobie—was formally accorded the right to "exercise supreme responsibility and authority" not only in the war zone but also in the event of any "serious state of disorder." As the chasm widened between the Communists and other groupings after liberation, it

68. J. S. Koliopoulos, *Greece and the British Connection 1935–1941*, 294–300.
69. P. Papastratis, *British Policy towards Greece during the Second World War 1941–1944*, 198–200, 211, 217–25.

became increasingly likely that the expeditionary force would be called upon to fight. As already noted, this did indeed happen in December 1944, when British troops engaged in bitter clashes with ELAS guerrillas in Athens. By the end of January 1945 the British presence in Greece totaled more than seventy-five thousand men.[70]

Before long, the suspicion that Stalin was no longer intending to honor his part of the bargain created the prospect of a far more serious conflict. Although the British doubted whether the Soviets were willing to "risk an open clash," it was taken for granted that Moscow would "take advantage" of any weakening of Britain's influence in Greece, possibly by sponsoring aggressive moves by its Balkan satellites, Yugoslavia and Bulgaria. Any such developments would inevitably undermine Turkey, with serious implications for the entire Middle East. London was convinced that its military presence was the only factor preventing such a disaster. To help deter the Communist threat, the British, who had steadily been withdrawing their own forces, undertook to build up a one hundred thousand–strong Greek army. The key role of the remaining British military presence was even more keenly felt in Athens, where ambassador Reginald Leeper predicted that the country would fall under the "bondage of the Kremlin" if such support was withdrawn. Increasingly, the British came to see the "Greek problem" as primarily one of "Anglo-Russian relations."[71] As the international political climate continued to deteriorate, it was the growing fears of Soviet expansionism, coupled with London's obvious inability to counter the Communist threat alone, which finally brought in the Americans as a serious player in Greek affairs.

The "Choice of Evils"

The British desire to restore their influence in post-liberation Greece inevitably led to considerable interference in the country's internal affairs. This had not been

70. FO371/48452 R20925, Lascelles to Hayter, November 11, 1945; FO371/48338 R20299, Athens to FO, Telegram no. 2406, November 30, 1945; G. M. Alexander, *The Prelude to the Truman Doctrine: British Policy in Greece 1944–1947*, 48, 59, 65; T160/1265/18217/014/1, Key to Rugman, June 30, 1944; WO204/8760, Leeper to Papandreou, November 24, 1944 (Enclosure: Memorandum of Agreement Regarding Questions Concerning Civil Administration, Jurisdiction and Relief Arising out of Military Operations in Greek Territory, November 24, 1944); Close, *Origins of the Greek Civil War*, 139; H. Butterfield Ryan, *The Vision of Anglo-America: The US-UK Alliance and the Emerging Cold War 1943–1946*, 196.

71. FO371/58673 R1992, C.O.S. (46) 35 (0), February 6, 1946; FO371/48276 R13082, Leeper to Sargent, August 2, 1945 (Enclosure: Note by Sir R. Leeper on the Present Situation in Greece, August 2, 1945); FO371/58678 R3496, Leeper to Sargent, February 27, 1946; FO371/58680 R4219, Athens to FO, Telegram no. 59, March 1, 1946.

Prime Minister Papandreou helps to load the first sack of flour into a truck brought in by ML, while Lieutenant General Scobie looks on, October 21, 1944. Photograph courtesy of the Imperial War Museum, London.

necessary before World War II. While the British had played no part in the creation of the Metaxas dictatorship and felt no particular affection for it, they could be reasonably pleased with a regime that was essentially pro-British and accordingly lent it their support.[72]

As the war progressed, the direction that Greek society took under Axis occupation presented particular problems for British long-term aims. With the radicalization of the populace and the rapid growth of the organized Left, it became increasingly obvious that the institutions in exile—the monarch and the discredited

72. Koliopoulos, *Greece and the British Connection*, 295–96.

remnants of the old regime—could not easily return after liberation without some degree of social friction. Because the British were slow to understand the nature and extent of the changes within Greece, and supremely convinced of their own correct appreciation of the situation, they spent most of 1943–1944 pondering the future of the king and the composition of the first post-liberation government.

Even before World War II, the Anglophile George II had been the cornerstone of British attention in Greece, a view reinforced by Churchill, both a close friend of the king and an admirer of constitutional monarchy as the ideal form of government. Thus in Whitehall, the restoration of the king as the "indisputable guardian" of the "British connection" seemed the most obvious avenue to restore British influence in postwar Greece. Such thinking, based on the assumption that the majority of Greeks genuinely desired the king's return after liberation, undoubtedly involved either a "gross misinterpretation" of the facts or a "serious self-deception." The British stubbornly stuck to their original policy despite hostility from republican politicians and representatives of the resistance within Greece. Not until the summer of 1944 was it widely accepted that the king should remain abroad until a new plebiscite could be staged.[73]

The British genuinely believed that the post-liberation Greek government should be more representative and that the old dictatorship should not be restored. However, officials in Whitehall failed to foresee the rapid rise of the organized Left under EAM and eventually became worried that the movement might seize power after the German withdrawal. At first they hoped that EAM could be weakened by enticing away its more moderate elements. By the spring of 1944, it was clear that this was unlikely to succeed, and a new approach sought to embrace EAM in a coalition government. The organization could thus be partly neutralized if it accepted, or ostracized and isolated if it refused.[74]

The desire to prevent a Communist takeover remained paramount in British thinking long after liberation. Thus the various moves against EAM have dominated the attention of later historians, who have sought to present the British as largely responsible for both the civil war and the coming to power of the Right.[75] The reality was much more complex. In 1945, in a discussion concerning the future of the monarchy, a senior embassy official bemoaned the fact that the British were

73. T. Sfikas, "People at the Top Can Do These Things, Which Others Can't Do: Winston Churchill and the Greeks, 1940–1945," 311–12; Papastratis, *British Policy towards Greece*, 91; Alexander, *Prelude to the Truman Doctrine*, chap. 1.

74. Papastratis, *British Policy towards Greece*, 219–24.

75. For an expansion of this view of British responsibility for the civil war and the rise of the Right, see especially T. Sfikas, *The British Labour Government and the Greek Civil War 1945–1949: The Imperialism of 'Non-Intervention.'*

faced by a "choice of evils."[76] This statement could be applied to most of the dilemmas confronting the British in their dealings with Greek politics during 1944–1947. Whitehall's determination to ensure a friendly government in Athens free from Communist domination was never synonymous with uncritical support for the Right. By the end of 1944 the Labour partners in the coalition could hardly be unaware of the strength of grassroots feeling condemning the apparent suppression of the Left in favor of the reactionary Right. Calls to the Labour party to prevent a right-wing domination of Greece continued to flood in throughout the whole crisis.[77] Leeper needed no such urgings. Bemoaning the impotence of the Center as Greece's "great weakness," he consistently sought to build up a "Third Force"—a moderate Center—in the hope that a gradual return to economic normality would steer a radicalized population away from political extremism. Increasingly fearing the Right as much as they did the Left, the British endeavored to prevent Greece from turning either "Communist, or Fascist."[78]

To this end, Leeper was instrumental in propping up a series of ineffectual provisional governments dominated by republicans and moderates, anxious that some stability be achieved before the all-important elections and plebiscite on the future of the monarchy. He claimed that everything possible had been done to stop public opinion from "swinging too far to the Right," and the British even acknowledged that they had lost much right-wing support by demonstrating they had not fought a "left-wing terrorist dictatorship" simply to hand over power to the "opposite extreme." However, they were aware that their efforts to bolster the Center had been a failure.[79] In such circumstances, the main beneficiaries of British intervention were the parties of the Right. Following the Right's electoral victory of March 1946, the British were forced to extend support to a grouping that was certainly not to their taste. Nevertheless, they were hardly in a position to withdraw their backing from a government with a popular mandate, even when the new regime embarked upon distinctly undemocratic and unconstitutional measures against its left-wing opponents.

76. FO371/48277 R14008, Caccia to Sargent, August 14, 1945.

77. For several appeals to the Labour party to block right-wing domination from constituency parties and trade union branches, see National Museum of Labour History, Manchester: Labour Party Archives, International Department, Correspondence on Greece.

78. Sir R. Leeper, *When Greek Meets Greek,* 209; Alexander, *Prelude to the Truman Doctrine,* 64; N. Clive, "British Policy Alternatives 1945–1946," 214; F0371/58804 R14062, Norton to Bevin, September 12, 1946.

79. FO371/58677 R3338, Leeper to Bevin, February 22, 1946; FO371/58680 R4219, Athens to FO, Telegram no. 59, March 1, 1946 (Enclosure: Political Summary 1945); FRUS, 1946: Rankin to the Secretary of State, February 28, 1946, vol. 7, 116.

Sir Reginald Leeper, British
ambassador to Greece, 1943–
1946. Photograph courtesy of
the British Embassy, Athens.

Even if the British frequently appeared to be shortsighted, it would be unfair to
accord them sole responsibility for the outcome of developments in Athens. Despite their substantial influence in the country's internal affairs, it is rather naive to
assume that they were automatically in a position to impose their will on specific
issues. There is no doubt that by the time Greece was liberated, the British held
"exceptional power" in a country that was little more than a "British protectorate,"
with Leeper behaving more like a "colonial governor" than a normal diplomat.[80]
However, the British ability to dictate the course of events should not be overstated.
While Leeper could wield considerable influence over the composition of cabinets
and could invariably prevail upon individual ministers to agree in principle to various measures, it was a vastly different matter when it came to persuading the Greeks
either to implement unpopular policies or to abandon favored ones. This would be

80. Clive, "British Policy Alternatives," 213–14.

Sir Clifford Norton, British
ambassador to Greece, 1946–
1951. Photograph courtesy of
the British Embassy, Athens.

demonstrated time and time again through the economic developments of 1944–
1947, and was also valid for most of the major political issues during the period.
As an example, far from acquiescing in the White Terror, the British protested with
depressing regularity without any success in changing the policy.[81]

A final recurring feature of British policy in Greece was the reluctance to accept
that the country's political polarization made it largely unreceptive to orthodox
economic advice. The British consistently believed that solving the economic crisis
had to take priority over political differences and felt certain that the public could be
galvanized by a resolute governmental stance. They frequently criticized successive
ministers for neglecting the propaganda and publicity aspects of the fight against
inflation. In May 1945, Leeper believed that it was enough for the government to
"explain the facts plainly to the public" and reminded Admiral Voulgaris of the
mobilizing effect of Churchill's "blood and sweat and tears" speech. Later that autumn another British official was surprised that the Varvaressos program should

81. A recent study has shown that the British Police Mission genuinely sought to create an impartial demilitarized and depoliticized police force, but was ineffective in the face of interference
from successive ministers and the extremist anticommunist stance of the leadership of the Greek
security services; Mazower, "Policing the Anti-Communist State in Greece," 143–46.

be attracting such hostility, precisely when the country should "so obviously be pulling together."[82] Nevertheless, from the Greek perspective, nothing was so obvious, as comparisons with wartime Britain were of doubtful validity. A "blood and sweat and tears" speech might well have galvanized public opinion in the autumn of 1940, when the nation stood united in the face of a single external threat. It was clearly inadequate in 1945, when the removal of the occupying forces had left a country torn by internal divisions. Severe political polarization, aggravated by the experience of the occupation, had left little consensus as to Greece's future.

Perhaps the real failure of British involvement in Greece was that despite the appearance that they held all the keys to an acceptable solution, the outcome proved so unsatisfactory. It was an unfortunate consequence of internal Greek politics that the natural supporters of an anticommunist policy—the Right and the Center— proved such unattractive allies. The Center, which the British cultivated so assiduously, lacked both credibility and vision, while the Right demonstrated timidity, small-mindedness, and a ruthlessness matching that of the Communists. That the British should have sought to neutralize the Far Left—first as an alien, undemocratic force, and later as a potential agent of a Soviet takeover—should not come as a surprise, but perhaps the real tragedy was that earlier developments in Greek politics—which the British had done nothing to oppose—had left so few of the country's progressive elements committed to genuine democracy.

British insistence on promoting their own view of the future Greece might seem arrogant, but if the only apparent alternative was a Greece in the Soviet orbit, then the eventual outcome—unsatisfactory as it was—probably justified the effort. In hindsight, the likelihood that the country would fall into the Communist bloc seems debatable, but it seemed a genuine possibility at the time. The experience of the Soviet satellites after 1945 suggests that almost anything was preferable to the fate of the so-called people's democracies. Whether British determination to maintain a sphere of influence in the world of the Atlantic Charter and the newly created United Nations smacks of a certain hypocrisy is beyond the scope of this work, but it would be disingenuous to single out the British as the chief villain of the postwar world.

As already noted, the Anglo-Greek connection throughout this period typified the unequal relations between a major power with global interests and a minor state preoccupied with its own more limited considerations. The relationship was permeated with frequent misunderstandings, usually resulting from Greek failure

82. T236/1044, Athens to FO, Telegram no. 1242, May 25, 1945; FO371/48330 R7924, Athens to FO, Telegram no. 1108, May 4, 1945; FO371/48336 R17044, EAC(45) 7th Meeting, August 25, 1945.

to comprehend the wider nature of British interests, with an according overestimation of the importance London placed on Greece. The British were invariably guilty of failing to keep their Greek clients informed of the exact nature of their aims and actions. The secret percentages agreement was only the most blatant example of a tendency to take major decisions without the knowledge of those most concerned. The British approach was both well meaning and essentially selfish, being based on the assumption that a parliamentary democracy and close links with Britain were in the country's best interests. Nevertheless, it was also marked by a dismal failure to perceive the true nature of political developments within Greece and an unshakable belief in the righteousness of its actions.

Despite the determination to retain a Greece friendly to imperial interests, the British were never keen to assume a wider degree of formal responsibility for the country. This had been a problem even before World War II, when Metaxas had sought a concrete alliance, in contrast with the close but informal collaboration that the British had preferred. The unwillingness to commit scarce land forces to an essentially indefensible territory reduced the real value of any help the British could offer. The policy remained in force after the outbreak of war and the Italian invasion, and was reversed only after it became clear that the Germans were preparing to attack Greece. Even then, the policy shift derived from the hope to cement a common Balkan front against the Axis threat rather than a desire to save Greece alone. The British refusal to enter into any wider formal commitment continued during the occupation, when a Greek request for a postwar political alliance was turned down as premature. Instead, the British opted for a standard military agreement on the lines of those already signed with the other governments in exile.[83]

The issue became more complicated after liberation, as the British-sponsored governments in Athens were clearly unable to restore economic stability. This undermined Whitehall's political aims and exacerbated the threat of communism from both within and without. Initially hopeful that Greece would recover quickly, the British were not only unable to free themselves from financial obligations taken on for the duration of the war but also became drawn ever deeper into the country's internal affairs. Both problems caused considerable unease within Whitehall: the former proved particularly costly at a time when Britain's own balance of payments

---

83. Koliopoulos, *Greece and the British Connection,* 296–300; Papastratis, *British Policy towards Greece,* 25, 43–44. For the text of the military agreement, see FO371/32206 W3793, Agreement between the Royal Hellenic Government and the Government of the United Kingdom Concerning the Organization and Employment of the Greek Armed Forces, March 9, 1942.

situation approached disaster, while the latter generated fears that the British would have to assume extensive responsibility for a situation they felt they could do little to change.

The "Clear Conflict": Security versus Finance

Even before the defeat of Germany, London sought to disengage from its 1942 undertaking to equip and maintain the Greek armed forces. In practical terms, the military agreement had obliged Britain to pay for these forces for as long as they remained under British High Command. Political and economic considerations within Greece were to prolong the commitment far beyond the scope of the original treaty. As early as January 1945, Leeper had complained of the "anomaly" that the British were still paying for repatriated units, which were now rightly the responsibility of the Athens government. At first, beset with economic problems, the latter sought a loan to enable Greece to assume the burden. However, Whitehall rejected both the continuation of subventions and the prospect of a loan, and the Greeks were duly informed.[84] Despite the finality of this statement, nothing came of it. The extent of the British commitment was brought up again in early May, when the Treasury sought clarification of many aspects of what had become an extremely confused issue. Following consultations with the Foreign and War Offices, it was decided that London should complete the initial equipping of a new Greek army, up to one hundred thousand strong, but that the Athens government should assume the costs of subsequent maintenance from the beginning of June. The Cabinet endorsed this, although the date on which payments would cease was left open.[85]

At this point, final decisions were complicated by the intervention of the British embassy in Athens, which warned of the likely internal and regional consequences of any withdrawal of funding. Harold Caccia, who took charge of the embassy during Leeper's stay in London, feared that the Greeks could not readily afford to finance their own armed forces, and that it was politically inopportune to force

84. FO371/48326, including R1054, Athens to FO, Telegram no. 183, January 14, 1945; R1719, Athens to FO, Telegram no. 18 Remac, January 22, 1945; FO371/48327, including R2022, FO to Athens, Telegram no. 392, February 5, 1945; R3216, Leeper to Sophianopoulos, February 6, 1945.

85. T236/1044, Minute by Davidson, May 1, 1945; Howard to Waley, May 16, 1945 (Enclosure: Draft Note); Waley to Howard, May 17, 1945; FO371/48330, including R4682, Davidson to Laskey, May 5, 1945 (Enclosure: Greece, May 3, 1945); R7682, Notes of a Meeting Held at the Foreign Office, November 9, 1945; Cash to Howard, May 23, 1945; T236/1045, Laskey to Cash, June 16, 1945; CAB65/53, Cabinet 10 (45), June 20, 1945.

them to do so at a time when Varvaressos was staging a "desperate fight" to save the economy. Quintin Hill, Leeper's financial adviser, added that the request would be akin to asking the government to commit financial and political suicide, and would send potentially disastrous signals to the country's northern neighbors. Still reeling from the sudden termination of Lend-Lease, Whitehall was adamant that the funding had to cease, but conceded that the Greeks should be given an indication of this decision rather than be simply presented with a date. However, after the resignation of Varvaressos in early September, the Foreign Office admitted it would be impossible to press the Greeks on the matter given the likelihood of total political and economic collapse in Athens. Even so, the need to take action was still clear: while the Foreign Office suggested that the payments should stop at the end of the year, the Treasury warned that the British should lose no time in ridding themselves of the "burden."[86]

By late October it was obvious that things could not be put off any longer. Overruling warnings from Leeper, the British duly informed the Greeks that the subventions would cease as of January 1, 1946.[87] The response was predictable. Grigorios Kasimatis, the minister of finance, warned that the news would have an "exceptionally unpleasant" effect on public opinion, while both the regent and Emmanuel Tsouderos, the minister of coordination, felt that the burden would be impossible to bear. The latter complained of the "irreparable" damage that would result from the decision and stressed that the additional expenses would bankrupt the country, given the already huge demands of balancing the budget and reconstruction.[88]

With the arrival of 1946, the deadline was quietly forgotten, and the subventions continued without a break. Tsouderos was informed that the British were not prepared to foot the whole bill for 1946, but was given vague promises that some assistance would be forthcoming. The concessions inevitably reawakened conflict-

---

86. FO371/48273 R11299, Caccia to Hayter, June 26, 1945; FO371/48334 R12941, Hill to Rowe-Dutton, July 25, 1945; FO371/48373 R14471, Sargent to Rowe-Dutton, August 28, 1945; Rowe-Dutton to Hill, August 31, 1945; FO371/48335 R14823, Sargent to Rowe-Dutton, September 4, 1945; FO371/48374 R15230, Rowe-Dutton to Sargent, September 7, 1945.

87. FO371/48374, including R17924, FO to Athens, Telegram no. 2137, October 19, 1945; R17925, FO to Athens, Telegram no. 2154, October 21, 1945; R17985, Athens to FO, Telegram no. 2151, October 22, 1945; FO to Athens, Telegram no. 2173, October 24, 1945; R18036, Athens to FO, Telegram no. 2156, October 23, 1945.

88. FO371/48285 R19830, Record of Conversation Held at His Majesty's Embassy, November 16, 1945; FO371/48338 R20282, Record of Discussion Held at the Palace of the Regency, November 19, 1945; FO371/48416 R21249, Record of Meeting at H.B.M. Embassy, November 22, 1945; FO371/48375 R21120, Athens to FO, Telegram no. 2508, December 18, 1945; FO371/58765 R1789, Tsouderos to MacNeil, January 23, 1946.

ing views on the whole issue, with added urgency arising from the seriousness of Britain's own balance of payments crisis. By this time the chancellor was issuing dire warnings to minimize the difficulties by avoiding all nonessential outlays abroad, while Treasury officials predicted an imminent plunge in the British standard of living unless the Foreign Office halted its "political overseas expenditure."[89]

Such gloomy forecasts cut little ice with the Chiefs of Staff, for whom the answer was clear: given the strategic importance of Greece, a necessary defense effort had to be maintained, and as the Greeks could not afford this the British had no choice but to keep up their payments. While not disagreeing with the strategic priorities, both the Foreign Office and the Treasury felt little enthusiasm for such recommendations. They pointed out that Whitehall was itself unable to afford the sums involved, and that as the maintenance of a one hundred thousand–strong establishment was clearly beyond everybody's means, a force half that size would surely be more appropriate. Unsurprisingly, the Chiefs of Staff were unimpressed. They dismissed the proposed reductions, which they claimed would destroy both the operational effectiveness and the deterrence value of the Greek armed forces. Moreover, they stressed that the overall savings from such a move would be more illusory than real, as British troops would have to prolong their stay in the country if the Greek army was not brought up to the necessary strength.[90]

Such discussions typify the fundamental British dilemma: the choice between security and financial considerations. Unless the British paid for a substantial Greek force, they would have to retain their own military presence in the country, which would not only prove equally expensive, but would also complicate negotiations over a general Balkan settlement. Given the continuing uncertainties, London could do little more than propose a review of the situation after the elections. Within weeks it was being suggested that the review should take place at the end of the summer. By now it was apparent that the British felt unable to resolve the "clear conflict" between their "strategic requirements" in Greece and the "financial aspect" of the commitment. However, it was equally obvious that the Greeks were facing their own dilemma: the choice between "having an army" and "economic ruin." A decision was finally prompted by the repeated urgings of the British representatives in

89. FO371/58765, including R1789, Sargent to Tsouderos, January 30, 1946; R1775, Minute by Waley, January 28, 1946; FO371/58673 R1992, Sargent to Hollis, February 20, 1946.

90. FO371/58673 R1992, C.O.S. (46) 35 (o), February 6, 1946; Minute by Laskey, February 11, 1946; Minute by Williams, February 13, 1946; Waley to Hayter, February 14, 1946; Hayter to Waley, February 20, 1946; Sargent to Hollis, February 20, 1946; Fo371/58679 R3861, Stapleton to Sargent, March 11, 1946.

Athens, who warned that the Greeks were clearly unable to pay for anything more than a token force. In such circumstances, Whitehall eventually agreed to prolong its payments until the end of March 1947.[91]

The "Second Egypt"

Given the British dismay over the prolongation of temporary wartime commitments, it is hardly surprising that the prospect of assuming additional responsibilities in Greece seemed particularly unattractive to many Whitehall officials. Such anxieties led to rejecting an early ML proposal to attach British advisers to various ministries in Athens. However, by the spring of 1945, following the signing of the Varkiza Agreement, London decided to expand British involvement by creating new bodies to help consolidate government authority. These were advisory missions designed to reorganize the armed forces and security services.[92] Thus, despite the disbanding of the ML, which was to be superseded by UNRRA in April 1945, most of its nonrelief functions and much of its personnel were transferred to the British embassy.

While the temporary necessity for a large Allied establishment had seemed acceptable in the transitional period after liberation, the Treasury had substantial doubts about maintaining a sizable British presence in postwar Greece. Its officials worried that the British commitment appeared to have escalated rather than diminished, and bemoaned the fact that Whitehall had chosen to become "involved up to the hilt." The Treasury officials felt that given the open-ended nature of the new arrangement, there was no clearly defined limit of British liability. Moreover, they observed that the potential price of failure continued to rise: while inflation was increasing the cost of maintaining British forces in the country, the growing possibility of civil unrest would inevitably involve additional troops and expenditure. They

91. FO371/58681 R4711, Minute by Hayter, March 14, 1946; FO371/58683 R5167, D.O. (46) 43, March 25, 1946; FO371/58688 R6515, Waley to Warner, April 23, 1946; Warner to Waley, April 30, 1946; FO371/58766, including R4847, Tsouderos to Sargent, March 15, 1946; R6356, Norton to Sargent, April 15, 1946; Summary of Comments on M. Tsouderos' Letter to Sir Orme Sargent of 15th March; R7246, Norton to Sargent, May 8, 1946; FO371/58729 R7947, Athens to FO, Telegram no. 1201, May 27, 1946; CAB128/5, Cabinet 54 (46), June 3, 1946; FO371/58814 R11052, D.O. (46) 91, July 22, 1946.

92. FO371/43726 R21946, Caserta to FO, Telegram no. 970, December 27, 1944; FO to Athens, Telegram no. 248, January 23, 1945; FO371/48257 R3559, Discussion on Greece at the British Embassy, February 15, 1945; W.P. (45) 138, Memorandum by Eden, March 5, 1945; CAB65/49, War Cabinet 29 (45), March 12, 1945.

feared that if the situation collapsed Britain would certainly be blamed, and would probably be expected to play a major role in financing Greek reconstruction.[93]

It was not only the size of the new establishment that generated disquiet within Treasury circles. The exact functions and powers were issues requiring clearer definition. Officials questioned the wisdom of maintaining advisers without obtaining any assurance that their counsel would be heeded by the Greeks, and warned that Britain might find itself held responsible for any failure to solve the crisis while having no real power to enforce appropriate measures for its solution. It was felt that London had to choose between either scaling down the commitment to Athens or becoming more effectively involved. Without real power to act, it was likely the British would end up with "all the blame and the bills" if the situation could not be saved.[94]

The anxieties were temporarily allayed during the summer of 1945 when it seemed that Varvaressos would be able to restore stability. However, once such hopes evaporated, calls for a further escalation of British involvement were renewed. In September, Leeper felt that action to end the crisis was "beyond the capacities" of the government and suggested that in cooperation with UNRRA, the British should consider a "much closer" degree of "control" over the "Greek economic administration." In addition, he proposed that a special mission be sent to help reorganize the country's civil service. This met with a frosty response in Whitehall, which had consistently shied away from such calls to take on additional responsibilities. In recent months, the Foreign Office had been reluctant to accede to requests that the military and police missions should assume executive powers. The latest suggestion from Leeper seemed to go even further, causing officials to warn of the dangers of moving down a "slippery slope," as this would inevitably end in "turning Greece into a second Egypt." Amid fears that the British would be "saddled with the blame" for the "shortcomings" of the Greeks, Leeper's ideas were rejected.[95]

Such misgivings were soon overtaken by events, as the Greek economy deteriorated rapidly during the following months. The growing likelihood of total economic collapse, threatening to neutralize all British efforts to maintain political stability, soon overrode the fear of the "slippery slope." The British launched a

93. T236/1044, Minute by Sandberg, April 20, 1945; Minute by Davidson, April 21, 1945.
94. Ibid.
95. Alexander, *Prelude to the Truman Doctrine*, 92, 119–21; T236/1046, Athens to FO, Telegram no. 1959, September 25, 1945; FO371/48282, including R16628, Athens to FO, Telegram no. 1982, September 28, 1945; FO to Athens, Telegram no. 2071, October 10, 1945; R16720, Minute by Hayter, October 3, 1945.

series of broader initiatives culminating in the London Agreement of January 1946, which amounted to a degree of control over several aspects of Greek economic life. Inevitably, this involved a greater responsibility for the country's future. Thus within months of dismissing suggestions for a moderate degree of supervision in conjunction with an international agency, the British single-handedly took on an even more extensive commitment. Such a solution, almost approaching a "second Egypt," was the price London had to pay in order to secure the kind of Greece that accorded with wider British interests. It had become clear that the price would spiral still further unless the venture was successful, while the political costs of failure would have been inordinately higher in terms of lost prestige.[96]

Nevertheless, this policy shift was not embraced with equal enthusiasm by all sections of the British establishment. Officials at the Treasury and the Bank of England clung tenaciously to the orthodox anti-inflation line, dismissing any other consideration as secondary. The initiatives that led to the London Agreement came from the politicians and the diplomats rather than the economists. The decision to widen the British commitment came firmly from Ernest Bevin, the secretary of state for foreign affairs, and his department. With Greece sliding toward disaster, Foreign Office officials became exasperated by the Treasury emphasis on budgetary measures. Leeper warned London not to take a "narrow financial view" of what was essentially a political matter and poured scorn on the idea that a "bankrupt state" could be "braced into becoming solvent." By this time, even some Treasury representatives were coming around to such views, with one eminent expert criticizing the constant strictures on budget austerity as akin to "telling a beggar . . . to live within his income." However, most financial experts were unwilling parties to the packages resulting from the Bevin initiative. Horrified by any suggestion that balancing the budget could be anything but top priority, they were unconvinced that any other solution could be successful and felt that financially unsound measures had been dictated by the wider agenda of the politicians. The most notable example occurred in early 1946 when the size of the British loan to back the latest stabilization plan was doubled as a result of Foreign Office pressure. The only purpose of this move, which cost the Exchequer £5 million, was to make the

---

96. FO371/58720 R531, Athens to FO, Telegram no. 75, January 10, 1946. Other possibilities mooted at the time included the incorporation of Greece into either the Empire or the Commonwealth. Even Leeper seriously recommended the granting of "Dominion status" as the most satisfactory guarantee of Greek independence and stability. Unsurprisingly, such suggestions met with a frigid response from Foreign Office officials; FO371/58678 R3496, Leeper to Sargent, February 27, 1946; Minute by Hayter, March 8, 1946; Minute by Warner, March 11, 1946; Minute by McNeil, March 29, 1946.

London Agreement more palatable to the Greeks. With wider interests at stake, Foreign Office considerations were allowed to override the cautious orthodoxy of the Treasury.[97]

The arrangements resulting from the London Agreement marked the high point of British involvement in Greece. As in the summer of 1945, optimism that solutions might still be attainable temporarily quieted fears about the extent of the commitment. However, when the relative ineffectiveness of British efforts became fully apparent, dissenting voices were raised once again. In August 1946 the head of the British Economic Mission (BEM)—the main institution arising out of the London Agreement—complained that the body he chaired had not only achieved little so far but also would be unlikely to achieve anything in the future unless it assumed yet more extensive powers and responsibilities. Refusing even to consider such a possibility, he recommended instead a winding down of British involvement. Although the Foreign Office dismissed the suggestions as unsatisfactory and "extremely defeatist," it also rejected the opposite view: as both the Americans and international agencies were beginning to show an interest in Greek affairs, there was no longer a need to contemplate any further escalation of the British role.[98]

The internal disagreements over the extent of the commitment to Greece highlight the tortuous course of British attempts to deal with the country's problems. While London never lost sight of the desirability of retaining its "outpost in South-Eastern Europe," there was little consensus as to how this was to be achieved. Instead of a single monolithic stance, Whitehall adopted a whole series of policies reflecting both the differing preoccupations of its departments and its latest perceptions of the Greek situation. Thus an essentially consistent strategy was accompanied by frequent and substantial shifts in tactics. These changes in emphasis, invariably in response to developments within Greece, created much friction between not only various ministries but also the civilians and the military. While the war lasted, alternative viewpoints were understandably subordinated to the overriding aim of achieving victory. However, different perspectives soon resurfaced to generate endless complications for British decision-makers. Inevitably, the concerns

97. FO371/48289 R21543, Athens to FO, Telegram no. 2573, December 27, 1945; FO371/58720 R531, Athens to FO, Telegram no. 75, January 10, 1946; T236/1048, The Greek Currency Problem, F. Leith-Ross, December 11, 1945; T236/1049, Minute by Eady, January 10, 1946. For details of the conflict between the Foreign Office and the Treasury, see section entitled The Treasury Plan, chap. 5.

98. FO371/58803 R13630, The Future of the British Economic Mission to Greece, Lt. General Clark, August 30, 1946; Minute by Williams, September 20, 1946; Minute by Selby, September 20, 1946.

of some British agents were often divergent from—and even contradictory to—those of their colleagues in other departments. Whereas the Foreign Office naturally saw matters in the grandest of terms, emphasizing international relations and Britain's place in the world, British representatives in Athens had to be exceptionally sensitive to the most minute of changes in the Greek psychological climate. The Treasury was primarily concerned with demands on the public purse and the need for sound fiscal policies, while the Chiefs of Staff were preoccupied with the practicalities of maintaining a force capable of deterring Communist aggression. Unsurprisingly, each agency's preoccupation with its own remit led to suggestions that were anathema to officials elsewhere in Whitehall. The two examples previously mentioned—the Foreign Office insistence on sacrificing £5 million as a psychological gesture to Greek public opinion, and the joint Treasury/Foreign Office initiative to save money by halving the Greek army—must have provoked sighs of exasperation among those responsible for the prosecution of sound fiscal and defense policies.

It would be an oversimplification to claim that all policy disagreements within Whitehall arose from the "clear conflict" between the need to maintain Britain's international standing and its growing economic inability to keep up its worldwide commitments. After all, although the Foreign Office and the Treasury squabbled frequently on these issues, they readily moved close to a common front against the Chiefs of Staff. Nevertheless, the narrowing financial restraints played an increasingly central role in the heated debates over the need to withdraw from Greece. Before the severity of the postwar balance of payments crisis was understood, the Foreign Office still thought of Britain as a world power and acted accordingly. However, it rapidly became increasingly difficult to justify extensive British involvement in Greece given the depressing combination of economic difficulties at home, the apparent futility of efforts that had been undertaken, and continuing uncertainty over the American commitment to prevent Communist expansion within Europe.

The Decision to Withdraw Aid

To understand the growing British misgivings over foreign commitments, it is necessary to appreciate the country's precarious economic situation after 1945. Britain had emerged from the war impoverished and close to bankruptcy, as the cumulative balance of payments deficits since 1939 had created unprecedented levels of debt. Exports had dwindled to a third of prewar levels as industry switched to war production, while invisible earnings, which had once financed 35 percent of imports, had also suffered following the loss of half of the country's merchant fleet and the sale of more than a quarter of overseas investments. Despite the Lend-Lease and other arrangements, a total wartime balance of payments shortfall of £10 billion had left international debts worth more than £3.5 billion by the end of 1945. This was the largest external debt in history, far in excess of anything incurred by any other belligerent, and dwarfed the gold and dollar reserves worth a mere £600 million.[99]

To make matters worse, there was little hope for any rapid improvement in the immediate postwar period. Until industry could be reoriented to peacetime production, exports would remain insufficient to prevent further balance of payments deficits. Coupled with the diminished returns from invisibles and the need to service the huge external debt, it was predicted that exports would have to rise by 75 percent over prewar levels, while maintaining strict controls over imports, to close the gap. This was not likely to occur for at least three years, by which time the balance of payments would have deteriorated by a further £1.25 billion. Even this gloomy prediction contained several optimistic assumptions.[100]

The wartime mobilization of resources that had led to such levels of indebtedness had only been possible thanks to the availability of Lend-Lease from the United States. Britain had relied on earlier assurances that such support would continue through the crucial postwar period, but the abrupt termination of Lend-Lease in August 1945 left the British economy in an extremely vulnerable position. Given the desperate urgency to obtain dollars to pay for vital imports from North America, breathing space was secured only by recourse to a new American loan worth $3.75 billion, topped by a further $1.25 billion lent by Canada. The loan had been conditional on making sterling fully convertible in mid-1947, three years earlier than the British had expected. The brief episode of convertibility had disastrous effects on Britain's foreign reserves, and only the first receipts of Marshall Aid in 1948 stemmed the drain. Despite an impressive recovery, the country's external position did not approach normality until 1951 and continued to suffer occasional crises thereafter.[101]

Such were the considerations that dominated the Treasury and the chancellor. Hugh Dalton had been the main opponent of the extension of military subsidies to Greece and was insistent that Britain was in no position to maintain a high level of

99. Sir A. Cairncross, "Reconversion, 1945–51," 26–27; S. Pollard, *The Development of the British Economy 1914–1990*, 193–94.

100. Cairncross, "Reconversion, 1945–51," 26–27; Pollard, *Development of the British Economy*, 193–94.

101. Cairncross, "Reconversion, 1945–51," 27–32; Pollard, *Development of the British Economy*, 193–99.

foreign commitments. However, political considerations still carried much weight. In December 1946 the Chiefs of Staff reemphasized Britain's strategic interests in Greece but stated that American help was "essential" to defeat the guerrillas. Thereafter, the decision as to future actions in Greece became inextricably linked with the question of Washington's future intentions. The subsequent negotiations between British and American representatives will be described more fully in chapter 6, but disagreements within the cabinet continued to confuse the British stance. In late January, Dalton had demanded that Greece be abandoned, but no one in the Foreign Office appeared to share this view. In mid-February, following further pressure from Dalton, Bevin was apparently won over. On February 21 the Americans were informed that the British could not extend their commitment beyond the end of March. This decision was not revoked. Apart from interim payments worth £6 million, and some continuing involvement in such areas as the training of Greece's security forces, the British commitment was scaled down rapidly. Within months, the British role in Greece was passed to the Americans.[102]

The sudden *volte-face* of the British withdrawal has been interpreted in many ways. Some have suspected that Bevin used the Greek issue to force the hand of the Americans and thus launch the Cold War, but this cannot be proved, and is in any case beyond the scope of this book. As Frazier points out, much remains unclear as to the exact reasons for the decision to withdraw, and the relative weight of political, strategic, and economic factors is impossible to assess. The decisions of February 1947 brought an abrupt end to a policy in which the British had invested large sums of money and immense amounts of time. The escalating cost of the British involvement in Greece, coupled with the disappointing results the policy had yielded, must have suggested that little improvement could be expected, and must have given weight to Prime Minister Attlee's remark that Greece was not "worth the candle."[103]

---

102. Frazier, *Anglo-American Relations with Greece*, chap. 8.
103. Ibid., 132; FO800/475/ME/46/22, Attlee to Bevin, December 1, 1946.

3

STABILIZATION POLICY CHOICES
IN POST-LIBERATION GREECE

§

The legacy of occupation ensured that the returning National Unity Government would face a monumental task of restoring political, economic, and social stability to a devastated, deeply divided, and thoroughly demoralized country. Before reconstruction could begin, the Papandreou government would have to confront the immediate breakdown resulting from the complete collapse of the currency by breaking the seemingly unstoppable upward spiral of prices. Yet faced with meeting the immediate needs of the population, and with only limited possibilities of collecting tax revenue, it could hardly avoid further accelerating the disintegration of the drachma before any positive measures could bear fruit. This chapter considers the policy choices and performance of successive post-liberation governments, and the outcome of the first British-sponsored stabilization scheme.

Pre-Liberation Planning

As 1944 progressed, two points became increasingly obvious: first, with the tide of war moving rapidly against the Germans, most if not all of Greece would soon be liberated by Allied forces; second, this realization was tempered by the knowledge that the Greek economy was sliding ever deeper into chaos as a result of the occupation. It was thus imperative for some degree of economic planning to take place before liberation, so that effective measures could be enacted as soon as the government returned. Understandably preoccupied with conducting the war and determined to avoid direct interference in economic matters, the British were concerned with only the most practical issues that were to follow in the wake of liberation, while details of the policies to promote the country's recovery were to be left to the Greeks themselves.[1]

As early as March 1944, Kyriakos Varvaressos, the governor of the Bank of Greece, had pointed out the necessity for a coordinated approach to the difficulties that had to be faced upon liberation. He emphasized the need to ensure adequate supplies of foodstuffs to maintain an impoverished population and the necessity of establishing an immediate exchange rate for the drachma, so that relief supplies could be priced appropriately. Above all, he stressed the need for government controls over not only imported goods but also domestically produced commodities. Although these views were communicated to Prime Minister Tsouderos, the sense of urgency was apparently not shared by others in Cairo, and the government-in-exile failed to take the initiative on matters of economic planning. In such circumstances, it was British concerns that set the agenda for the subsequent policy discussions between the two sides. These hinged upon three essential issues: the immediate post-liberation exchange rate of the drachma, the means of payment to be used by Allied forces after entering Greece, and prices to be charged for relief supplies.[2]

Initially, setting a new exchange rate seemed a relatively straightforward matter of agreeing on a specific number. However, the growing crisis of the drachma ruled out simplistic solutions. With both prices and note circulation spiraling out of control, it was not only impossible to predict an appropriate rate for the drachma but also increasingly difficult even to establish a formula to calculate the rate. In March 1944, Varvaressos suggested that the prewar parity should be multiplied by a factor corresponding to the rise in note circulation and adjusted to take account of both the smaller quantity of goods and services available in the country as well as changes in world prices. Before long it was clear that such calculations, based on data from late 1943, were no longer appropriate. As it became obvious that inflation was spiraling even faster than the rise in note circulation, the original formula would have left the drachma seriously overvalued. To compensate, Varvaressos felt that an upward adjustment of 50 percent in favor of the pound would be necessary. However, as the pace of inflation continued to accelerate, even this was considered inadequate, and within a week Varvaressos was suggesting that the rate needed to be adjusted upwards by 100 percent.[3]

---

1. T160/1265/18217/014/1, Key to Rugman, June 30, 1944.

2. LBG/KVA/Δ3(B), Varvaressos to Tsouderos, March 17, 1944; Patterson, *Financial Experiences of Greece*, 14–24; T160/1265/18217/014/1, Key to Rugman, June 30, 1944.

3. WO204/3561, The Immediate Economic Problems in Greece at the Time of Liberation and the Means for their Solution, K. Varvaressos, March 1944; LBG/KVA/Φ11/Δ3(B), Varvaressos to Svolos, Telegram no. 95, August 29, 1944; Varvaressos to Svolos, Telegram, September 5, 1944.

From left to right: Kyriakos Varvaressos, Emmanuel Tsouderos, and Char. Simopoulos (Greek ambassador to Britain) visiting the Foreign Office. E. Venezis, *Emmanuel Tsouderos* (Athens, 1966).

At this point, Alexandros Svolos, the minister of finance, expressed agreement in principle with Varvaressos and declared that the new exchange rate would be fixed twenty-four hours after liberation, when the full extent of inflation would be known. He warned that as prices were likely to fall immediately upon liberation, some way had to be devised to minimize speculative gains, and that general monetary policy guidelines should be announced publicly as soon as possible. In response, Varvaressos suggested abandoning his original formula and establishing a new exchange rate, and recommended instead that two major issues should be considered. The first question was as much social as economic: he believed that the drachma should be devalued sufficiently to rule out instant profits from speculation, but not so drastically as to price imported goods out of the reach of ordinary wage earners. The second question involved deciding which value of the note circulation would provide an adequate supply of means of payment. Given the severe curtailment of economic activity, Varvaressos recommended that the note circulation be set at either 25 percent or 40 percent of its prewar value, suggesting the lower figure as a more appropriate way of taxing immediate gains from speculation. The new rate of exchange would be fixed to reflect whichever of the levels was chosen. He argued that if the government pursued suitable policies, note circulation could be increased in line with the expansion of the economy without generating inflation.[4]

In reply, Svolos claimed that such measures would still not prevent huge instant gains by speculators taking advantage of the massive readjustment of the exchange rate. He therefore proposed either setting note circulation at half the lower level suggested by Varvaressos or an immediate 50 percent reduction of the nominal value of the drachma as a means of taxing such profits. He also recommended that the state of the Athens stock market be taken into account when making a final decision. Varvaressos dismissed all these suggestions as inappropriate. He claimed that an automatic reduction of the value of the currency was entirely unnecessary in addition to devaluation, while setting note circulation at too low a level would have an adverse effect on the purchasing power of urban wage earners. Moreover, he pointed out that the fluctuations of the Athens stock market, being essentially speculative in nature, should not be used as the basis for any decisions. He stressed that there were no simple solutions to the unequal distribution of wealth and that a much more general economic policy had to be devised, and that important decisions needed to be taken soon.[5]

While these exchanges were taking place, continued Allied anxiety had led to the commissioning of an UNRRA report to consider the issue. Unaware of the amendments and provisos added by Varvaressos over the previous month, the report criticized his original formula as likely to overvalue the drachma and pointed out that an alternative formula based on wage increases would produce a much lower rate. Allied observers believed that this was far more realistic, but there is no apparent evidence that the suggestions were passed on to the Greek government.[6]

In any case, both the Varvaressos/Svolos debate and the Allied deliberations in Cairo were rendered irrelevant by the government's decision to adopt the views of Xenophon Zolotas, one of the leading economists at the University of Athens before the war. Starting from different interpretations of the crisis, Zolotas proposed contrasting solutions to the problem of the exchange rate. He predicted that the

4. LBG/KVA/Φ11/Δ3(B), Svolos to Varvaressos, Telegram no. 18141, September 5, 1944; Varvaressos to Svolos, Telegram no. 106, September 9, 1944.

5. LBG/KVA/Φ13/Δ3(B), Svolos to Varvaressos, Telegram no. 77, September 12, 1944; Varvaressos to Svolos, Telegram no. 116, September 15, 1944.

6. WO204/8608, The Drachma Exchange Rate, C. Coombs, September 30, 1944; DSR 868.51/10–1044, MacVeagh to the Secretary of State (Enclosures: Three Memoranda Concerning Rate of Exchange to Be Fixed in Greece after Liberation), October 10, 1944.

promise of significant quantities of relief supplies would have immediate effects after liberation, including the dishoarding of commodities, a substantial fall in prices,
and a move away from the gold sovereign. He warned that in such circumstances,
fixing note circulation at too low a level would lead to serious deflation and liquidity
shortages. Instead, he suggested that note circulation should be increased, primarily via such means as the purchase of sovereigns and new issues to central and local
government. He proposed that no immediate action should be taken on setting a
new external value for the drachma, which should not be fixed for several weeks.
For the time being, temporary parities could be devised for each issue of drachmae
to the Allied forces stationed in Greece, but the establishment of a "natural" rate
of exchange would be left to the market. Zolotas claimed that speculation would
be substantially minimized if the Bank of Greece endeavored to take full advantage
of the move away from gold by purchasing as many sovereigns as possible. He envisaged that up to a million sovereigns could be acquired by the bank during the
initial period after liberation.[7]

Varvaressos was dismayed by the suggestion to leave the exchange rate to market
forces. He dismissed the idea as entirely "repugnant" and predicted grave implications for the postwar economy. He believed that the inevitable outcome would be
further speculation, and warned that Greece would require rigorous control of both
foreign exchange and trade as well as the prevention of capital exports. However,
the views of Varvaressos did not prevail. Distrusted by the cabinet, ostensibly for
having originally accepted his post during the Metaxas dictatorship, Varvaressos
was snubbed by the appointment of Zolotas as cogovernor of the Bank of Greece.
Whether the decision was based on policy or personal reasons remains unclear, but
it amounted to a practical endorsement of Zolotas' views. Varvaressos promptly
resigned from the governorship of the bank.[8]

The issue of means of payment of the Allied forces after entering Greece was not
finally decided until the date before liberation. Given the virtual worthlessness of
the drachma, the British were determined to introduce the so-called British Military Authority (BMA) note as a stopgap until local currency could be made avail-

7. LBG/KVA/Φ13/Δ3(B), Επί του Νομισματικού Ζητήματος (On the Monetary Question,
X. Zolotas), September 22, 1944.
8. LBG/KVA/Φ13/Δ3(B), Varvaressos to Svolos, Telegram no. 129, October 5, 1944; DSR 868.51/
9–3044, MacVeagh to the Secretary of State, September 30, 1944 (Enclosure: Memorandum Regarding Inflationary Developments in Occupied Greece, H. A. Hill, September 30, 1944); LBG/
KVA/B/1, Papandreou to Varvaressos, Telegram no. 19443, October 6, 1944; Varvaressos to Papandreou, Telegram no. 510, October 9, 1944.

Xenophon Zolotas giving
a speech at the Bank of
Greece, October 1944.
Photograph courtesy of
the Bank of Greece.

able at a definite rate of exchange. The government-in-exile was worried about the
psychological effect of such a currency, and was particularly anxious to secure sterling credits to the equivalent value of the notes issued. It thus delayed a decision on
accepting the BMA note, agreeing only after the British threatened a unilateral fixing of the exchange rate. Further delays arose from British plans to circulate BMA
notes in Yugoslavia and Albania, fueling Greek fears that their country might be
obliged to finance Allied military expenditure elsewhere in the Balkans. This was
resolved only when London agreed to redeem all BMA notes presented to the Bank
of Greece. The final agreement stipulated that the BMA note was an emergency
measure to be employed until the bank could provide a stable currency in sufficient

quantities. The exchange rate was to be set twenty-four hours after liberation. Once a stable currency was available, the notes would be withdrawn and redeemed in the form of sterling credits.[9]

The third major issue—the pricing of relief supplies—was not settled prior to liberation. Although the British had recognized that the decisions had to be made on the spot, they were concerned that prices would have to bear some relation to landed costs. Once again, this would require definite decisions on the rate of exchange. Despite the intention of the government-in-exile to use the sale of relief supplies as an important source of revenue, it admitted that it possessed "no clear method" to reconcile the prices of such goods with local wage rates. Up until liberation, no one on the Greek side produced any initiatives on this subject.[10]

Thus by the time the country was liberated, no major policies had been formulated to address the formidable economic problems. Such debates as had arisen had resulted from British insistence on clarifying practical issues. Only Varvaressos had responded by consistently stressing the need for a comprehensive set of policies, but his views were not adopted in Cairo, and he himself was sidelined in the weeks prior to liberation. Thus instead of a definite program, the Papandreou government possessed only a vague collection of ideas by Zolotas saying little about specific measures to be taken. Even worse, these ideas appeared to be based on highly optimistic assumptions, including the rapid balancing of the budget, a stampede away from the sovereign, and a substantial inflow of relief supplies. Almost immediately this optimism proved to be hollow.

The Stabilization Scheme of November 1944

The National Unity Government arrived in Athens on October 18 and soon proved powerless in the face of the economic crisis. Relief supplies were delayed

9. FO371/43723, including R13936, Cairo to FO, Telegram no. 658, September 4, 1944; FO to Cairo, Telegram no. 432, September 5, 1944; WO to AFHQ, Telegram no. 74056, September 5, 1944; R14054, Cairo to FO, Telegram no. 662, September 6, 1944; R14460, Cairo to FO, Telegram no. 50 Saving, September 6, 1944; R14510, Varvaressos to Fraser, September 12, 1944; Varvaressos to Fraser, September 13, 1944; Key to Fraser, September 15, 1944; FO371/43724 R16985, Cadogan to Aghnides, October 17, 1944; Aghnides to Cadogan, October 17, 1944. BMA notes circulated in Greece until June 1945, although British forces had been receiving local currency from April. The bilateral accounts resulting from the arrangement were not finally cleared until 1948; Patterson, *Financial Experiences of Greece,* 19–20, 168–71.

10. FO371/43723 R13322, Cairo to FO, Telegram no. 619, August 25, 1944; Patterson, *Financial Experiences of Greece,* 22–23.

The British Military Authority Note. Alpha Credit Bank, *The Banknotes of Greece* (Athens, 1995).

by the need to repair port facilities, and fresh drachmae had to be printed to maintain services and pay wages long before any tax revenue could be collected. The seriousness of the situation was compounded by the government's complete lack of preparation. Contrary to expectations, liberation failed to restore confidence in the drachma, and the rush to sell sovereigns never materialized. The currency continued to plummet, but the government delayed any decision on setting a new exchange rate. Within days, ministers came to stress large-scale foreign aid as the only feasible solution. At first, requests for Allied help were linked to specific difficulties arising from inflation. Zolotas pressed Military Liaison for increased relief supplies to provide a crucial source of revenue. Svolos, pointing out that the payment of foodstuffs in lieu of wages could minimize the use of the printing press, asked for a one-off doubling of ML monthly shipments, together with additional financial assistance and transport facilities. Before long, the government and the Bank of Greece became convinced that inflation as expressed by the sovereign rate could be stabilized only by official gold sales. Zolotas, who had recently predicted a huge inflow of gold into the vaults of the Bank of Greece, was forced to ask ML for two hundred thousand sovereigns, to be paid out of Greek bullion reserves held abroad. In addition, he pressed ML to use BMA notes as payment for labor.[11]

The British response was mixed. ML supported the request for sovereigns, and called for an immediate Allied announcement of substantial financial assistance for Greece. ML was also in favor of increasing relief supplies, but refused to consider a one-off doubling of shipments, fearing that such levels could neither be maintained nor distributed effectively. Leeper echoed the government's call for additional external aid and requested that a Treasury expert be sent to Athens, stressing that a collapse of public security was imminent unless a rapid solution was forthcoming.[12] Outside Greece, British responses were far less favorable. Both Harold Macmillan, Minister Resident at the Allied Forces Headquarters (AFHQ) in Caserta, and General Henry Maitland Wilson, Supreme Allied Commander in the Mediterranean (SACMED), were opposed to gold sales and suggested that large amounts of BMA notes should be given to the government for use as a temporary currency until a stabilization scheme was implemented. Officials at the Treasury and the Bank of England were equally unenthusiastic about the request for gold. David Waley felt certain that the sale of gold coins would not restore confidence in the drachma, and the situation would ultimately deteriorate even further. Cameron Fromanteel Cobbold scathingly dismissed gold sales as a "stupid plan" that would render the later use of a paper currency even more difficult. Nevertheless, Whitehall approved the release of 200,000 sovereigns, but warned the Greeks that they had to solve their own financial problems. However, another 250,000 sovereigns were dispatched within days following further pleas from Athens.[13]

11. FO371/43724, including R17640, Greekaid to WO, Telegram no. FI-1, October 20, 1944; R17044, Athens to FO, Telegram no. 12, October 21, 1944; FO371/43726 R21396, MLHQ (G), Progress Report No. 1, October 15, 1944–November 10, 1944.

12. Ibid.

13. FO371/43724, including R17640, Caserta to FO, Telegram no. 583, October 21, 1944; Minute by Laskey, October 21, 1944; WO to Greekaid, Telegram no. 86968, October 21, 1944; R17836, Wil-

Despite the unwilling concession on the gold issue, the British remained deeply opposed to all the other requests. They were adamant that relief shipments could not be increased, and neither ML nor London was willing to sanction the use of BMA notes beyond the minimum requirements of the British forces. Nevertheless, ML was forced to relent after Piraeus dock laborers refused to accept drachmae as back payment for unloading relief supplies. This brought a lukewarm response from Whitehall. Despite claims that the BMA notes seemed the most practical alternative to the drachma, the British were afraid they would soon lose all value if large numbers were brought into use. London remained convinced that internal measures—such as heavy taxation, price controls, and rationing—had to form a solution rather than financial and material assistance from abroad. However, the British were still determined that suggestions would be offered only if specifically requested by Athens, and that major initiatives should come from the Greeks themselves. In the absence of any such indications, they turned to Varvaressos, hoping he would devise a suitable plan to deal with the crisis.[14]

Varvaressos, excluded from decision-making since resigning his post, was openly critical of the government's inaction. Blaming the continuing depreciation of the drachma on the failure to fix a new exchange rate immediately after liberation, he urged that this should be done as soon as possible. He also called for controls over prices of essential goods, action to suppress speculation, and closer attention to the distribution of relief supplies. In addition, he stressed the need for public declarations of Allied support and urged that the international relief effort should be substantially increased.[15]

The Treasury was enthusiastic about the Varvaressos proposals, and its officials even suggested that the continuing crisis of the drachma was largely the result of the government's refusal to follow his advice. Nevertheless, the British were aware that given his exclusion from power, it would be difficult to press the issue. Although the proposals were discussed at the British embassy in Athens, it appears

son to WO, October 22, 1944; Key to Wilson, November 4, 1944; R17001, AFHQ to WO, Telegram no. F42200, October 22, 1944; BE OV80/21, Minute by Cobbold, October 23, 1944.

14. FO371/43724, including R17640, Minute by Laskey, October 21, 1944; R17044, FO to Athens, Telegram no. 5, October 23, 1944; WO204/3562, Memorandum of a Meeting at the Treasury, October 24, 1944; BE OV80/21, Note on Meeting at the Treasury (October 24, 1944)—Greek Currency Situation, Minute by Cobbold, October 26, 1944; Catto to the Chancellor of the Exchequer, October 26, 1944; FO371/43726 R21396, MLHQ(G), Progress Report No. 1, October 15, 1944–November 10, 1944.

15. FO371/43724 R17391, The Solution of the Present Monetary Crisis in Greece, K. Varvaressos, October 25, 1944; BE OV80/21, Note on Meeting at the Treasury (October 25, 1944) to Discuss Greek Currency Situation with Varvaressos, Minute by Lithiby, October 26, 1944; LBG/KVA/Φ13/Δ3(B), Varvaressos to Svolos, Telegram no. 140, October 26, 1944.

they were never formally presented to the government.[16] By the end of October, it was obvious that the Papandreou government had neither adopted nor formulated any economic policy and seemed totally incapable of restoring monetary stability, preferring to resort to the printing press and to rely on the prospect of foreign help. The prime minister, who had refused to accept the resignation of Varvaressos, instructed him to seek credits and relief supplies from any quarter. Despite his resentment that his advice had been ignored, Varvaressos offered to represent the country's interests abroad, but pointed out that the policy vacuum was aggravating the crisis and warned that foreign credits would be of little use unless backed up by the measures he had repeatedly advocated.[17]

In the meantime, inflation accelerated faster than ever. The government printed huge quantities of currency to overcome the virtual absence of revenue in the initial period. To underline the grim absurdity of the situation, the government was soon faced with an acute shortage of banknote paper. Up to November 11, the budget deficit exceeded 99 percent.[18] In such circumstances, the British were forced to abandon their avowed policy of noninterference, and an advisory body was set up to offer assistance on economic, financial, and relief issues. Alarmed by what he had seen during his visit to Athens, Anthony Eden, the secretary of state for foreign affairs, warned Churchill that anarchy would ensue unless significant measures were undertaken immediately. He stressed the need to increase relief shipments and to supply additional means of transport to distribute foodstuffs, and also suggested the dispatch of certain luxury goods to provide revenue. Moreover, he requested that the Treasury send a financial expert to advise both the government and the British authorities in Athens. While agreeing that heavy taxation and internal loans formed the most appropriate long-term policy, he pointed out the obvious irrelevance of such a policy at a time when the government was able neither to impose taxation nor raise internal loans.[19]

16. FO371/43724, including R17044, Minute by Laskey, October 23, 1944; FO to Athens, Telegram no. 5, October 23, 1944; R17391, Fraser to Taylor, October 26, 1944; BE OV80/21, Waley to (?), October 29, 1944; Patterson, *Financial Experiences of Greece*, 37.

17. LBG/KVA/B/1, Papandreou to Varvaressos, Telegram no. 19886, October 12, 1944; Varvaressos to Papandreou, Telegram no. 7088, October 14, 1944; LBG/KVA/Φ11/Δ3(B), Papandreou to Varvaressos, Telegram no. 20892, October 26, 1944; Varvaressos to Papandreou, Telegram no. 144, October 28, 1944.

18. Patterson, *Financial Experiences of Greece*, 27–28, 32.

19. FO371/43724, including R17302, Athens to FO, Telegram no. 25, October 26, 1944; R17391, Minute by Laskey, October 30, 1944; WO204/8760, Meeting Held at the British Embassy, October 29, 1944; FO371/43726 R21396, MLHQ(G), Progress Report No. 1, October 15, 1944–November 10, 1944. The advisory body for economic, financial, and relief issues was the Economic and Supply

Galloping inflation continued even after the withdrawal of the Germans from Athens. The two notes pictured bear the signature of the first post-liberation cogovernor of the Bank of Greece, Xenophon Zolotas.

In the meantime, the Greeks had asked the British to supply a further five hundred thousand sovereigns. Waley, the Treasury expert appointed following Eden's appeal, was unenthusiastic, and warned that intervention in the gold market without a clear strategy would do little to prevent financial disaster. Instead, he urged the government to devise a comprehensive stabilization scheme as quickly as possible, and promised that the request would be considered if such a scheme was produced

Committee (ESC) set up on October 29, 1944, under the chairmanship of Lt. General Scobie. The ESC contained mainly British personnel but also several Americans, including Gardner Patterson who was to play an influential role in later developments. Patterson had previously acted as the U.S. Treasury representative in London; Patterson, *Financial Experiences of Greece*, 39–40.

before his return to London. The British assured the Greeks that they were doing everything possible to increase supplies of food and raw materials, particularly cotton. Although the government had hoped to defer stabilization until the arrival of substantial relief shipments, Waley's stance persuaded them to undertake immediate measures, to be launched on November 10. Given this change of heart, Waley recommended that the gold be released, and 250,000 sovereigns were duly dispatched during the first week of November. In a similar spirit, Macmillan pressed London to write off the 1940 war debt, warning that if the government collapsed, the British would lose not only their money but also much political credibility.[20]

In response to Waley's urgings, a broad outline of a stabilization scheme—including the introduction of a new currency—was formulated by Zolotas at the Bank of Greece. He emphasized that the scheme could be successful only if huge quantities of goods were imported immediately. A second precondition was a "comparative equilibrium" of the budget, which would be achieved by such measures as the introduction of taxes on war profits and luxury items, the sale of imported goods at market prices, and the dismissal of surplus employees. With the budget balanced, the government would not be obliged to undermine the new drachma by printing money to finance its current deficits. In Zolotas' opinion, a final precondition of success would be full convertibility into sterling, which would be sold freely until stability had been achieved, after which restrictions would be imposed. He claimed that the sterling link alone could create sufficient confidence in the new currency, and argued that the state's foreign reserves, worth £43 million, could well afford the probable loss of up to £2 million. He envisaged that the sale of foreign exchange would eliminate demand for gold. Although he claimed that it was unacceptable for the Bank of Greece to conduct gold transactions, he argued that sovereigns should be offered to the public as an additional safety valve during the initial period. He believed that there was little to fear from such a move, as the entire note circulation in Greece was worth less than one hundred thousand sovereigns, but argued that a reserve of half a million would be necessary to regulate the market. He repeated his earlier claim that the restoration of normality would provoke a rush to sell gold back to the bank. Zolotas added that once prices had been stabilized, wages would no longer need to be pegged to the cost of living. He recommended that the old drachma remain in use until the new currency gained widespread acceptance, and that the government should deliberately refrain from establishing an official

20. FO371/43724, including R17611, Athens to FO, Telegram no. 90, October 31, 1944; R17612, Athens to FO, Telegram no. 97, October 31, 1944; FO to Athens, Telegram no. 75, November 1, 1944; R17842, Athens to FO, Telegram no. 127, November 3, 1944.

conversion rate between the two, leaving the task to market forces. The government would continue to issue old drachmae to cover its budget deficit, but would not be allowed to print new drachmae in the same way.[21]

The following days saw lengthy discussions over details of the stabilization scheme, the first post-liberation budget, and the government's wage and price policies. The main point of disagreement was whether the new currency was to be convertible into sterling, as advocated by Zolotas, or into BMA notes only. The British, fearing a flight from the drachma, preferred the latter option, despite concerns that the BMA note itself might suffer as a result from its association with the new currency. Following a warning from Waley that the scheme had little chance of success without BMA-drachma convertibility, Whitehall concurred, with the proviso that BMA notes would be redeemable for drachma only, and that gold sales be suspended as soon as the new currency was introduced.[22] A hastily finalized stabilization scheme was formally agreed to on November 10, to come into effect the next day. The new drachma was to be fully convertible into BMA notes at the rate of six hundred to the pound, while the old drachma would temporarily remain in circulation, at the rate of 50 billion to one new drachma. Existing drachma assets and obligations were not revalorized, and were thus effectively wiped out. Government

The new drachma.

21. WO204/8765, The Conditions and the Realization of Currency Stabilization, X. Zolotas, November 1, 1944.

22. FO371/43725, including R19108, Minutes of the First Meeting Held at the Bank of Greece, November 4, 1944; Minutes of the Second Meeting Held at the Bank of Greece, November 6, 1944; R19113, Minutes of the Third Meeting Held at the Bank of Greece, November 7, 1944; Minutes of the Fourth Meeting Held at the Bank of Greece, November 8, 1944; FO371/43724, including R17841, Athens to FO, Telegram no. 125, November 3, 1944; R17924, Athens to FO, Telegram no. 136, November 5, 1944; R17929, Athens to FO, Telegram no. 138, November 5, 1944; R18740, FO to Athens, Telegram no. 123, November 6, 1944; CAB65/44, War Cabinet Conclusions 146(44), November 6, 1944; BE OV80/22, Minute by Cobbold, November 6, 1944.

loans from the Bank of Greece were to continue subject to strict limits. To ensure adequate supplies of currency, the British agreed to provide £3 million of BMA notes.[23]

Initial public reaction seemed quietly favorable as the sovereign rate remained fairly stable, with little immediate demand for BMA notes. A competent Allied observer saw the prospects as encouraging, despite the obvious difficulties that lay ahead. Similarly, Waley felt confident that the scheme would succeed if the government honored all its commitments.[24] However, several related issues still awaited a satisfactory solution. Detailed discussions on budgetary reforms did not proceed smoothly, despite declarations of ministerial determination to enact drastic measures such as heavy taxes on war profits. A set of estimates was drawn up, only to be dismissed by the British as too basic and completely inadequate. Within days, a revised version anticipated an almost perfectly balanced budget. This assumed that taxes would provide 27 percent of revenue, with the rest deriving from the sale of relief supplies, while 80 percent of planned expenditure was to cover current expenses, including salaries, pensions, and administration. The British conceded that the revised budget was probably the best that could be expected in the circumstances, but expressed serious reservations. They were unhappy about the size of the government payroll and pensions list, and warned against the assumption that income from relief supplies could be treated as ordinary revenue without the prior approval of the donor agencies. They insisted that the situation could be improved only by immediately enacting such measures as the imposition of strict limits on public sector salaries and military expenditure, the sale of relief supplies at prices sufficiently high to yield a reasonable revenue, huge increases of all indirect taxes, and the introduction of heavy taxation on war profits and luxury goods.[25]

With budgetary issues still unresolved, a further disagreement arose as government proposals for new wage rates provoked immediate opposition from the British, who regarded them as "dangerously high." Highlighting the close connection between wages and food prices, Papandreou resisted British pressure by making the acceptance of lower wages conditional upon assurances of increased relief supplies. In turn, the British made the promise of food shipments conditional upon

23. FO371/43725, including R19951, Law No. 18, *Government Gazette,* November 9, 1944; R19115, Leeper to Papandreou, November 10, 1944; Papandreou to Leeper, November 10, 1944; FO371/ 43724 R18201, Athens to FO, Telegram no. 173, November 8, 1944.

24. WO204/3564, Greek Currency Stabilization, F. A. Southard, Jr., November 14, 1944; FO371/ 43725 R18538, The Stabilization of Greek Currency, Sir D. Waley, November 14, 1944.

25. Patterson, *Financial Experiences of Greece,* 47; FO371/43724 R18738, Athens to FO, Telegram no. 165, November 8, 1944; Athens to FO, Telegram no. 166, November 8, 1944; FO371/43725 R18796, Athens to FO, Telegram no. 4 Saving, November 9, 1944.

an official announcement that wages and the price of imported rations would be fixed at appropriate levels. Despite further pledges to do so, continued government inaction led the British to issue an ultimatum withdrawing the offer of additional supplies unless agreement was reached. This brought an immediate response from the Greek side, and new levels of wages and ration prices were agreed on November 30.[26]

The growing frustration of the British, which had led to the unprecedented tone expressed in the ultimatum, took place against a background of mounting tension, as it became painfully clear that the currency reform had not brought lasting success. After a few days of relative stability, the sovereign rate began to rise again. While little was done to increase receipts either from taxation or the sale of imported supplies, government spending spiraled rapidly, resulting in a budget deficit of almost 94 percent during the three weeks after the stabilization attempt. In the same period, note circulation increased by 900 percent, while free market prices of essential consumer goods rose more than 50 percent.[27]

By now, even Zolotas was openly critical of the government for its failure to create any of the conditions necessary for the stabilization to succeed. He claimed that nothing had been done to establish confidence in either the currency or the government's management of the economy, while official statements had only fueled public anxiety and uncertainty. He was particularly scathing of the lack of action on public finance. Promises on increased taxation had not been kept, imported supplies were being sold at ridiculously low prices, no checks had been introduced to ensure that only genuine indigents were receiving free food rations, and the pruning of the state bureaucracy had made little progress. By losing much potential revenue and failing to check expenditure, the government was still compelled to use the printing press to finance its daily operations. In such circumstances, the currency reform had scant hope of success. Zolotas claimed that gold sales alone had prevented a total collapse, but added that this policy could not by itself save the drachma unless swift action was taken on all the other issues.[28]

26. FO371/43725, including R18652, Athens to FO, Telegram no. 238, November 15, 1944; R18662, Athens to FO, Telegram no. 249, November 16, 1944; R19528, Athens to FO, Telegram no. 9 Remac, November 28, 1944; R19833, Athens to FO, Telegram no. 14 Remac, December 1, 1944; R19811, Athens to FO, Telegram no. 15 Remac, December 1, 1944; FO371/43726 R21873, Leeper to Eden, December 6, 1944 (Enclosures: Scobie to Papandreou, November 20, 1944; Papandreou to Scobie, November 22, 1944); WO204/8760, Meeting of November 30, 1944 to Fix Wages and Prices, December 1, 1944.

27. Patterson, *Financial Experiences of Greece*, 66–67, 70, 73, 80–82.

28. FO371/43725 R18418, Athens to FO, Telegram no. 8 Remac, November 27, 1944; WO204/8765, On the Evolution of the Monetary Question, X. Zolotas, November 24, 1944.

As Zolotas had indicated, the sale of gold was the only policy actively promoted in support of the stabilization scheme. This move, which had not been envisaged by the scheme, was taken without prior consultation with the British. On November 21 the National Bank of Greece (not to be confused with the central bank) was authorized to conduct gold transactions on the state's behalf. Various mechanical means were employed to inconvenience purchasers and thus reduce the volume of sales. Nevertheless, over eleven working days, net sales of sovereigns totaled more than 44,000. Contrary to Zolotas' expectation, this did nothing to stem the new tide of price rises, and the Bank of England was asked to provide another 250,000 sovereigns. The request was turned down on the grounds that the policy was merely reinforcing the public distrust of the paper currency. In such circumstances, fears that the country's gold reserves would soon be exhausted led to the suspension of the policy on December 2.[29]

Thus by the beginning of December the stabilization scheme was already virtually moribund, but any prospect of a return to normality was destroyed by the outbreak of fighting in Athens. This caused considerable destruction and forced the suspension of all relief operations, not only aggravating material hardship but also depriving the state of urgently needed revenue. The political situation forced concern over immediate economic issues into the background. As ministers seemed still unable to propose "anything plausible" on such matters, British observers became increasingly alarmed by the way the problems were "not being faced" and suggested that it was now up to London to take the initiative in formulating constructive policies.[30] Although this call for wider responsibility was eventually rejected, the British authorities in Athens took their own initiative in defining a set of measures they expected the Greek government to undertake once order was reestablished in the capital. They were particularly concerned that the wage levels agreed in November should be adhered to once relief deliveries were recommenced, and looked for a much more vigorous approach to the budget. While recognizing this could not be balanced in the near future, they demanded that the government should at least furnish "realistic" estimates and take decisive action on curbing expenditure and raising additional revenue. Moreover, they insisted that fixed prices be set not only for relief foodstuffs but also for a wide range of domestically pro-

29. FO371/43725, including R18963, Athens to FO, Telegram no. 2 Remac, November 21, 1944; R19607, Athens to FO, Telegram no. 378, November 28, 1944; FO to Athens, Telegram no. 327, December 1, 1944; R19687, Athens to FO, Telegram no. 12 Remac, November 30, 1944; Patterson, *Financial Experiences of Greece*, 80–82; LBG/KVA/B/2, Varvaressos to Maben, September 29, 1945.

30. WO904/8611, Tait Smith to Rugman, November 17, 1944; FO371/43726 R21510, Athens to FO, Telegram no. 26 Remac, December 21, 1944.

duced goods and services including fuel, tram fares, rents, electricity, and basic items of clothing.[31]

The "Easy Way Out"

In any event, these recommendations were not passed on to the Papandreou government, as it collapsed before the fighting had ceased. A new government under General Plastiras took office on January 4, and the British immediately presented their summary of economic priorities to Georgios Sideris, the new minister of finance, who also held the potentially conflicting post of minister of labor. Disappointed by the previous government's performance, they sought a more vigorous stance from Plastiras. Despite pressure from the British, Sideris displayed little enthusiasm for either their recommendations or their suggestion that Varvaressos be reappointed to the governorship at the Bank of Greece, vacated by the dismissal of Zolotas. Although Varvaressos was indeed reinstated shortly afterwards, there was little progress on other issues. While Sideris assured Allied advisers he would maintain the wage levels agreed in November until the end of January, he refused to commit himself beyond that point without commitments on the extent of ML imports to be provided in the near future. However, within days the government made several concessions on state salaries and seemed likely to extend these to the private sector. While Allied advisers complained that Sideris had done "virtually nothing" on price controls, the minister continued to make far-reaching concessions on wages. In early February he ignored the wishes of ML by agreeing to increase the daily wage rate for unskilled labor by 20 percent and to make corresponding increases in other categories. As many private employers were already paying more than the official wage levels, the new rates of pay were mainly ignored, with increased wage costs simply passed on to the consumer. In spite of strong opposition from ML, it was clear that Sideris was unwilling to draw up a comprehensive wage policy, preferring to grant concessions to individual groups of workers whenever successive waves of protest arose.[32]

31. FO371/43726, including R21496, FO to Athens, Telegram no. 248, January 23, 1945; R21946 Caserta to FO, Telegram no. 970, December 27, 1944; WO204/8760, Paper No. ESC(44) No. 2, C-in-C's Policy Following the Withdrawal of ELAS Forces from the Athens Area, December 24, 1944.

32. WO204/8760, Paper No. E&SC (45) 6, Aide Mémoire, January 5, 1945. Technically, the Plastiras government dismissed Zolotas by abolishing the post that had been especially created for him; FO371/48347 R16322, Greek Personalities Report, September 17, 1945; FO371/48326, including

Throughout this period, it was evident that the post-liberation governments had done little to secure sufficient revenue to finance public spending. During January the budget deficit was a staggering 98 percent, and was covered only by fresh loans from the Bank of Greece, which pushed the government well beyond the limit—two billion drachmae—agreed as part of the November stabilization scheme. Sideris proved as unresponsive on budgetary issues as he had been on price controls, declining to suggest any figures for more than a month or two in advance. As with wages, he was unwilling to commit himself to any longer-term forecast until he knew the exact cost of the proposed military program and the extent of ML imports. Sideris not only refused to prepare a budget but also requested that the British foot the bill for the new Greek army, which he hoped would be paid according to British scales. Realizing that London would not provide funds or loans for this purpose, Sideris eventually set new rates of pay at levels lower than those of the British army but still higher than those in the Greek civil service. The civil servants were themselves already agitating for higher salaries, and at the end of March they were given a bonus equal to one month's basic pay. As further concessions were granted during each successive crisis, it was obvious that the wage structure agreed in November 1944 had already disintegrated.[33] Thus the major Allied expectation expressed back in early January had been completely ignored.

Greek ministers continued to display little confidence that they could manage without external help. Sideris warned ML that the drachma could not be saved without a foreign loan, while Plastiras stressed to Whitehall that the country could not survive without financial and material support. The Allies emphasized that

R503, Athens to FO, Telegram no. 2 Remac, January 6, 1945; R627, Athens to FO, Telegram no. 98, January 8, 1945; R905, Athens to FO, Telegram no. 4 Remac, January 11, 1945. WO204/8760, including Paper No. E&SC (45) 9, Implementation of Agreed Policy for the Period Following the ELAS Withdrawal from the Athens Area, January 18, 1945; E&SC (45) 2nd Meeting, January 19, 1945; FO371/48330 R7298, Leeper to Eden, April 16, 1945 (Enclosure: Paper No. E&SC [45] 28, Wages and Salaries in Greece, April 7, 1945); WO204/8761, JCC (45) 3rd Meeting, February 8, 1945; E&SC (45) 6th Meeting, February 12, 1945; E&SC (45) 7th Meeting, February 19, 1945; JCC (45) 5th Meeting, February 22, 1945; E&SC (45) 10th Meeting, March 12, 1945; Patterson, *Financial Experiences of Greece*, 116, 118, 122.

33. Patterson, *Financial Experiences of Greece*, 264; WO204/8760, E&SC (45) 2d Meeting, January 19, 1945; E&SC (45) 3d Meeting, January 23, 1945; WO204/8761, E&SC (45) 4th Meeting, January 29, 1945; E&SC (45) 9th Meeting, March 5, 1945; JCC (45) 9th Meeting, March 22, 1945; FO371/48328, including R5326, Athens to FO, Telegram no. 795, March 20, 1945; R5343, Athens to FO, Telegram no. 796, March 20, 1945; FO371/48329, including R6140, Athens to FO, Telegram no. 888, April 3, 1945; R6315, Paper No E&SC (45) 26, New Scales of Pay for Greek Armed Forces, March 25, 1945; FO371/48334 R14166, Economic and Financial Developments in Greece November 1944–June 1945, C. Coombs, 1945, 52.

a loan to save the drachma not only would be unlikely but also would produce no immediate results. Furthermore, given the worldwide shortage of commodities and means of transport, it was most important that the Athens government should make more efficient use of resources at its disposal. The Greeks were adamant that unless transport facilities were improved, there was little chance of industrial and agricultural recovery, and thus no hope for raising government revenue. Both sides appeared to be at cross-purposes, with consistent Allied emphasis on budgetary measures and economic controls invariably countered by equally consistent Greek complaints about transport infrastructure difficulties and the necessity of increased material supplies and loans from abroad.[34]

In such circumstances, the British authorities in Athens lost patience. They were particularly dissatisfied with Sideris and even considered trying to remove him from power. Varvaressos, who continued to impress the Allied advisers after returning to the Bank of Greece, seemed an obvious replacement. However, given the political circumstances, the British decided not to press this matter further.[35] Nevertheless, they maintained the line that immediate austerity measures were necessary, and that Greece would have to look to its own resources rather than external aid to promote economic recovery.

As Sideris could offer nothing to revive the economy, senior British officials were becoming increasingly worried about the state of public finances and the stability of the drachma. In mid-February, Waley warned that the currency might collapse within a "week or two," unless swift action was taken on prices and wages. Soon afterwards, British exasperation with the inertia in Athens led to strong words from Eden, who met leading Greek politicians on his way back from Yalta. He made it clear that they had to take greater responsibility for their country, in language that was "blunt to the verge of rudeness." At the same time, Eden pointed out that measures taken by the Greeks themselves would have to be of paramount importance, as there was little prospect that the extent of Allied assistance could be increased given current international circumstances. A few days later, Churchill gave a highly public expression of British dissatisfaction with the situation. Speaking in the House of Commons, he declared that the Greeks could not expect the Allies to shoulder the main burden of responsibility for the country's recovery. The Athens government

34. WO204/8761, JCC (45) 1st Meeting, January 25, 1945; Scobie to Plastiras, January 21, 1945; Scobie to Sideris, January 24, 1945; Sideris to Scobie, February 6, 1945; Plastiras to Scobie, February 9, 1945; Scobie to Sideris, February 12, 1945; Sideris to Scobie, February 15, 1945; FO371/48257 R3657, Plastiras to Churchill, Telegram no. 216, February 6, 1945.

35. WO204/8761, E&SC (45) 4th Meeting, January 29, 1945; E&SC (45) 6th Meeting, February 12, 1945; FO371/48257 R3475, Athens to FO, Telegram no. 565, February 19, 1945.

From left to right: Archbishop Damaskinos, Winston Churchill, and Anthony Eden attending a mass meeting in Athens, February 14, 1945. Photographic Archive of the Benaki Museum, Athens. Photo by Dimitrios Charisiadis.

had to ensure that the budget was balanced, and that inflation was kept within reasonable limits.[36]

Sideris was careful to defend the government's record, asserting that efforts had been made to implement the Allied recommendations. Nevertheless, he observed the practical difficulties involved: it was almost impossible to impose price controls

36. A. Eden, *The Eden Memoirs: The Reckoning*, vol. 3, 521; FO371/48257 R3559, Discussion on Greece at the British Embassy, February 15, 1945 (Annex IV, Aide-Mémoire, February 15, 1945); 408 H.C. DEB. 5 s., 1291.

on domestically produced goods, while increases in indirect taxation would yield next to nothing until there was actual production of taxable goods. Moreover, superfluous state employees could not be dismissed until an unemployment benefit scheme was established. Other ministers also sought to paint an "optimistic picture" of the government's plans of the economy in interviews and statements. The British, however, consistently felt that the Greeks were not doing enough to address the country's economic problems. Despite their optimism, Plastiras and Sideris achieved little while in office. The finance minister's few serious initiatives proved ineffectual. His new tax on war profits turned out to be a dead end. His long overdue attempt to prohibit dealings in gold, when he threatened to "bring all speculators before the firing squad," came only days before his departure from the ministry and was immediately dropped by his successor.[37]

The few concessions that Greek ministers made to British advice during this period were inspired by Varvaressos at the Bank of Greece rather than any government figure. One important breakthrough was the adoption of a slightly more "economic than philanthropic" approach to the price of the ML/Joint Relief Commission ration. A further achievement owing much to Varvaressos was the setting up of a Joint Price Fixing Sub-Committee within the Joint Coordinating Committee (JCC).[38] This was to address the shortcomings of existing price-fixing measures, as until then individual ministries had conducted uncoordinated ad hoc policies covering a limited range of commodities including kerosene, matches, salt, newspapers, playing cards, tram fares, and certain road haulage freights. As prices had been frequently set at inappropriate levels, and as few guidelines had been provided to local authorities in the provinces, it was clear that a permanent body was necessary to coordinate policies at all levels. Varvaressos was the obvious choice to chair this subcommittee. Nevertheless, it had advisory powers only and spent

37. WO204/8761, Sideris to Scobie, February 15, 1945; FO371/48262 R5444, AIS Weekly Report No. 21, March 4–10, 1945; FO371/48330 R7205, Compulsory Law No. 182, *Government Gazette*, March 12, 1945; FO371/48329, including R5917, Athens to FO, Telegram no. 64 Remac, March 29, 1945; R5957, Athens to FO, Telegram no. 65 Remac, March 30, 1945; FO371/48266 R6723, AIS Weekly Report No. 24, March 25–31, 1945; FO371/48267 R7138, AIS Weekly Report No. 25, April 1–7, 1945.

38. WO204/8761, JCC (45) 2d Meeting, February 1, 1945; JCC (45) 3d Meeting, February 8, 1945; Patterson, *Financial Experiences of Greece*, 145–46. The JCC was set up in early 1945 to provide a forum in which British and American advisers belonging to the ESC could discuss policy issues with Greek ministers. The JCC was replaced by the Joint Policy Committee (JPC) after the UNRRA takeover of the relief effort in Greece. It included Greek, British, and UNRRA officials; DSR 868.50/4–2145, MacVeagh to the Secretary of State, April 21, 1945 (Enclosure: JPC (45) 1st Meeting, April 16, 1945). For the reasons for the absence of American officials in the JPC, see section entitled "Contrasting Fears," chap. 6.

most of its time fixing prices of UNRRA and ML supplies. It achieved little as far as domestically produced commodities were concerned, since government ministers did virtually nothing to enforce controls on such items.[39]

Aggravated by government inactivity, the Greek economy languished through-out the first quarter of 1945 and remained as dependent on external relief as it had been shortly after liberation. Holders of surplus currency continued to prefer more stable stores of value. Gold maintained its multiple role as a medium of exchange, saving, and investment, as the drachma lost further credibility. With confidence low as a result of political tensions and the weakness of the currency, hoarding be-came commonplace, leading to further shortages and inflationary pressures. Public finances remained precarious as the gradual recovery of revenue was outpaced by massive rises in expenditure. Despite the warnings of Varvaressos, the government's relentless use of the printing press to cover chronic budget deficits ensured rapid increases in note circulation. As the country became locked in a vicious cycle of price and wage inflation, persistent demands for wage increases placed the govern-ment under severe pressure. Civil unrest seemed inevitable if such demands were not met, but concessions would have led just as inevitably to further inflation and a crisis of the drachma.[40]

Such were the circumstances inherited by Admiral Voulgaris, who succeeded as prime minister in early April. The change of government added to the general uncertainty over the economy, and the sovereign rate reached new heights on the Athens market. When it soon became apparent that the new government, univer-sally regarded as temporary, had failed to produce any major statement on eco-nomic policy, the British continued to press for action.

Before long, Voulgaris was warned that heavy taxation, ruthless expenditure cuts, and administrative reform had to be enacted immediately, while Georgios Mantza-vinos, the new minister of finance, was pressed for a budget statement. In response, a set of revenue estimates was produced within days. These emphasized the signifi-cance of receipts from the sale of UNRRA supplies (62 percent) and the special tax on war profits (17 percent), rather than those from direct or indirect taxation (5 percent and 15 percent respectively). The British were extremely skeptical. Returns

39. WO204/8761, Paper No. E&SC (45) 16, Fixing of Prices, February 11, 1945; Paper No. E&SC (45) 6th Meeting, February 12, 1945; Paper No. JCC (45) 9, Fixing of Prices, February 13, 1945; Paper No. JCC (45) 4th Meeting, February 17, 1945; Patterson, *Financial Experiences of Greece*, 147–51.

40. LBG/KVA/B/2, Varvaressos to Sideris, March 15, 1945; FO371/48334 R14166, Economic and Financial Developments in Greece November 1944–June 1945, C. Coombs, 1945; DSR 868.50/4–2345, MacVeagh to the Secretary of State, April 23, 1945 (Enclosure: Memorandum by H. A. Hill, April 21, 1945).

from the sale of relief supplies were almost impossible to predict as the financial arrangements between UNRRA and the Greek government had not yet been finalized. Furthermore, the deliveries were to last for six months only and not for the whole fiscal year. The war profits tax seemed even more dubious as assessment would be difficult and collection would be subject to legal proceedings. The British felt that much more should be done to increase yields from direct and indirect taxation. On the government side, while Voulgaris was afraid that higher taxes would provoke strikes, Mantzavinos replied that he was urgently studying taxation issues and would soon propose further increases. To Leeper, the only real choice was to take unpopular action immediately while the situation could still be saved, or to take similar action at a later stage after the currency had collapsed.[41]

Within days, Mantzavinos produced a revised version of the budget, taking partial account of British criticisms of his original proposals. While the share of direct taxation remained at 5 percent, it was now assumed that indirect taxes would contribute 25 percent, thanks mainly to a 50 percent increase on tobacco duties and the levying of import duties on UNRRA goods. Despite this increase, the budget still relied heavily on the sale of relief supplies (39 percent) and the war profits tax, which saw its predicted share doubled to 29 percent. Anticipated revenue was to exceed expenditure, producing a surplus of 4 percent.[42]

Despite the minor concessions, the British regarded the estimates as "pure window dressing." Hill was still skeptical about the predicted yields from the war profits tax and the sale of UNRRA goods, but he was most upset by Mantzavinos' refusal to introduce a meaningful income tax. While even before the war such a tax was levied at 4 percent in the public sector and 5 percent in the private, the minister now suggested a maximum 1 percent. The government was adamant that a general strike would follow if a higher rate was imposed, although it was prepared to raise the rate for higher incomes. Mantzavinos claimed that a heavier income tax was "economically and politically impossible," and said he would rather resign than attempt such a move. Hill was equally adamant that only a more substantial income tax could mop up surplus purchasing power and stop inflation. He therefore concluded that such decisions were political in nature, and were dependent on the

41. FO371/48330, including R6859, Athens to FO, Telegram no. 90 Remac, April 16, 1945; R7093, Athens to FO, Telegram no. 1016, April 20, 1945; R7164, Athens to FO, Telegram no. 1017, April 20, 1945; T236/1044, Hill to Davidson, April 22, 1945.

42. T236/149, Greek Revenue and Expenditure, Conversations Held on 21st, 23d and 25th April 1945, between the Minister of Finance (M. Mantzavinos) at the Bank of Greece and Mr. Harry Hill, Sir Quintin Hill, Mr. Lingeman, and Mr. Patterson; Hill to Davidson, April 27, 1945; T236/1044, Hill to Davidson, April 26, 1945.

degree of resolution that the government was willing to display. He was anxious not to provoke a general strike, particularly if the Greeks were to claim that "unreasonable demands" from the British had caused the tax crisis. In the face of government insistence that heavier taxation entailed risks of social unrest, the British grudgingly accepted that little progress appeared possible on budgetary issues. While Hill recognized that the latest proposals were probably the best which could be expected in the circumstances, he nevertheless emphasized that large capital outlays would be required to revitalize the economy and warned that the "whole bottom" would "fall out of the budget" if either the war profits tax or the sale of UNRRA goods failed to produce the anticipated sums. His distrust increased considerably following a subsequent meeting with a senior official from the finance ministry. The finance official virtually admitted that the expected amounts deriving from the war profits tax and the sale of UNRRA supplies were "fictitious," but was "bankrupt in suggestions" as to other possible sources of revenue.[43]

Preaching the "Gospel of Control"

By the end of April the British authorities in Athens had come to realize that circumstances dictated a change of emphasis in the advice they were recommending to the Greeks. Although far from happy with the latest budget proposals, they accepted that the government had at least made some progress on increasing tax revenue. However, it was only during this period that the British finally seemed to appreciate the full extent of the poverty in the country.[44] They came to believe that until the economy began to revive, little more could be gained by forcing the taxation issue. Thus in answer to the Treasury's continued strictures about the need to mop up purchasing power, Hill replied that the incomes of wage earners were so low that "sterilizing purchasing power" would be tantamount to "sterilizing them out

43. T236/1044, Hill to Davidson, April 26, 1945; Hill to Davidson, May 2, 1945; T236/149, Greek Revenue, T. St. Quintin Hill, April 23, 1945; Hill to Davidson, May 11, 1945 (Enclosure: Greek Revenue, Note of Discussion with M. Pesmazoglou, Under-Secretary for Finance on 11th May 1945); Hill to Waley, June 2, 1945 (Enclosure: Greek Budget 1945/1946, Summary Statements Furnished by M. Pesmazoglou on 11th and 15th May 1945).

44. FO371/48331 R8915, Caccia to Hasler, May 5, 1945 (Enclosure: Hill to Waley, May 5, 1945); T236/1044, Hill to Davidson, April 26, 1945. The recently completed report of the Trades Union Congress representatives present in Athens since February had a particularly strong influence on the British advisers. The delegation had been sent to observe the trade union elections, but had taken careful note of the living conditions of wage earners in the capital; FO371/48331 R8915, Caccia to Hasler, May 5, 1945 (Enclosure: Comment on Conditions in Athens and Piraeus, V. Feather).

of existence." Despite this admission, Hill agreed that the taxation of the rich would still remain a priority, and promised he would continue to pay close attention to public finance. Nevertheless, recent events had demonstrated that economic as well as budgetary pressures were fueling inflation, and that these problems needed to be addressed swiftly. With rising prices provoking wage demands in a vicious circle, and commodities and raw materials being hoarded when finished goods were desperately needed, the British felt it was obvious that the Greek government had to accept what was universally recognized elsewhere: the need to impose controls of supply, distribution, and price. Accordingly, the focus of British advice was switched, with a new emphasis on "preaching day in and day out" on the "gospel of control." This "preaching" took many forms. The Anglo-Greek Information Service (AGIS) distributed literature on the topic, while articles appeared in the Athens press describing the economic controls used in Britain during the war.[45] Such publications were designed to influence public opinion and to gain wider acceptance for the concept of controls.

By this time, however, another strand was emerging in the British policy in Greece, in response to the move to bring Varvaressos into the government as an economic troubleshooter. As will be shown in chapter 4, further action would wait for more than a month until Varvaressos returned in late May from official business abroad. Realizing that little could be expected until he came back, the British preferred to wait to discuss policy details with him rather than with the cabinet, although in the meantime, ministers were still urged to take immediate action. In early May the British complained to Voulgaris that next to nothing had been achieved since Eden's outburst in February, and stressed once again the need for increased state control over the country's economic life. The distribution of raw materials and finished goods, the stimulation of private industry, the control of prices of basic commodities, the tight control of wages to avoid inflation spirals—all were emphasized as absolute necessities without which the economy could not survive.[46]

45. T236/1044, Hill to Davidson, April 26, 1945; Hill to Davidson, May 2, 1945; FO371/48330, including R7752, Athens to FO, Telegram no. 99 Remac, May 1, 1945; R7921, Athens to FO, Telegram no. 1107, May 4, 1945; FO371/48266 R6723, AIS Weekly Report No. 24, March 25–31, 1945; FO371/48268 R7816, AGIS Weekly Report No. 27, April 15–21, 1945. A leading newspaper, Ελευθερία (Eleftheria), carried a series of articles by a Professor Pintos entitled "Organization or Anarchy." According to AGIS, these were probably inspired by the economist Rena Zafiriou, who had completed a doctorate at the London School of Economics while working as assistant to Varvaressos during the war. Both were to serve under Varvaressos during the summer of 1945; FO371/48269 R8082, AGIS Weekly Report No. 28, April 22–29, 1945.

46. FO371/48331 R8189, Leeper to Sargent, May 2, 1945 (Enclosure: Aide Mémoire, May 2, 1945).

Fresh disagreements appeared almost immediately. As a surge of labor unrest reached alarming proportions, senior Greek officials made a series of visits to Leeper, seeking advice on how to defuse the escalating wave of strikes. Most recent stoppages had been resolved by surrendering to the demands of the strikers, but Voulgaris felt particularly threatened by the latest agitation for an Easter bonus. He warned Leeper that a refusal would lead to even more serious civil disorders. Leeper repeated the standard advice given so many times before, reminding Voulgaris that the Greeks had undermined the progress achieved in recent discussions by opposing British suggestions on the introduction of income tax. Leeper took pains to show his disappointment with such avoidance of vigorous action. Citing Churchill's reference to "blood and sweat and tears," he hoped that the Greek government would also display determined leadership and demand sacrifices of the population. Leeper conceded the wisdom of immediate wage increases in order to prevent civil unrest, but extracted assurances from Voulgaris that the public would be informed of the seriousness of the situation and the necessity of the policies to be introduced.[47]

Voulgaris eventually admitted that economic stability required increased taxation and price controls, and claimed that concrete steps had already been taken in both areas. Nevertheless, he continued to stress that Greece still needed extra supplies from abroad. He explained that until the new policies were enforced, wage increases had to be granted given the threat of a general strike. Within days, Voulgaris sought further British help to overcome the latest wave of labor unrest. Tobacco workers were demanding a 250 percent pay raise, and the government was afraid that any concessions would provoke similar demands from others while a refusal could trigger a general strike. Voulgaris was unable to take any decision. The British were unwilling to give a definite answer on the spot, but observed that the pay raises already offered to the tobacco workers (150 percent) suggested huge profits that should be taxed by the state. They stressed that given the political dimension, Voulgaris would have to take his own decisions, but that any wage increases conceded by the government should be as small as possible, and should be granted solely for the purpose of buying time for a policy of economic controls.[48]

Despite consistent pressure from the British, the policy vacuum in Athens continued throughout the whole of May, with the Greeks appearing reluctant to under-

47. FO371/48330, including R7868, Athens to FO, Telegram no. 1104, May 3, 1945; R7921, Athens to FO, Telegram no. 1107, May 4, 1945; R7924, Athens to FO, Telegram no. 1108, May 4, 1945.

48. FO371/48331, including R8738, Athens to FO, Telegram no. 108 Remac, May 18, 1945; R9017, Athens to FO, Telegram no. 1227, May 22, 1945; T236/1044, Hill to Waley, May 31, 1945 (Enclosure: Diary of Events from Saturday 19th May to Wednesday 30th May).

take any serious measures before the return of Varvaressos. By the time he finally arrived on May 27, the economic situation was becoming desperate. The sovereign rate had doubled within a week, and rapid inflation seemed imminent. With Varvaressos back, events moved rapidly. Within days the full extent and scope of the UNRRA relief program was finally announced, while Voulgaris publicized the government's determination to rebuild the country, stressing that the success of the measures depended on a universal willingness to make sacrifices and work for the common good. Varvaressos assumed the posts of deputy prime minister and minister of supply on June 3. With this move, the long months of "delay and indecision" finally came to an end, and Greece entered into a period of economic reforms that came to be known as the "Varvaressos Experiment."[49]

Conclusions

During the seven and a half months between liberation and the return of Varvaressos to the government, efforts to undo the economic legacy of the occupation largely met with failure. As a result, the Greek economy remained in much the same state of disarray as it had been in October 1944. Although the presence of Varvaressos in the cabinet indicated that vigorous action would at last be taken, it is clear that the new approach could no longer count on the frenzied enthusiasm that had greeted liberation but had long since evaporated in the face of continuing uncertainties.

While the task of restoring even a modicum of normality to such a devastated country was clearly never going to be straightforward, the difficulties were compounded by the stance of successive governments in Athens. Even before liberation, ministers were unable to devise any program to foster recovery. This total neglect of economic planning, coupled with the exclusion of the one man who had appreciated the problems and suggested concrete solutions, ensured that the returning National Unity Government was entirely unprepared to cope with the reality it encountered.

Even worse was the fact that successive governments seemed content to follow this pattern. No member of any of the three governments appeared willing to take

49. FO371/48331 R8745, Athens to FO, Telegram no. 1182, May 16, 1945; T236/1044, Hill to Waley, May 31, 1945 (Enclosures: Diary of Events from Saturday 19th May to Wednesday 30th May; Maben to Voulgaris, May 28, 1945); Broadcast by Admiral Voulgaris from Athens Radio, May 29, 1945; Patterson, *Financial Experiences of Greece*, 178–79.

any serious initiatives to reconstruct the country's economic life. Ministers were essentially reactive, enacting short-term policies on an ad hoc basis. The official stance on economic matters was invariably more about the tactics of day-to-day survival than plans for the future. When the problems of the economy generated specific challenges requiring a decisive response, no government was able to offer anything more constructive than hasty capitulation in the face of social unrest.

Varvaressos aside, the hopes of all ministers appeared to lie solely in the prospect of help from abroad. As Leeper later wrote, they seemed to assume that the crisis could be "put right by foreign assistance." In a situation where austerity measures would inevitably arouse popular protest, extensive aid from the Allies had obvious attractions. The British wondered whether ministers were using the prospect of external help as an excuse to avoid unpopular decisions, and believed they had become convinced that nothing could be achieved "without a foreign loan." One observer even suggested that they had deliberately done nothing in the expectation that London would "save them from the mess" which their "delay and indecision" had created, while another sensed that the British were being blackmailed into bailing them out. Despite recent attempts to blame royalists alone for the view that outside aid was the main solution, Varvaressos seems far more correct in stressing that such beliefs were almost universal.[50] Certainly, apart from Varvaressos himself, this assumption does not appear to have been questioned by any minister, regardless of political ilk.

This apparent expectation that Allied assistance would be forthcoming was an unfortunate distraction, diverting attention away from the seriousness of the task ahead. The British were adamant that such attitudes would lead "nowhere." In a similar vein, Varvaressos criticized politicians, both within and outside of successive cabinets, for living in a "world of make-believe" while the economy continued to deteriorate. It is not possible to single out any of the governments as either more or less effective in facing the crisis, as all three demonstrated a remarkable consistency in their approach. Some attempts have been made to absolve the Papandreou government of the failure of the November stabilization scheme, which several authors see as prematurely aborted by the outbreak of fighting in Athens. Despite the proximity of the two events, such views ignore the fact that the reform was already moribund by the first days of December. The claim that the fighting "left

50. Leeper, *When Greek Meets Greek*, 155–56; FO371/48331, including R9017, FO to Athens, Telegram no. 1219, May 25, 1945; R9037, Athens to FO, Telegram no. 1230, May 23, 1945; Hadziiossif, "Economic Stabilization and Political Unrest," 27; LBG/KVA/B5, Memorandum on the Greek Economic Situation, K. Varvaressos, August 2, 1946, 75–79.

the government no time to complete its economic program" seems questionable given that no such program ever existed.[51]

The chronic lack of an effective stance on economic matters derived partly from the fragility of successive governments, which felt they lacked both the political mandate and the real power necessary to enact unpopular measures. Few ministers, apart from Varvaressos, had any confidence in their ability to combat the mounting crisis. One British observer remarked that the Greeks felt there was "so little" they could do to "help themselves" that it was simply "not worth starting to do it." Varvaressos was also scathing of this belief that the country could do nothing to help itself. Such hesitancy was perhaps not surprising given the makeup of the provisional governments, which, mindful of the weakness of their popular support, shied away from painful anti-inflationary policies. As Politakis observes, an austerity package would have to be paid for at the ballot box.[52] Nevertheless, the crisis could not be overcome by "delay and indecision," and drastic measures were clearly required. This reality, so forcibly repeated ad nauseam by the British, was acknowledged by Varvaressos alone.

The dismal record of successive governments prevented the successful implementation of any coherent policy to restore economic normality to the country. Even if ministers had chosen to entirely disregard British advice, they displayed little enthusiasm in carrying out schemes devised by leading Greek economists, namely Varvaressos and Zolotas. While Varvaressos was the first to point out the need for a clear and coordinated approach to post-liberation economic problems, he was excluded from decision-making even before the government-in-exile returned to Athens. While the British continued to hold him in high regard, the Papandreou government chose to ignore his ideas, instructing him instead to travel the world with a begging bowl on the country's behalf. Even after his return to the Bank of Greece, ministers proved no more ready to accept his advice. In many respects, Zolotas fared no better. Even though his ideas had been preferred to those of Varvaressos, little was done to ensure their success.

The pre-liberation disagreements between the two economists have been misrepresented by subsequent authors, who choose to contrast Varvaressos' initial

51. WO204/8761, Public Works in Greece, February 2, 1945; LBG/KVA/B5, Memorandum on the Greek Economic Situation, K. Varvaressos, August 2, 1946, 80; Hadziiossif, "Economic Stabilization and Political Unrest," 27; Politakis, *Greek Policies of Recovery and Reconstruction,* 103, 340; W. O. Candilis, *The Economy of Greece, 1944–66: Efforts for Stability and Development,* 27.

52. FO371/48331 R9037, Athens to FO, Telegram no. 1230, May 23, 1945; T236/139, Hugh-Jones to Waley, January 30, 1945; LBG/KVA/B5, Memorandum on the Greek Economic Situation, K. Varvaressos, August 2, 1946, 76; Politakis, *Greek Policies of Recovery and Reconstruction,* 106.

proposals from the spring and autumn of 1944 with a Zolotas memorandum writ-ten in November.[53] This distorts the options available to the Papandreou govern-ment by presenting them as a choice between Varvaressos' simplistic formula for the exchange rate and Zolotas' comprehensive package. Such accounts totally ig-nore the constant evolution of Varvaressos' views on the exchange rate, his con-sistent calls for a clear and coordinated policy, and his emphasis on the need for economic controls. On the other hand, Zolotas has been applauded for not ignor-ing the "realities of liberation" and for demonstrating "pragmatic liberalism" and a "carefully managed approach," balanced throughout by "continuous corrective intervention."[54] Such praise fails to consider Zolotas' complete misjudgment of the climate likely to prevail after liberation, as demonstrated by his predictions of rapid dishoarding of gold.

It would be equally simplistic to dismiss the views of Zolotas out of hand. After all, he had pointed out the necessity of balancing the budget and halting the print-ing presses. Furthermore, he could claim with much justification that his ideas had not been given a full chance to succeed, as little had been done to create the nec-essary preconditions he had deemed essential. However, he seemed unable to offer any real solutions to the crisis. For practical purposes, his "continuous corrective intervention" appears to have amounted to nothing more than the desperate sale of sovereigns. Even though this had clearly failed in November, he still advocated resuming the policy after his dismissal.[55]

The Zolotas approach seemed to absolve the government from enacting sev-eral measures already taken for granted in other countries. His noninterventionist stance, with its tolerance of free market operations, transactions in gold, sales of foreign currency, and capital flight, was entirely out of step with policies to combat scarcity anywhere else at the time. For Varvaressos, reliance on the free market was "repugnant" and could serve only the interest of "profiteers and speculators," who were to be left "completely unmolested." This view was fully endorsed by Patterson,

53. Candilis, *Economy of Greece*, 23–30; Politakis, *Greek Policies of Recovery and Reconstruction*, 85–103. Both authors accepted the somewhat biased accounts given in two later histories of the Bank of Greece, *Τα Πρώτα Πενήντα Χρόνια της Τραπέζης της Ελλάδος* (The First Fifty Years of the Bank of Greece), 242–47; E. Venezis, *Χρονικόν της Τραπέζης της Ελλάδος* (Chronicle of the Bank of Greece), 318–23. These accounts contained introductions written by Zolotas, who remained governor of the bank for several decades. A third source of distortion was Zolotas' own work, which includes the text of all his post-liberation statements only; X. Zolotas, *Η Πολιτική της Τραπέζης της Ελλάδος: Από 19 Οκτωβρίου 1944 μέχρι 8 Ιανουαρίου 1945* (The Policy of the Bank of Greece).

54. Politakis, *Greek Policies of Recovery and Reconstruction*, 103, 339.

55. WO204/8765, Reflections on the Proper Monetary Policy, X. Zolotas, January 8, 1945.

who pointed out that the implicit "attitude towards war profiteers and tax evaders [. . .] compared unfavorably" with that of "most other post-liberation governments of Europe."[56] Despite such damning criticisms, the essentially laissez-faire approach found much more favor, and was consistent with the actions of virtually every Greek government between 1944 and 1947. Such measures as the sale of gold and foreign currency received widespread support within Greece not only in late 1944, but as will be seen, also in subsequent years.

Thus the first seven and a half months after liberation demonstrated the considerable conflict between two very divergent approaches, broadly articulated by the views of Varvaressos and Zolotas. To a large extent, Varvaressos' vision of state management as a solution to scarcity reflected his awareness of the success of measures undertaken in wartime Britain. Unsurprisingly, his views largely accorded with British thinking, but seemed alien in a country that had little understanding of what had been achieved elsewhere. In contrast, Zolotas' noninterventionist ideas appeared to either ignore or reject lessons learned elsewhere, but seemed much more appealing to Greek politicians and business circles. The violent disagreement over which of these stances should be adopted remained unresolved throughout the whole period of British involvement in Greece.

56. LBG/KVA/B5, Memorandum on the Greek Economic Situation, K. Varvaressos, August 2, 1946, 75; Patterson, *Financial Experiences of Greece,* 43.

4

THE
"VARVARESSOS EXPERIMENT"

§

While the first five months of 1945 were characterized by government inertia and unwillingness to take any decisive action to improve the economic situation, this changed once Varvaressos joined the cabinet. Technocrat Varvaressos' energy and courage offered a striking contrast to the timidity of the politicians. For the first time, a minister launched a bold program designed to overcome the immediate crisis and initiate economic recovery. Most of this package enjoyed the full blessing of the British, containing as it did all the main policies that they had long been urging the Greeks to adopt. Nevertheless, despite initial success, Varvaressos failed to achieve any of his major objectives, and his decisive stance proved as fruitless as the vacillations of his predecessors. This chapter explains the nature and course of the so-called Varvaressos Experiment and the opposition it aroused, and analyzes the controversy surrounding its failure.

The Return of Varvaressos

To understand why Varvaressos had suddenly become so important in British eyes, it is necessary to recount his activities since the autumn of 1944. As already noted, the British had looked to him to suggest a definite policy as an alternative to the total inertia prevailing in Athens, and were enthusiastic about his ideas. However, given the apparent distrust of Varvaressos in Greek government circles, the matter was allowed to drop. British respect for Varvaressos grew steadily from January 1945, when he returned to Athens to resume the governorship of the Bank of Greece. Officials at the Treasury welcomed the move. John Maynard Keynes felt confident that Varvaressos would be able to "bring a breath of responsibility" into the country's economic affairs. In a final meeting before his departure, Waley was pleased to note how much Varvaressos' views concurred with those of Whitehall.[1] It was precisely this perception of a common ground which gradually convinced the British that Varvaressos could be their most important ally in the struggle to restore economic stability.

His ideas had been explained at length to Allied representatives immediately after his return to Athens. Varvaressos was deeply worried about the state of the economy and was convinced many government policies needed to be changed. He was alarmed by the twin spirals of prices and wages, which he felt would lead to inevitable chaos. He believed that domestically produced commodities should be subject to price controls, while ML supplies would have to be sold at realistic prices rather than simply distributed free of charge. At the same time, wages would have to be pegged to the controlled prices rather than to open market rates. He was appalled by the prevailing attitude that only external assistance could solve the country's problems. Although he wished for continued British financing of the armed forces, he hoped that their size and cost could be kept at levels the country could maintain in the future. He believed that the drachma was seriously overvalued, but felt that political and psychological factors ruled out any adjustments in the near future. He emphasized the need to provide low-interest credit to revitalize local industry, but stressed that such credits would have to be targeted toward firms which were committed to restarting production and selling their output at designated prices. He was adamant that neither industrialists nor financiers should be allowed to make vast profits by exploiting the current situation. Finally, he condemned the gold sales policy previously pursued by the Bank of Greece.[2]

The governor's audience had been particularly impressed with his views, which contrasted so sharply with the apparent lack of policy and drive from the current government. An admiring Leeper claimed that while Sideris was content to beg for further Allied help, Varvaressos was tackling essential problems with "clarity and energy" and seemed to be the "only man" able to "grasp Greece's postwar problems."[3] Within weeks Varvaressos had impressed even further, with his

1. FO371/43724 R17044, Minute by Laskey, October 23, 1944; FO to Athens, Telegram no. 5, October 23, 1944; T236/139, Minute by Keynes, January 22, 1945; FO371/48326 R1120, Waley to Hugh Jones, January 12, 1945.

2. FRUS, 1945. MacVeagh to the Secretary of State, January 30, 1945, vol. 8, 196–97; FO371/48327 R2286, Athens to FO, Telegram no. 24 Remac, January 31, 1945.

3. FO371/48327, including R3109, Athens to FO, Telegram no. 28 Remac, February 13, 1945; R3263, Athens to FO, Telegram no. 538, February 15, 1945; FO371/48257 R3475, Athens to FO, Telegram no. 565, February 19, 1945.

initiatives on price fixing and relief supplies. As mentioned previously, by the middle of February the British authorities were discussing the possibility of suggesting Varvaressos as a likely replacement for Sideris. Nevertheless, they feared that such an appointment might be resisted by many in the cabinet, or that even if appointed, Varvaressos could be forced from office if the government fell. Given the political uncertainty, and not wishing to risk the support that Varvaressos was providing from the Bank of Greece, it was decided not to press the matter.[4]

However, the British quickly changed their minds and sought to bring about what they had dubbed the Varvaressos Solution by securing him a place within the cabinet. Initial discussions with senior Greek officials led to the suggestion that Varvaressos should become a minister with overall "authority to control and co-ordinate economic and financial measures." At first the regent was very "noncommittal" and suggested that such an appointment might entail political difficulties, but within days, both Damaskinos and Plastiras seemed agreeable to the idea. The regent admitted that the proposal was attracting "much discussion," while widespread rumors in Athens predicted that Varvaressos would soon be joining the government (albeit as finance minister).[5]

Despite the apparent inevitability that Varvaressos would assume the post, events took a different turn. While still believing that Varvaressos would be a useful addition to the Plastiras government, by mid-March the British decided not to stir up "personal jealousies and antipathies," as it seemed that Sideris was opposed to granting wider powers to Varvaressos.[6] In any case, Varvaressos chose to remove himself from the Greek political scene by visiting Britain and the United States. In Washington he wished to publicize the difficulties facing Greece, which he felt the Americans insufficiently understood. In London he wanted to discuss more concrete matters, and was particularly determined to secure increased supplies of raw materials and industrial equipment.[7]

4. WO204/8761, E&SC (45) 4th Meeting, January 29, 1945; E&SC (45) 6th Meeting, February 12, 1945. For the original idea of replacing Sideris, see section entitled "The Easy Way Out," chap. 3.

5. FO371/48257, including R3769, Athens to Cairo, Telegram no. 98, February 16, 1945; R3565, Athens to FO, Telegram no. 586, February 21, 1945; R3566, *The Times*, February 23, 1945; FO371/48327 R3263, Athens to FO, Telegram no. 538, February 15, 1945; FO371/48262 R5390, Notes on Interview with the Regent, February 28, 1945.

6. FO371/48261 R5072, Athens to FO, Telegram no. 762, March 15, 1945. This was not the first time that Sideris had demonstrated such hostility: back in January, he had seemed particularly unenthusiastic about the prospect of Varvaressos' return to Athens (see section entitled "The Easy Way Out," chap. 3).

7. FO371/48328 R5780, Athens to FO, Telegram no. 58 Remac, March 27, 1945; FO371/48263 R5989, Athens to FO, Telegram no. 869, March 31, 1945; T236/1044, Athens to FO, Telegram no. 72 Remac, April 4, 1945; Minute by Waley, April 7, 1945.

It is not clear why Varvaressos made such a choice at this time. Moreover, an additional government request that he should join its delegation at the San Francisco conference after completing his talks has further clouded the issue. Some Allied observers speculated whether the foreign trips were merely a device to remove Varvaressos from Athens. Hill wondered if this was an attempt to "side-track" him, while the American ambassador Lincoln MacVeagh felt it was possible that his political opponents were happy to see him out of the country. Several later historians have accepted such speculation at face value, and have suggested that Varvaressos was practically prevented from taking office by his enemies in the Greek establishment. Thus Politakis repeats the MacVeagh quote, and goes on to claim that Varvaressos had been kept from power by "significant domestic opposition" and that his opponents had won "a temporary victory." Richter goes even further to claim that other ministers' delight about the prospects of Varvaressos' absence amounted to a "rejection of his policy of economic austerity." Hadziiossif also exaggerated individual statements by various Greeks to build up an unsubstantiated picture of a coherent anti-Varvaressos opposition.[8]

It is possible that the San Francisco leg of the trip—which Varvaressos neither wanted nor regarded as necessary—may be interpreted in such a light. As already noted, the events of September 1944 indicated much personal hostility toward Varvaressos from politicians. In addition, he was also disliked by many sectional interests, particularly bankers, who opposed his strict credit policies. However, there is no evidence to confirm he was kept out of office by a concerted opposition. It seems clear that Varvaressos had little intention of joining the government and regarded his foreign trips—San Francisco excepted—as vital. On several previous occasions he had already declined offers of cabinet posts. In December 1944 he had refused the finance ministry, preferring to reassume the governorship of the Bank of Greece. According to Sideris, Varvaressos had turned down similar offers in early February and mid-March. Even when finally invited to become minister of coordination after the change of government in early April, he still indicated great reluctance to accept. Moreover, in interviews with the British, Varvaressos took pains to justify his decision to visit London and Washington, making it clear how much importance he attached to the move.[9]

8. FO371/48328 R5780, Athens to FO, Telegram no. 59 Remac, March 27, 1945; FRUS, 1945: MacVeagh to the Secretary of State, March 24, 1945, vol. 8, 204–5; Politakis, *Greek Policies of Recovery and Reconstruction*, 110–11; H. Richter, *British Intervention in Greece: From Varkiza to Civil War, February 1945 to August 1946*, 210; Hadziiossif, "Economic Stabilization and Political Unrest," 29–30.

9. FRUS, 1945: MacVeagh to the Secretary of State, March 24, 1945, vol. 8, 204–5; FO371/48330 R6984, Athens to FO, Telegram no. 92 Remac, April 18, 1945; FO371/48347 R16322, Greek Person-

Between Varvaressos' announcement of his trips in late March and his departure some two weeks later, the question of his assuming office continued to be raised many times during the flurry of activity that accompanied the accession of Voulgaris. Although his name was not mentioned during the cabinet reshuffle of April 2, when it was rumored that Sideris would be made minister of coordination, the arrival of the Voulgaris government rekindled speculation that Varvaressos would soon be brought in. On April 8 further rumors suggested that he would be offered the ministry of finance, but by the next day it was claimed he was finally to be brought in as minister of coordination. On April 10, Mantzavinos urged Varvaressos to accept the post. Later that day he claimed to have "no enthusiasm" for the idea, and still seemed unwilling to join the cabinet three days later, before finally accepting on April 17. Before taking office, Varvaressos had insisted on the removal of certain ministers and civil servants, and later admitted that he was prepared to take responsibility for the economy only if granted suitably sweeping powers.[10]

In any event, his foreign trips achieved little despite a series of high-level meetings with British and American officials. The San Francisco leg of his journey was cut short after only a few days, as the deteriorating state of the Greek economy moved the British to press Voulgaris to recall him from abroad as quickly as possible. Accordingly, on April 20 Voulgaris promised to order him back upon completion of his business in Washington. The British had long regarded Varvaressos as the man most likely to implement appropriate economic policies, and the way was now clear to address the most pressing problems of the Greek economy. With his imminent return to Athens, the British decided to take advantage of his stopover in London to explain the course they wanted him to pursue. The agenda for the forthcoming talks was based on a memorandum drawn up by E. Lingeman, Leeper's economic adviser, after consultations with Zafiriou and Hill.[11]

The memorandum contained an analysis of those areas of the Greek economy

alities Report, September 17, 1945; FO371/48328 R5780, Athens to FO, Telegram no. 58 Remac, March 27, 1945; T236/1044, Waley to Hill, April 13, 1945; Athens to FO, Telegram no. 72 Remac, April 4, 1945.

10. FO371/48264, including R6182, Athens to FO, Telegram no. 893, April 4, 1945; R6432, Athens to FO, Telegram no. 932, April 8, 1945; R6477, Athens to FO, Telegram no. 943, April 9, 1945; FO371/48329 R6519, Athens to FO, Telegram no. 82 Remac, April 10, 1945; Minute by Laskey, April 11, 1945; Minute by Howard, April 11, 1945; T236/1044, Waley to Hill, April 13, 1945; FO371/48267 R7363, Athens to FO, Telegram no. 36 Saving, April 17, 1945; FO371/58680 R4219, Athens to FO, Telegram no. 59, March 1, 1946 (Enclosure: Political Summary 1945); G. Kasimatis, Το Οικονομι-κόν Πρόβλημα: Τι Έγινε. Τι Πρέπει να Γίνει (The Economic Problem), 26–27; Patterson, Financial Experiences of Greece, 178.

11. While in London, Varvaressos had talks with Dalton, Eden, and Bevin. In Washington he met the president of the Ex-Im Bank and several government officials; T236/1044, Waley to Hill,

where state controls over distribution and price would yield tangible benefits. It highlighted many absurdities resulting either from the absence of suitable controls or from the uneven implementation of existing controls. Thus while certain districts suffered severe shortages of commodities, the same goods were often in plentiful supply on the free market elsewhere. Other much-needed items were hoarded in anticipation of future price rises in the absence of official willingness to requisition stocks. While the government experienced huge difficulties with the distribution of relief supplies, owners of private transport were apparently making huge profits. Such anomalies were clearly unacceptable. Lingeman thus recommended that the government should assume far greater control over all modes of transport and freight charges. Moreover, a system of registration of stocks and powers to requisition goods were vital to combat hoarding and ensure a more equitable distribution of existing supplies. Only such measures would enable the successful operation of price controls, which would embrace both basic foodstuffs and other essential commodities. In addition, greater care was needed to prevent relief supplies from reaching the black market, and given huge local variations in the free distribution of UNRRA goods, consistent guidelines on these issues were clearly necessary. To this end, Lingeman suggested appointing a British official with relevant experience, together with experts on publicity and control policies, to advise the ministry of coordination.[12]

With minor amendments from the Treasury, the Lingeman recommendations formed the basis for the subsequent discussions in London.[13] The talks revealed broad agreement on strategy, but disagreement on priorities and the timing of individual measures. For the Treasury, the main priority was to construct a "simple and striking" program designed to create public confidence. Varvaressos pointed out the practical difficulties he would face. He emphasized that prices had risen out of all proportion to prewar price and wage levels, and thus had to be reduced

April 13, 1945; FRUS, 1945; Clayton to Diamantopoulos, May 4, 1945, vol. 8, 213–15; Memorandum by Baxter, May 4, 1945, vol. 8, 215–16. FO371/48330, including R7093, Athens to FO, Telegram no. 1016, April 20, 1945; R7164, Athens to FO, Telegram no. 1017, April 20, 1945; R7752, Athens to FO, Telegram no. 99 Remac, May 1, 1945. FRUS, 1945. MacVeagh to the Secretary of State, April 21, 1945, vol. 8, 211–12; T236/1044, Hill to Davidson, April 26, 1945 (Enclosure: Minute by Hill, April 24, 1945); Hill to Davidson, May 2, 1945 (Enclosure: Economic Reconstruction of Greece: Notes for Program as Evolved in Conversations with Miss Zafiriou, April 30, 1945).

12. FO371/48331 R8904, Laskey to Caccia, May 16, 1945 (Enclosure: Controls in Greece, E. R. Lingeman, May 9, 1945).

13. FO371/48331, including R8508, Sandberg to Laskey, May 15, 1945 (Enclosure: Economic Measures and Controls in Greece, May 14, 1945); R8743, Davidson to Laskey, May 17, 1945; Laskey to Davidson, May 19, 1945.

rather than merely frozen. So far, price controls extended only to relief supplies, but all local produce needed to supplement the UNRRA ration was disproportionately expensive. He therefore queried whether controls should embrace essential goods only or a much wider range of items. He realized the former option would be much easier, but warned that this would allow the continued production of luxury items. Worried that this would divert labor and capital from the production of essentials, he felt controls should be extended widely. He warned that strict control of each commodity price might take months to achieve, and thus suggested imposing maximum prices that could not be increased without special authority. He believed that introducing a wage freeze should be accompanied by immediate price reductions with further reductions to follow. He also hoped that increased production of most essential commodities would ease the upward pressure on prices. Varvaressos suggested that prices should be reduced to March levels, but the British doubted whether this was feasible. The meeting ended without clarifying the apparent differences of opinion. General agreement was reached on the broad strategy to be pursued, with Varvaressos receiving complete freedom to work out the details.[14]

The "Varvaressos Experiment"

As already noted, Varvaressos returned to Athens on May 27 to find the country in the midst of economic turmoil. Following last-minute assurances that he would have a free hand in pursuing any policies he deemed necessary, he assumed the posts of deputy prime minister and minister of supply on June 3, without relinquishing the governorship of the Bank of Greece. With sweeping powers to control and coordinate all government policies on economic and financial matters, he was eager to take immediate action. On the eve of his appointment, Varvaressos confidently assured Leeper that he would tax the rich and put an end to the "feasts of Kolonaki," a euphemism for the extravagant lifestyle of the affluent minority in Athens. Almost at once, transactions in gold and foreign currency by private individuals were outlawed, on pain of severe fines or imprisonment, while the foreign exchange value of the drachma was reduced by 70 percent in order to encourage export trade and to treat fairly remittance receivers.[15]

14. FO371/48331, including R9195, Draft Note of a Meeting Held at the Treasury to Discuss the Greek Financial Position: Gold and Exchange Rate, May 18, 1945; R9208, Note of a Meeting Held in the Treasury to Discuss Economic Measures and Controls in Greece, May 22, 1945; T236/1044, Davidson to Hill, May 24, 1945; T236/1045, Waley to Hill, June 6, 1945.

15. FO371/48332, including R9386, Athens to FO, Telegram no. 1281, May 30, 1945; R9475, Athens to FO, Telegram no. 1301, June 1, 1945; FO371/48334 R12776, Compulsory Law No. 362, *Government*

The Varvaressos program appeared in the newspapers only three days after he took office. In introducing it, he claimed that the country had failed to recover after liberation because of two main obstacles: successive governments exercised little control or supervision over the economy, and despite the goodwill of the Allies, relief supplies from abroad had fallen far short of the country's actual needs. The recent announcement of the UNRRA program was expected to solve the latter. The most pressing need therefore was to assume sufficient powers to ensure speedy recovery and increased material welfare. Varvaressos pointed to the substantial role of the state in the economic life of other countries, and argued that the lack of any controls in Greece had allowed a disproportionate share of the country's wealth to be concentrated in a few hands. He added that some of these few were undermining the drachma and fueling inflation by speculating in gold, while others were contributing to inflation by restricting production or hoarding goods and raw materials. In such circumstances, living standards could not be improved unless the existing maldistribution of incomes was reduced.[16]

Varvaressos announced several measures to address this problem. Wage rates were increased by 50 to 60 percent, while the prices of UNRRA foodstuffs other than bread were reduced by 50 percent. In addition, price controls were to be imposed on domestically produced goods, beginning with staples, and gradually extended to all other commodities. He also demanded that retailers reduce their prices to levels prevailing before the recent wave of inflation. Claiming that the rich had profited from the country's misfortune, he promised heavy taxation. He called on traders and industrialists to comply with his program, and warned that the period of "excessive gains" was over. He added that if cooperation was not forthcoming, the government would not hesitate to take action to "safeguard the people's interests." He appealed to the public not to buy goods at inflated prices from the open market, promising that their purchasing power would soon increase as a result of his measures.[17]

The British were relieved that the policies they had long recommended were about to be implemented, but had reservations about the substantial reductions in the prices of UNRRA goods. Nevertheless, as Hill observed, since Varvaressos seemed to have "turned politician" in pursuit of popular support, "100 percent financial purism" could no longer be expected. The most serious doubts centered on the government's ability to implement the measures, but the British strengthened

Gazette, June 4, 1945; Compulsory Law No. 395, *Government Gazette,* June 12, 1945; Patterson, *Financial Experiences of Greece,* 178, 180, 236–39.

16. FO371/48334 R12776, Leeper to Eden, June 8, 1945 (Enclosure: Economic and Financial Program of the Government, June 5, 1945).

17. Ibid.

From right to left: Admiral Voulgaris, Herbert Lehman (director general of UNRRA), Kyriakos Varvaressos, and an unidentified official at the port of Piraeus. Photographic Archive of the Benaki Museum, Athens. Photo by Voula Papaioannou.

their resolve to offer full support. The initial Greek reaction was also largely favorable. On the Athens market, both the sovereign rate and commodity prices reacted positively and goods such as cheese and sugar reappeared for sale.[18]

To implement his program, Varvaressos set up the so-called Economic Service of the Vice President within the Bank of Greece, a team of experts with cabinet authority to coordinate policies and issue instructions to ministries. To head this body, Varvaressos recruited Zafiriou, who had previously been involved with all his initiatives. Professor Ieronymos Pintos, who had publicized price controls in the Athens press back in May, was made deputy minister of supply. Varvaressos also created a new body to ensure more effective collaboration with UNRRA and the British authorities. The Economic Advisory Committee (EAC) replaced the Joint Policy Committee (JPC) and its various sections. Unlike the previous bodies, no Greek ministers or officials were to be included in the EAC, which would consist of the foreign advisers and Varvaressos with his allies Zafiriou and Pintos. Apart from creating new structures, Varvaressos also initiated a reorganization of the ministry of supply, including the setting up of a new department to supervise all matters relating to UNRRA supplies.[19]

The first concrete control scheme came on June 10, when Varvaressos imposed retail price ceilings on seventeen locally produced goods, mainly foodstuffs. The new official prices were considerably lower than those currently prevailing in the open market and represented a return to levels of May 5. A second list, involving a far wider range of commodities and further price reductions, was issued on June 17, after which regular updatings were issued on a weekly basis. As a result of these measures, Varvaressos claimed an early victory. Within three weeks he announced that the ceilings were being observed, and that the cost of living had consequently dropped by 30 percent. Competent observers confirmed this, adding that the prices of some items had even fallen below official levels. However, some deterioration in the quality of market goods was noted, and several commodities were becoming increasingly scarce. Varvaressos recognized some shortages, but claimed these were the result of increased purchases rather than hoarding. The undeniable

18. T236/1045, Hill to Waley, June 5, 1945; Minute by Sandberg, June 5, 1945; Rowe-Dutton to Hill, June 7, 1945; FO371/48332 R9975, Athens to FO, Telegram no. 1361, June 9, 1945; FO371/48272, including R10796, AGIS Weekly Report No. 34, June 3–9, 1945; R10344, Athens to FO, Telegram no. 107 Saving, June 11, 1945.

19. T236/1045, Hill to Rowe-Dutton, June 14, 1945; FO371/48272 R10344, Athens to FO, Telegram no. 107 Saving, June 11, 1945; FO371/48333, including R10910, Minutes of a Meeting Held at the Bank of Greece, June 14, 1945; R11265, Paper No. EAC (45) 1; R11266, EAC (45) 1st Meeting, June 23, 1945; R11601, Paper No. EAC (45) 2; FO371/48334 R12776, Compulsory Laws No. 451, No. 452, Government Gazette, July 9, 1945.

initial success was limited mainly to foodstuffs, as no manufactured goods had been covered by the June announcements. At first the measures were introduced in the Athens area only, but the swift establishment of a network of provincial committees allowed the imposition of a uniform policy throughout the country by the end of June. By this time, a market police corps had been set up to enforce the policy.[20]

To further discourage violations of his control schemes, Varvaressos enacted a measure designed to combat "offences threatening the vital interests of the public." Actions falling under this heading included the closure or suspension of any industrial or retail business for the purpose of evading government regulations, the concealment or hoarding of goods of basic necessity, and infringements of the newly imposed price controls. Producers or traders failing to comply were to be punished by heavy fines or imprisonment, together with the withdrawal of licenses to operate their businesses for a period of at least six months, during which time their enterprises would be administered by the state.[21]

Shortly afterwards, Varvaressos announced major initiatives designed to balance the budget. To reduce expenditure, he declared his resolve to end severe overmanning within the civil service.[22] To increase revenue he devised a new form of taxation, recalling his earlier promise to tax the rich. Given the inadequacies of the tax-collecting machinery and the need to produce immediate yields, he rejected increases in conventional direct taxation, choosing instead to introduce the so-called "Special Contribution," to be paid by almost all commercial, industrial, and professional enterprises for a period of nine months. Each month, every business renting its premises was to be charged a multiple of its rent, while those owning their premises were to pay a similar multiple of imputed rental values of their properties. The special contribution was to be levied at three different rates varying between six and fifteen times the rental value. Varvaressos justified this measure by claiming that as rents had become nominal as a result of a general rent moratorium, businesses had made large savings in a period when all other goods and services had experienced considerable inflation. Although Varvaressos was in effect taxing these savings, he admitted the special contribution hardly constituted a "scientific" form of taxation.[23]

20. Patterson, *Financial Experiences of Greece*, 216–18; FO371/48334, including R14166, Economic and Financial Developments in Greece November 1944–June 1945, C. Coombs, August 1, 1945, 47–48; R12776, No. 21367 Decision of the Deputy Prime Minister and Minister of Supply, June 14, 1945; *Η Καθημερινή* (Kathimerini), June 26, 1945.

21. FO371/48334 R12776, Constitutional Act No. 57, *Government Gazette*, June 22, 1945.

22. FO371/48334 R12776, Constitutional Act No. 59, *Government Gazette*, June 26, 1945.

23. FO371/48334, including R12776, Compulsory Law No. 431, *Government Gazette*, June 21, 1945; R14166, Economic and Financial Developments in Greece November 1944–June 1945, C. Coombs, August 1, 1945, 33–37; Patterson, *Financial Experiences of Greece*, 183–86.

With the announcement of the new tax, the Varvaressos program ran into immediate problems. The special contribution attracted a huge wave of hostility from those who felt it threatened their interests. Many organizations representing traders or industrialists issued vigorous protests, most notably the Athens Federation of Traders and Small Manufacturers. Within days the federation attempted to send a delegation to Varvaressos, and announced plans for a shopkeepers' strike after the minister refused to meet them. The press reported that industrialists had asked for the special contribution to be suspended until all affected groups could be consulted. Varvaressos refused to compromise. In protest, the federation announced an indefinite shopkeepers' strike to begin on July 9. Varvaressos restated his determination to collect the tax and warned that failure to pay the first installment on time (by July 10) would be punished with draconian fines. He promised that individual complaints would be addressed, but only after the July installment was paid. As for the threatened strike, Varvaressos warned that the full force of the law would be applied to those who undertook such an illegal act. Stronger warnings were issued by Pintos, who announced that any shop closed for more than twenty-four hours would be reopened and operated by his ministry. This resolute stance had the desired effect. Instead of the indefinite stoppage, a one-day strike was called for July 9. Even this was unsuccessful. No more than 15 percent of shops in Athens and Piraeus joined the strike, of which very few remained shut for the entire day.[24]

Varvaressos encountered further problems when he attempted to fulfill a previous promise to ensure an adequate supply of cloth and clothing at reasonable prices. This brought conflict with both government inertia and stout resistance from industrialists. As the textile industry had not yet recommenced production, the country had experienced severe shortages of clothing, and prices of material had risen more quickly than those of almost any other commodity. These shortages had been further aggravated by the woeful inefficiency of successive governments in distributing the huge amounts of finished textiles supplied by ML/UNRRA. ML alone had furnished more than three million of yards of cloth between February and May, with further quantities being delivered by UNRRA. In addition, both agencies had provided large amounts of ready-made garments. Up to this time, these items had simply been allowed to pile up in Piraeus warehouses, a situation that Hill described as an "outstanding scandal." Varvaressos ended months of government inaction by introducing a ration system in late July, and fixed moderate prices for all imported textiles. Administrative difficulties ensured that the distribution of these goods did

24. FO371/48273 R11371, AGIS Weekly Report No. 36, June 17–23, 1945; FO371/48274 R12219, AGIS Weekly Report No. 38, July 1–7, 1945; FO371/48275 R12702, AGIS Weekly Report No. 39, July 8–14, 1945; Patterson, *Financial Experiences of Greece*, 187–89.

not begin until late August. A further problem arose from UNRRA deliveries of raw cotton, of which seventy-five hundred tons had been received by late summer. This was sufficient to allow the country's cotton industry to work at full capacity for a year. Negotiations on how to allocate these supplies had begun in June, but produced few results. Varvaressos was determined that the industry should produce only utility goods, with all products, prices, and profit margins to be decided by the government. Mill owners resented what they saw as an unprecedented degree of state control over all aspects of the production process. Particular disagreement was raised over estimates of production costs and profits for the manufacturers. Stubborn opposition by the industrialists ensured that negotiations dragged on for two months. The textile producers secured relatively generous terms. Officially, they were allowed 8 percent profits on government contracts. However, as competent observers were convinced that the mill owners had deliberately overstated their production costs, actual profits were likely to be considerably higher.[25]

While Varvaressos was engaged in such struggles, cracks had begun to appear in the entire control system. By mid-July analysts were noting a "slackening" of the program's momentum. For the first time since Varvaressos joined the cabinet, the cost of living began to rise again. On July 21 the sovereign rate returned to June 5 levels. The initial success of the fixed prices began to evaporate as the availability of several commodities started to drop alarmingly. During July, olive oil virtually disappeared from the Athens markets. By the first weeks of August, cheese, sugar, butter, and soap were also in short supply, at controlled prices, though more and more goods were being sold at higher prices in open defiance of the government. Varvaressos could only increase the number of policemen patrolling the markets and threaten severe penalties for those who ignored the controls. By this time, British observers were ruefully noting that early enthusiasm for the Varvaressos program had "faded sadly."[26]

The return of inflation brought a new series of demands for higher wages, mainly from groups that had not benefited from the raises announced on June 5. Varvaressos fulfilled his promise to grant substantial wage increases to civil servants on June 22, but was determined not to make similar concessions to the armed forces.

25. FO371/48332 R9723, Athens to FO, Telegram no. 120 Remac, June 5, 1945; FO371/48334 R12776, *Η Καθημερινή* (Kathimerini), June 26, 1945; FO371/48273 R11371, AGIS Weekly Report No. 36, June 17–23, 1945; FO371/48276 R13678, AGIS Weekly Report No.41, July 22–28, 1945; FO371/48277 R13868, AGIS Weekly Report No. 42, July 29–August 4, 1945; Patterson, *Financial Experiences of Greece*, 222–25; FO371/48337 R18405, Economic and Financial Developments in Greece July–August 1945, C. Coombs, September 17, 1945, 7–8.

26. FO371/48275 R12961, AGIS Weekly Report No. 40, July 15–21, 1945; FO371/48278 R14422, AGIS Weekly Report No. 43, August 5–11, 1945.

Sellers of olive oil in the center of Athens. Photographic Archive of the Benaki Museum, Athens. Photo by Dimitrios Charisiadis.

This move failed to satisfy any of the interested parties. The civil servants regarded the raise as insufficient and were generally opposed to the redundancy measures announced on the same day. The military was obviously dissatisfied at missing out, and Varvaressos came under relentless pressure from members of the armed forces and the police. In early August he was forced to grant both groups pay raises comparable to those given in the civil service. At the same time, he bowed to similar pressure to grant massive raises to pensioners. Despite these unwelcome concessions, Varvaressos was adamant that he could not allow another series of general wage increases, and refused to accede to the demands of the Piraeus dock workers who had threatened strike action. Even in this case, he was forced to make compromises. Instead of higher wages, he conceded extra payments in the form of foodstuffs and more generous working conditions.[27]

The wage concessions undid much of Varvaressos' good work on public finance. Despite the extra revenue produced by the special contribution, spiraling expenditure meant that Varvaressos had little chance of achieving budget equilibrium. This was tacitly admitted in early August, when new budget estimates were presented to the British authorities and UNRRA. Varvaressos seemed confident that by increasing revenue, he could reduce the deficit to 20 percent over the coming year. This admission was far more honest than the unrealistic predictions made back in April, but the August estimates also contained doubtful assumptions. Varvaressos anticipated that less than a third of total revenue would come from direct and indirect taxes (4 percent and 19 percent respectively). Sales from UNRRA goods were to furnish 28 percent, but the biggest doubts surrounded three items that were to produce almost half of government revenue. The special contribution was to furnish 20 percent, based on the projection that the amounts collected in July could also be collected throughout the following eight months. As will be shown, such assumptions proved far from accurate. The second item was the war profits tax, which was to bring in an anticipated ten billion drachmae or 13 percent of total revenue. However, this had so far produced pitiful results, yielding only one hundred million drachmae since its creation. The final problematic heading was war prizes, also predicted to provide 13 percent. Varvaressos was vague as to the basis for such a high estimate, as no revenue had yet been obtained from the sale of any article falling into this category. Competent analysts were convinced that neither the special contribution nor the two war-related taxes would furnish anything like the sums envisaged in the estimates.[28]

The initial results of the special contribution had seemed very promising, with a total of 1.7 billion drachmae being collected in July. During that month, Varvaressos made considerable progress toward his goal of balancing the budget as the deficit fell to 25 percent, less than half of the figure for June (52.8 percent). Nevertheless, vigorous opposition ensured that the success would not continue for long. At the end of July, Varvaressos responded by introducing a series of amendments. These included the raising of rates paid by industrial establishments, the reclassification of

27. Patterson, *Financial Experiences of Greece,* 198–206.

28. T236/149, Notes of Discussion on Revised Greek Budget, August 3, 1945; Muir to Sandberg, August 23, 1945 (Enclosure: Notes of Discussion on the Revised Greek Budget of August 1945, August 13, 1945); August Budgetary Estimates of the Greek Government, C. Coombs, September 10, 1945.

several categories of small businesses into lower bands of payment, and the granting of total exemptions to regions that had suffered particular damage during the war. Although Varvaressos wished to shift the burden from small to larger enterprises, the immediate consequence was a reduction in receipts for August, when only 1.3 billion drachmae was collected. As a result, the budget deficit rose to 42.5 percent in August. The concessions did little to soften the general hostility toward the tax, and opposition continued to mount. While shopkeepers considered another one-day strike, the increasing incidence of refusal to pay the levy forced Varvaressos to issue dire threats, warning that defaulters would face confiscation of their property. This provoked a mass meeting of Athens and Piraeus tradesmen, who denounced both the tax and the punitive measures. As hostility escalated, Varvaressos was forced to climb down, and on September 1 he announced that no penalties would be imposed for nonpayment of the special contribution as long as all outstanding sums were paid in by September 10.[29]

As the Varvaressos reforms stalled in the face of growing opposition, its central element—price controls—began to collapse completely during August. With official prices ignored as totally irrelevant, foodstuffs could be bought only at ever higher free market prices. As the cost of manufactured goods rose unabated, farmers felt little incentive to cooperate with a program that offered increasingly meaningless returns for their produce. Many farmers chose to withhold commodities, particularly olive oil, the first article to disappear from markets. As far back as June, Varvaressos had conceived a barter plan, offering other foodstuffs and UNRRA clothing in exchange for olive oil. Instead of the envisaged two thousand tons, the scheme yielded a mere three tons by the beginning of August. By this time Varvaressos had become increasingly convinced that organized groups within society, primarily merchants and industrialists, were conspiring to thwart his policies. He saw the failure of the olive oil scheme as further evidence of such a conspiracy, singling out traders rather than farmers as responsible for the crisis. By the middle of August he decided that even stronger measures were necessary to break the opposition. On August 22 he attempted to solve the olive oil shortage by decreeing a state monopoly on sales of the product. Two days later, a further decree commanded all industrialists and traders to declare their stocks of staple articles and raw materials, with direct state control to be imposed on any businesses failing to comply. By the end of August it was clear that the Varvaressos program had failed to achieve most of its objectives. In an angry exchange of open letters, the Greek Union of

29. Patterson, *Financial Experiences of Greece*, 190–93, 264; T236/149, August Budgetary Estimates of the Greek Government, C. Coombs, September 10, 1945.

Industrialists denied the charge of obstruction and complained that Varvaressos had done nothing to secure their cooperation. They expressed a willingness to invite British experts to advise on industrial organization and investigate the charges. In reply, Varvaressos refused to accept any blame for the situation. However, his tendency of blaming everybody else finally backfired, and earned him almost universal hostility. The press, which had been relatively moderate in its criticisms of the measures, launched a violent campaign against him, with papers representing both the Left and the Right attacking his handling of the economy in similar tones.[30]

With few cards left to play, Varvaressos turned to the British. He asked them to deliver large quantities of vital commodities such as olive oil, cheese, and soap, in addition to the prearranged UNRRA quota, to improve the supply situation and "break the ring of profiteers." He warned that failure to assist would lead to the abandonment of his entire program. Although determined to do everything possible to help, the British made it clear that the delivery of large quantities of scarce supplies at such short notice was almost impossible. Varvaressos repeated that if the shipments were not forthcoming he would have to resign. He predicted that his departure would usher in a "brief period of chaos," resulting in "widespread trouble and discontent," which would convince his opponents of the necessity of his policies. The British advised him to remain in the government and make fundamental changes to his program to address its "most glaring weaknesses," including the delegation of responsibilities and the forging of a new relationship with industry and commerce. Although Varvaressos agreed to reconsider his position, on the evening of September 1 he resigned from all his cabinet posts. In the wake of his resignation, the government at first assured the British and the country that existing policies would be continued. On September 4 Voulgaris reiterated that price controls were the "sole means of recovery" for Greece. Three days later, all price controls on foodstuffs were abolished.[31] The "Varvaressos Experiment" was over.

30. Patterson, *Financial Experiences of Greece*, 225–30; T236/1046, *Το Βήμα* (To Vema), August 24, 1945; *Η Καθημερινή* (Kathimerini), August 25, 1945; FO371/48277 R13868, AGIS Weekly Report No. 42, July 29–August 4, 1945; FO371/48278 R14422, AGIS Weekly Report No. 43, August 5–11, 1945; FO371/48279, including R14971, AGIS Weekly Report No. 44, August 12–18, 1945; R15076, AGIS Weekly Report No. 45, August 19–25, 1945; R15586, AGIS Weekly Report No. 46, August 26–September 1, 1945; FO371/48337 R18405, Economic and Financial Developments in Greece July–August 1945, C. Coombs, September 17, 1945, 8–9.

31. LBG/KVA/B/2, Note by the Vice-President of the Council Mr. Varvaressos to the American and British Embassies, August 20, 1945; Varvaressos to Caccia, August 28, 1945; Caccia to Varvaressos, August 30, 1945; Lingeman to Varvaressos, August 31, 1945; T236/1045, Athens to FO, Telegram no. 1733, August 21, 1945; Athens to FO, Telegram no. 1734, August 21, 1945; LBG/KVA/Δ.4(B), Lingeman to Varvaressos, August 27, 1945; FO371/48335, including R14794, Athens to FO,

Conclusions

The period between the closing of the civil war and the departure of Varvaressos can be divided into two highly contrasting phases. During the first, from January until the end of May, successive Greek governments played only a passive role in managing the economy. As Richter observes, this early period is notable for the "virtual non-existence of an economic policy."[32] In contrast, the second phase, from June until the end of August, saw the implementation of a well-defined package of policies, which enjoyed initial success but provoked an avalanche of hostility from diverse groups within Greek society.

Both contemporaries and later historians offered several reasons to explain Varvaressos' failure. These fall into two broad categories: one concerned with the sources of opposition to the Varvaressos program, and the other concentrating on the shortcomings of the policies and the man himself. Reasons adduced for the former include the inadequacies of the administrative machinery, the lack of support within the government and the civil service, insufficient backing from the Allies, the hostility of the opposition parties, and the conspiracies of an economic oligarchy determined to bring down the program. Arguments from the second category concentrate on specific details of the policies and the damaging effects of Varvaressos' lack of flexibility. All these reasons need to be addressed, although none can be dealt with in isolation.

From the point of view of fiscal orthodoxy, the basic tenants of his program were undeniably correct. The economy could not recover unless the currency was stabilized by putting a brake on inflation, which required the elimination of the budget deficit. Nevertheless, implementing his policies was fraught with problems. As even the Nazi occupation authorities had recognized, no state controls would function properly in a country such as Greece, with its tradition of "economic individualism." Predictably, many Greeks resented the seemingly authoritarian tone of Varvaressos' pronouncements. The left-wing press compared him with Hjalmar Schacht, the president of the Reichsbank under the Nazis, and accused him of introducing "totalitarian methods" reminiscent of "Hitlerite Germany." Varvaressos'

Telegram no. 1801, September 1, 1945; R14795, Athens to FO, Telegram no. 1804, September 1, 1945; R14822, Athens to FO, Telegram no. 1808, September 2, 1945; R14823, Athens to FO, Telegram no. 1808A, September 2, 1945; Athens to FO, Telegram no. 1810, September 2, 1945; R14863, Athens to FO, Telegram no. 1819, September 3, 1945; R16253, Prime Minister Voulgaris' Broadcast, September 4, 1945; FO371/48279 R15349, Athens to FO, Telegram no. 175 Saving, September 4, 1945; FO371/48280 R16135, AGIS Weekly Report No. 47, September 2–8, 1945.

32. Richter, *British Intervention in Greece*, 202.

determined stance alarmed not only the Left: a later historian commented on the similarities between the language of Varvaressos and communist jargon, and noted its frightening effect on the middle classes.[33]

Varvaressos was thus faced with an unenviable task. The vacillations of previous ministers had allowed the situation to deteriorate to a point where only drastic measures could save the economy. Fiscal orthodoxy dictated policies almost guaranteed to arouse the opposition of many sections within Greek society. While increases in government revenue would inevitably attract hostility from those obliged to shoulder the burden, reductions in expenditure would evoke a similar response from affected groups such as civil servants or pensioners, and controls over prices and supplies would be liable to impinge upon the interests of farmers, industrialists, and traders. For Varvaressos to have any chance of success, all these interest groups needed to be handled with a mixture of tact, judgment, and resolution. If the tact and judgment had to come from Varvaressos himself, resolution required the complete backing of his cabinet colleagues and the civil service.

Despite the basic soundness of the Varvaressos program, it did contain some hasty half measures and misjudgments. He introduced price controls in the full knowledge that the government was clearly unable to impose any controls over supply, distribution, or transport, and had made no plans to ration foodstuffs in particularly short supply. Moreover, despite some tinkering with personnel, he was unable to improve the administrative machinery, and created no viable body to oversee his reforms. To embark on a policy of price controls without appropriate levels of control over supplies was clearly risky. Varvaressos did not even seek to ascertain the extent of existing supplies until the end of August, with his attempt to conduct a census of stocks. By then, his program was already doomed, and a British observer described the move as "locking the stable door after the horse has bolted."[34] The Varvaressos price controls were also fundamentally flawed in that they offered no real incentives for many producers and traders to continue their activities. The imposition of price ceilings on foodstuffs, without similar controls on manufactured goods, alienated farmers, who increasingly withheld output from the market. Retailers and middlemen, who had seen their profit margins slashed, also chose to hoard stocks. Varvaressos' punitive laws were of little avail in the face of such resistance, as the state could not realistically take over private businesses.

33. Ritter, *Hermann Neubacher and the German Occupation of the Balkans*, 128; Alexander, *Prelude to the Truman Doctrine*, 269; FO371/48274 R12219, AGIS Weekly Report No. 38, July 1–7, 1945; Hadziiossif, "Economic Stabilization and Political Unrest," 33.

34. FO371/48279 R15076, AGIS Weekly Report No. 45, August 19–25, 1945.

A more cautious approach, demonstrating a more realistic attitude toward price levels and profit margins, could have avoided many of these problems.

In terms of his personal qualities, it is possible to question to what extent Varvaressos was suited to fulfill the role entrusted to him. Although he vigorously defended himself against claims that he had acted in a "dictatorial, authoritarian [and] inflexible" manner, he later confessed to using "high-handed methods." Even the British readily testified to his difficult nature, reporting his "violence in discussion," "unconcealed distrust of all but his immediate circle," "doctrinaire rigidity," and "his high-minded manner, and his refusal to listen to critic or to friend."[35] Given the nature of the opposition he faced, some degree of exasperation might be perfectly understandable, but the implementation of such a bold program would have required possibly superhuman levels of diplomacy, which Varvaressos clearly did not demonstrate.

Varvaressos was also unable to maintain popular support for his reforms. He never organized an adequate publicity machine to present clear explanations of his policies, despite persistent British appeals and a clear awareness within his own circle of the crucial importance of this issue. His major initiatives were announced solely through the press. His first radio broadcast did not come until August 17, by which time it was almost certainly too late to rekindle any enthusiasm for his program. The British were adamant that the failure to keep the public informed was a serious mistake. As Leeper wrote later, any statesman unable to get his way by force would have to "get it by persuasion."[36] Varvaressos seemed unwilling or unable to pursue the latter approach. In his dealings with various interest groups, he possessed neither the ability to secure cooperation nor sufficient powers to punish noncooperation.

The austerity program had little chance of success unless backed by a government of sufficient strength and confidence to carry it through. As indicated earlier,

---

35. LBG/KVA/B2, Varvaressos to Sophianopoulos, December 20, 1945; LBG/KVA/B5, Memorandum on the Greek Economic Situation, K. Varvaressos, August 2, 1946, 115; FO371/48335 R15140, Athens to FO, Telegram no. 1835, September 6, 1945; FO371/48280 R15829, Athens to FO, Telegram no. 179 Saving, September 10, 1945; FO371/48282 R16649, Athens to FO, Telegram no. 2000, September 30, 1945.

36. T236/1044, Hill to Davidson, April 26, 1945 (Enclosure: Minute by Hill, April 24, 1945); Hill to Davidson, May 2, 1945 (Enclosure: Economic Reconstruction of Greece: Notes for Program as Evolved in Conversations with Miss Zafiriou, April 30, 1945); FO371/48335 R14491, Statement on the Economic Program—Broadcast by M. Varvaressos, August 17, 1945; FO371/48333 R10860, Athens to FO, Telegram no. 1430, June 24, 1945; T236/1045, Hill to Rowe-Dutton, June 26, 1945; FO371/48275 R12961, AGIS Weekly Report No. 40, July 15–21, 1945; FO371/48279 R14971, AGIS Weekly Report No. 44, August 12–18, 1945; Leeper, *When Greek Meets Greek,* 177.

unconditional government support had been one of the major conditions demanded by Varvaressos before joining the cabinet. Whether he actually enjoyed such support is a moot point. He subsequently claimed that his colleagues took a neutral attitude to his reforms, acting as "spectators in the economic fight" rather than offering him assistance. Later historians went much further, alleging that the lack of government support was a key cause of his failure.[37] Once Varvaressos had accepted his post, it was rumored that the minister of national economy, Grigorios Kasimatis, an advocate of contrasting policies, had threatened to resign along with several cabinet colleagues. By August the British authorities in Athens were certainly aware that many ministers were said to be deliberately obstructing Varvaressos' moves and undermining his policies, and later reported that Kasimatis had conducted a "whispering campaign" against the reforms.[38] The very nature of such allegations makes them difficult to prove. Although widespread sabotage cannot be established in the absence of concrete evidence, the lack of any apparent endorsement of the program from other ministers does not suggest any great enthusiasm for Varvaressos within the cabinet.

Civil service support largely evaporated as early as June, with the announcement of redundancies and the cancellation of wartime promotions. For the rest of his period in office, Varvaressos found himself locked in a fruitless struggle with the civil service employees' union, which successfully resisted the attempted purge. As will be discussed later, there were also suspicions that KKE members within the civil service were actively sabotaging the measures. Varvaressos scathingly dismissed the bureaucracy as a "sick" organism, and it seems that few implemented his policies with any vigor.[39]

Even without deliberate obstruction, Varvaressos found his options severely limited by the traditional shortcomings of the state administration. This had a particularly damaging effect on his taxation promises. As he had pledged, tax increases would target the rich. Nevertheless, the woeful inadequacies of the tax-collecting machinery ensured that the rich could not be squeezed via the normal means of higher rates of income and business taxes. In May 1945, annual revenue from taxes

37. FO371/48337 R18546, Note of Conversation with Mr. Varvaressos, October 23, 1945; Richter, *British Intervention in Greece*, 214; Politakis, *Greek Policies of Recovery and Reconstruction*, 132; J. V. Kofas, *Intervention and Underdevelopment: Greece during the Cold War*, 25.

38. Kasimatis, Οικονομικόν Πρόβλημα (*Economic Problem*), 26–27; T236/1045, Conversation with Miss Zafiriou, August 7, 1945; FO371/48284 R19491, AGIS Weekly Report No. 55, October 28–November 3, 1945; T236/1047, Hill to Davidson, November 3, 1945.

39. Papastratis, "Purge of the Greek Civil Service," 41–53; T236/1046, Translation of a Statement by Mr. Varvaressos, September 3, 1945.

on company profits and private salaries had been estimated to produce less than half the amounts to be collected from levies on theaters and cinemas, and roughly one-fifteenth of the expected revenue from the tobacco tax.[40] Varvaressos was fully aware that the shortcomings of the system could not be overcome quickly. Moreover, it had become obvious that the only other suggestion for taxing the rich—the war profits tax—was failing to deliver the anticipated sums. Given the desperate need for immediate returns, Varvaressos was forced to rush through an imaginative measure to secure increased revenue from businesses, hence the creation of the special contribution.

At first, the levy fulfilled all expectations. In the first month alone, it produced a sum nearly three times greater than the revenue Varvaressos expected to receive from direct taxation during the entire fiscal year. In terms of popular support, the results were far less positive, as Varvaressos was forced to pay a high price for his windfall. The business community condemned the tax as excessive and unfair. Unable to tax profits by normal methods, Varvaressos chose to tax rental values as a proxy for profits. While the absence of statistical data rules out any definitive assessment, it is very unlikely that there was a high correlation between 1940 rental values and 1945 profits, although Coombs' suspicion that the tax had been set too high cannot be proved or disproved.[41] Neither Varvaressos' admission that the contribution was hardly "scientific," nor the modifications introduced in response to the protests, can alter the fact that the contribution was a deeply flawed mechanism for taxing the rich. Increases in direct income and business taxes would have been a much fairer solution, but Varvaressos possessed neither the means to implement such increases nor the time to await the results.

The taxation problems underline the difficulties of imposing any kind of economic controls in a country with such an inefficient administrative machinery. The failure to distribute the ML/UNRRA clothing and cloth was a particularly striking example of official ineptitude. Neither government fears of unpopularity nor the stubbornness of industrialists offer any convincing explanation for the inability to distribute finished and semi-finished goods so desperately needed by the population. This failure had several serious consequences. The government deprived itself of a considerable amount of revenue that would have been generated by the sale of the textiles, while many Greeks were forced to pay higher than necessary prices

40. T236/149, Comparative Statement of Budget of May and of August 1945.
41. T236/149, August Budgetary Estimates of the Greek Government, C. Coombs, September 10, 1945; FO371/48334 R14166, Economic and Financial Developments in Greece November 1944–June 1945, C. Coombs, August 1, 1945, 36.

for their clothing, thus further fueling inflation. Bottlenecks were created by the failure to empty much-needed warehouses precisely when UNRRA deliveries were arriving in unprecedented quantities. Finally, by exacerbating the clothing short- ages, the government reduced its bargaining power vis-à-vis mill owners, whose cooperation was vital if the country's industries were to be revived.

The textile fiasco was merely the worst of many examples of state inability to organize production and distribution, suggesting that little had improved since the embarrassing disasters of the earlier period.[42] The British felt that the Greeks seemed entirely unsuited to the task of administering economic controls. Leeper suggested that price controls seemed to have no appeal to "the Greek mind," while Hill was frequently exasperated by the attitudes of senior officials who claimed that "what Greece needed was [economic] freedom."[43] To be fair to the Greeks, the recent experience of dictatorship and enemy occupation, as well as hostility to Communist programs, must have made the concept of a managed economy far less attractive. However, such Hellenocentric perceptions of the recent past remained blissfully unaware that state intervention in the economy had proved compatible with democracy and private enterprise in Britain and other Western democracies.

British observers wondered to what extent hostility toward control schemes was linked to corruption in ministerial circles, suspecting that "everyone in power" was "connected with everyone else who matters." One even seemed to take it for granted that the entire cabinet was "hand-in-glove" with the rich, and that many were pros- pering because they had "friends at court." The charges of corruption are hard to refute. The official UNRRA history described the Greek government as one of the

42. Months after liberation, the British berated the ministry of public works for failing to even consider the drawing up of plans and estimates. In another case, while the government was press- ing ML to help with the transport problem, the British were able to point out that coastal shipping was frequently making empty return journeys despite the desperate need to move cargoes, and that many lorries, tyres, and caiques already delivered had never been used. In addition, nothing had been done to salvage the large numbers of steamers scuttled in coastal waters. Many of these vessels were lying in shallow water and could thus be raised relatively easily. Ministers seemed to have little grasp of developments affecting their departments. One embarrassing example con- cerned large shipments of highly valuable coffee in early 1945. The ministers of supply and the economy were unaware of these deliveries long after their arrival, and they discovered this fact only after conversations with the Allied advisers; WO204/8761, Public Works in Greece, February 2, 1945; JCC (45) 1st Meeting, January 25, 1945; E&SC (45) 7th Meeting, February 19, 1945; Paper No. JCC (45) 37, April 3, 1945; JCC (45) 11th Meeting, April 5, 1945; DSR 868.50/4–345, MacVeagh to the Secretary of State, April 23, 1945 (Enclosure: Memorandum by H. A. Hill, April 21, 1945).

43. FO371/48331 R8189, Leeper to Sargent, May 2, 1945; T236/1044, Hill to Davidson, May 2, 1945.

major obstacles to its operations, while a later historian felt compelled to emphasize the "inertia, venality, political biases, and corruption" of the Athens government.[44]

The lack of a clear commitment from the Allies has also been cited as a factor explaining the failure of the Varvaressos program. Varvaressos himself seemed convinced of this and expressed great bitterness toward the British, accusing them of withdrawing support once his policies began to generate serious opposition. Several recent studies have echoed this theme. One author highlights Allied reluctance to support Varvaressos, while another stresses that Varvaressos had been misled as to the extent of UNRRA supplies, and that his resignation was triggered by the Allied refusal to offer full backing during the final crisis. The latter study also suggests that Whitehall had always been reluctant to support Varvaressos in a conflict with industrialists and the middle class, as these groups "formed the social foundations" of British policies for Greece. Another work offers a series of bold statements, claiming that initial British support for Varvaressos turned into neutrality by August, that the British flatly refused to accede to Varvaressos' request for emergency supplies, and that the change of government in London had created a "vacuum of authority," which Varvaressos interpreted as a "betrayal." Yet another study makes equally bold claims, citing the "counterproductive role" of UNRRA supplies as a major cause of Varvaressos' downfall, because of the hostility such supplies aroused among traders and industrialists.[45]

All these arguments seem to misread events and misunderstand several wider issues, mainly because of ignorance of British policy as explained in Foreign Office and Treasury documents. As already shown, Whitehall's commitment to the reforms, which offered the only hope of achieving the kind of economic solutions advocated by the British, was never in doubt. Varvaressos was not misled as to the extent of supplies Greece would be receiving, and his resignation followed a declaration from the British that they were simply unable to fulfill his request for large additional consignments of foodstuffs at such short notice. The "vacuum of authority" argument ignores the continuity of British personnel in Athens, and of

44. T236/1044, Hill to Davidson, May 2, 1945; Davidson to Hill, May 7, 1945; Davidson to Hill, May 15, 1945; Woodbridge et al., *History of the United Nations Relief and Rehabilitation Administration*, 105; L. S. Wittner, *American Intervention in Greece, 1943–1949*, 48.

45. LBG/KVA/B5, Memorandum on the Greek Economic Situation, K. Varvaressos, August 2, 1946, 116; Varvaressos to Nicolson, February 10, 1947; T. Kalafatis, "Νομισματικές Διαρρυθμίσεις και Κοινωνικές Επιπτώσεις (1944–1946)" ("Monetary Reforms and Their Social Impact [1944–1946]"), 51; Hadziiossif, "Economic Stabilization and Political Unrest," 34; Politakis, *Greek Policies of Recovery and Reconstruction*, 135; Kofas, *Intervention and Underdevelopment*, 23.

general British policies for Greece. Criticisms of the effect of UNRRA supplies seem to overlook the realities of the post-liberation Greek economy. While UNRRA deliveries inevitably reduced excess demand for certain commodities, supplies were never sufficiently abundant to reduce the profit margins of traders or producers. Moreover, with most of the country's industrial capacity lying idle, UNRRA supplies were hardly competing with locally produced goods. The claim about the "social foundations" of British policies for Greece seems highly questionable. As noted previously, British policies sought to secure broad support for the middle ground.

Direct contacts between British advisers and Greek officials seem far less frequent during the Varvaressos period, but this should not imply any withdrawal of support. In late July, Hill reminded Whitehall that British support was the "one rock" on which Greece was standing, and he was not alone in warning against any actions that could embarrass the Athens government during such a critical period. In sharp contrast to the claims that London was downgrading its commitment to Varvaressos, there is evidence to suggest that Varvaressos himself was reluctant to accept some British offers of help. Thus, British proposals to send several experts to Greece were not taken up because Varvaressos had not been enthusiastic about the idea. Only at the end of August did he agree to receive experts connected with textile production.[46]

The problems within the government and the civil service might not have proved insurmountable had the country pulled together as the British had intended. Unfortunately for Varvaressos, not only did the lack of any real support from within the machinery of state severely weaken his ability to confront opposition arising from other quarters, but also resistance to his program was to escalate steadily throughout his period in office. By the end of August it was clear he was unable to survive without strong government backing, which was never forthcoming.

Contemporary observers and later historians expressed very definite views as to the sources of opposition to Varvaressos. However, such attempts have all too frequently reflected the political sympathies of their authors. Varvaressos himself had no doubt that powerful economic interests had undermined his program. While he could later express admiration for the "capitalist class" of both Britain and the United States for their "self-discipline and voluntary sacrifices" and their "commendable social conscience," his attitudes toward their Greek counterparts were far less positive. He claimed that he had been defeated by the actions of an "economic oligarchy." Later historians, particularly from the Left, accepted the idea, and used

46. FO371/48273 R11299, Caccia to Hayter, June 26, 1945; FO371/48334 R12941, Hill to Rowe-Dutton, July 25, 1945; T236/1045, Laskey to Dennehy, August 31, 1945.

the language of the class struggle to conclude that Varvaressos had indeed been the victim of a coherent group, alternatively described as the "nouveaux riches" or the "new bourgeoisie." Several terms seem to be used interchangeably, with another historian from this group appearing to equate the economic oligarchy with a *parakratos*—a state within a state.[47]

Although right-wing opposition to Varvaressos was considerable, and probably included many influential members of the Greek establishment, claims of an effective conspiracy emanating from an economic oligarchy are difficult to substantiate. Despite the consistency and apparent sincerity of Varvaressos' belief in such a cabal, the evidence is inconclusive. Even the British—whose wholehearted support for Varvaressos and relative naiveté about Greek realities might have led them to embrace any conspiracy theory—refused to believe such claims. While readily acknowledging continuous hostility from the Communists, and some degree of concerted opposition from elsewhere toward the end, they were totally dismissive of the Varvaressos allegations.[48]

The rejection of the single conspiracy argument need not be inconsistent with the notion of several smaller but equally opportunistic conspiracies to exploit the crisis. Many supporters of the Right were obviously working against the reforms, but the motivation for opposition was unlikely to be solely ideological. In the case of Varvaressos' particular bête noire—the industrialists and traders—economic rationality could go hand-in-hand with ideological prejudice. In reacting to price controls, it is not unreasonable to suppose that producers and traders were behaving rationally in seeking the best possible deal for themselves. Similarly, the textile manufacturers, who had held out for the most favorable terms, were acting effectively in their own self-interest. Such a relentless pursuit of self-interest inevitably conflicted with the welfare of other individuals. Although less repugnant than the wartime profiteering, such blatant exploitation of the immediate postwar crisis can only be viewed with distaste. Thus, the moral arguments used by Varvaressos may well have much validity, but still do not prove the conspiracy of which he complained.

Those who highlight the hostility of the economic oligarchy do not seem to have

47. DSR 868.51/2–149, Memorandum by Cromie, February 1, 1949; K. Varvaressos, "Ανοικτή Επιστολή προς τον κ. Αλέξανδρον Διομήδην" ("An Open Letter to Mr. Alexandros Diomidis"), 297–99; K. Varvaressos, "Απολογισμός και Κριτική της Οικονομικής Πολιτικής των Τελευταίων Ετών (Απάντησις εις τον κ. Αλέξανδρον Διομήδην)" ("Review and Criticism of Recent Economic Policy [A Reply to Mr. Alexandros Diomidis]"), 337–63; K. Vergopoulos, "The Emergence of the New Bourgeoisie, 1944–1952," 305; Kofas, *Intervention and Underdevelopment*, 24; Richter, *British Intervention in Greece*, 214.

48. FO371/48335 R14795, Athens to FO, Telegram no. 1804, September 1, 1945.

considered the possibility of organized opposition from the Left. One study blames Varvaressos for compromising with the oligarchy rather than securing the support of the masses as "represented by EAM." This interpretation ignores Varvaressos' strenuous attempts to gain popular support by granting substantial wage increases and reducing the prices of UNRRA rations—his only major divergence from British advice. It also assumes that the Left would have been willing to cooperate with Varvaressos had such cooperation been sought.[49]

In reality, EAM's main component—the KKE—felt no inclination to support Varvaressos. Unlike the Right, it also resented the British presence in Greece. Thus, it would have had a double interest in undermining government policies. According to American intelligence, it instigated several campaigns expressly designed to obstruct individual measures. KKE members within the taxation department were instructed to create confusion over the special contribution payments, while the party was actively involved in attempts to boycott the tax. The KKE was particularly concerned not only to mobilize the workers against the Varvaressos program but also to secure the support of other groups opposed to its provisions, such as small shopkeepers.[50] In contrast with the Right, which was represented by loosely structured parties and several competing interest groups, the KKE was well organized, highly disciplined, and driven by one overriding motivation. If there was a grand conspiracy to topple Varvaressos, the very tangible Communists deserve to be considered as conspirators no less than the ill-defined *parakratos,* new bourgeoisie, or economic oligarchy.

In the end, Varvaressos was brought down by what one study described as a "coalescence of hostile factors,"[51] a coming together of individuals and interest groups implacably opposed to his reforms. Attempts to put the entire blame on one or another set of extremists seem highly disingenuous, as both the Left and the Right contributed to Varvaressos' downfall and must share responsibility for the continuation of the chaos. After a brief interlude when bold policies were pursued energetically, the country returned to a policy vacuum that could only exacerbate the economic crisis and strengthen the hand of the extremists.

The Varvaressos reforms were the first serious attempt to address both the most acute and the most chronic problems of the Greek post-liberation economy. Varvaressos had tried to overcome the crisis by updating the country's essentially laissez-faire capitalism with the hasty introduction of several aspects of state economic

49. Richter, *British Intervention in Greece,* 214.
50. P. J. Stavrakis, *Moscow and Greek Communism 1944–1949,* 75.
51. Ibid.

management as practiced in the Western democracies during the war. However, the impressive results achieved in Britain and the United States could not be easily replicated in a country so devoid of the tradition, mentality, and consensus required to accept such measures, and the machinery to administer and enforce them. The American ambassador, Lincoln MacVeagh, was probably correct in claiming that Varvaressos had attempted to do "too much too quickly." The failure to gain wider acceptance for closer state involvement in the economy ensured that Greece would continue to suffer the disastrous effects of what Zafiriou described as "full nineteenth-century economic practice operating uncontrolled in conditions of nightmare scarcity," which allowed powerful interest groups full rein to prosper to the detriment of others within society.[52]

52. DSR 868.51/9–11.45, MacVeagh to the Secretary of State, September 11, 1945; T236/1044, Hill to Davidson, April 26, 1945.

5

THE LONDON AGREEMENT
OF JANUARY 1946

§

With the departure of Varvaressos, the forceful policies he had pursued were quietly laid aside. Apart from sporadic well-publicized though abortive initiatives, successive governments lapsed back into inertia, while the economy continued to slide. In the face of a new catastrophe, the persistent British emphasis on fiscal orthodoxy appeared increasingly insufficient to redress the situation, prompting Bevin and the Foreign Office to propose a much broader initiative amounting to increased involvement in Greece's economic affairs. Despite Greek misgivings and Treasury skepticism, this new approach culminated in the London Agreement of January 1946. The London Agreement and its implementation over the following fifteen months marked the climax of British intervention in Greece. Political and strategic considerations had forced Whitehall to mount an increased effort to address Greece's major economic problems. This chapter explains the shift in British thinking that produced the new approach. It describes the two institutions—the British Economic Mission (BEM) and the Currency Committee—arising out of the initiative, and analyzes the consequences of Greek government actions and inaction during the period up to the annunciation of the Truman Doctrine. It ends by assessing the significance of the London Agreement and the nature of the obstacles that undermined it.

The British Response to the New Policy Vacuum

At first, the departure of Varvaressos triggered nothing more than a cabinet reshuffle, with the government insisting that the existing policies would be maintained. The British applauded this continuity and offered full support as long as policies were conducted "on the same lines."[1]

Nevertheless, within days, the government abolished price controls on all major foodstuffs. This decision was taken without any prior consultation with either the British authorities or UNRRA, despite recent meetings.[2] Privately, although British observers felt that the removal of price controls was a practical measure, they were alarmed by the absence of clear government policies coupled with rising inflation. Reconsidering their priorities, the Treasury acknowledged that the Greeks were not only clearly unable to administer efficient economic controls but also unwillingly disposed to the concept. They were thus willing to accept a more liberal economic policy, but they were becoming increasingly concerned about public finances and felt that revenue had to be increased via heavier taxation and the more profitable sale of UNRRA goods.[3]

The British in Athens shared the Treasury concerns, but took pains to stress the urgency of the situation. Hill felt it would be "intolerable" to simply "sit and watch" while the economy faced potential collapse, believing that the only appropriate course was to keep "pegging away" for a suitable policy. Accordingly, Leeper and Hill pressed the government to take immediate action on the budget and gold speculation, and suggested that the danger of inflation meant that a policy of controls was still appropriate, although this would have to be administered with "greater flexibility" than before. In reply, the prime minister promised drastic measures, but the British were unconvinced that such "brave words" could be translated into similar deeds. Voulgaris had continued to claim that controls were central to government policy, despite the abandonment of price controls and the halfhearted application of related schemes.[4]

---

1. FO371/48335, including R14822, FO to Athens, Telegram no. 1860, September 4, 1945; R15140, Athens to FO, Telegram no. 1835, September 6, 1945.

2. Following this move, Athens markets saw the reappearance of olive oil and most other commodities, in abundant quantities at prices well below black market rates but still very much higher than the previous controlled prices. Thus olive oil, which had cost 440 drachmae per oka (1.28 kilograms) under controlled prices (at which none was obtainable in the marketplace) and at 1,300 drachmae on the black market (at which only small transactions could be made) was selling at an average price of 700 drachmae. Other commodities followed the same trend; FO371/48335 R15242, Athens to FO, Telegram no. 1853, September 8, 1945.

3. FO371/48335 R16112, Hill to Davidson, September 11, 1945; T236/1046, Rowe-Dutton to Hill, September 25, 1945.

4. T236/1046, Hill to Davidson, October 2, 1945; Athens to FO, Telegram no. 1959, September 25, 1945; FO371/48282 R16628, Athens to FO, Telegram no. 1982, September 28, 1945; FO371/48336 R16773, Athens to FO, Telegram no. 2022, October 2, 1945. As an example of other control schemes, an agreement had been reached in early September, by which various industrialists were to re-

Before long, Hill warned Mantzavinos that another month without energetic countermeasures would lead to severe inflation. He reemphasized the need to outlaw the gold market and warned against official sales of gold by the Bank of Greece, a move commonly advocated in Athens. Although the minister was in general agreement with Hill, he admitted that it was extremely difficult for a provisional government to pursue vigorous policies, since it must avoid offending powerful interest groups. However, he opposed any moves against the gold market, claiming this was a symptom and not a cause of the country's problems. By now, Hill had severe doubts whether any serious measures would be enacted to save the economy.[5]

In an analysis of the causes of the economic crisis, Hill singled out chronic budget deficits as the main factor leading to inflation, gold speculation, industrial stagnation, and commodity shortages, leading in turn to labor unrest, higher wages, and a vicious circle of rising volume and velocity of circulation, destroying confidence in the currency. Despite this gloomy assessment, Hill was optimistic about the country's prospects, claiming that Greece was still in a healthier position than other liberated states. It had no internal debt and was thus spared the burden of interest and redemption payments, while its foreign debts were not being serviced. It also possessed substantial foreign exchange reserves, amounting to approximately £40 million in sterling, dollars, and gold. Moreover, for the time being, it was receiving massive foreign aid: both in volume and value the ML/UNRRA supplies considerably exceeded prewar levels of imports. Britain was carrying the sole cost of maintaining the armed forces and much of the cost of reorganizing the police, while also providing occasional aid for relief and reconstruction purposes. Hill concluded that Greece possessed a uniquely "favorable basis for reconstruction and recovery," but warned that inflationary pressures could be checked only by overbalancing rather than simply balancing the budget. He urged drastic increases in state revenue via higher taxation and returns from the sale of UNRRA goods, together with cuts in expenditure. He suggested setting up a special committee, including members from outside the government, to oversee all aspects of public finance. He also proposed various measures to reduce price levels, including action against speculation in gold, and the imposition of economic controls to supervise production and distribution.[6]

---

sume production under official control. However, this foundered amidst general confusion due to the vagueness and contradictory nature of the guidelines issued by the minister concerned; FO371/48335 R15242, Athens to FO, Telegram no. 1853, September 8, 1945; FO371/48280 R16154, Athens to FO, Telegram no. 181 Saving, September 18, 1945.

5. T236/1046, Hill to Davidson, October 5, 1945.
6. T236/1046 and T236/1047, The Finances of Greece, T. St. Quintin Hill.

The Hill recommendations became the cornerstone of British advice to the Greek government, and discussions over their implementation formed the core of endless meetings over the following weeks. As will be shown, the proposals remained central to the wider plans that culminated in the London Agreement. Sharing Hill's concern over public finances, inflation, and the gold market, the Treasury nevertheless felt little hope of achieving cuts in public spending although they advocated strong discouragement of all new expenditure. Instead, they emphasized the need to augment revenue by increasing existing duties on entertainment, alcohol, and tobacco, and by creating new forms of taxation, particularly a purchase tax, and new levies on commercial and residential property. Moreover, as huge profits were being made from the resale of UNRRA supplies on the black market, the prices of such goods should be raised substantially, while the number of indigents receiving free rations would have to be reduced drastically. As for speculation in gold, they stressed that existing government powers to curtail the market should actually be enforced, and that the Bank of Greece should not sell gold. Within days British thinking was articulated even more clearly, when advisers in Athens produced the first detailed proposals on ways to raise additional revenue. They suggested that receipts could be almost doubled by a series of tax increases ranging from 50 percent (the special contribution) to 200 percent (tobacco duties), coupled with a new tax based on controlled rents and a trebling of the price of UNRRA supplies.[7]

Despite British insistence that immediate action was crucial, their sense of urgency was not shared by the Greek side. Matters were delayed by the fall of the Voulgaris government, while the regent claimed that as the head of a provisional government he had no authority to act.[8] Although Mantzavinos was finally compelled to study both the Hill recommendations and the concrete suggestions on taxation, he too refused to commit himself, preoccupied as he was with his own proposals for a new budget. In the meantime, the press was optimistically suggesting that budgetary equilibrium would at last be achieved in the current fiscal year. Indeed, the second Mantzavinos budget was far more optimistic than that drawn up by Varvaressos in August, anticipating increases of revenue and expenditure of 30 percent and 12 percent respectively, resulting in a deficit of less than 6 percent. However, his revenue estimates assumed that only 3 percent would derive from direct taxation, while almost 22 percent would come from war-related taxes (on war

7. T236/1046, Davidson to Hill, October 9, 1945; Davidson to Hill, October 17, 1945; Davidson to Hill, October 20, 1945; FO371/48282 R16628, FO to Athens, Telegram no. 2072, October 10, 1945; FO371/48337 R18575, Davidson to Laskey, October 30, 1945 (Enclosure: Greek Budget, Annex C, Suggested Additional Taxation).

8. T236/1046, Athens to FO, Telegram no. 2122, October 18, 1945.

profits and prizes of war, together with a new tax on merchants who had imported supplies during the occupation). The prices of UNRRA goods and tobacco duties were to be raised considerably to yield 41 percent and 11 percent of total receipts respectively, but the special contribution was to provide only 12 percent. On the expenditure side, wages and pensions were to absorb 44 percent, with 15 percent going to the distribution of UNRRA supplies, 13 percent on public health and social welfare, and 10 percent on public works including reconstruction.[9]

Although the Mantzavinos estimates had appeared deceptively sound on paper, the minister had in effect wasted precious time on a document amounting to nothing more than a "happy-go-lucky shot in the dark."[10] While applauding the action on UNRRA supplies and tobacco duties, the British were decidedly unimpressed with a budget containing so many "illusory" and "dubious" figures. They were particularly annoyed that the proposals almost entirely ignored their recent suggestions on taxation, while continuing to attach so much importance to such unreliable sources as the war-related taxes that had failed to yield meaningful sums. They were exasperated by the minister's obstinate stance in subsequent discussions, when he not only resisted further pressure to amend his estimates but also maintained his determination to publicize the existing version as widely as possible.[11] Thus, when the British were doing their utmost to emphasize the need for swift and decisive action, time was being squandered on a budget that was no more realistic than any other since liberation. Despite these charades, nothing came of the episode in any case, as the minister left office within days with the passing of the Damaskinos government.

The new Kanellopoulos government immediately indicated a more resolute stance, with the prime minister promising "vigor and decision" and determination to "end the economic chaos."[12] Mantzavinos was succeeded by Kasimatis, recently one of the fiercest opponents of Varvaressos and his reforms. In previous weeks, Kasimatis had given wide publicity to his own ideas to address the country's problems. He emphasized that given the extent of Greece's wartime losses, only extensive foreign loans could make good the damage. The bulk of the foreign exchange reserves had to be mobilized to finance commercial imports. Such imports would

9. Patterson, *Financial Experiences of Greece*, 255; FO371/48337 R18575, Davidson to Laskey, October 30, 1945 (Enclosure: Greek Budget); FO371/48336 R17885, Athens to FO, Telegram no. 2139, October 20, 1945.

10. Patterson, *Financial Experiences of Greece*, 255.

11. FO371/48337 R18575, Davidson to Laskey, October 30, 1945 (Enclosure: Greek Budget); FO371/48336 R17885, Athens to FO, Telegram no. 2139, October 20, 1945.

12. FO371/48284, including R18726, Athens to FO, Telegram no. 2218, November 3, 1945; R19491, AGIS Weekly Report No. 55, October 28–November 3, 1945.

stimulate the productive machinery of the country and lower domestic price levels, leading to dishoarding. He claimed it would be better if the foreign exchange ran out than if it simply sat doing nothing. He stressed that the deep-rooted gold mentality ensured that commodity prices were driven by the sovereign rate, and that the latter would have to be stabilized before price stability could be achieved. Convinced that the "gold sickness" could be cured only with gold itself, he underlined the necessity of using Greek sovereign reserves to take control of the gold market. He was adamant that a strenuous reconstruction effort must not be delayed out of fear of inflation. He advocated granting widespread credit and rapidly distributing raw materials to further industrial recovery, and proposed removing all restrictions on internal commerce. He acknowledged the need to impose certain economic controls on production, but dismissed price controls as unenforceable. He also advocated devaluation of the drachma, significant pay raises for civil servants, and adjustments to the taxation system in order to increase the tax burden of the rich.[13]

Shortly after assuming his new post, Kasimatis informed the British of his intentions to launch a comprehensive program on the above lines. Hill recognized that the abolition of controls merely reflected current realities, but urged caution as the ideas offered little to balance the budget. He was unhappy about the use of gold, and feared the immediate inflationary effects of devaluation. Above all, he felt uneasy about the possible consequences of commercial imports. However, he believed the idea might have some merit if it could be proved that certain imports could stimulate industry and dampen down inflation, and that suitable safeguards could prevent the flight of capital. In reply, Kasimatis stood his ground on the imports issue, threatening resignation if he could not get his way. He repeated his determination to implement the program and rejected Hill's emphasis on balancing the budget to the exclusion of other considerations. Hill could only repeat his advice and requested that Kasimatis should inform the British of the government's intentions. The minister agreed, but took pains to wring an admission from Hill to the effect that all the details were still "open for discussion."[14]

13. Kasimatis, Οικονομικόν Πρόβλημα (Economic Problem), 42–61. See also T236/1047, Hill to Davidson, November 3, 1945 (Enclosure: Economic Program of M. Kassimatis: Summary of a memorandum published by him in "PARON" monthly political review special edition of October 12 and submitted to the Regent and Admiral Voulgaris).

14. FO371/48337, including R18716, Athens to FO, Telegram no. 151 Remac, November 3, 1945; R18717, Athens to FO, Telegram no. 152 Remac, November 3, 1945; R18754, Athens to FO, Telegram no. 153 Remac, November 4, 1945; T236/1047, Summary of Proceedings of a Meeting Held in the Greek Ministry of Finance, November 4, 1945.

Hill's reservations over the Kasimatis proposals were shared in London, with officials at the Treasury and the Bank of England equally hostile to the ideas. The Treasury bemoaned what it saw as Greek unwillingness to introduce stern measures to combat the crisis, accusing them of still looking for an "easy way out." Treasury officials felt that any relaxation on the sale of gold and foreign exchange would only aggravate the situation and refused to consider a loan, believing that the country possessed ample foreign exchange reserves. They reiterated that the budget deficit would have to take priority over every other issue, stressing that the "hard way" was the "only way" out of the crisis, and that "almost penal taxation" was called for. The Treasury views were largely mirrored by those of the Bank of England, which rejected the possibility of sterling credits and expressed considerable skepticism about plans to intervene in the gold market. Although they recognized that gold sales could mop up purchasing power, they felt that de facto confirmation of the weakness of the drachma could prove far more damaging.[15]

Despite British skepticism, Kasimatis was able to win virtually unanimous Greek support for the majority of his program, the proposal on gold sales having been withdrawn following the opposition of leading Greek financial experts. The amended proposals were duly presented to the British. Privately, Leeper admitted that the ideas should be supported despite their clear shortcomings, as any British veto could bring down the government. Moreover, London was hardly in a position to impose any alternative policies. Meanwhile, British and American officials met the minister once more. Hill attempted yet again to persuade Kasimatis to postpone devaluation, and after heavy pressure the minister agreed to keep existing rates for a month. In addition, commercial imports were to be subject to the approval of the government rather than that of UNRRA or the British, and surcharges were to be imposed on all foreign exchange sold to prospective importers. Following the concession on exchange rates, the British and American embassies together with UNRRA local representatives endorsed the amended proposals. Whitehall approved, but ruled out any form of British loan, offering instead to provide support for internal reform and reorganization.[16]

15. FO371/48337 R18717, FO to Athens, Telegram no. 121 Camer, November 3, 1945; T236/1047, Minute by Davidson, November 5, 1945; Minute by Rowe-Dutton, November 5, 1945; BE OV80/26, Bolton to Davidson, November 5, 1945.

16. Kasimatis, Οικονομικόν Πρόβλημα (Economic Problem), 79–82, 85–90; FO371/48337, including R18833, Athens to FO, Telegram no. 2237, November 6, 1945; R18868, Athens to FO, Telegram no. 2236, November 6, 1945. R18869, Athens to FO, Telegram no. 2239, November 6, 1945; FO to Athens, Telegram no. 2271, November 8, 1945; R18941, Athens to FO, Telegram no. 2242, November 7, 1945. Surcharges were to be set at three levels according to the category of goods:

The Kasimatis economic program was duly broadcast to the country amid solemn speeches underlining the seriousness of the crisis. At the same time, the minister announced a new budget. This was by far the most optimistic set of estimates produced since liberation, in that it assumed that budgetary equilibrium would be achieved over the coming fiscal year. The minister anticipated unprecedented levels of revenue, of which only 3.1 percent was to derive from direct taxation, and 8.4 percent from the special contribution. Sales of UNRRA supplies were to provide a massive 60 percent, while a further 27 percent was to come from the war-related taxes and the sale of war booty. The expenditure figures were far more vague, but assumed large rises in the cost of salaries and pensions and the distribution of UNRRA supplies. The estimates even provided for the creation of a "budgetary reserve," to be used for "real and absolute needs." The budget failed to arouse any enthusiasm among foreign observers. The figures proved "quite beyond the understanding" of one competent analyst, while another dismissed the entire budget as "even less satisfactory [. . .] than any of its predecessors," with public spending "grossly underestimated" and revenue "sufficiently inflated" in order to achieve the "required arithmetic."[17]

This apparent flurry of activity did not last for long. The budget was never published, and within days both the government and the regent were pleading for financial assistance from the British. Kasimatis called for an indication from London that such assistance would be forthcoming, while Damaskinos demanded a public recognition of the Greek plight. The latter complained that Greece's economic

---

110 percent for articles of primary necessity, 125 percent for articles of nonprimary necessity, and 150 percent for all other articles. The amended proposals contained the following points: "(1) Readjustment of taxation and augmentation of prices of UNRRA supplies in order to balance the budget on a strong foundation; (2) Increase of imports. Foreign currency will be definitely allotted without obstruction for import of every item considered useful and permitted to be imported by the state. The price and use of imported goods will be controlled; (3) Credit will be issued under control in order to support production and internal trade; (4) Foreign exchange will be sold to importers at official rates but subject to surcharges, varying with types of goods in order to absorb difference between world and domestic price levels; (5) An application for financial assistance from Allied sources on a broader basis will be made and when allotted will be used mainly for immediate rehabilitation of the country; (6) UNRRA supplies will be distributed and valorized quickly; (7) Effective control of prices with regard to particular peculiarities of the country will be organized." See Kasimatis, Οικονομικόν Πρόβλημα (*Economic Problem*), 96-97, 125.

17. FO371/48285 R19827, AGIS Weekly Report, No. 56, November 4–10, 1945; Kasimatis, Οικονομικόν Πρόβλημα (*Economic Problem*), 101–2, 108–32; T236/1047, Statement to Be Made by M. Kasimatis Announcing His Program over the Radio. Translation of a Document Handed to Financial Advisor on 9th November 1945; Patterson, *Financial Experiences of Greece,* 260.

problems could hardly be solved by "sympathy, advice [or] declarations of friend-ship" alone; neither could the crisis be overcome by taxation measures or police action. He warned that the country simply could not survive without foreign aid.[18]

Shortly afterwards yet another government was sworn in, but the new minis-ters merely reiterated what their predecessors had said. Tsouderos, the minister of coordination, repeated the need for external aid, while the minister of finance, Alexandros Mylonas, dismissed British emphasis on the budget by claiming that the economy could not bear any additional taxation. In subsequent meetings, Tsoud-eros attempted to gain leverage by hardening his position, stating he would not make any public declaration on the economic and financial situation unless the Allies promised extensive assistance. The British were unimpressed, as the govern-ment was doing little to improve public finances or to suppress the gold market. In reply, Tsouderos claimed that gold speculation was merely a political weapon used by the Right to undermine the government, and dismissed fiscal measures as a solution to the problem.[19] Further contacts between the two sides merely pro-duced a repetition of the fundamental positions: while the Greeks emphasized the need for foreign help, the British continued to stress the budgetary situation as the real key to the problem. Despite Hill's insistence on a much closer control of public spending, Mylonas could offer no helpful suggestions. Claiming that the maximum taxable capacity of the country had been reached following the Kasimatis measures, the minister felt he could neither increase revenue nor reduce expenditure. Hill warned that only vigorous action on the budget could prove effective and added that taxes would not only have to be raised drastically in order to bring them in line with current prices, but also would have to be pegged to inflation to avoid future depreciation. Similarly, officials at the Treasury were adamant that only internal measures could solve the country's problems. Douglas Davidson was convinced

18. FO371/48285, including R19828, Record of a Conversation between the Prime Minister, Mr. McNeil and His Majesty's Ambassador, November 14, 1945; R19830, Record of a Conversation Held at His Majesty's Embassy, November 15, 1945; FO371/48338, including R20280, Record of Conversation Held at His Majesty's Embassy, November 16, 1945; R20282, Record of a Discussion Held at the Palace of the Regency, November 19, 1945; FO371/48286 R20281, Discussion Held at the Palace of the Regency, November 19, 1945.

19. FO371/48416, including R21248, Record of Meeting Held at the British Embassy, November 21, 1945; R21249, Record of Meeting Held at H.B.M. Embassy, November 22, 1945; FO371/48338, including R20171, Athens to FO, Telegram no. 155 Remac, November 29, 1945; R20320, Athens to FO, Telegram no. 2403, November 30, 1945; R20382, Athens to FO, Telegram no. 2416, December 2, 1945; R20299, Athens to FO, Telegram no. 2405, November 30, 1945; R20345, Athens to FO, Telegram no. 2414, December 1, 1945.

that room for improving public finance did exist, and dismissed the notion that Greek taxable capacity had been reached as a dangerous idea likely to cause trouble in the future.[20]

The dispatch of Hector McNeil—the undersecretary of state for foreign affairs—to Athens, heralding the preparation of a sizable advisory economic mission, signaled the advent of a much broader British approach to the Greek crisis. For the adherents of fiscal orthodoxy, preoccupied as they were with public finance, this new initiative created a double danger. For one thing, they felt that the Greeks would avoid any vigorous action on the budget pending the outcome of the London talks. Hill was convinced that the government believed that British assistance would remedy all the country's problems and planned to "let things slide," and to blame Britain for the crisis should such assistance be refused. He deplored the numerous press rumors about an impending British loan, which the government was doing nothing to dispel, and even suggested that these had originated within the cabinet itself.[21]

For Hill and Davidson, the very breadth of the proposed mission posed an even greater danger. They felt anxious that the initiative would divert attention away from what they saw as the only guaranteed solution to the crisis. Davidson was appalled by the priorities of McNeil, who seemed to emphasize "supply and production" rather than "financial problems." Although he acknowledged that the former issues were important, he did not believe that recovery could be possible unless the budget was balanced. Hill went even further. While admitting that the mission could achieve much in reviving industry and assisting distribution, he felt this would not be enough unless inflation could be checked. By now, he doubted

20. FO371/48338 R20704, Davidson to Laskey, December 6, 1945 (Enclosure: Greek Finances, November 28, 1945); T236/1048, Report of Proceedings of a Meeting in the Ministry of Finance, December 5, 1945; Greek Finance, D. Davidson, November 23, 1945; Greek Financial Situation, D. Davidson, November 26, 1945; Minute by Davidson, November 28, 1945. The total government inertia on public finance contrasted with other actions it took in response to the escalating political and economic crisis. At the end of November, after sharp rises in the sovereign rate, it finally heeded British advice and passed a law prohibiting transactions in gold. As this had no effect, it was shortly followed by a second law promising drastic penalties (including confiscation, imprisonment, and exile) for those who continued to trade. This proved no more effective than the first, and within days the Bank of Greece resorted to secret sales of gold, without informing the British. By these means, 97,000 sovereigns were sold by the end of January 1946; Patterson, *Financial Experiences of Greece*, 304–8.
    21. FO371/48338 R21506, Hill to Rowe-Dutton, December 13, 1945.

whether an economic solution could be found to the crisis given the country's "free economy," coupled with "the Greek temperament and lack of efficiency."[22]

The only vigorous action taken by the government during this period was to demand participation in the London talks, where the details of the economic mission and other forms of British support were to be finalized. Both Tsouderos and Georgios Kartalis, the minister of supply, sought invitations to London to state the Greek case. Kartalis warned that the government would fall unless immediate measures were enacted, and threatened to resign unless he was invited to join the discussions. A worried Leeper urged the Foreign Office to comply in the interests of political stability. As he warned, a "narrow financial view" could completely destroy British policy in Greece, whereas a "wide and realistic" approach could yield "big results." Officials at the Foreign Office resented the idea of various "visiting Greek ministers" seeking to obtain an "immediate cut-and-dried scheme" that would "get them out of all their troubles," and were annoyed that Kartalis was not prepared to remain at his post. Nevertheless, given the political circumstances, they relented on condition that the ministers should not expect any immediate results from the forthcoming discussions.[23]

Upon arrival in London, the ministers emphasized that Greece's financial problems were entirely dependent upon immediate reconstruction. They claimed that any attempt to deal with the two questions in isolation would lead to further collapse, as they believed that only a long-term reconstruction program would make it possible to stabilize the currency and balance the budget. They added that Greece was utterly unable to provide resources required for such a program, as revenue could not be increased, nor could expenditure be reduced. Thus in their view, reconstruction would only be possible through massive Allied assistance and a greater relief effort from UNRRA.[24]

The British fully acknowledged the urgent need for reconstruction, but pointed out that immediately stabilizing the currency was of at least equal importance. This would require much more efficient use of Greece's own resources. They agreed that Greece would need a great deal of help from abroad, but stressed that reconstruction could not be wholly dependent on Allied aid, as UNRRA resources were

22. T236/1048, Minute by Davidson, November 28, 1945; T236/1047, Hill to Rowe-Dutton, November 21, 1945 (Enclosure: Note by Hill, November 21, 1945).

23. FO371/48338, including R21366, Athens to FO, Telegram no. 2535, December 21, 1945; FO to Athens, Telegram no. 2538, December 22, 1945; FO371/48289, including R21403, Athens to FO, Telegram no. 2548, December 23, 1945; R21543, Athens to FO, Telegram no. 2573, December 27, 1945; FO to Athens, Telegram no. 2575, December 28, 1945; T236/1048, FO to Athens, Telegram no. 2555, December 24, 1945.

24. FO371/58720 R398, The Greek Ministers' Memorandum, January 2, 1946.

limited and Greece was already receiving a "disproportionately large share" of what was "available." Such high levels of aid could be maintained only if the Greeks could demonstrate they were putting it to constructive use. They declared that the British government was anxious to provide technical assistance, together with limited aid for rebuilding housing, industrial plants, and transport infrastructure. However, they underlined that London was neither able nor willing to undertake long-term financial obligations, and that British assistance could be provided for a limited period only, after which Greece would have to carry on alone. They added that in any case, foreign credits would be of little help unless the government stopped covering budget deficits by resorting to the printing press. They urged a greater effort to restart industrial and agricultural production, but as Waley warned, "printing more paper money" would not "make the chickens lay more eggs." Only stabilization of the budget could diminish speculation and restore confidence in the economy.[25]

The Broader Approach

Throughout the autumn, British advice had been limited to issues relating to the immediate crisis. As the situation deteriorated, it became increasingly clear to most observers outside Treasury circles that fiscal orthodoxy alone would not be enough to solve Greece's problems. This realization forced the British to broaden their approach in order to concentrate on the wider underlying weaknesses of the Greek economy as much as on the immediate threat of inflation. This prompted a series of initiatives culminating in the London Agreement of January 1946, by which the British assumed a far more direct role in Greek economic affairs.

Suggestions for wider Allied involvement came from the Greeks themselves, and were made shortly after the departure of Varvaressos.[26] In the end, fears of a political breakdown forced the British to rethink their approach toward the economic crisis. In a radical departure from previous practice, Bevin's swift conversion to a policy of active intervention produced an offer to send McNeil to Athens to discuss a program of technical advice and expert assistance. Bevin envisaged that Britain could soon offer the Greeks a full economic mission consisting of experts attached to various ministries. These would advise on matters relating to the army, public

25. FO371/48289 R21668, FO to Athens, Telegram no. 14, January 2, 1946; FO371/58720 R398, Minute by Sargent, January 1, 1946; T236/1049, Minute by Waley, January 7, 1946; FO371/58721 R793, Waley to Laskey, January 8, 1946 (Enclosure: Points for Reply to the Greek Ministers' Memorandum, January 2, 1946).

26. FO371/48280 R16154, Athens to FO, Telegram no. 181 Saving, September 18, 1945.

finance, transport, and distribution. In addition, Britain would assist the Greek import program, with special emphasis on acquiring capital goods and raw materials. In exchange, Bevin expected the Greeks to undertake a series of measures dealing with industry, distribution, and transport infrastructure, along with various political measures.[27]

While in Athens, McNeil communicated the British government's willingness to send a mission to assist with the "task of economic reconstruction." Its ultimate aim would be to reestablish the country as a "going concern" after which it would be withdrawn. However, such a mission would not be sent unless the Greek government gave an undertaking to "implement and operate" any program it devised. The Greeks professed astonishment at the British proposals and claimed that as an interim government they had no right to commit future administrations to such an arrangement. Nevertheless, with the formation of the Sophoulis government, Tsouderos accepted the program in principle and gave a "gentleman's assurance" that the mission's advice would be accepted.[28]

The Grove Plan

In mid-December, two of the key figures in the planned economic mission visited Athens for a further fact-finding trip ahead of the London talks. These were Vyvyan Board and Edward Grove, responsible for industry and finance respectively.[29] Within days, Grove concluded that the measures that had hitherto been central to British advice to successive Greek governments were "inappropriate to the present circumstances." Accordingly, he devised a plan that reflected changed priorities. He claimed that although budgetary equilibrium would probably stabilize prices, it would not dispel the general distrust of the drachma, and thus could not in itself overcome the crisis. He believed that as it would be difficult to restore public

27. FO371/48284, including R18571, FO to Athens, Telegram no. 2224, November 1, 1945; R18832, FO to Athens, Telegram no. 2266, November 7, 1945; CAB129/4/C.P. (45) 266, Greece, Memorandum by the Secretary of State for Foreign Affairs, November 3, 1945; CAB128/2/C.M. 49(45), Greece, November 6, 1945.

28. FO371/48285, including R19826, McNeil to Kanellopoulos, November 14, 1945; R2344, Athens to FO, Telegram no. 2344, November 22, 1945; FRUS, 1945: MacVeagh to the Secretary of State, November 17, 1945, vol. 8, 270–71.

29. FO371/58667 R155, Athens to FO, Telegram no. 283 Saving, December 21, 1945. Board was chairman of the Distiller's Company, and had acted as alcohol, molasses, and rubber controller at the Ministry of Supply during the war; Grove had worked for Lazard Brothers in London. FO371/48416, including R20671, FO to Athens, Telegram no. 2466, December 9, 1945; R20906, FO to Washington, Telegram no. 12455, December 12, 1945.

confidence in any currency other than gold, the only possible solution would be a currency with a 100 percent backing in gold or foreign exchange. As an interim measure, he advocated the complete withdrawal of the drachma, and its replacement by gold coins as the standard medium of exchange. Believing that the Bank of Greece held sufficient reserves for this purpose, he claimed the arrangement would effectively prevent the government from resorting to the printing press. He doubted whether a foreign loan would be necessary, but pointed out that a small loan of £5 million, for the purchase of industrial plant and capital goods, would be an encouraging gesture. He agreed that the Greek government would have to act decisively to balance the budget, no matter how drastic the necessary measures might be. Moreover, they would also have to accept a rigid financial control by a mission from the British Treasury. Finally, he assumed that the country would require foreign assistance until at least the end of 1948, and urged that the Greeks should be assured they would not be allowed to starve in the period between the end of the UNRRA program and the complete recovery of the economy.[30]

No other British financial expert betrayed any enthusiasm for the plan. Whereas one was content to describe it as "far-reaching" and "revolutionary," another dismissed it as "egregious."[31] Hostility centered on particular proposals. Officials at the Treasury disliked the idea of a gold-backed currency. Wilfrid Eady claimed that such a move essentially amounted to a "confidence trick," with "no avenue of retreat" in the event of failure. Waley was equally skeptical, but added that any objection to the use of gold would be removed if the budget could be balanced quickly. However, both had severe doubts whether anything drastic would be done to save the economy. Eady acknowledged that Greece would need extensive assistance, but felt Britain could not commit itself to any financial help beyond the end of 1946. Nevertheless, he was prepared to recommend that the British government offer the Greeks substantial aid until that time.[32]

Officials at the Bank of England also displayed marked reserve toward the use of gold, with Harry Siepmann and George Bolton equally hostile to the idea. Instead,

30. T236/1048, Meeting with M. Tsouderos, M. Kartalis, Sir Vyvyan Board, Mr. Grove, Financial and Economic Advisers at the Bank of Greece, December 20, 1945; FO371/48416, including R21223, Athens to FO, Telegram no. 2524, December 21, 1945; R21309, Athens to FO, Telegram no. 2529, December 21, 1945; R21314, Athens to FO, Telegram no. 2530, December 21, 1945.
31. T236/1048, Hill to Davidson, December 19, 1945; T236/1049, Minute by Eady, January 10, 1946. The unanimous hostility toward the plan belies Hadziiossif's bizarre claim that "Grove's ideas reflected the findings of the British Embassy in Athens"; Hadziiossif, "Economic Stabilization and Political Unrest," 38.
32. FO371/48338 R21610, Laskey to Reily, January 4, 1946 (Enclosure: Record of Meeting Held in Mr. McNeil's Room in Foreign Office, December 24, 1945).

the bank proposed the establishment of an international currency commission, operated by one British and one American representative with additional members
from other European countries, to issue a new currency backed by gold and foreign exchange. The commission would include several advisers, who would seek
to "bring some order into the Greek administration," while the Bank of Greece
would lose its note-issuing authority. The suggestions met with the approval of the
Treasury, which duly incorporated them into its own plan.[33]

The Treasury Plan

The Treasury was convinced that fiscal orthodoxy could no longer ensure a successful stabilization unless excessive money issues could be prevented. Accordingly,
they proposed setting up a currency control committee consisting of up to four
members: the Greek minister of finance and the governor of the Bank of Greece,
together with a Briton and an American if possible. Their unanimous agreement
would be required for new note issues. The new currency would be fully backed
by foreign exchange, but the British representative on the committee would have
to be consulted as to the appropriate measures to prevent any possible flight of
capital. The Greek government would have to deposit £15 million out of its foreign
exchange reserves into a special note cover account, to which the British would add
a further £5 million on condition that vigorous action be taken on public finance.
In addition, the British would provide experts to advise Greek ministers on taxation measures and budgetary control as well as an adviser for the sole purpose
of reforming the Greek civil service. The proposals concluded that although no
further financial assistance would be extended, Britain should waive repayment
of wartime loans amounting to £46 million if the Greeks undertook appropriate
financial measures.[34]

Although the chancellor approved the suggestions, Cobbold, the deputy governor of the Bank of England, was less than enthusiastic. While claiming there was
nothing wrong with the plan itself, there was little likelihood that the Greeks would
"carry it out." Without political stability and a willingness to "do what is necessary"
he felt the proposals amounted to "putting new money down the same old drain."
He firmly believed that the proposed currency committee would have to possess
executive powers, but doubted whether even this would be enough. He objected

33. BE OV80/26, Minute, Greece, December 31, 1945; Minute by Bolton, Greece, December 31,
1945.
34. T236/1049, Memorandum by Davidson, January 1, 1946.

to full convertibility into sterling, but felt little confidence that the new currency would be viable without such convertibility.[35]

Despite such misgivings, the Foreign Office supported the idea of full convertibility into sterling, claiming that this alone could guarantee the prerequisite degree of confidence in the new currency. They argued that the dangers of capital flight could be avoided if convertibility were accompanied by sufficiently "watertight arrangements." Nevertheless, the Treasury continued to emphasize the possibility of capital flight as a major objection to convertibility, concluding that the measure was in any case pointless unless the Greeks were prepared to take the "painful and difficult" measures that the situation demanded.[36]

Following two weeks of largely theoretical discussions, the subsequent course of events was heavily influenced by political considerations. Believing that the British proposals were insufficiently generous, the Greek ministers threatened to return to Athens. Not for the first time, an angry Leeper warned the Foreign Office of the potentially disastrous consequences of treating the Greek crisis as a "purely financial problem." He feared the impasse could bring down the government, after which the most likely outcome would be a "regime of the Extreme Right" followed by a "Communist dictatorship." To avoid "bloodshed and famine," he urged a more "generous approach."[37]

The Foreign Office was of similar mind. It suggested that the £5 million earmarked to back the stabilization plan should be doubled, feeling this would appear more impressive to the Greeks. The Treasury was anything but impressed. They argued there was little financial justification for such a move, particularly as Britain's own balance of payments was so unsatisfactory. They reluctantly accepted that the Foreign Office had its own agenda for Greece based on criteria other than financial. The Treasury objections were overruled as the broader Foreign Office agenda prevailed. After consulting with Bevin, Dalton consented to the proposal, despite his clear lack of enthusiasm for the Greek leadership. Claiming he had little confidence in "Tsouderos and Co.," he urged Bevin to ensure that the £5 million would not be simply thrown "down the drain."[38]

35. T236/1049, Minute by Eady, January 3, 1946; Davidson to Laskey, January 7, 1946; BE OV80/26, Minute by Cobbold, January 4, 1946; Minute by Cobbold, January 7, 1946.

36. FO371/58790 R209, McNeil to Waley, January 4, 1946; Waley to McNeil, January 5, 1946.

37. FO371/58722 R1310, Record of a Meeting Held in Mr. McNeil's Room, January 8, 1945; FO371/58720, including R532, Athens to FO, Telegram no. 76, January 10, 1946; R531, Athens to FO, Telegram no. 75, January 10, 1946; R595, Athens to FO, Telegram no. 87, January 11, 1946; Athens to FO, Telegram no. 88, January 11, 1946.

38. T236/1049, Minute by Eady, January 10, 1946; FO371/58720 R485, Minute by Laskey, January 10, 1946; FO371/58721 R979, Dalton to Bevin, January 14, 1946.

As a result of the political pressure, the Treasury produced a revised set of proposals. These included the £10 million stabilization loan, the waiving of the £46 million wartime debt, some material assistance, and British advisers to be placed within Greek ministries, in addition to the economic mission. In return, the Greek government would have to issue a new currency and set new exchange rates. The government would have to provide £15 million from their own foreign exchange reserves to supplement the British loan. The new currency would be freely convertible, with all new issues subject to the unanimous approval of a currency committee comprised as in the original plan. Safeguards to prevent capital flight were left to the discretion of the Greek government. The proposals demanded austerity in public finance, with expenditure cuts to be achieved by reducing the size of the state bureaucracy. New taxes would have to be introduced, while all existing taxes would have to be revalorized to take account of inflation. Revenue from the sale of UNRRA supplies would have to be increased, partly by raising their price and partly by cutting the numbers of nonpaying recipients.[39]

The Greek ministers' response was guarded. They declared that the amended plan offered a "satisfactory basis for discussion," but refused to commit themselves at first. They accepted the need to balance the budget, and claimed that they would not be deterred by the likely unpopularity of some of the proposed measures, but took pains to reemphasize that increased taxation would have to await the recovery of industrial production and foreign trade, and that the whole stabilization plan would be jeopardized unless UNRRA supplies were increased. Eventually, they accepted, feeling this would "ensure continued foreign interest in Greece's welfare." In the meantime, both sides had agreed to set up a committee to control public finance. This would include British and Greek officials and would have advisory functions only. Rather than creating an entirely new currency, the existing drachma would be retained. Following a final compromise, the drachma was to be freely convertible for "imports and for other approved purposes including approved capital transactions." The stabilization plan was formally adopted on January 24, and the details of the agreement were announced the next day.[40]

39. T236/1049, Economic and Financial Situation in Greece, January 15, 1946.

40. T236/1049, Minute by Somerville Smith, January 16, 1946; Athens to FO, Telegram no. 117, January 17, 1946; Minute by Waley, January 18, 1946; FO371/58790, including R1221, Record of a Meeting Held at 21 St. James's Square, January 17, 1946; Minute by Laskey, January 18, 1946; R1049, FO to Athens, Telegram no. 19 Camer, January 18, 1946; FO371/58722, including R1311, Greek Ministers' Comments, January 16, 1946; R1308, Waley to Tsouderos, January 23, 1946; R1355, FO to Athens, Telegram no. 162, January 24, 1946; Financial and Economic Agreement between His Majesty's Government in the United Kingdom and the Greek Government, January 24, 1946.

Signing the London Agreement, January 24, 1946. From left to right: Emmanuel Tsouderos, Ernest Bevin, and Georgios Kartalis. E. Venezis, *Emmanuel Tsouderos* (Athens, 1966).

The London Agreement and Its Instruments

The London Agreement superseded all previous forms of British economic aid to Greece. Apart from the stabilization loan to back convertibility, little material assistance was offered. Instead, the most important result was the creation of two new institutions: the British Economic Mission (BEM) and the Currency Committee, both of which were designed to play central roles in subsequent events.

As the British were already largely familiar with the major problems of the Greek economy, the areas in which the economic advisory mission would operate were clearly defined from the very beginning. Thus within weeks a provisional body had been devised to deal with issues relating to finance, industry, agriculture, labor, and transport. By February 1946 the BEM consisted of six sections: Cooperative Movement, Supply and Distribution, Labor, Transport, Finance, and Industry.[41] With

41. FO371/48416 R20139, Minute by McNeil, November 28, 1945; FO371/58723 R2967, British Economic Mission to Greece, Fortnightly Report no. 1.

slight amendments, this basic structure remained in force until the termination of its activities.

Whereas the scope of the BEM was thus well defined, its aims were never clearly formulated. Originally, it was stated that the proposed body would strive to "get [the] Greek economy working again" and transform the country into a "going concern." However, the directive drawn up in December 1945 merely specified that the mission would cooperate with Greek officials in planning the "various phases of reconstruction," and would seek to ensure that "any decisions reached" would be acted upon. These general statements were never formally refined or redefined. Instead, as the work of the BEM progressed, each section developed an independent list of priorities and objectives, ranging from general topics to extremely specific courses of action.[42]

An even more contentious issue was the extent of the powers that the BEM could wield. The Greeks had been particularly anxious to avoid the granting of executive authority to any foreign experts, and warned against any arrangement that could offend "rather touchy circles" or "certain susceptibilities." Accordingly, the British took great pains to emphasize the advisory nature of the BEM, and never officially departed from the line that its members were effectively "servants" of the Athens government. The BEM would thus merely provide advice, with responsibility for its adoption or otherwise to lie entirely with the Greek government.[43] As will be shown, this arrangement was to prove one of the most serious weaknesses of the entire Bevin initiative.

When the BEM was first proposed, British authorities optimistically suggested that it would operate for between three and six months. As set out in the London Agreement in January 1946, this became eighteen months, with the possibility of a further six months' extension by mutual agreement.[44] The BEM was headed by Lieutenant General John Clark, with Thomas Rapp acting as deputy from July 1946. Initially, its most important members included Edward Grove and Vyvyan Board as heads of the finance and industry sections. Both had played central roles in the

42. CAB129/4/C.P. (45) 266, Greece, Memorandum by the Secretary of State for Foreign Affairs, November 3, 1945; FO371/48285 R19826, McNeil to Kanellopoulos, November 14, 1945; FO371/48416 R20906, Economic Advisory Mission to Greece (Draft Directive), December 10, 1945. For a list of objectives of each section as defined in April 1946, see FO371/58798 R6681, English Text of a Memorandum Submitted in Greek by the British Economic Mission to His Excellency M. S. Stephanopoulos, Minister of Coordination, April 1946.

43. FO371/58790 R1221, Record of a Meeting Held at 21 St. James's Square, January 17, 1946; FO371/67101 R2377, Interim Report of the British Economic Mission to Greece, January 31, 1947, 1.

44. FO371/48416 R20906, Economic Advisory Mission to Greece (Draft Directive), December 10, 1945; FO371/58722 R1355, Financial and Economic Agreement between His Majesty's Government in the United Kingdom and the Greek Government, January 24, 1946.

negotiations leading to the London Agreement. In May 1946, Grove was replaced by John Nixon, who combined BEM duties with his existing role as British member of the Currency Committee.[45]

In contrast with the BEM, the scope, aims, and powers of the Currency Committee were much more clearly defined. The London Agreement had laid down that the proposed committee was to have "statutory management of the note issue," and its unanimous approval was required if further drachma issues were contemplated. These stipulations were duly enshrined in Greek law, but another clause, stating that the £25 million note cover account could be used only in agreement with the Bank of England, was omitted. Likewise, a suggestion that the account should be subject to the Currency Committee's control was vetoed by Tsouderos on political grounds, although it was agreed in practice that no unilateral action would be taken. However, the Currency Committee eventually assumed additional duties not covered in its original statute, such as the approval of major commercial loans and private imports, and the sale of foreign exchange. The Currency Committee, or for practical purposes its foreign members, was thus furnished with powers the BEM never possessed, in that it was authorized to veto any government actions it deemed inappropriate. The Bank of Greece initially undertook to provide regular statistical updates on note circulation and foreign exchange and bullion assets, but within weeks it was agreed that this obligation should be extended to cover virtually every aspect of public finances, the balance of payments, and the money supply. Like the BEM, the Currency Committee was designed to function for an eighteen-month period, with the possibility of a six-month extension.[46] The foreign members invited to participate were the already mentioned Nixon (replaced by Theodore Gregory in November 1946) and Gardner Patterson, previously of the ESC, as the American representative. In their official capacity, both were to play important roles in subsequent events, and their names frequently recur in the narrative.[47]

45. Lieutenant General Clark had headed the SHAEF Mission responsible for the military relief effort in the Netherlands; Nixon had filled a series of senior posts within the Indian civil service; Rapp had served previously as consul general in Thessaloniki; FO371/58723 R1776, FO to Athens, Telegram no. 227, December 4, 1946; FO371/48416 R20906, FO to Washington, Telegram no. 12455, December 12, 1945.

46. FO371/58722 R1355, Financial and Economic Agreement between His Majesty's Government in the United Kingdom and the Greek Government, January 24, 1946; FO371/58726 R4590, Common Law No. 1015, *Government Gazette*, February 20, 1946; T236/1050, BEM/SEC/18/46/1, February 14, 1946; BEM/FIN/8/46/17, February 22, 1946; T236/1051, Currency Committee, First Informal Meeting, March 21, 1946.

47. The role of the Bank of Greece personnel in the Currency Committee has been misinterpreted by Pepelasis Minoglou, who rightly underlined the bank's subservience to the govern-

The Bevin initiative that culminated in the London Agreement thus led to the establishment of two institutions designed to address and eliminate some of the most obvious shortcomings of the Greek economy. While the BEM's remit was extremely broad, the brief of the Currency Committee was limited to a relatively small number of key issues. While the BEM could merely advise, with no effective mechanism of ensuring that its advice was heeded, the Currency Committee was empowered to block government measures running counter to its objectives. If the purpose of the BEM was to offer constructive solutions and promote positive actions, the Currency Committee's task was primarily one of damage limitation, in that it sought to minimize the potentially harmful effects of government policy. Although both instruments were independent of each other, their general objectives were convergent and mutually supporting. Despite differences in their scope and power, the success of each depended largely on the degree of cooperation offered by the Greeks.

Inflationary Factors

British advice to successive governments in Athens had emphasized the need to combat inflation by pursuing sound fiscal and monetary policies. This implied a much greater effort to improve the budget situation and avoid recourse to the printing press. Despite persistent British pressure, developments over the following fifteen months increased rather than reduced inflationary forces, which were held in check only by measures that had little to do with fiscal orthodoxy. The following section describes the factors contributing to inflation: continuing budget deficits, escalating expenditures on wages and the military, and granting huge credits to agriculture.

Budgetary Developments

Under the terms of the London Agreement, the government undertook to reduce, and as soon as possible eliminate, the budget deficit by increasing revenue

---

ment in Athens, but failed to mention the powers of the foreign members; I. Pepelasis Minoglou, *Transplanting Economic Ideas: International Coercion and Native Policy,* 47; and the same author's "Transplanting Institutions: The Case of the Greek Central Bank," 57. As the foreign members of the Currency Committee later stated, its primary task was to remove monetary and credit policy from the sphere of "Greek party politics." See T. Gregory, J. W. Gunter, and D. C. Johns, *Report and Recommendations on Certain Aspects of the Greek Banking System,* 13.

from taxation and minimizing unnecessary expenditure. To assist the Greeks in this endeavor the BEM provided two advisers, Blackburn and Macintosh from the Inland Revenue and the Treasury respectively. This pair formed the nucleus of a committee of leading British, Greek, and UNRRA officials set up to scrutinize public finances, and preliminary estimates for a new budget were prepared by the end of March. In the meantime, following additional pressure from Whitehall, specific recommendations on tax increases were presented to Tsouderos. Given the proximity of the elections, however, little immediate action was taken.[48] While the budget was being discussed, the situation continued to deteriorate. State receipts as a share of expenditure amounted to only 44.6 percent in January and fell to 36.5 percent in February. In March the share rose to 51.1 percent, but this improvement was due almost solely to massive increases in revenue from ML/UNRRA supplies rather than to higher tax yields, which had been entirely absorbed by rising expenditure.[49]

Once the newly elected government was installed, attention was quickly refocused on the pressing economic issues. Within days of taking office, Stephanos Stephanopoulos, the new minister of coordination, highlighted budgetary equilibrium as one of the most urgent tasks to be addressed.[50] An analysis of the actual budget figures for 1945–1946 demonstrates the enormity of the task facing the Tsaldaris government. During the fiscal year, total revenue covered slightly less than 60 percent of expenditure. State receipts were still heavily dependent on extraordinary sources (48 percent). Proceeds from the sale of ML/UNRRA supplies were the biggest single component (37 percent), while extraordinary taxes on wartime profits, on which such hopes had been placed by successive finance ministers since liberation, produced disappointing results, yielding less than 8 percent. Ordinary taxation provided 52 percent, but a detailed breakdown suggests that many potential sources of revenue were undertapped. The largest sums were derived from duties on tobacco consumption (17 percent), easily dwarfing yields from direct taxation (less than 15 percent). The special contribution generated significant sums— 11 percent, or 74 percent of all direct tax revenue. In sharp contrast, the returns from income and corporate taxes were pitifully small, providing a mere 1.1 percent.[51]

---

48. FO371/58722 R1355, Financial and Economic Agreement between His Majesty's Government in the United Kingdom and the Greek Government, January 24, 1946; FO371/58725 R4369, Note on the Financial Policy of Greece, E. Grove, March 8, 1946; FO371/58726 R5252, Budget 1945/46 and 1946/47, J. Nixon, March 25, 1946; FO371/58724, including R3488, FO to Athens, Telegram no. 467, March 5, 1946; R3862, Athens to FO, Telegram no. 499, March 11, 1946; FO371/67101 R2377, Interim Report of the British Economic Mission to Greece, January 31, 1947, 80

49. Patterson, *Financial Experiences of Greece,* 339–41.

50. FO371/58727 R6134, British Economic Mission to Greece, Fortnightly Report no. 5.

51. Percentages calculated from data in Patterson, *Financial Experiences of Greece,* 344.

Public spending was dominated by the current costs of administration, distribution, and security, rather than reconstruction. By far the largest single expenditure item was the government payroll, which accounted for 31 percent of the total. The burden of pensions for former employees constituted a further 13 percent. Thus almost half of all expenditure was devoted to the maintenance of current and former state personnel. The huge cost of distributing ML/UNRRA supplies also absorbed a large share (28 percent), as did the security forces (21 percent). The latter figure did not include the substantial costs of equipping and maintaining the armed forces, which were still borne by the British. Conversely, expenditure on reconstruction and public works was negligible, amounting to a mere 11 percent.[52]

These figures make grim reading and illustrate two major points. First, the tax-gathering capability of the state fell woefully short of even its current requirements, let alone the enormous long-term demands of reconstruction. Second, the surprising contrasts between the different shares of items on both the expenditure and revenue sides suggested obvious means by which the overall budgetary situation could be improved. As Patterson notes, the "regressive nature" of the tax system was readily apparent.[53] Yields from income and corporate taxes were so low as to be virtually symbolic, and the special contribution remained the only meaningful mechanism for taxing the business community and the professions. By contrast, duties on tobacco consumption alone yielded sixteen times more than taxes on income and profits, and more than all direct taxation combined. Given the extent of poverty in postwar Greece, the poor were shouldering a disproportionately large share of the tax burden. The problem of how to tap the large profits and incomes enjoyed by a narrow section of society, so frequently discussed back in 1945, still awaited a solution. As for the expenditure side, it was clear that drastic measures were needed to address both the excessive costs of the state machinery and distribution. On the former, the bloated government payroll required urgent trimming to reduce chronic overmanning. On the latter, only substantial improvements in infrastructure and administration could avoid the absurdity of a situation where the costs of distributing UNRRA supplies to the population exceeded proceeds from the sale of those supplies.

British pressure on public finances took two complementary forms: the drawing up of a comprehensive budget statement, coupled with the need to improve the

52. Ibid.
53. Ibid., 345.

existing system of taxation, to examine the feasibility of additional levies, and to maximize receipts from the sale of UNRRA supplies. As noted previously, progress on a budget statement was painfully slow. However, both the pre- and post-election governments enacted several measures to increase returns from both ordinary and extraordinary sources.

Between January and May, a series of increases of the tax on tobacco consumption raised duties by 275 percent on basic tobacco and 176 percent on luxury grades, bringing prices roughly in line with prewar levels. In February the special contribution, which had not been adjusted since the departure of Varvaressos, was raised to 225 percent of the August levels. This still fell short of the original burden, as retail prices had risen by more than 1,400 percent in the meantime. From the beginning of April, the special contribution was revamped as the "professional tax." This worked on the same principles as the original levy, though it involved a further reduction in real terms. Also in February, import duties were fixed at forty times the 1941 levels, and the rates of the "net proceeds tax" were raised by 40 percent. In March stamp duties were set at twenty to thirty times the prewar rates, while in May the land tax was increased fivefold. Apart from adjustments of the basic threshold, no serious action was taken on income taxes, which remained fixed at 1 percent. The so-called turnover tax also remained unchanged. During the overall period, all other indirect levies were raised substantially, particularly those involving state monopolies or various forms of entertainments. Several measures were also enacted to increase yields of extraordinary sources, especially from the sale of UNRRA supplies.[54]

As demonstrated previously, successive governments had made some genuine efforts to increase revenue. However, the formulation of a comprehensive budget statement was a long process, involving persistent pressure from the British. Estimates were finally presented in early June and were the result of close collaboration between the new minister of finance, Dimitrios Helmis, and the BEM. The new budget was much more realistic than any of its predecessors, in that it recognized that the deficit would not be eliminated during the fiscal year. Instead, the main priority was to keep this deficit down to a minimum without compromising the efficient functioning of the government.[55]

---

54. Ibid., 339, 360–81.

55. FO371/58728, including R7298, Nixon to Waley, April 26, 1946; R7297, Bevin to Aghnides, May 15, 1946; R7338, Athens to FO, Telegram no. 1090, May 15, 1946; FO371/58729, including R7744, Athens to FO, Telegram no. 1174, May 22, 1946; R7870, Athens to FO, Telegram no. 1196, May 25, 1946; FO371/67101 R2377, Interim Report of the British Economic Mission to Greece, January 31, 1947, 80.

In drawing up the estimates, it was assumed that wages and prices had returned to equilibrium, and that future price stability could be ensured through the increased availability of consumer goods. In addition, it was taken for granted that UNRRA supplies would continue until the end of 1946 and that the British government would cover all military expenditure until the end of the fiscal year. Moreover, it was finally recognized that few rapid improvements could be expected from taxation on incomes or business profits, and that indirect taxes offered far more immediate potential for raising revenue. Expenditure estimates were largely based on actual figures from February and March 1946, with a small additional provision for reconstruction purposes. Revenue estimates were based on yields from the preceding fiscal year, adjusted to take account of the various increases enacted in recent months and the anticipated improvements in assessment and collection of taxes.[56]

The 1946–1947 budget estimates assumed that revenue would cover 88.8 percent of total expenditure. This figure, although less optimistic than the various predictions of the preceding year, represented a huge improvement compared with the actual performance during 1945–1946. It was anticipated that 57 percent of total revenue would come from extraordinary sources. As before, proceeds of the sale of UNRRA supplies were to constitute the biggest single item (40.5 percent). Ordinary revenue was to provide only 43 percent, while a mere 6.6 percent would derive from direct taxation. On the expenditure side, it was assumed that government salaries and pensions (32 percent), the distribution of UNRRA supplies (28.6 percent), and internal and external security (20.8 percent) would continue to be the major areas of public spending. Expenditure on reconstruction and public works was set at a mere 9.2 percent. This was recognized as completely inadequate, but it was hoped that savings in other departments could be channeled into additional reconstruction projects.[57]

The budget estimates of June 1946 proved reasonably accurate. On the revenue side, positive results were achieved, as receipts fractionally exceeded anticipated sums. For the first time since liberation, direct taxes surpassed all expectations: actual yields were 86 percent higher than estimated, and contributed 12.1 percent of total revenue. Proceeds from income and corporate taxes were particularly encouraging, exceeding estimates by almost 3,000 percent. Other direct taxes and the duty on tobacco consumption were more disappointing, but all other sources of ordinary revenue were largely in line with expectations. Extraordinary receipts fell

56. Patterson, *Financial Experiences of Greece*, 80–81.
57. Percentages calculated from data in ibid., 83, 352, 395–96.

12 percent short of the anticipated sums, despite favorable returns from the sale of UNRRA supplies (7 percent more than planned). Nevertheless, the undeniable progress was dissipated by substantial increases in public spending, which over-shot estimates by 23 percent. As will be described below, the most important sin-gle source (almost 60 percent) of overspending resulted from concessions on state salaries and pensions, with increased military expenditure (also largely consisting of pay increases to armed forces personnel) accounting for another 31 percent, and additional outlays on reconstruction contributing 5.5 percent. As a result, only 73 percent of total expenditure was covered by revenue.[58]

Wages

Ever since liberation, British officials had regarded wage restraint as one of the primary weapons in the fight against inflation and repeatedly advised successive Greek governments to resist excessive pay demands. While acknowledging the low purchasing power of the labor force, they felt that wage levels had to be based on what the country could afford rather than the cost of living, and should not be raised before the economy had recovered. Accordingly, the London Agreement laid down that wages would be "kept stable," after initial adjustments to take account of the simultaneous devaluation of the drachma.[59] At the beginning of February, new scales for wages and pensions were set at ten times the June 1945 levels. However, even these increases were deemed insufficient by the trade unions, which demanded that pay be automatically pegged to changes in the cost of living. The government resisted at first, but at the end of February it announced the free distribution of locally produced clothing to civil servants. The new scales remained relatively in-tact throughout the spring, as stable prices kept strikes to a minimum. Although concessions were granted to Piraeus stevedores in March, the government seriously undermined its principles by awarding the traditional Easter bonus, despite oppo-sition from the BEM and UNRRA. In the meantime, official wage rates outside the state sector were being surreptitiously replaced by piecework and bonus schemes. Before long, the banks were also paying salaries above the legal scales.[60]

In June the government itself made a mockery of the official rates by resorting to the practice of advancing half-monthly salaries and pensions every fourteen days.

58. Percentages calculated from data in ibid., 383, 395–96.
59. FO371/67101 R2377, Interim Report of the British Economic Mission to Greece, January 31, 1947, 7, 71; FO371/58722 R1355, Financial and Economic Agreement between His Majesty's Gov-ernment in the United Kingdom and the Greek Government, January 24, 1946.
60. Patterson, *Financial Experiences of Greece,* 403–12.

According to Patterson, this move added approximately 7 percent to the government wage and pension bill. Moreover, it was enacted without the consent of the Currency Committee, which had not even been informed. In early July another disguised pay raise appeared in response to strong pressure from state employees. Once again the government attempted to circumvent official wage scales by distributing UNRRA imported food and clothing free of charge without first seeking permission from the agency. The goods were distributed despite UNRRA's refusal to give its consent.[61]

Notwithstanding these thinly disguised pay raises, fresh wage demands erupted by the end of the month. During early August, individual strikes in Athens were resolved only by granting open raises. Three weeks later, while maintaining the facade of the official scales, the government announced another free distribution of UNRRA foodstuffs to civil servants, and declared that the practice of advanced payments would be continued, with half-monthly salaries to be paid every twelve days. By this time, the February wage structure had become an empty fiction completely superseded by an intricate system of monetary and nonmonetary payments, euphemistically described as bonuses, loans, special allowances, overtime pay, or fees for attending functions.[62]

Nevertheless, even this failed to satisfy the trade unions, which demanded a doubling of the legal wage rates in mid-October. Within days, civil servants joined the agitation for pay increases. When the Currency Committee refused to sanction these fresh demands, the government briefly resisted. Throughout November strikes for higher wages became widespread. Unable to grant open pay raises, the government attempted to defuse the situation by announcing a cut-price sale of UNRRA imported goods to all lower-paid employees, public or private. Similarly, it made no attempt to refuse the annual Christmas bonus. However, it did accede to demands to scrap advanced salary payments, although these were replaced with the promise of a fresh 25 percent wage rise.[63]

Within the private sector, labor unrest was resolved through further unofficial pay increases, but civil service agitation continued unabated following government refusals to agree to their latest demands, culminating in a weeklong strike in January. In the face of steadfast opposition from the foreign members of the Currency Committee, the new prime minister, Dimitrios Maximos, threatened to resign. Unwilling to risk the political repercussions, Gregory and Patterson felt forced

61. Ibid., 384–85, 413–15.
62. Ibid., 415–18.
63. Ibid., 419–23.

to back down, although they made their disapproval clear with a formal protest. The government chose to ignore both this and the later call for a pay freeze. Although substantial concessions placated the civil servants, periodic strikes by various occupational groups remained an almost permanent feature throughout the spring.[64]

While the struggle over civilian wages was played out in a series of demands and concessions, the parallel issue of payments to the armed forces took an equally serious turn away from the public gaze. The major initiative came neither from the government nor from below, but from the war ministry, which unilaterally awarded extra payments to army officers in early August. As with civilian wages, fierce opposition from the foreign members of the Currency Committee proved to no avail. Thereafter, pay raises within the armed forces took on familiar fictitious forms, masquerading as various special allowances and bonuses. With the escalation of fighting, military expenditure, consisting primarily of payments to personnel, was virtually the sole responsibility of the minister of war. As such it was effectively outside the control of even the ministry of finance, not to mention the Currency Committee.[65]

Loans to Agriculture

A final source of inflationary pressure arose from the granting of huge loans to farmers by the Agricultural Bank of Greece from the spring of 1946. Initially happy to approve individual requests for specific purposes, by October 1946 the Currency Committee became alarmed at the sheer scale of the bank's operations, which were putting vast sums of drachmae into circulation. The foreign members of the Currency Committee threatened to suspend approval for further loans until a full agricultural credit program was drawn up. A comprehensive program was duly presented, in which the bank announced its intention of issuing loans totaling 655 billion drachmae in the year up to September 1947. As this would have represented a net increase of note circulation amounting to 332 billion drachmae, compared to the existing circulation of 496 billion as at the end of August 1946, the inflationary potential was enormous. Following pressure from the Currency Committee, the program was modified, but up to the end of April 1947 its operations had added

64. Ibid., 423–27; DSR 868.515/2–447, Groves to the Secretary of State, February 4, 1947 (Enclosures: a) Gregory and Patterson to Maximos, January 28, 1947; b) Record of Meeting of Currency Committee, January 31, 1947); FO371/67013 R5587, Gregory and Patterson to Maximos, February 28, 1947.
65. Patterson, *Financial Experiences of Greece,* 386–91.

nearly 160 billion to note circulation. Even after the British withdrawal, credits to agriculture were to remain a serious threat to the stability of the drachma.[66]

Throughout the period of British involvement with Greece, the necessity of improving public finances and of maintaining stable wages formed a crucial part of the advice given to the government. Accordingly, the BEM devoted a huge amount of time to these issues, and their painstaking efforts finally bore some fruit, at least as regards the budget, where persistent pressure resulted in an unprecedented level of cooperation from Greek officials. The budget estimates of June 1946 were the first since liberation to be based on solid research rather than wishful thinking. The accuracy of the revenue predictions suggests a thoroughly realistic appraisal of potential yields and far greater efficiency in the assessment and collection of taxes. On the expenditure side, greater discipline was imposed, much waste was eliminated, and some degree of central control was established over the spending of individual departments. Compared with previous years, this represented a serious step forward.

However, despite undeniable achievements, the situation at the end of the 1946–1947 fiscal year was far from rosy. The budget deficit, although drastically reduced in relative terms, was still considerable. Moreover, the growing intensity of the civil war, coupled with the still enormous demands of reconstruction, ensured that a balanced budget was likely to remain as elusive as ever. British persistence had indeed instilled a large measure of efficiency and discipline into collecting revenues, but the institutional mechanisms of the London Agreement proved powerless to control government spending, as the foreign members of the Currency Committee found themselves either forced into reluctant acquiescence or completely circumvented when they attempted to oppose Greek demands for increased expenditure. Moreover, despite the claims of the BEM that they had wielded a restraining influence over the government on the wage issue, this influence was far from decisive.[67]

On the revenue side, public finances could not be put on a modern footing until the taxation system was completely overhauled. Given the enormity of the task, the British had mainly concentrated on refining the existing system and had not seriously challenged its regressive nature. Despite some new levies, both personal income and corporate profits still remained severely undertaxed by Western standards. The British recognized that little could be achieved until proper and honest

66. Ibid., 496–508.
67. FO371/67101 R2377, Interim Report of the British Economic Mission to Greece, January 31, 1947, 73–74.

accounting practices had been adopted by firms, and until the government possessed a cadre of suitably trained accountants and auditors. Moreover, the continued survival of many anachronistic taxes, particularly at the local level, unnecessarily complicated a system that was in clear need of simplification.[68]

Nevertheless, the relative success on the revenue side was more than neutralized by increases in expenditure. Although the Currency Committee vetoed "literally hundreds of . . . proposals" for additional spending, this stance was undermined by the frequent authorization of new outlays passed without the knowledge of either the Currency Committee or even the finance minister. In their understandable urge to complete reconstruction projects, ministries used up their funds with scant regard for budget estimates.[69] Less understandable was the disastrous government tendency to make continuous compromises on wages. Neither the provisional nor the elected government even attempted to draft a comprehensive wage policy, and their measures were essentially ad hoc panic responses to demands from below. The only major departure from previous practice was the manner in which concessions were granted. Formally bound by the promise to maintain the February wage structure, the government largely avoided open raises. Instead, it resorted to a series of underhanded measures, including free distribution of supplies and granting periodic bonuses, subsidies, and bogus loans. Whatever the outward appearance, the end effect was the same.

Developments on the expenditure side ensured that by the spring of 1947 public finances had returned to the precarious state of previous years. The budget was still heavily overreliant on external assistance: the international relief effort and the British financing of the armed forces, which were to cease at the end of 1946 and the end of March 1947 respectively. During the fiscal year 1946–1947, the sale of UNRRA supplies had yielded large profits for the first time, with returns exceeding distribution costs by 29 percent. If all UNRRA-related transactions are subtracted from the actual figures for 1946–1947, and if British military assistance (which did not figure in the budget) was added, revenue would cover a mere 43 percent of expenditure.[70] Even if the lag between the arrival of goods and their sale delayed the full shock of the post-UNRRA reality until well into 1947, it was clear that fresh problems were imminent. Moreover, although increased military spending had proved so damaging to public finances, the sums involved were merely the tip of the iceberg, as the British were still bearing most of the cost. By the spring of 1947 the govern-

68. Patterson, *Financial Experiences of Greece*, 363, 367, 398.
69. Ibid., 382, 391–93.
70. Percentages calculated from data in ibid., 352, 395–96.

ment faced grim choices: without massive increases in tax revenue, a tighter rein on expenditure, or renewed large-scale external assistance, the coming fiscal year would inevitably bring inflationary pressures as violent as those that had caused such chaos back in 1944–1945. However, an even more ominous danger was emerging: with the intensification of the civil war and the imminent cessation of British military funding, the price of resisting the Communist threat was clearly about to rise way beyond the means of the Greek state.

Anti-inflationary Policies

The practical consequences of government action or inaction and the resumption of credit operations caused an inevitable expansion in note circulation. As Table 5.1 demonstrates, between January 1946 and March 1947 advances to the state to cover current expenditure and loans to agriculture and industry contributed 43.7 percent and 53 percent respectively to a gross increase of 1,236.6 billion drachmae. However, this was largely neutralized by other factors, leaving a net increase of only 427.9 billion drachmae. Note circulation rose rapidly during the earlier part of the period—363.9 billion drachmae between January and August 1946—but the corresponding rise between September 1946 and March 1947 was only 64 billion drachmae, with some months actually witnessing a contraction (Table 5.2). Two policies slowed down this expansion: the sale of gold coins by the Bank of Greece, and the lifting of restrictions on commercial imports coupled with the unconditional issuing of foreign exchange to prospective importers. Both were designed to restore and maintain price stability by reducing inflationary pressure through the mopping up of surplus currency. Both were pursued with great vigor by successive Greek governments, in sharp contrast to their lukewarm reaction to British insistence on fiscal orthodoxy.

Gold Sales

The main aim of the gold policy was to stabilize the drachma by creating what amounted to an internal gold standard or rather sovereign standard, with the drachma firmly pegged to the sovereign. There was nothing new in this. As noted previously, the German occupiers had used gold sales as a last desperate means of keeping the economy afloat until the military situation improved. The National Bank of Greece had also sold sovereigns after liberation in late 1944. For most of 1945, while Varvaressos was in charge, no sales were permitted, but the practice

TABLE 5.1. The Drachma Note Issue (in billions of drachmae)

	From November 11, 1944, to		Jan. 31, 1946-March 31, 1947
	Jan. 31, 1946	March 31, 1947	
SOURCES OF INCREASE			
Advances to the State (a)	96.2	637.0	540.8
Payments to UNRRA (b)	2.6	33.1	30.5
Loans, Advances etc.	37.6	693.1	655.5
Net Purchases of Foreign Exchange (c)	33.9	-	-33.9
Miscellaneous	-	43.7	43.7
	170.3	1,406.9	1,236.6
SOURCES OF DECREASE			
Deposits of the State	12.3	77.0	64.7
Other Deposits	25.0	166.0	141.0
Proceeds of Sale of Gold	0.1	304.1	304.0
Net Sales of Foreign Exchange (c)	-	300.4	300.4
Miscellaneous	1.5	-	-1.5
Total New Drachma in Circulation	131.4	559.4	(428.0)
Old Drachma Circulation	-	-	-
Subsidiary Notes of the State	0.6	0.5	0.1
Total Currency in Circulation	132.0	559.9	(427.9)

Source: Patterson, *Financial Experiences of Greece*, 510.

(a) Payments by the Bank of Greece to the Greek state less receipts effected by the Bank of Greece for the account of the state.
(b) For internal administrative costs of the UNRRA, Greece Mission.
(c) Including BMA notes and foreign exchange on London representing advances to the British Forces in Greece.

TABLE 5.2. Note Circulation and Sovereign Rate, 1946-1947

Period	Drachmae (in billions)	Sovereign Rate
January 31, 1946	132.0	148.346
February	218.6	141,709
March	278.7	135,875
April	363.5	136.000
May	389.4	134.750
June	412.0	136.982
July	444.1	134.585
August	495.9	134.962
September	511.7	135.587
October	505.3	135.696
November	468.0	136.264
December	537.5	136.212
January 31, 1947	499.3	139.116
February	523.5	138.583
March	559.9	134.980

Source: Patterson, *Financial Experiences of Greece*, 508; Delivanis and Cleveland, *Greek Monetary Developments*, Statistical Appendix.

was resumed after his departure. From November 1945, substantial amounts of sovereigns were sold secretly in order to bolster the drachma. Having received a promise of five hundred thousand sovereigns from the Bank of England, the Sophoulis government felt able to pursue an open policy of massive gold sales to the public. On February 12 all internal gold transactions were legalized, and three days later a law was passed authorizing free sales of gold on the Athens Stock Exchange.[71]

The move achieved its immediate aim: the sovereign rate, which had peaked at 180,000 in December 1945, reached a new equilibrium around 135,000 before the end of February. This was bought dearly, as during the first two months the Bank of Greece sold 646,000 sovereigns, representing nearly 21 percent of the country's gold reserves. Despite this steady attrition of gold, the bank defended its actions at the end of April. Claiming that gold sales had steadied the sovereign rate, thus contributing to general price stability, the bank expressed confidence that the associated risks had been removed by the psychological changes resulting from the establishment of the country's first elected government. Believing that the policy was the best means of shoring up the drachma pending economic recovery and a return to budget equilibrium, and aware that the country's gold reserves would allow sales to be maintained at current rates for another six months, the bank committed itself to further sales as long as the favorable psychological climate remained unchanged.[72]

As noted previously, British hostility to gold sales was almost unanimous, with only one expert supporting the policy. Despite the rejection of his original plan, Grove continued to recommend the use of gold as a means of stabilizing the drachma.[73] However, he was isolated in this view, and all the other British officials, both in Whitehall and in Athens, were hostile to the idea. While they recognized that central bank intervention in the gold market was a valid instrument for correcting temporary exchange rate fluctuations, they were prepared to sanction sizable gold sales by the Greeks only as long as the latter were implementing the "energetic measures" they had undertaken to enact under the London Agreement. Reluctantly, they gave conditional support on the understanding that gold sales were merely a means to buy time for more fundamental economic reforms. Nevertheless, as it rapidly became clear that no drastic action was being taken on the central issues of public finances and a recovery plan, the policy seemed increasingly ludicrous. Whitehall had obvious misgivings about a measure that did nothing to

71. FO371/67101 R2377, Interim Report of the British Economic Mission to Greece, January 31, 1947, 95; FO371/58790 R1049, FO to Athens, Telegram no. 19 Camer, January 18, 1946; T236/1050, Siepmann to Tsouderos, January 23, 1946; Patterson, *Financial Experiences of Greece*, 536.

72. FO371/58728 R7072, Nixon to Waley, April 29, 1946.

73. T236/1051, Athens to FO, Telegram no. 88 Saving, February 27, 1946; FO371/58725 R4369, Note on the Financial Policy of Greece, E. Grove, March 8, 1946; FO371/67102 R10370, Final Report of the British Economic Mission to Greece, July 10, 1947, 11.

British gold sovereigns. Pictured are a number of the sovereign types issued during the
reigns of Victoria (1837–1901), Edward VII (1901–1910), and George V (1910–1936).
Swiss Bank Corporation, *Gold Coins* (1969).

address the "root causes" of the crisis and felt that it should be discontinued as soon
as possible.[74]

Gold sales forced the Greeks to seek new supplies of sovereigns from the British,
as immediate stocks became periodically depleted. Whitehall recognized they had
no powers to prevent the government from using its gold reserves in whichever way
it saw fit, but were both reluctant and occasionally unable to convert Greek bullion
into sovereigns to allow sales to continue. Nevertheless, in the absence of any other
source of stability, they were forced to acquiesce to continued demands for gold
coins. Three hundred thousand sovereigns were duly delivered in March. Whatever
their general views, the British were particularly anxious to avoid instability at any

74. FO371/58725, including R4092, Waley to Laskey, March 12, 1946 (Enclosure: Clark to Waley,
March 4, 1946); R4259, FO to Athens, Telegram no. 603, March 20, 1946. T236/1051, Siepman
to Waley, March 12, 1946; FO371/58727 R5625, Minute by Laskey, March 15, 1946; BE OV80/27,
Greece—Gold Sales, Memorandum by Sandberg, March 21, 1946.

cost in the period leading up to the election. They thus agreed to further requests to provide another five hundred thousand before the polling day.[75]

However, British tolerance finally ran out once it became clear that the Tsaldaris government, despite its popular mandate, was as content to rely on gold sales as its predecessors had been. Upon hearing that Stephanopoulos intended to continue the gold policy for a possible "four or five months" until confidence returned, Nixon retorted that the measure was merely an excuse to do nothing and would end in failure long before confidence could be restored. Dismissing gold sales as a "frail reed," he warned that no more sovereigns would be forthcoming and that public confidence would return only if the government presented a resolute budget. Despite this rebuff, the Greeks made yet another request for 750,000 sovereigns within days. This annoyed the British. Having accepted gold sales before the elections as a dangerous "palliative," they refused to condone further sales in the light of the government's failure to comply with the London Agreement. The Greeks were informed that the delivery of such an amount of sovereigns was logistically impossible, and added that in any case Whitehall regarded gold sales as "highly undesirable."[76]

Despite unanimous British mistrust of the gold policy, by the middle of May the BEM came to stress the need for flexibility. Recognizing that the Tsaldaris government had at least made an effort to understand the situation, and fearing that the termination of gold sales would prove immediately disastrous, they felt that the prospect of the 750,000 sovereigns should be used to gain leverage over the government, in that the sovereigns would be delivered only after the latter had taken irreversible steps to honor its promises. In the meantime, the British refusal had created considerable unease inside the government, which realized that its sovereign reserves would be exhausted within three weeks unless the volume of sales was curtailed. Afraid that such a move would simply create a new black market in gold, inevitably pushing up commodity prices, the Greeks could only reiterate the desperate need for further sovereigns. However, they did resolve to explore possibilities of limiting gold sales and promised to produce a new budget within days. Given these concessions, the BEM recommended to Whitehall that the possibility of further

75. FO371/58724, including R3855, Athens to FO, Telegram no. 515, March 12, 1946; R3856, Athens to Cairo, Telegram no. 33, March 12, 1946; FO371/58725, including R4160, Athens to FO, Telegram no. 52 Remac, March 15, 1946; R4259, Athens to FO, Telegram no. 586, March 18, 1946; FO to Athens, Telegram no. 603, March 20, 1946; R4321, Athens to FO, Telegram no. 593, March 19, 1946; R4345, FO to Athens, Telegram no. 660, March 28, 1946.

76. FO371/58728, including R7298, Nixon to Waley, April 26, 1946; Somerville Smith to Selby, May 4, 1946; FO to Athens, Telegram no. 935, May 7, 1946; R7297, Somerville Smith to Selby, May 7, 1946; Minute by Hayter, May 13, 1946; Bevin to Aghnides, May 15, 1946.

shipments of sovereigns should be suggested to the Greeks, as long as a "threatening attitude" was employed to force them to make further irreversible concessions on restricting gold sales and balancing the budget. At the Bank of England, Siepman bemoaned the "fatal policy," but recognized that the Treasury had little alternative but to agree. The Foreign Office sanctioned the conditional release of five hundred thousand sovereigns, on the strict understanding that the consignment would have to last until the budget was finally balanced.[77]

Expressing disappointment that so little had been done since the signing of the London Agreement, the BEM demanded concrete action on the budget and a drastic reduction of the volume of gold sales. This de facto ultimatum and the British insistence on "deeds not words" worried the government, which appeared "willing to agree to almost anything." Clifford Norton, who had replaced Leeper as British ambassador in March 1946, expressed confidence that more had been achieved in a few days than in the previous five months, and London duly authorized the shipment.[78]

However, British optimism was not borne out by subsequent events. The government did indeed attempt to reduce the volume of gold sales by discontinuing transactions on the Athens Stock Exchange. Sovereigns could be purchased only in person from a handful of counters at the Bank of Greece, which had sold gold coins directly to the public since early April. This created considerable inconvenience to buyers, as massive queues formed at the bank. However, such crude restrictions on supply rapidly proved ineffective in the face of undiminished demand. Within days a dual sovereign rate emerged, with open market prices rising up to 15 percent above the official selling rate. Blaming speculators for this fiasco, the government temporarily succeeded in stabilizing open market prices by reducing its official selling rate and resorting to large-scale secret sales. After a week an attempt to restrict purchases per customer triggered another rise in open market quotations, which was controlled only by increasing the volume of secret sales. Between June 5 and June 27, when this practice was discontinued, secret sales accounted for 84 percent of the 206,000 sovereigns sold to the public.[79]

77. FO371/58728, including R7238, Athens to FO, Telegram no. 1080, May 14, 1946; R7338, Athens to FO, Telegram no. 1090, May 15, 1946; R7309, Athens to FO, Telegram no. 1091, May 15, 1946; R7339, Athens to FO, Telegram no. 1092, May 15, 1946; FO to Athens, Telegram no. 1028, May 16, 1946; R7340, Athens to FO, Telegram no. 105 Remac, May 15, 1946; BE OV80/27, Minute by Siepman, May 16, 1946.

78. FO371/58729, including R7744, Athens to FO, Telegram no. 1174, May 22, 1946; R7785, Athens to FO, Telegram no. 1186, May 23, 1946; R7870, Athens to FO, Telegram no. 1196, May 25, 1946; R8069, FO to Athens, Telegram no. 94 Camer, May 31, 1946.

79. Patterson, *Financial Experiences of Greece,* 542–46.

Stability in the gold market returned from the end of June, as demand plunged temporarily. Far from reflecting any genuine return to confidence in the drachma, this situation arose from a combination of incidental and external factors. First, with the gradual decline of gold prices on the Alexandria market, arbitrage transactions by Athens dealers were no longer profitable. The process was reversed on a smaller scale as "significant" amounts of sovereigns were smuggled back into Greece from Egypt during the summer. Second, with the arrival of privately sponsored imports, traders were forced to cash in large numbers of gold coins to repay government credits. A third factor was seasonal: as demand for nonperishable goods customarily plummeted during the summer, many shopkeepers were obliged to part with sovereigns in order to meet current expenses. Finally, it was increasingly felt that the price stability achieved during the year had at last reestablished public faith in the drachma. As a result of all these factors, gold purchases by the Bank of Greece actually exceeded sales by a narrow margin between the end of June and August 21.[80]

Superficially, this period of relative calm suggested that the gold policy had indeed been correct. However, continued efforts by Greek officials to obtain gold coins on international markets during the summer indicated anxiety that massive sales would probably have to be resumed in the future.[81] In the absence of any fundamental improvement in the economy, confidence in the drachma remained acutely sensitive to both internal and external shocks. The inherent weakness of the "frail reed" was demonstrated by developments in late August, when growing international tensions triggered a new flight from the drachma. On August 22 the deterioration of relations between the United States and Yugoslavia created a massive increase in demand for sovereigns. By the next day the Bank of Greece was forced to resume secret sales to defend the drachma. Despite a temporary lull at the beginning of September following the plebiscite on the future of the king, continued anxiety over the international situation kept demand for gold at high levels. At the end of the month, armed clashes within Greece itself, coupled with instability inside the government, ensured that the clamor for gold and the prospect of further inflation assumed alarming proportions.[82]

---

80. Ibid., 546–48.

81. Without consulting the foreign members of the Currency Committee or any other British-sponsored body, the Greeks made a series of deals to convert remaining bullion into gold coins. Napoleons worth half a million sovereigns were bought from France, and a similar deal was negotiated with the Canadian government; FO371/58731 R12321, Somerville Smith to Selby, August 17, 1946.

82. Patterson, *Financial Experiences of Greece,* 548–52.

By the end of October, British anxieties over the dire state of Greek sovereign reserves led to demands that action should be taken to discourage public purchases
and suggested closer screening of all commercial credit applications in the belief
that drachma loans had been used primarily to buy gold. Given the political turmoil, nothing was done. In the meantime, gold sales continued to escalate, and an
immediate crisis was averted only by a delivery of 250,000 sovereigns from the Bank
of England in mid-November. By this time Gregory and Patterson had completely
lost patience, and declared that without the implementation of other economic
reforms gold sales were a waste of irreplaceable reserves and should be stopped as
quickly as possible. Despite these strictures and the increasingly desperate state of
the country's foreign exchange position, the Greeks were still reluctant to abandon
gold sales. Gregory noted a government tendency to assume that something would
"turn up" to remedy the situation, and a reluctance to accept the inevitable termination of the policy. Within days, Helmis could only repeat that stopping sales
would simply lead to new inflation.[83]

Demand for gold eased off following the imposition of restrictions on commercial credits, fueling perceptions that these had been routinely used to finance purchases of sovereigns. Temporary reductions in international tensions arising from
some conciliatory Soviet moves also helped calm the situation. As a result, gold
sales in December fell by 85 percent compared to the previous month. Once again,
the respite proved to be short-lived. By sanctioning the payment of a Christmas
bonus amounting to a month's salary for all employees, the government ensured
a massive cash injection into the economy. By the middle of January the surplus
drachmae had found their way to retailers and producers, who apparently lost no
time in converting them into sovereigns. In addition, the escalation of fighting in
northern Greece and continued instability within the government contributed to
a new flight from the drachma. This roused Gregory and Patterson into demanding that gold sales be stopped immediately before stocks were finally exhausted, in
order to maintain a last reserve to deal with any temporary crisis. In reply, Greek
ministers claimed that the current problems constituted precisely such a crisis and
vigorously refused to stop selling gold. When the Maximos government was finally
formed on January 24, Gregory and Patterson gave added urgency to their calls
to put an end to the policy. Nevertheless, within days the new ministers declared
that the sales must continue if a complete financial collapse was to be avoided. In

83. Ibid., 553–56; FO371/58806 R17388, Memorandum by Gregory and Patterson, November
25, 1946; FO371/58732 R16957, Athens to FO, Telegram no. 2481, November 22, 1946; FO371/58733
R17072, Athens to FO, Telegram no. 2497, November 25, 1946.

desperation, the government sought the return of a large consignment of bullion previously pledged to the Federal Reserve Bank of New York (FRBNY) as security for a $10 million loan. The foreign members of the Currency Committee warned that such a measure would be considered only if the government committed itself to a vigorous anti-inflationary program. Thus thwarted, the government exchanged almost the entire remainder of its bullion for ninety thousand sovereigns from India. By the end of February the Bank of Greece possessed less than twenty days' supply at the current rate of sales. With financial disaster looming, the situation changed dramatically as a result of the Truman speech on March 12. The confidence created by the prospect of extensive material and moral support from the world's greatest economic and military power provoked a dramatic turnaround in perceptions: within days massive queues reappeared at the Bank of Greece, with the difference that this time the rush was to sell rather than buy gold.[84]

Between February 1946 and the end of March 1947, net sales of sovereigns amounted to more than two million.[85] Thus, a perfectly valid instrument for correcting temporary fluctuations in international exchange rates came to be adopted as the primary mechanism for maintaining the internal value of the drachma. Furthermore, the longer this mechanism was employed, the more it assumed an air of permanence, with successive ministers appearing increasingly reluctant even to consider its dismantling. They frequently made references to buying time, claiming that an extended period of price stability would allow ample time for fundamental reforms to address the underlying problems of the economy. Moreover, by creating a de facto sovereign standard, they hoped to increase public willingness to hold on to drachmae and to help wean Greeks away from their obsession with gold.[86]

The gold policy achieved its primary objectives for long periods, as the sovereign rate remained relatively stable. Even the British opponents of the policy reluctantly admitted that convertibility into gold allowed the drachma, and thus the entire economy, to "function more smoothly."[87] Nevertheless, the measure was hardly an unqualified success. In terms of its secondary objectives, it failed miserably,

84. FO371/67013, including R1758, Athens to FO, Telegram no. 20 Remac, February 7, 1947; R2609, Gregory and Patterson to Maximos, February 7, 1947; FO371/67102 R10370, Final Report of the British Economic Mission to Greece, July 10, 1947, 26–27; Patterson, *Financial Experiences of Greece*, 557–64. For the FRBNY loan, see sections entitled "Commercial Imports," chap. 5, and "The Pursuit of U.S. Aid," chap. 6.

85. Patterson, *Financial Experiences of Greece*, 564.

86. FO371/67101 R2377, Interim Report of the British Economic Mission to Greece, January 31, 1947, 97.

87. Ibid., 96.

achieving little and creating fresh problems for the future. Moreover, this partial success was bought at a potentially high price.

Gold sales involved considerable risks, both immediate and long-term. By relying on a particularly scarce form of gold the government frequently courted disaster, being almost forced to suspend sales as its supply of sovereigns approached zero. However, the effect on overall reserves was much more serious. The policy proved an expensive means of shoring up the drachma, swallowing up almost all the country's gold stocks. By failing to create any incentive for this gold to return to its coffers, successive governments deprived themselves of considerable resources that could have been earmarked for other purposes. Few countries could afford to sacrifice such huge sums to so little effect.

British approval for gold sales was secured only on the assumption that a breathing space would be used effectively to address other chronic problems within the economy, a view with which American observers largely concurred.[88] Unfortunately, this assumption proved misplaced. Much to the disgust of the British, the gold policy came to dominate the thinking of successive ministers, almost to the exclusion of any other consideration. As little was done to implement any of the fundamental measures of the London Agreement, the British became exasperated as the time so dearly bought was being squandered, and resented the fact that gold was being "poured down the Athenian drain."[89] Throughout the period between the conclusion of the London Agreement and the announcement of the Truman Doctrine, the monotony of continuous British appeals that the Greeks should concentrate on areas such as public finances, and the equally insistent reply that gold sales had to continue, make depressing reading.

By creating an illusion of stability, gold sales reduced the urgency to undertake fundamental economic reforms. Apart from perpetuating past and current shortcomings, the policy also led to further negative consequences. Gold sales generated their own momentum independent of other economic factors. Once the possession of gold became a means of profit via arbitrage and resale, demand for sovereigns rose accordingly, giving rise to a vicious circle that made it increasingly difficult to terminate the policy. Rather than striking blows at the speculators, the government inadvertently provided a new source of handsome profits. Moreover, the attractiveness of gold as a source of both security and profit diverted resources away from productive investment, thus delaying economic recovery. Far from eradicating the

88. DSR 868.515/3–2847, Groves to the Secretary of State, March 28, 1947 (Enclosure: Gregory and Patterson to Maximos, March 10, 1947).

89. BE OV80/28, Lithiby to Waley, June 14, 1946.

gold mentality, the ease of acquiring gold coins actually weakened public willingness to hold on to drachmae. The Bank of Greece admitted that gold sales had
almost certainly undermined public confidence in the currency.[90] The longer the
policy was maintained, the more it reinforced the very mentality it sought to overcome.

Commercial Imports

Alongside gold sales, the liberalization of commercial imports formed the second
central pillar of Greek economic policy, both before and after the elections. Under
Varvaressos private imports had been strictly regulated by a licensing system, but
after his resignation these restrictions were gradually relaxed. Thus in September
1945 the Voulgaris government gave its approval to private imports of industrial
equipment, and certain concessions were made regarding private trade with the
United States. By October, the short-lived Damaskinos government was declaring that privately sponsored imports would relieve pressure on domestic prices,
but it was the succeeding Kanellopoulos government that embraced the liberalization of private trade as part of its economic program. Having made references to
the desirability of using the country's foreign exchange reserves to combat price
rises, it declared that although licensing requirements would still be maintained,
foreign exchange would be sold to finance all "useful imports." While recognizing that nonessential items could also be imported, this was discouraged by heavy
surcharges on currency sales for such goods.[91]

Shortly after the London Agreement was concluded, the Sophoulis government
scrapped most of the remaining controls on private imports. In a decree passed
on February 15, licensing requirements were removed for a wide range of essential commodities, for which foreign exchange could be purchased from the Bank
of Greece. The surcharges were also abolished, thereby removing the differentials
discouraging nonessential imports. In addition, prospective importers already possessing their own foreign exchange could ship in any items without restriction. By a
subsequent decree of February 23, importers were promised almost total freedom in
pricing and distribution of imported commodities, and were required to lodge only

90. DSR 868.516/4–1048, Smith to the Secretary of State, April 10, 1948 (Enclosure: Bank of
Greece, *The Economic Situation in Greece and the Bank of Greece in 1946: Report for the Years 1941,
1944, 1945, and 1946*, 47–48).

91. Patterson, *Financial Experiences of Greece*, 309–11. For the surcharges, see section entitled
"The British Response to the New Policy Vacuum," chap. 5.

moderate deposits, ranging from 30 to 60 percent, in support of foreign exchange applications.[92]

These liberalizing measures had significant effects, as private imports flourished and associated sales of foreign exchange attained alarming levels. In the first three months prospective importers bought foreign currency worth $61 million, with total sales reaching $109 million by the end of August. By this time, unrestricted private imports were threatening to exhaust the country's foreign exchange (sterling and dollars) and gold assets, which had amounted to only $193 million at the beginning of the year. During the first eight months of 1946, outflows of foreign exchange more than doubled receipts, leaving a deficit of $53 million. As almost all available dollar holdings had been either spent or committed for imports, the government approached the Federal Reserve Bank of New York (FRBNY), seeking credits worth $10 million against an equivalent amount of Greek bullion. Within weeks the government withdrew £4 million out of the £25 million currency cover account at the Bank of England to provide funds for further imports.[93]

In curious contrast to the close attention paid to gold sales, neither the BEM nor Nixon seemed unduly concerned about the consequences of the imports policy until the seriousness of the situation became apparent. As late as August the latter felt optimistic about the general state of the economy, and failed to mention the rapid depletion of the foreign exchange reserves. Patterson was more cautious. Although in late July he described the general economic situation as "gratifyingly quiet," he pointed out that the lack of import controls was hardly likely to help Greece's foreign exchange position. To be fair, the British themselves had demonstrated some earlier unease. Back in April the BEM had suggested drawing up a detailed summary of Greek commodity requirements in order to formulate a national import program, under which priority would be given only to the most essential goods. To administer the program, the BEM proposed the establishment of a new body, the Greek Commercial Cooperation (GCC). The government chose to ignore these recommendations, despite subsequent pressure on Tsaldaris.[94]

92. Ibid., 577–78; United Nations Relief and Rehabilitation Administration, *Foreign Trade in Greece,* 12–13.

93. United Nations Relief and Rehabilitation Administration, *Foreign Trade in Greece,* 13–14, 28–29; Patterson, *Financial Experiences of Greece,* 576, 580–82.

94. FO371/58731 R11916, Nixon to Somerville Smith, August 6, 1946; DSR 868.51/8–1246, Mac-Veagh to the Secretary of State, August 12, 1946 (Enclosure: The Financial Situation in Greece, G. Patterson, July 22, 1946); FO371/58798 R6681, English Text of a Memorandum Submitted in Greek by the British Economic Mission to His Excellency M. S. Stephanopoulos, Minister of

By October it was obvious that the country's freely accessible foreign exchange reserves would soon run out completely, but the Greeks and the foreign members of the Currency Committee held very different views as to the most appropriate solution. Tsaldaris desperately sought help from London and Washington in order to continue the existing policy. By contrast, Gregory and Patterson pressed for the abandonment of unrestricted imports in favor of a carefully planned import and export program. By the end of November, Greek officials had at least attempted to tackle the less urgent task of drawing up an import program for 1947. Based on unrealistic assumptions, this proved to be of doubtful value. Unable to complete the task, the officials handed over the whole problem to the foreign members of the Currency Committee. It was not until mid-December that the government finally heeded the calls to amend those aspects of the import policy that required immediate action. First, the Bank of Greece agreed to review all credit applications already approved but not yet taken up, canceling those that did not cover essential goods. Second, new applications for foreign exchange were made subject to the Currency Committee's approval. Within days, the final demise of the unrestricted imports policy was hastened by a new crisis when the government found itself unable to pay for two crucial import deals. From December 26, all future commodity imports required the approval of a newly created Special Imports Committee composed of representatives of several ministries but effectively controlled by the Bank of Greece. In February 1947 this body was reorganized with overall control passing to the ministry of national economy. In the same month, after consulting with Buell Maben, the UNRRA chief of mission in Greece, Gregory and Patterson suggested the creation of a centralized agency, to be known as the Foreign Trade Administration (FTA), to oversee both imports and exports. Although accepted in principle, nothing was done until the arrival of the American Mission of Aid to Greece (AMAG) later in the year.[95]

. . .

Coordination, April 1946; FO371/58727 R6718, Athens to FO, Telegram no. 978, May 2, 1946; FO371/58729 R7744, Athens to FO, Telegram no. 1174, May 22, 1946; T236/1053, Bevin to Norton, July 20, 1946 (Enclosure No. 8); FO371/58804 R13646, Report on the British Economic Mission and its Activities, C. Mackenzie, September 9, 1946, 24–25.

95. FO371/58732, including R16019, Athens to FO, Telegram no. 2369, November 2, 1946; R16020, Athens to FO, Telegram no. 2370, November 2, 1946; FO371/58806 R17388, Memorandum by Gregory and Patterson, November 25, 1946; Patterson, *Financial Experiences of Greece*, 583–95, 597–603; FO371/67013, including R2609, Gregory and Patterson to Maximos, February 7, 1947; R5587, Gregory and Patterson to Maximos, February 28, 1947; DSR 868.515/3–747, Groves to the Secretary of State, March 7, 1947 (Enclosure: Economic Program of Maximos Government). For the FTA, see section entitled "The American Mission for Aid to Greece," chap. 6.

The rationale behind the liberalization of commercial imports was twofold. Clearly, normal trade had to be resumed, particularly as UNRRA supplies alone could not satisfy all the country's needs, and were in any case planned to terminate after the end of 1946. Moreover, an additional inflow of imports onto the domestic market, through sales of foreign exchange, could complement gold sales as a mechanism for neutralizing inflationary pressures.[96] Although closely interrelated, the two sets of policy objectives were driven by partly divergent factors.

Much of the pressure to free imports from government controls appears to have come from within the Greek business community, which resented official interference in economic matters. Competent observers felt that this pressure was a major factor behind the partial lifting of restrictions in late 1945, and described the February measures as a total capitulation to the "demands of private importers." However, belief in the need for a more liberal policy was shared by not only leading financial experts but also many politicians, who saw commercial imports as an effective means to alleviate commodity shortages and inflationary pressures. After assuming power, the Tsaldaris government made firm pledges to allow private enterprise to flourish without hindrance.[97]

As indicated earlier, the British were initially more inclined to regard privately sponsored imports as a means to stimulate industrial recovery rather than as a way to combat inflation. However, this longer-term stance soon gave way to more immediate considerations. Before long the British were emphasizing the anti-inflationary aspect of increased imports, as the short-term expedience of maintaining price stability totally eclipsed the broader goals of economic recovery. Apart from the BEM recommendations in April, Bevin's original belief that imports should provide machinery rather than food was quietly forgotten, as the British were now highlighting the desirability of consumer goods to absorb surplus drachmae. Thus, in February both Grove and Nixon warned that stability could be ensured only if sizable quantities of imports arrived soon. In April Nixon interpreted the larger than expected volume of imports as a definite "sign of hope." Even in July, Waley claimed that Greece needed to import "as many consumer goods as possible," while in a similar tone, another Treasury official felt that "more energetic steps" had to be taken to increase imports. None of these statements indicated any particular

96. Patterson, *Financial Experiences of Greece*, 567–68.
97. United Nations Relief and Rehabilitation Administration, *Foreign Trade in Greece*, 12; HANBG 32 (file 38), Commercial and Industrial Chamber of Athens, Memorandum to T. Sophoulis, Prime Minister, January 15, 1946; Kasimatis, Οικονομικόν Πρόβλημα (*Economic Problem*), 79–82, 85–90; LBG/KVA/B5, Memorandum on the Greek Economic Situation, K. Varvaressos, August 2, 1946, 118, 133; Coombs, *Financial Policy in Greece*, 14.

concern about the country's foreign exchange reserves. Grove had even declared that the required imports could be secured only if foreign exchange was sold off "sufficiently quickly." In August, Nixon warned that the danger of inflation was "much more imminent" than the exhaustion of Greek foreign exchange reserves. Even as late as October, Norton singled out inflation as the most serious threat and suggested that "flooding" the country with "imported consumer good[s]" was the "only immediate remedy," ruefully adding that there was little likelihood that this would happen.[98]

Given the gradual shift away from the view that imports should assist economic recovery and toward an increasing emphasis on the anti-inflationary aspect, any assessment of the unrestricted imports policy has to take account of both aims by analyzing such factors as the composition and utility of imports, the contribution of customs duties to public finances, and effects on note circulation and commodity prices.

At first glance, aggregate trade figures suggest that private imports did consist mainly of "useful" goods, in accordance with the original justification of the policy. During 1946, agricultural products, textiles, clothing, and minerals accounted for more than half the total value of imports. When pressed to abandon the unrestricted imports policy, the government defended its record by claiming that practically all the acquired goods had been necessary. However, aggregate statistics give a misleading picture of the utility of private imports, and suggest less favorable interpretations. Neither raw materials nor capital goods materialized in large quantities, while many frivolous items were imported. At the same time, purchases of nonessential goods, including many which were considered luxuries in the immediate postwar period, were far from negligible. Thus, expenditure on machinery was almost equaled by that on coffee and perfumes. Indeed, in comparison with 1938–1939, imports of the latter commodities rose fourfold in 1946. Such figures question the credibility of government claims, and eyewitness descriptions of shops full of foreign luxuries in the midst of poverty-stricken Athens provoked scathing comments from observers.[99]

98. FO371/58724 R3352, Grove to Waley, February 20, 1946; T236/1050, Nixon to Waley, February 26, 1946; FO371/58727 R6383, Nixon to Waley, April 15, 1946; T236/1052, Visit of Greek Prime Minister, Memorandum by Somerville Smith, July 6, 1946; T236/1053, Notes of a Meeting Held in the Treasury, July 9, 1946; FO371/58731, including R11682, Nixon to Somerville Smith, August 7, 1946; R14873, Athens to FO, Telegram no. 2210, October 7, 1946.

99. FO371/58733 R17114, Athens to FO, Telegram no. 2498, November 26, 1946; Ministry of National Economy and General Statistical Service of Greece, *Bulletin Mensuel du Commerce Special de la Grece avec des Pays Etrangers, January–December 1947*; Politakis, *Greek Policies of Recovery*

Whatever the wider merits or demerits of the unrestricted imports policy, the generation of revenue in the form of customs duties was a positive consequence given the overall state of public finances. Levies on imports had played an important role in the prewar budget, contributing 26 percent of total revenue in 1938–1939. The budget estimates for 1946–1947 anticipated eighty-one billion drachmae from this source, amounting to 5.8 percent of total revenue. Thus, the actual yield of eighty billion drachmae almost entirely fulfilled expectations. However, this was not quite the success it appeared to be. Patterson felt that the returns could have been far higher. As noted previously, customs duties had been set at forty times the 1941 levels. As commodity prices had risen about eighty times in the same period, import duties were roughly 50 percent lower in real terms. Importers were thus able to enjoy substantial profits. Complaints about the inadequacy of the new tariffs led to the creation of a study group, but this achieved virtually nothing. Patterson was convinced that the government was extremely reluctant to raise customs duties to previous levels, fearing that the additional costs would simply be passed on to consumers in the form of higher prices.[100] Having allowed importers total freedom in pricing their commodities, the government thus sacrificed a source of considerable extra revenue, thereby diluting one of the few beneficial effects of a doubtful policy.

Given their composition and their meager contribution to public finances, it is extremely questionable whether commercial imports provided any significant basis for economic recovery. Competent observers outside the government made frequent allegations highlighting the more undesirable consequences of the policy. Thus many commodities were shipped in solely to provide high or fast profits. In addition, importers often hoarded their goods in the expectation that even higher profits could be obtained in the future. More seriously, foreign exchange, allocated for prospective imports, could be diverted for other purposes, offering both security against depreciation of the drachma and the possibility of capital export.[101] In a close parallel with gold sales, the indiscriminate allocation of foreign exchange created its own momentum, appearing to serve the interests of a small section of the population rather than the long-term needs of the country. Such a development could only aggravate existing social tensions and economic inequalities. As

---

and Reconstruction, 201–2; FO371/67017 R2882, Report of the British Parliamentary Delegation to Greece, October 10, 1946, 12; A. W. Sheppard, Britain in Greece: A Study in International Interference, 19–20.

100. Patterson, Financial Experiences of Greece, 372–74, 395, 398–99.

101. Ibid., 373, 398–99, 578–79, 595–96; United Nations Relief and Rehabilitation Administration, Foreign Trade in Greece, 15; Varvaressos, "Απολογισμός και Κριτική της Οικονομικής Πολιτικής" ("Review and Criticism of Recent Economic Policy"), 358.

Varvaressos contemptuously noted, the policy had created a "heaven" for private importers in one of the poorest countries of the world, where the "poverty of the masses" went hand in hand with the "impunity of profiteers."[102]

Before the full impact of the imports had become apparent, the government had attempted to launch a policy even more obliging to the holders of surplus wealth in Greece. In June the minister of finance indicated his intention of authorizing transfers of dollars by individuals to the United States, up to a maximum four hundred dollars per month. While attempts to sell sterling had created little damage because of the considerable unattractiveness of Britain's inconvertible currency, the free sale of dollars was an altogether more serious prospect. Patterson, alarmed that the measure would actively encourage capital flight, protested vigorously, and the matter was allowed to drop.[103]

As both the liberalization of commercial trade and the gold policy shared the aim of restoring and maintaining price stability by mopping up surplus drachmae, their effectiveness should be assessed in conjunction with each other. Given almost permanent budget deficits, periodical wage increases, and the granting of huge loans for agricultural and industrial recovery, note circulation continued its inexorable rise. However, as Table 5.1 indicates, between January 1946 and March 1947 nearly 60 percent of the increase was absorbed by the sale of foreign exchange and gold, with each contributing in roughly equal measure to this result. With increases in the stock of paper money thus moderated, private imports also played an obvious role in preventing a recurrence of inflation by reducing commodity shortages. Consequently, the period from the London Agreement to the announcement of the Truman Doctrine witnessed remarkable price stability, with none of the inflationary upheavals so characteristic of previous years. Between February and July 1946 the retail price index actually fell by almost 19 percent, and thereafter rose only 9 percent by February 1947.[104] In this respect, both policies made an undeniable contribution to short-term stability.

However, this stability was bought at a considerable cost. According to Patterson, the end result was nothing short of a "reckless and irresponsible dissipation" of the country's foreign exchange reserves. The limitations of both policies have been

102. LBG/KVA/B5, Memorandum on the Greek Economic Situation, K. Varvaressos, August 2, 1946, 131.

103. DSR 868.5151/6–2446, Rankin to the Secretary of State, June 24, 1946 (Enclosure: Memorandum by G. Patterson, June 19, 1946).

104. Percentages calculated from data in Patterson, *Financial Experiences of Greece,* 528.

succinctly put by Coombs: such huge outflows were feasible only if fundamental reforms were undertaken in the meantime, or if another country was willing to "underwrite the expense."[105] With the Greeks unwilling to act on the former, and the British both unwilling and unable to act on the latter, the policies were doomed to failure.

By using irreplaceable foreign exchange and bullion holdings to subsidize its current deficits, the government was sparing itself the painful task of balancing the budget by imposing heavier taxation and reducing expenditures, as recommended ad nauseam by the British. This evasion offered certain political advantages, removing the necessity to take on either the rich or the civil service, both of whom would have lost out had more orthodox measures been applied. However, in both economic and social terms the move proved disastrously shortsighted. By the beginning of 1947 the country faced an uncertain future, still having to confront the economic problems it had failed to solve since liberation, with the major difference that its foreign exchange reserves had been exhausted and the international relief effort had come to an end.

Such apparent shortsightedness on the part of the government suggests that the Greeks did indeed believe that others would underwrite their losses. Despite British exhortations that Greek problems would have to be solved internally rather than by a "fairy godmother" in the form of foreign aid or reparations, a point repeated time after time by Allied representatives, significant assistance from abroad was virtually taken for granted by the Greek political establishment. Patterson was convinced this was the case, although no senior Greek official would admit as much. However, leading politicians frequently referred to promises of Allied aid or reparations in public speeches, raising popular expectations that salvation would come from abroad. Varvaressos, by far the best informed and most perceptive of all Greek observers, complained derisively about such "demagoguery" with its assurances of "astronomical" sums that would shortly be flooding into the country.[106]

If the motives of the Greek government in launching the gold and imports policy appear to be relatively straightforward, British motives and perceptions in the same episode are more difficult to explain. Patterson, who subsequently regarded

105. Ibid., 511–12; Coombs, *Financial Policy in Greece,* 33–34.
106. FO371/58727 R6718, Athens to FO, Telegram no. 978, May 2, 1946; LBG/KVA/B5, Memorandum on the Greek Economic Situation, K. Varvaressos, August 2, 1946, 135; Patterson, *Financial Experiences of Greece,* 535; Varvaressos, "Απολογισμός και Κριτική της Οικονομικής Πολιτικής" ("Review and Criticism of Recent Economic Policy"), 346–47.

the depletion of Greek foreign exchange reserves as an unparalleled catastrophe, took frequent pains to emphasize British responsibility for the debacle.[107] As such a statement raises important questions regarding British priorities and the resulting quality of advice given to the Greeks, this issue requires careful attention.

As described previously, the British were always unenthusiastic about gold sales, and the measure was not embodied in the London Agreement. Nevertheless, fears about political instability ensured a reluctant acquiescence. Successive Greek demands for sovereigns invariably produced admonitions, repetitions of earlier advice, and attempts to gain leverage, but the requests were always granted in the end. Thus, British exasperation over the failure to act on more fundamental issues was tempered by the unwelcome realization that they could not force the government to abandon a policy it was determined to continue.

The imports policy was another Greek initiative that met with a doubtful response from British officials. However, on this point, the British can not be exonerated so easily. As already indicated, when the original Kasimatis proposals had been announced, Hill had warned that capital flight would be a likely outcome. During discussions over drachma convertibility in January 1946, the fear of capital flight had been paramount in the minds of Treasury and Bank of England officials. Despite Foreign Office assurances that watertight arrangements could prevent such an occurrence, the necessary safeguards were left to the discretion of the Athens government once it became clear that Tsouderos and Kartalis were equally opposed to luxury imports and capital flight. Thus the London Agreement sanctioned the provision of foreign exchange for prospective importers and approved capital transactions, embodying a compromise that Waley feared could produce the "worst of both worlds."[108]

As the British were becoming increasingly enthusiastic about the potential impact of imports on inflation, this consideration soon eclipsed both their original emphasis on imports as a source of capital goods and raw materials, and their fears of capital flight. Thus, the London Agreement made no reference to either the utility of imports or the prevention of capital flight. Moreover, neither issue was raised following the relaxation of restrictions and thus the abandonment of

107. Patterson, *Financial Experiences of Greece*, 568, 577.
108. T236/149, Minute by Waley, January 18, 1946; FO371/58790, including R1049, FO to Athens, Telegram no. 19 Camer, January 18, 1946; R1221, Record of a Meeting Held at 21 St. James's Square, January 17, 1946; FO371/58722 R1308, FO to Athens, Telegram no. 154, January 23, 1946. Waley had consistently warned about the dangers of capital flight. A year earlier he had criticized an idea from Zolotas to mop up purchasing power by selling sterling cheques, claiming that such a move would simply add to the dissipation of Greek external reserves to "all their present troubles"; FO371/48326 R1120, Waley to Hugh Jones, January 12, 1945.

safeguards in February. Although the BEM eventually made suggestions that a controlled import/export program should be adopted, this was not done until a third of the Greek foreign exchange reserves was committed for imports. In any case, the suggestion was allowed to drop, and it was not until the autumn, when the failure of the policy was becoming increasingly obvious, that the British became concerned. Even then, Bevin and others tended to emphasize the scale of remaining reserves rather than bemoan the huge sums that had already been dissipated.[109]

This apparent lack of concern about the fate of Greek foreign exchange reserves seems particularly curious when compared with the almost permanent pressure the British were applying to end the gold policy. To a large extent, this reflected the British view that imports represented a "better method of using foreign exchange reserves than selling gold."[110] However, even this does not entirely explain the contrasting British reactions to both policies. Thus, while they agonized over the latest statistics on gold sales, they did not seem unduly worried about the almost complete disappearance of the country's dollar holdings, preferring to take heart from the continued availability of the note cover account.

Possibly, the delayed British response partly reflects a lack of up-to-date information. Nixon complained that the BEM had not been furnished with the promised monthly statements on the foreign exchange position, and eventually they came to realize that foreign exchange sales were far larger than had previously been assumed. Nevertheless, this does not seem to excuse the readiness with which the British chose to ignore initial fears about commercial imports and capital flight, and their neglect in failing to ensure that adequate safeguards were maintained. Once the restrictions on imports were lifted, the only dissenting voice was that of Varvaressos, who was soon issuing dire, and ultimately accurate, predictions of the likely outcome of the policy.[111]

A final assessment of the British stance on the imports episode would have to concur with Patterson's strongly expressed and frequently repeated conviction that their preoccupation with suppressing inflation overrode every other consideration to an excessive degree.[112] Although not initially responsible for the liberal-

109. T236/1053, Nixon to Somerville Smith, September 20, 1946; FO371/58732, including R16020, FO to New York, Telegram no. 2058, November 11, 1946; R16478, FO to Athens, Telegram no. 2319, November 15, 1946; FO371/58733 R17258, Norton to Tsaldaris, November 22, 1946.

110. FO371/58728 R7339, FO to Athens, Telegram no. 1028, May 16, 1946.

111. FO371/58733 R17067, Nixon to Somerville Smith, November 4, 1946; LBG/KVA/B5, Memorandum on the Greek Economic Situation, K. Varvaressos, August 2, 1946, 141–49; Varvaressos, "Απολογισμός και Κριτική της Οικονομικής Πολιτικής" ("Review and Criticism of Recent Economic Policy"), 356–58.

112. Patterson, *Financial Experiences of Greece,* 334.

ization of commercial imports, the British embraced it with enthusiasm, eagerly forgetting not only earlier reservations but also their original emphasis on longer-term goals. Increasingly obsessed with the immediate threat of inflation, the British failed to prevent the very catastrophe that Hill and Waley had feared. Undoubtedly, they must therefore shoulder a large measure of blame for the foreign exchange debacle.

Economic Trends up to 1946

The period under review witnessed a gradual but uneven recovery of the Greek economy. The most satisfactory feature was the strong resurgence of certain branches of agriculture, notably the cultivation of cereals, fruits, and vegetables, which benefited from particularly favorable weather conditions. Grain productivity exceeded prewar levels as gross yields approached the 1935–1938 averages, while the output of potatoes far surpassed pre-1939 figures. However, yields of tobacco, raisins, and currants, previously the country's biggest export earners, reached only 66 and 42 percent of prewar levels respectively. In contrast to arable production, livestock farming did not recover so swiftly. Although by the end of 1946 stocks had registered satisfactory increases over the previous year, they were still roughly a third lower than in 1938. With the substantial capital assistance provided by UN-RRA deliveries of machinery, livestock, and seeds, and the generous provision of credit, agriculture was slowly returning to its prewar state, but much remained to be done.[113]

As with agriculture, industry also recovered unevenly. By December 1946, to-tal output was calculated at 67 percent of prewar levels. Substantial progress was achieved in the production of consumer goods, notably cotton and woolen textiles, and electrical appliances. Production of wine, spirits, cigarettes, and pharmaceutical items performed even better, approaching or exceeding prewar output. Electricity generation was actually 23 percent higher than in 1939. In contrast, the metal, wood, and leather-based industries were slow to revive, with the production of capital goods lagging behind other sectors. Equally disappointing was the meager

---

113. Coombs, *Financial Policy in Greece*, 19–21. The need to rejuvenate Greek agriculture by overcoming its traditional backwardness was emphasized by the report of an investigative mission from the UN Food and Agriculture Organization (FAO), which visited Greece in May 1946. This recommended several long-term measures to raise the efficiency and the diversity of production; *Report of the FAO Mission for Greece*.

progress of the extractive industries, which had played such an important role in the prewar balance of payments.[114]

Clearly, the pace and extent of recovery was far from encouraging. All sectors of the economy continued to suffer as a result of the economic and political problems facing the country. Budgetary restraints delayed badly needed reconstruction measures, particularly the rebuilding of the communications network. Consequently, transport costs remained excessive. The resulting high prices reduced the viability of producing many commodities, discouraging investment and expansion. In addition, the continuing instability of the drachma, reinforced by the psychological effects of political uncertainties, proved equally damaging by encouraging hoarding rather than processing of raw materials, and investment in gold or foreign exchange rather than in productive assets. The inability or unwillingness of successive governments to address the most urgent needs of the economy thus created additional obstacles hampering recovery. The failure to curb both the exorbitant profits charged by carriage firms and port facilities, as well as the high levels of local taxation imposed on the movement of all goods, ensured that huge cost increases would be borne by potential producers.

Even when action was taken to tackle various aspects of the crisis, it frequently proved counterproductive. While imports flourished during 1946, exports failed to recover to any similar degree. To a certain extent, this reflected the continuing problems of both the lost European markets and the reduced demand for goods such as tobacco and dried fruit, which were still regarded as "luxuries" in the prevailing circumstances. However, other factors helped retard the recovery of the export trade, particularly the exchange rate set in January 1946. As the year progressed, it became increasingly clear that the new rate overvalued the drachma, raising local costs and prices above world levels with detrimental consequences to potential exporters, and one attempt to find a way around this problem was the revival of barter trade and bilateral arrangements. Accordingly, several agreements were concluded with various European countries.[115] By August 1946 the slow recovery of exports led to divisions between the foreign members of the Currency Committee, which revealed significant differences of opinion on the exchange rate issue. Patterson, anxious about the damaging effects of the overvalued drachma on the export trade and thus the balance of payments, argued that a further devaluation was essential. Nixon, equally worried about the inflationary threat and the psychological blow

---

114. Coombs, *Financial Policy in Greece*, 21–24.
115. For details, see Patterson, *Financial Experiences of Greece*, 606–25.

that devaluation would bring, chose to disagree, claiming that internal prices would instead have to readjust to the existing exchange rate. Enjoying Whitehall's support for his views, Nixon refused to compromise, and there were no further adjustments during the period under review.[116]

Apart from the general problems affecting the whole economy, industry continued to be plagued by more specific problems, many of which remained unresolved at the end of the period under review. Several obstacles needed to be overcome before production could return to prewar levels. Some of these obstacles resulted from government policy, while others reflected deeper problems of the manufacturing sector, exacerbated by wartime neglect and the uncertainties of the immediate postwar years. The damaging effect of the overvalued drachma and delays in the reconstruction have already been noted. In addition, producers were seriously hit by the new tariffs of 1946, which made little distinction between raw materials and finished articles. Legislation governing relationships in the workplace also proved troublesome for employers. Although the obligation to retain redundant employees was finally abrogated in May 1946, the difficulties and costs of discharging surplus personnel ensured continued overmanning. The labor force created additional problems, with its continuing inefficiency and its high propensity to threaten or take strike action in support of wage claims.

A further obstacle adding to production costs was the credit policy of commercial banks. By early 1946, little had been done to overcome the deficiencies of the banking system. The Bank of Greece still had no meaningful control over the multitude of commercial banks, which remained overstaffed and unprofitable. Private banks retained obsolete organizational structures, with little distinction between commercial and investment functions. They were able to operate only with the assistance of loans from the Bank of Greece. Nevertheless, relations between the Bank of Greece and the private institutions were still strained. Moreover, the latter were fiercely competitive with each other and charged "usurious" interest rates, but lack of confidence in the drachma kept bank deposits at low levels.[117] Clearly, without streamlining and a total overhaul, the plethora of overstaffed, unsophisticated,

116. Ibid., 574; FO371/58731 R11682, Nixon to Somerville-Smith, August 7, 1946; BE OV80/28, Waley to Siepman, August 13, 1946; Siepman to Waley, August 14, 1946; DSR 868.5151/8–1946, MacVeagh to the Secretary of State, August 19, 1946 (Enclosure: The Drachma Exchange Rate, Memorandum by G. Patterson, August 12, 1946). A further negative consequence of the overvalued drachma was the bypassing of the Bank of Greece by dollar remittances: it was estimated that at least two thirds of the total went straight into black market channels; Patterson, *Financial Experiences of Greece*, 571.

117. Patterson, *Financial Experiences of Greece*, 435–36.

and virtually bankrupt credit institutions had little chance of facilitating economic recovery, particularly as interest rates remained prohibitively high.

Accordingly, the BEM investigated the issue and recommended several measures, especially the establishment of proper divisions between commercial and investment banking and the reduction of interest rates. The Currency Committee was also quick to involve itself with such matters, sought to obtain reliable estimates of the credit needs of industry, and assumed the right to refuse applications for commercial credit. From May onwards the Currency Committee continued to emphasize the need to reform the banking system and to formulate a credit policy, and during the following month a separate Banking Committee was established to examine the topic. Its report in August called for the imposition of maximum interest rates and proposed greater central bank control over the commercial banks to ensure that their credit policies were consistent with state guidelines, with the "usefulness" of the relevant economic activity the sole criterion for assessing loans. The suggestions aroused the concerted hostility of the private banks, which were particularly opposed both to interference from the Bank of Greece and the concept of a ceiling on interest rates. The recommendations also met with a negative response from industrialists, who regarded them as far too lenient toward the banks. By March 1947 it was clear that the main thrust of the proposals had been almost entirely ignored by the private institutions, and virtually nothing had been achieved to reform the banking system, which as a competent observer ruefully admitted, remained a "frightful muddle."[118]

Industry thus suffered from the self-interest of several groups and institutions: central and local government, labor, and the transport and banking sectors. Moreover, as the capital requirements and entry costs within manufacturing were so much higher than in any other sector, internal and external insecurities acted as an even more powerful disincentive to investment, as demonstrated by the meager levels of private imports of industrial equipment. In addition, the absence of a rigorous reconstruction program provided little stimulus for expansion, particularly in the capital goods industries. However, many of the problems hampering recovery were deeply rooted within industry itself. Most of the plants were small and inefficient, with much obsolete and poorly maintained capital equipment. Efficiency was further reduced by the absence of modern cost-accounting and record-keeping practices. The attitudes of the industrialists, particularly those who had resumed

118. FO371/58728 R6878, British Economic Mission to Greece, Fortnightly Report No. 6 (Appendix B: Memorandum Concerning Banking Submitted by the British Economic Mission to the Greek Currency Committee); FO371/67101 R2377, Interim Report of the British Economic Mission to Greece, January 31, 1947, 88; Patterson, *Financial Experiences of Greece,* 435–37, 445–65.

production, also complicated the picture. They were as much motivated by self-interest as any other group within the country. As the BEM ruefully noted, profit margins that seemed excessively high in Britain were condemned as scandalously low in Greece, and the mission's cost accountants encountered considerable hostility in their investigations. Furthermore, the monopolistic abuses that had caused such bitterness back in the previous year were still very much in evidence. Competent observers suspected that textile mill owners were acting as a cartel in late 1946, restricting output in order to maintain high prices, and it was hinted that such practices remained the norm rather than the exception.[119] As indicated earlier, these were not the only allegations of dishonesty leveled at the industrialists: other observers believed that despite complaints about credit difficulties, not only did many manufacturers find ample funds to invest in gold, but these funds themselves had been derived from commercial loans.

Thus by the first months of 1947, the Greek economy remained precarious and the country was in no position to fend for itself. According to the Bank of Greece's own figures for 1946, the balance of payments was still severely unfavorable, with current receipts amounting to less than a quarter of expenditures. The total current account deficit of $317 million was financed only by foreign aid ($224 million) and a loss of reserves ($96 million).[120] With the termination of the UNRRA program in the end of 1946, it was clear that huge amounts of foreign aid would be needed long into the future.

Conclusions

The period between January 1946 and March 1947 marked the culmination of British intervention in Greek affairs. While the political and strategic motives remained unchanged, the continuing economic turmoil forced Whitehall to launch an initiative designed specifically to address the country's major economic problems. This assumption of wider involvement found expression in the London Agreement. As already noted, this offered two new institutions, drachma convertibility into sterling and relatively scant material assistance. In the broadest terms, the package was clearly unsuccessful. By the end of the period the Greek economy

119. FO371/67101 R2377, Interim Report of the British Economic Mission to Greece, January 31, 1947, 30; FO371/58805, including R15662, Clark to Warner, October 18, 1946; R16045, Minutes of a Meeting Held at the Foreign Office to Discuss Certain Aspects of the British Economic Mission to Greece, October 30, 1946; Coombs, *Financial Policy in Greece*, 23.

120. Cited in Coombs, *Financial Policy in Greece*, 28.

was barely "working again," and in no way could the country be described as a "going concern." In many respects, the economy was still poised as precariously as it had been back in late 1945. In early 1947 the BEM admitted that the country's "fundamental problems" not only remained "unsolved," but were becoming even worse. In March, following the British decision to withdraw, the mission's head confessed it could no longer achieve anything useful in the circumstances. In April it became clear that the Americans had no interest in a joint economic mission with the British, and the BEM was formally terminated in July, although Gregory remained as a member of the Currency Committee.[121]

Such was the end of the London Agreement, which found few friends among either contemporary observers or later researchers, and has usually been dismissed as inadequate, irrelevant, or even harmful. However, oversimplistic judgments have blurred a complex picture, which deserves much more careful analysis, as a full explanation of the fate of the London Agreement is central to understanding the outcome of the entire British involvement in Greece. First, the performance of both institutions has to be considered carefully, taking into account the very different problems arising from their respective briefs. Second, the episode should not be judged simply in terms of British success or failure, as the Greek side of the equation also needs to be addressed. Third, the course of events must be appraised in the light of the widely held belief that the London Agreement imposed extraordinary levels of foreign control over Greece. Fourth, no assessment can be complete without an exploration of the internal dilemmas of the British, particularly the coherence of their motives. Finally, as critics have all too often focused on policies not actually forming part of the London Agreement, a separation of fact from fiction is necessary in order to distinguish between the consequences of British moves and those of successive governments in Athens.

The performance of the new institutions was decidedly mixed, as notable examples of success went hand in hand with equally notable failures. The most undeniable achievement of the BEM was the excellent work it undertook in the field of public finances, where unprecedented levels of revenue were both accurately predicted and collected. It also made less spectacular though tangible contributions to improvements in administration, distribution, and many other areas of the economy. The Currency Committee could claim much success in instilling a large degree of discipline into the government's monetary and credit policies, and was able to

---

121. FO371/67101, including R2377, Interim Report of the British Economic Mission to Greece, January 31, 1947, 2; R3893, Athens to FO, Telegram no. 685, March 22, 1947; R4616, Minute by Williams, April 11, 1947; Washington to FO, Telegram no. 2044, April 4, 1947; Rapp to Warner, April 5, 1947; R10309, Athens to FO, Telegram no. 1469, July 25, 1947.

force the abandonment of unrestricted imports. Nevertheless, the success of both bodies was limited. The Currency Committee could not prevent considerable rises in note circulation, wages, or government expenditure, and proved virtually powerless to stop the sale of gold. Even the BEM's finance section, which helped achieve so much in augmenting state revenue, shied away from the colossal task of overhauling the taxation system. Despite its strenuous efforts, the BEM felt that little had been accomplished compared with what remained to be done, and at best it had created "valuable breathing space" for the country.[122]

However, the overall success or otherwise of BEM/Currency Committee involvement in any particular area provides a merely partial picture of the reality, as it fails to take account of Greek actions and attitudes. As Whitehall appreciated from the start, the British never expected to be able to transform the country single-handedly, and understood that the effectiveness of the package depended upon both extensive cooperation and a vigorous response from the Greeks themselves. Thus Bevin candidly recognized that British assistance would prove valuable only if it formed part of a wider program to be devised and carried out by the Greeks.[123] Despite persistent British pressure, no such initiative was ever contemplated by any government in Athens.

Unlike the elusive program, cooperation from the Greek side was often forthcoming, although this was limited to a few specific areas. Thus the considerable success of Blackburn, the Inland Revenue adviser on taxation, reflected harmonious collaboration with the finance ministry. On the other hand, the experience of Macintosh, the Treasury adviser on public spending, was much more typical. His comparative ineffectiveness was largely indicative of government unwillingness to accept his advice. The contrasting fortunes of the two advisers, who both made equally strenuous efforts to grapple with their sides of the budget, illustrate the central problem of the BEM—and ultimately, of the entire British presence in Greece—in that Greek consent and cooperation formed one of the most fundamental restraints on what the British could achieve. Without such cooperation, good work could rarely be translated into good results.

The purely advisory role of the BEM rendered it powerless to ensure that its recommendations would be implemented. This was anticipated even before the first experts departed for Athens. Despite Greek promises that advice would be heeded, skeptical British officials doubted whether anything could be achieved unless the

122. FO371/67102 R10370, Final Report of the British Economic Mission to Greece, July 10, 1947, 10; FO371/67101 R2377, Interim Report of the British Economic Mission to Greece, January 31, 1947, 2.

123. FO371/58722 R1352, FO to Athens, Telegram no. 169, January 25, 1946.

advisers possessed "almost dictatorial" authority.[124] In the absence of any such power, the BEM recommendations could be simply ignored if deemed undesirable by the recipients.

The different legal status of the Currency Committee created a contrasting set of circumstances. Unlike the BEM, its statutory powers ensured that it could not be openly ignored. Instead, its presence forced various ministers into great feats of ingenuity in order to circumvent its power of veto. Thus, when the Currency Committee insisted that gold sales be stopped, the central bank simply switched to secret sales in the open market. As this soon became common knowledge, disgusted British officials wondered what the Greeks expected to gain from such "tricks," but were largely unable to prevent a repetition later in the year. A related example was the covert withdrawal of £4 million from the note cover account in order to finance more imports.[125] Similarly, ministers proved particularly creative in devising an entire arsenal of euphemisms to disguise wage increases. Finally, one of the most serious problems facing the Currency Committee was the government's failure to honor its promise to provide regular economic statistics. Without possessing complete and fully updated data, the foreign members of the Currency Committee frequently found themselves unable to ascertain the true picture of the economy. This often delayed or even prevented the formulation of an appropriate response, and proved particularly dangerous in the case of the foreign exchange crisis, where earlier action could have reduced the extent of the debacle.

The generally poor cooperation offered by the Greeks, coupled with the glaring inefficiencies of the administrative machinery, combined to further reduce the effectiveness of the BEM and the Currency Committee. Frustrated that appropriate action was not being taken, both became progressively involved with an ever-wider range of issues. This proved a time-consuming distraction from addressing the country's more strategic problems. Thus the BEM found itself unable to see the "wood for the trees," as it became increasingly bogged down in the minutiae of the Greek economy. Similarly, the Currency Committee took on additional responsibilities, to the point where its ultimate aims became obscured amidst a welter of

124. T236/1047, Davidson to Rowe-Dutton, November 19, 1945 (Enclosure: Note by Treasury Representative and Economic and Financial Advisers on Conditions to Be Exacted from Greek Government to Implement Mr. McNeil's Instructions, November 19, 1945).

125. FO371/58729 R9434, Somerville Smith to Forbes, June 24, 1946; FO371/58733 R17114, Athens to FO, Telegram no. 2498, November 26, 1946. As noted previously, withdrawal of foreign currency from the note cover account contravened a verbal promise rather than the statutory powers of the Currency Committee. Several authors were mistaken in failing to distinguish between the two; Politakis, *Greek Policies of Recovery and Reconstruction*, 175–76, 188; Kofas, *Intervention and Underdevelopment*, 44–45.

relatively minor items. As Patterson ruefully noted, processing credit applications took up a disproportionate amount of the Currency Committee's time. To have experts of the caliber of Nixon, Gregory, and Patterson dissipating their energies on such matters was clearly absurd, and the BEM bemoaned the fact that their "high qualifications" were "unable to find proper expression."[126]

Contemporary critics of the London Agreement resented what they saw as the imposition of foreign control over the Greek economy. Varvaressos, who had withheld his support partly for this reason, dismissed the dispatch of foreign experts as "contemptuous of elementary national dignity and pride." The Communist press denounced the convention as an act of "imperialism" and "colonialism," predicting a situation where ministers would be "ordered about" by their British advisers, and later portrayed the BEM as the "economic dictator of Greece." The American ambassador in Athens had gone even further, describing the British advisory role as a form of control more complete than that attempted by the German occupiers. Several later historians also chose to highlight this aspect of the London Agreement, with references to a new "form of foreign tutelage" and a "device" allowing "greater British control in Greece's internal affairs." Sfikas, for whom the "British approach to Greek politics" at this time displayed "some of the trappings of nineteenth century imperialism," interpreted the entire initiative as an attempt to restore the "British position in Greece by economic means." The strongest condemnation of all came from Tsoucalas, who completely misunderstood the whole episode. According to him, a "permanent" mission acted as an "independent ministry of economic affairs." Moreover, the country's "economic difficulties" were "exacerbated by the rigidity of British economic control."[127]

---

126. FO371/58697 R9619, British Economic Mission to Greece, Somerville Smith, June 27, 1946; Patterson, *Financial Experiences of Greece,* 436–37; FO371/67102 R10370, Final Report of the British Economic Mission to Greece, July 10, 1947, 4.

127. LBG/KVA/B4, Varvaressos to Tsouderos, January 16, 1946; LBG/KVA/B5, Memorandum on the Greek Economic Situation, K. Varvaressos, August 2, 1946, 127–28; S. G. Xydis, *Greece and the Great Powers 1944–1947: Prelude to the 'Truman Doctrine,'* 151; FO371/58722 R1373, Athens to FO, Telegram no. 198, January 26, 1946; FO371/58728 R6878, British Economic Mission to Greece, Fortnightly Report No. 6; FRUS, 1945: MacVeagh to the Secretary of State, November 16, 1945, vol. 8, 268–69; Hadziiossif, "Economic Stabilization and Political Unrest," 39; C. Hadziiossif, "Η Πολιτική Οικονομία της Μεταπολεμικής Ελλάδας, 1944–1996" ("The Political Economy of Postwar Greece, 1944–1996"), 295; Kofas, *Intervention and Underdevelopment,* 45; G. Margaritis, *Ιστορία του Ελληνικού Εμφυλίου Πολέμου 1946–1949* (History of the Greek Civil War 1946–1949), vol. 1, 122; Sfikas, *British Labour Government and the Greek Civil War,* 71–73; C. Tsoucalas, *The Greek Tragedy,* 95–96.

As the events of 1946–1947 demonstrate, such control was largely illusory. Successive Greek governments were usually able to pursue policies of their own choice despite the opposition of the two institutions. Notwithstanding the allusions to the dictatorial role of the BEM, the British clearly appreciated that it possessed nothing more than a "strong nuisance value."[128] Although the Currency Committee enjoyed considerable statutory powers, these were rarely exercised to any significant degree. While it did indeed possess the legal sanction to impinge upon the authority of the government and the central bank, it invariably found itself either circumvented or forced to give ground. As the compromises over wages demonstrate, the Currency Committee frequently refrained from asserting its authority when it wished to avoid the risk of political unrest, which would further undermine the government. Even when it did act decisively, as in the case of the foreign exchange crisis, the resulting measures placed no meaningful restraint on the government, which had already lost its freedom of action along with its foreign exchange reserves. Although the British occasionally felt that a tough stance could indeed force ministers to act, as in the sovereign crisis of May 1946, few tangible results were achieved. The apparent ease with which the Greeks successfully evaded most forms of economic interference makes a mockery of the claim of foreign control, and any comparison with the wartime experience is patently ludicrous. Far from acknowledging an unprecedented degree of control over the Greek economy, the British, who had consciously shied away from more drastic alternatives, were fully aware that the lack of any real means of coercion was a major constraint preventing the implementation of what they saw as appropriate solutions.

A further limitation on what the London Agreement could achieve derived from the fact that it failed to offer anything like the levels of material assistance the Greeks felt were necessary. The BEM was painfully aware that this failure weakened its influence and reduced Greek propensity to accept British advice. While the Greeks were prepared to recognize that Britain's own economic standing ruled out the possibility of substantial financial help, it was felt that the actual sums given were paltry. As Varvaressos remarked, in view of the extent of British involvement in the country, "she could have done more [. . .] than supply £500,000 worth of dyed battle-dresses and similar goods."[129]

128. FO371/58697 R9619, British Economic Mission to Greece, Somerville Smith, June 27, 1946.

129. FO371/58804 R13646, Report on the British Economic Mission and its Activities, C. Mackenzie, September 9, 1946, 4–5; LBG/KVA/B5, Memorandum on the Greek Economic Situation, K. Varvaressos, August 2, 1946, 124.

The lack of financial clout accompanying the London Agreement reflected Whitehall's consistent line that Britain was in no position to finance the reconstruction of Greece. Thus, British energies were devoted to making the most efficient use of existing resources, but within the BEM, divergent interpretations reflected the contrasting priorities of the individual sections. For the financial advisers, maintaining currency stability was all-important, and took precedence over the longer-term needs of reconstruction. This orthodox approach actively discouraged expenditure on reconstruction, fearing the inflationary effects of increased spending. However, several dissenting voices deplored this narrow view. Nixon, the chief proponent of fiscal orthodoxy, was criticized for his preoccupation with the budget to the exclusion of most other considerations. The transport experts warned that "reconstruction alone" could ensure economic progress and stressed the urgency of the task. Board called for a relaxation of restrictions on expenditure in order to place greater emphasis on the restoration of housing and transport links, claiming that in a "primitive country" such as Greece "there were worse things than a certain measure of inflation." Mackenzie, Board's successor as head of the industry section, indicated growing anxiety about Nixon's intransigence, stressing that additional outlays on reconstruction were vital if recovery was "not to be held up." Likewise, Lieutenant General Clark later regretted that the BEM had not advocated far greater expenditure on reconstruction, particularly on road repairs, even "at the cost of a bigger deficit and more inflation." These divergences of opinion reflect understandable differences of approach between the practically minded industrialists, transport specialists, and military men, and the economists. In the end, the economists invariably held sway, and the rest were forced to acknowledge that the "vicious circle" could not be broken as currency instability ruled out an extensive reconstruction program.[130]

It was precisely this preoccupation with the immediate stability of the drachma that led the British to support a measure which Patterson described as the most disastrous feature of 1946, namely the loss of foreign exchange as a result of the unrestricted imports policy. As already noted, initial British enthusiasm had concentrated on the positive developmental contribution of capital goods imports. The abandonment of this stance in favor of currency-absorbing imports of consumer goods can only demonstrate the ascendancy of fiscal orthodoxy, which remained

130. FO371/58697 R9619, British Economic Mission to Greece, Somerville Smith, June 27, 1946; FO371/67101, including R8888, Minute by McCarthy, July 29, 1947; R2377, Interim Report of the British Economic Mission to Greece, January 31, 1947, 55; FO371/58706 R13027, Minute by Sargent, August 30, 1946; FO371/58804 R13646, Report on the British Economic Mission and its Activities, C. Mackenzie, September 9, 1946, 18; FO371/67102 R11234, Reily to Warner, August 11, 1947.

unshaken despite the massive depletion of the foreign exchange reserves. Similar reasoning lay behind Nixon's refusal to contemplate a further devaluation of the drachma. Notwithstanding the likelihood that devaluation would help the country's balance of payments, Nixon feared that such a move could provoke another wave of inflation.

This approach was partly inevitable when a financial expert such as Nixon was preeminent among the British advisers in Greece. He not only held key positions in both the BEM and the Currency Committee but was also of much higher standing than Lieutenant General Clark. One observer wondered whether Nixon was not inadvertently distorting the entire policy of the BEM. The stance was modified once Nixon was replaced by Gregory. According to Patterson, who worked alongside both men, Gregory was far more flexible on many issues.[131] To a large extent, the conflict between fiscal orthodoxy and broader considerations was a recurrent theme, which reflected previous differences of priority between Whitehall's financial establishment and those responsible for British foreign policy. Although the Bevin initiative had suggested the ascendancy of the latter, the views of the former remained central to advice given to the Greeks.

The dilemma of the partly conflicting priorities was never fully resolved. For the British experts on the ground, this created additional confusion. As late as September 1946, halfway through the life of the BEM, one of its leading members claimed that its aims still required "clearer definition," as it was never apparent whether various Whitehall departments were "speaking [. . .] with one voice." Without a guiding framework to reconcile the concerns of its individual sections, it was hardly surprising that the BEM itself was unable to speak with "one voice."[132]

This lack of an overriding grand purpose illustrates the second major constraint on the economic goals of British policy in Greece: the lack of financial resources.

---

131. FO371/58715 R17040, Sargent to Norton, December 17, 1946; Patterson, *Financial Experiences of Greece*, 582–83.

132. FO371/58804 R13646, Report on the British Economic Mission and Its Activities, C. Mackenzie, September 9, 1946, 2; FO371/58697 R9619, British Economic Mission to Greece, Somerville Smith, June 27, 1946. A good example of the lack of a clear priority was the long-running disagreement over a solution to the problem of wage demands during the spring of 1947, when the Currency Committee, the BEM and Whitehall departments failed to reach a satisfactory compromise; FO371/67039 R4937, Athens to FO, Telegram no. 815, April 11, 1947; FO to Athens, Telegram no. 911, April 23, 1947; FO to Athens, Telegram no. 912, April 23, 1947; FO371/67013, including R5761, Reily to Warner, April 26, 1947; R6250, Athens to FO, Telegram no. 977, May 8, 1947; R6558, Draft Record of Meeting, Greek Wages Policy, May 14, 1947; R6250, Guildhaume Myrddin-Evans to Hampton, May 28, 1947; FO371/67014 R7500, Hampton to Guildhaume Myrddin-Evans, May 23, 1947.

Given Britain's own economic difficulties and the extent of its commitments else-where, the huge cost of maintaining the Greek armed forces meant that little could be spared to address the country's other problems. It was thus impossible to both preserve immediate currency stability and undertake extensive reconstruction in such a devastated country. The inability to fulfill both aims created an intractable dilemma: economic revival would be impossible unless confidence in the drachma could be rebuilt and sustained, while the pace of recovery would be delayed by any postponement of the reconstruction effort. The experience of 1946–1947 merely confirmed that Greece required huge levels of material assistance, far beyond what Britain was able to afford.

The two major constraints outlined above ensured that the London Agreement achieved far less than its initiators anticipated. Although its positive contribution was admittedly negligible, it is worth considering whether or to what extent it was responsible for the "calamitous" and "ruinous" consequences cited so forcefully by its critics.[133] The overall picture is much more complex than most authors ac-knowledge, as the latter have invariably failed to distinguish between three sep-arate factors: the provisions agreed in January 1946, the Greek interpretation of those provisions, and the subsequent measures initiated by the Greeks. As already demonstrated, the gold policy was not part of the London Agreement and was never supported by London, despite frequent claims to the contrary.[134] It was merely the continuation of similar policies carried out by several governments after liberation. Persistent attempts to force the cessation of gold sales foundered on the chronic British inability to impose their will on the Greeks. Similarly, although the sale of foreign exchange to finance imports did appear in the London Agreement, the actual implementation of this policy was hardly in accord with British intentions, even if the British must share responsibility for the consequences. Far from being foisted on the Greeks by the London Agreement, both policies were already be-ing proposed by the Kanellopoulos government back in late 1945, and must have appeared far more attractive alternatives than the British insistence on fiscal dis-cipline. The enthusiasm with which the first two policies were pursued contrasts strikingly with the reluctance to act on the budget.

Unfortunately, the combined effects of the gold and unrestricted imports poli-cies allowed speculation and capital flight to flourish as unproductive alternatives

---

133. Kofas, *Intervention and Underdevelopment*, 47–49.

134. Ibid., 47. A recent work repeats the claim that gold sales were a direct consequence of the London Agreement; see Hadziiossif, "Πολιτική Οικονομία της Μεταπολεμικής Ελλάδας" ("Political Economy of Postwar Greece"), 296.

to productive investment, protecting the assets of a narrow section of Greek society. Varvaressos had indeed criticized the London Agreement as an attempt to "win the confidence of vested interests" within the country.[135] However, rather than pandering to sectional interests, London anticipated that the package should promote general stability by restoring confidence in the currency. Such stability would offer a breathing space until the all-important elections and would encourage a gradual resumption of normal economic activity. As the British believed, the only alternative was chaos leading to a communist Greece. Whitehall had never intended that any "vested interests" should be able to exploit the terms of the London Agreement, but had little power to impose safeguards or prevent subsequent abuses of gold and foreign exchange. If the policies of 1946–1947 unduly benefited the rich, this was the result of actions and shortcomings of successive Greek governments rather than British design.

Whitehall had hoped to keep Greece afloat by means of a package that included neither the resources required to address the country's myriad problems, nor the powers to ensure that those problems would be addressed in a systematic manner. Greek disappointment with the material provisions reduced the levels of cooperation the British could expect to receive, and resentment over the sovereignty issue further diminished the effectiveness of the foreign advisers. The London Agreement was a compromise experiment involving a limited increase of commitment, and its failure hastened the British departure from Greece, as London recognized that its objectives were no longer tenable in view of the constraints. Unsatisfactory as this compromise was, it is difficult to see how these constraints could have been overcome. Any British attempt to acquire real executive power would probably have aroused universal condemnation, not only from the Greeks but also from Whitehall departments anxious to avoid such an apparently unlimited responsibility. Any British attempt to increase the levels of financial assistance to Greece would have provoked the wrath of a hostile Treasury and necessitated the downscaling of British commitments elsewhere. Given the relentlessly uninspiring record of successive governments in Athens, which made such poor use of the resources they were granted, it is hopelessly naive to assume that the country could have been magically restored had immense sums simply been handed over. The experience of 1946–1947 ensured that no external aid would be given unconditionally. Despite the failure of the London Agreement, its lessons were not lost on the Americans,

135. LBG/KVA/B5, Memorandum on the Greek Economic Situation, K. Varvaressos, August 2, 1946, 122.

who were soon to take over the British role in Greece. Careful to avoid the twin pitfalls that had plagued the British involvement, the United States proved willing to furnish the necessary resources to both maintain and rebuild the country, but only after assuming the powers to ensure compliance with their own view as to how those resources should be employed.

6

THE
AMERICAN AFTERMATH

§

I f Greece was a virtual British protectorate after its liberation from German occupation, then it came to rely exclusively on the United States by the middle
of 1947. At first, Washington ignored calls to become actively involved in Greece,
being reluctant to assist a country that demonstrated so little resolve to help itself and unwilling to be drawn into what it regarded as a British adventure. By the
spring of 1947, however, these twin misgivings were set aside as the United States
accepted sole responsibility for Greece, backed up by the promise of extensive assistance. This chapter outlines the gradual transition from initial detachment to
wholehearted espousal of the Greek cause, the evolution of American perceptions
of the crisis, and the practical results of the U.S. aid program during 1947–1948.

The International Dimension

Sharing the "Headache"

Although British statesmen took it for granted that Greece lay within their sphere
of interest, American moral and material support was accorded increasing significance as the price of extensive involvement in Greek affairs escalated without bringing even the appearance of a solution. Initially regarded as desirable, a greater role
for Washington came to be seen as crucial for Greece's survival, and also eventually
for allowing the British to reduce their own presence without sparking off a fresh
crisis.

The first manifestation of the British desire to formalize Anglo-American collaboration came with the establishment of the Military Liaison (ML) in 1944. This

was originally proposed as the Allied Military Liaison (AML), implying a degree of American responsibility for an area where no U.S. troops would be involved. As ML increased its role in Greece's internal affairs, the implication of American core-sponsibility could only be strengthened. Such efforts were not abandoned when UNRRA replaced ML. As early as March 1945 the British War Cabinet had approved Macmillan's proposal for a joint Anglo-American committee to coordinate advice on economic and financial matters, and suggested that everything should be done to promote collaboration between the two embassies in Athens.[1] As will be seen, the initiative was to prove abortive.

In contrast to this search for bilateral cooperation in Greece, the British reacted violently to Roosevelt's suggestion that a tripartite mission, including Soviet members, should be dispatched to advise on economic matters. Implacably opposed to any role for the Soviets, the British instead proposed a similar bipartite mission containing representatives of the Western Allies only. The idea lapsed with Roosevelt's death. Although raised one more time in cabinet discussions during the summer, there is no evidence that the proposal was actually put to the Americans.[2]

As the crisis dragged on, senior officials from international agencies joined the chorus calling for a more resolute stance from Washington. At first, such calls were more concerned with the U.S. relationship with UNRRA and with the nature of UNRRA's role in Greece. In the spring of 1945, Buell Maben, the UNRRA chief of mission in Greece, urged the U.S. State Department to consider "more active participation" in the relief effort on the ground and a "less standoffish policy" toward the Greek problem. In October the emphasis shifted when Commander Jackson, the senior deputy director of UNRRA, suggested that UNRRA should extend its functions to become the "controlling authority" in economic matters and that the major powers should strengthen their own direct involvement in the country. Washington was soon receiving more ominous signals. Lieutenant General Morgan, Supreme Allied Commander in the Mediterranean (SACMED), warned that Britain alone would not be able to shoulder the burden for assisting the Greeks indefinitely. He

---

1. Frazier, *Anglo-American Relations with Greece*, 60; FO371/48257 R3559, Discussion on Greece at the British Embassy, February 15, 1945; CAB65/49, War Cabinet 29 (45), March 12, 1945; FO371/48263 R5826, FO to Athens, Telegram no. 827, March 31, 1945; FO371/48265 R6627, Athens to FO, Telegram no. 962, April 11, 1945; FO371/48267 R7165, Athens to FO, Telegram no. 1026, April 20, 1945.

2. FO371/48264 R6104, Roosevelt to Churchill, Telegram no. 723, March 21, 1945; Churchill to Roosevelt, Telegram no. 932, April 3, 1945; FO371/48265 R6648, Roosevelt to Churchill, Telegram no. 737, April 8, 1945; CAB65/63, CM (45) 10, June 20, 1945.

insisted that the United States should assume some responsibility and that a wider long-term Allied policy should be devised for the country. Unless this was forthcoming, financial constraints might force Britain to withdraw completely from Greek affairs.[3]

British pressure was resumed in November following Bevin's new initiatives. At first the approach was indirect, with calls on Washington to endorse proposals for closer UNRRA involvement in Greece. Before long, more direct cooperation was sought. After proposing an economic mission, London indicated that it would "gladly consent" to American participation if Washington felt so inclined. The Foreign Office formally suggested that the two governments should "act together" in a "joint venture." Similarly, it recommended a joint declaration in support of the Athens government to boost confidence in the country.[4] These efforts brought little result. The joint declaration was not issued, and no significant American cooperation was secured.

The conclusion and subsequent enactment of the London Agreement took away much of the urgency of such attempts, and during the first half of 1946 British authorities do not appear to have exerted any direct pressure on Washington. In April an alleged remark by Secretary of State James Byrnes, stressing the importance of preventing a communist takeover of Greece, revived hopes in London that the Americans might be prepared to share the "financial burdens" of supporting the country. Officials in the Foreign Office and elsewhere, however, took the view that the Americans should not be pressed, particularly as their cooperation was being sought in other troubled areas such as Palestine. Thus plans for Bevin to discuss the issue at a meeting with Byrnes in June were dropped.[5]

Growing British anxieties about the costs of military aid to Greece, which came to a head during the late summer of 1946, brought new urgency to the search for American financial support. Hopes were rekindled by evidence of increasing American

3. FRUS, 1945: Memorandum by Baxter, May 5, 1945, vol. 8, 216–17; MacVeagh to the Secretary of State, June 18, 1945, vol. 8, 224–28; Jackson to Lehman, October 27, 1945, vol. 8, 246–47; Jackson to Lehman, October 28, 1945, vol. 8, 247–50; Jackson to Lehman, October 27, 1945, vol. 8, 250–51; Kirk to the Secretary of State, November 2, 1945, vol. 8, 251–52; Kirk to the Secretary of State, November 4, 1945, vol. 8, 253–55.

4. FRUS, 1945: Bevin to the Secretary of State, September 29, 1945, vol. 8, 238–40; MacVeagh to the Secretary of State, November 15, 1945, vol. 8, 267–68; The British Embassy to the Department of State (Aide-Mémoire), December 3, 1945, vol. 8, 276–77; The British Embassy to the Department of State (Memorandum), December 5, 1945, vol. 8, 277–80; FO371/48285 R19826, McNeil to Kanellopoulos, November 14, 1945; FO371/48416 R20388, FO to Washington, Telegram no. 12081, December 1, 1945; FO371/48338 R20345, FO to Washington, Telegram no. 12159, December 4, 1945.

5. Frazier, *Anglo-American Relations with Greece*, 108–9.

fears over the communist threat, the resulting offer to supplement British military assistance, and the decision to send the Porter Mission to Greece. Nevertheless, as Frazier points out, subsequent British approaches to Washington were confused and often misleading, reflecting the internal disagreements between Dalton and other policy makers in Whitehall. Lack of consensus within the cabinet interfered with formulating concrete overtures toward the Americans. Thus in October, when Bevin proposed that a large reconstruction loan could be secured from Washington if the British maintained their military payments until the end of 1947, the idea was vetoed by Dalton, who refused to retreat from his opposition to any extension of British subsidies beyond March 1947. Similarly, a fresh Foreign Office initiative in December, pledging large sums for the Greek armed forces on condition that the Americans granted similar credits for civilian purposes, was dropped once it became clear that Dalton would not agree.[6]

The full extent of the disagreements within the cabinet was not revealed to the Americans. As late as the end of January 1947, U.S. embassy officials in London were told that some British aid would continue beyond March. In early February the British ambassador in Washington was instructed to tell George Marshall, who had replaced Byrnes as secretary of state, that £70-£80 million would be needed in Greece in the nine months after March, and that the United States would have to provide the "lion's share" of the amount. This implied a partnership rather than a cessation of the British contribution. It was only on February 19 that the Foreign Office informed the Americans of its clashes with the Treasury and confessed that it was not confident of "gaining its point." Two days later the British communicated their decision to terminate all payments at the end of March. Pending the arrival of the aid promised by Truman, the British agreed to provide interim assistance worth up to £6 million over the following three months.[7]

The confused events of early 1947 culminated in success for Britain's long-running effort to secure some degree of American involvement in Greece. As early as 1945, a senior Foreign Office official admitted that the British had "always wished to get the Americans to help [. . .] in Greece." A year later a colleague expressed similar sentiments, confessing an anxiety to "interest the Americans in Greece in every possible way."[8] Toward the end of the period, this desire was complicated by

6. Ibid., 110–12.

7. Ibid., chap. 8.

8. FO371/48284 R18735, Minute by Hayter, November 6, 1945; FO371/58732 R16478, FO to Athens, Telegram no. 2319, November 15, 1946.

endless internal disagreements over the wisdom of extending the British commit-ment to Greece. The resulting uncertainties not only made it more difficult to agree on a coherent approach to Washington but also ensured that the Americans were given extremely short notice of the final decision to terminate all aid.

Given the clear British desire to secure American help, the apparent ambivalence with which the aim was pursued may seem puzzling. The probable explanation is that British statesmen were unwilling to make a direct request for substantial economic assistance for Greece, fearing it would be taken as a tacit admission that Britain's role as a major international player was over. It seems likely that they hoped the Americans, by participating in various collaborative committees and missions, would themselves come to the conclusion that their material support was required. Thus the British deliberately refrained from asking for aid until their economic difficulties seemed to outweigh political loss of face. The associated question—to what extent the British feared that American involvement in Greece would sup-plant their own influence in the country—is much more difficult to answer. At first, it is likely that material and moral backing from the Americans was seen as strengthening rather than weakening Britain's position in Greece. However, as the policy dragged on with limited success and maintaining British control became less and less feasible, an American-dominated Greece must have seemed infinitely preferable to the prospect of yet another Soviet satellite.

Contrasting Fears

Initially, the American response to British calls for closer involvement in Greece was cool. This partially reflected the fact that Washington felt it had no major in-terests in Greece, but more significantly it was the result of American suspicion of British motives. American hostility to the creation of spheres of influence in the postwar world was combined with a long-standing distrust of Britain as an imperial power devoted to the maintenance of an exclusive imperial bloc. On both counts, the percentages agreement with Stalin could only heighten Washington's distrust. With the outbreak of fighting in Athens in December 1944, the Americans objected to what they saw as a flagrant British policy to impose a client government in Athens against the wishes of the Greek people. Senior U.S. naval officers attempted to prevent the British from using U.S. ships to transport military supplies to Greece, while MacVeagh went to great lengths to demonstrate his neutrality in the conflict. Much publicity was given to a statement from Secretary of State Edward Stettinius expressing a hope that the "newly liberated countries" should not be subjected to "outside interference." Privately, he told the British ambassador in Washington that "British actions in the Mediterranean" amounted to "neo-colonialism."[9]

Given such tensions, the Americans were anxious to avoid any close association with British activities in Greece, and persistently rebuffed the invitation to enter into the formal bilateral arrangements sought by London. They thus refused to provide combat troops for the liberation of Greece, and agreed to participate only in the subsequent ML relief effort. Formal collaboration with the British was limited to relatively minor bodies such as the Joint Transportation Facilities Mission Greece (JTFMG). With the disbanding of ML, American distrust toward the British resulted in a hostile response to the proposals of new advisory bodies. MacVeagh suspected that the British were deliberately creating a false "impression of joint responsibility" and feared that the international relief effort would become an "instrument of British policy." Accordingly, he rejected the idea of an Anglo-American committee, and U.S. advisers in Athens were instructed not to participate at any formal meetings of the Joint Policy Committee (JPC). Such reticence did not rule out participation in a wider setup, as demonstrated by Roosevelt's suggestion of a tripartite mission. Although the proposal was dropped following Churchill's refusal, Roosevelt remained opposed to any bilateral Anglo-American arrangement, but stipulated that some support and advice would continue to be provided directly to Greece.[10]

This basic stance survived the change of administrations from Roosevelt to Truman. During the crisis of late 1945, when MacVeagh and Maben urgently appealed for closer attention to Greek affairs, Washington remained more concerned about maintaining its independent role.[11] Despite British calls for coordinated declarations and a "joint venture," the Americans refused to participate in the proposed economic mission and their representatives attended the London talks as observers only. Similarly, when U.S. authorities finally agreed to participate in the Currency Committee, it was only on condition that the U.S. member should act as a private

9. Frazier, *Anglo-American Relations with Greece,* chap. 5.

10. Ibid., 60–62; M. M. Amen, *American Foreign Policy in Greece 1944–1949: Economic, Military, and Institutional Aspects,* 61–63; FRUS, 1945: MacVeagh to the Secretary of State, March 14, 1945, vol. 8, 202–3; MacVeagh to the Secretary of State, April 21, 1945, vol. 8, 211–12; MacVeagh to the Secretary of State, June 18, 1945, vol. 8, 224–28; T236/1044, Hill to Waley, April 11, 1945; FO371/48264 R6104, Roosevelt to Churchill, Telegram no. 723, March 21, 1945; Churchill to Roosevelt, Telegram no. 932, April 3, 1945; FO371/48265 R6648, Roosevelt to Churchill, Telegram no. 737, April 8, 1945.

11. FRUS, 1945: MacVeagh to the Secretary of State, November 5, 1945, vol. 8, 256–57; MacVeagh to the Secretary of State, December 15, 1945, vol. 8, 284–88; FRUS, 1946: MacVeagh to the Secretary of State, January 11, 1946, vol. 7, 91–92. For Maben's advice, see DSR 868.50/1–1046, Hawkins and Taylor to the Secretaries of State and Treasury, Telegram no. 328, January 10, 1946.

individual rather than as a representative of the U.S. government, thus absolving Washington from formal responsibility for the Currency Committee's decisions. Instead of associating with the London Agreement, the United States indicated a willingness to send its own experts if requested.[12]

Such decisions demonstrated Washington's continued determination to steer clear of formal collaboration with the British, or as the latter saw it, to operate on "parallel lines." There was still little apparent urgency in Washington over Greek affairs. Patterson was not appointed until May 1946, and discussions over the dispatch of individual experts dragged on interminably until the matter was eventually dropped. As late as August, MacVeagh could quote Patterson's report that despite the many underlying problems, the country's immediate financial situation remained "gratifyingly quiet."[13] Within weeks, such cautious optimism was replaced by a growing sense of anxiety, originating not so much from any reassessment of the economic situation but instead from increasing fears arising from regional and international developments. Growing perceptions of the communist threat both within and outside Greece proved crucial in reshaping American attitudes. With wider issues at stake, reservations about becoming associated with the British rapidly became irrelevant.

At the end of September Byrnes privately expressed his anxiety about recent world developments, particularly the attitude of the Soviet Union. He emphasized the necessity of offering American support to Turkey and Greece. Such fears were fueled by dire warnings from MacVeagh, who stressed Greece's vulnerability in the face of overwhelming hostile forces and the risk that it would be overrun almost immediately if the British withdrew their military presence. Within weeks, the State Department cited a long list of anti-Greek activities undertaken by Moscow and its satellites to demonstrate that Greece and Turkey constituted the "sole obstacle to Soviet domination of the Eastern Mediterranean." It recommended that Washington should announce its readiness to "take suitable measures" to safeguard the "territorial and political integrity of Greece," including diplomatic and moral support, and practical assistance in the form of credits and military equipment.[14]

12. FRUS, 1945: MacVeagh to the Secretary of State, November 16, 1945, vol. 8, 268–69; The British Embassy to the Department of State (Aide-Mémoire), December 3, 1945, vol. 8, 276–77; Acheson to MacVeagh, December 17, 1945, vol. 8, 288–89; Acheson to Winant, December 27, 1945, vol. 8, 297; FRUS, 1946: Acheson to Winant, January 10, 1946, vol. 7, 89–90; The Secretary of State to Tsouderos (Memorandum), January 15, 1946, vol. 7, 95–96.

13. T236/1048, Washington to FO, Telegram no. 8544, December 22, 1945; FRUS, 1946: MacVeagh to the Secretary of State, August 12, 1946, vol. 7, 188–89.

14. FRUS, 1946: The Secretary of State to Clayton, September 24, 1946, vol. 7, 223–24; MacVeagh to the Secretary of State, September 30, 1946, vol. 7, 226–27; Memorandum by Henderson,

At first, the shift of emphasis did not imply the immediate adoption of any major commitment to Greece. In early November, Washington agreed to assume responsibility for economic assistance, while London would continue to supply military materiel. Nevertheless, there was still no overwhelming sense of urgency. Decisions on economic aid were to await the findings of an investigative mission, to be dispatched to Athens, partly to identify projects requiring American credits. The State Department declared that it would furnish only such equipment as the Greeks were unable to obtain from the British.[15]

During subsequent months, this relatively leisurely approach disappeared as Washington became increasingly preoccupied with the threat posed by the country's northern neighbors, as demonstrated by countless references to border incidents and political and economic instability in official exchanges. By early 1947 the tone of dispatches from U.S. personnel in Athens had become positively alarmist. MacVeagh pointed out that the combination of external pressure and internal unrest was likely to lead to revolution and "Soviet control," while Mark Ethridge, the U.S. representative on the UN Commission of Investigation, compared Greece to a "ripe plum" likely to fall into Soviet hands within weeks.[16]

Responding to these panic-laden signals, Washington moved closer toward concrete action. On February 21 Undersecretary of State Dean Acheson warned of the consequences of allowing Greece to fall under Soviet domination simply through the "lack of adequate support" from the United States and Britain. Aware that Britain was unable to supply necessary military equipment on schedule, he recommended that the United States extend its own assistance in that field. Above all, he urged that a special bill be rushed through Congress authorizing a direct loan to Greece.[17] Given the sense of urgency already pervading Washington, the receipt

---

October 21, 1946, vol. 7, 240; Memorandum Prepared in the Office of Near Eastern and African Affairs (Memorandum Regarding Greece), October 21, 1946, vol. 7, 240–45.

15. A full account of the mission is given later in this chapter. FRUS, 1947: Memorandum by Acheson to the Secretary of State, February 21, 1947, vol. 5, 29–31: FRUS, 1946: Memorandum by Baxter to Henderson, October 29, 1946, vol. 7, 247–49; Memorandum Prepared in the Office of Near Eastern and African Affairs (Memorandum Regarding Greece), October 21, 1946, vol. 7, 240–45; Memorandum by Hilldring to Acheson, October 29, 1946, vol. 7, 255; Acheson to MacVeagh, November 8, 1946, vol. 7, 262–63.

16. FRUS, 1946: vol. 7, 264–88; FRUS, 1947: MacVeagh to the Secretary of State, February 11, 1947, vol. 5, 16–17; Ethridge to the Secretary of State, February 17, 1947, vol. 5, 23–25. The Commission of Investigation was established by the UN Security Council on December 19, 1946, to examine alleged frontier violations by insurgent forces said to be using the territories of Yugoslavia, Albania, and Bulgaria as operational bases; see FRUS, 1946: Johnson to the Secretary of State, December 19, 1946, vol. 7, 284–85.

17. FRUS, 1947: Memorandum by Acheson to the Secretary of State, February 21, 1947, vol. 5, 29–31.

of the British note on February 21 had an immediate effect. Within weeks the Truman Doctrine had been articulated, and the way was open for the policy of all-out containment of Soviet communism and the accompanying ideological crusade.

The United States and Greece

If international developments largely explain the motives behind the escalation of American involvement in Greece, the story is only complete with the consideration of two other fundamental but less-publicized issues: the relentless pursuit of U.S. aid undertaken by successive governments in Athens after 1944, and the evolution of American perceptions of Greece's economic problems. The following section begins by describing the Greek efforts to secure financial assistance, and then charts the gradual change of heart within Washington, from an initial reluctance to go beyond a limited degree of help to a willingness to commit extensive resources in an all-out effort to achieve a combination of political, military, and economic objectives.

The Pursuit of U.S. Aid

The British were far from alone in their efforts to persuade the Americans to show greater interest in Greek affairs after 1944. The pressure from the Greeks themselves was even more intense and persistent. During World War II and in its aftermath, Greece's pursuit of American credits was almost relentless. As early as 1942 the government-in-exile sought a loan to finance its international obligations, but the story began in earnest shortly before liberation. In July 1944, Varvaressos formally applied for a loan of $25 million to cover the government's day-to-day expenses. When this was refused, for reasons that will soon be discussed, the matter dragged on interminably. The request was repeated several times over the following months, with an additional emphasis on the need to support stabilization, secure essential imports, and promote industrial recovery.[18]

The Greeks never allowed the matter to drop from the agenda, as demonstrated by the stance of Sideris in early 1945, but the next major offensive came with Varvaressos' return to prominence. He had brought up the question of U.S. aid during his

18. FRUS, 1944: Memorandum by Stettinius, July 28, 1944, vol. 5, 216–20; Memorandum by Kohler, August 5, 1944, vol. 5, 220–22; Memorandum by Miller, October 28, 1944, vol. 5, 223–24; Stettinius to MacVeagh, November 7, 1944, vol. 5, 224–26; DSR 868.51/9–844, Memorandum by Kohler, September 8, 1944; DSR 868.51/10–3044, Memorandum by Miller, October 30, 1944; DSR 868.51/11–244, Memorandum, November 2, 1944.

visit to Washington in the spring of 1945. Some success was achieved in July when the Foreign Economic Administration (FEA) agreed to provide short-term credits up to the value of $20 million. However, this was not the end of the matter. In August, with his program running into difficulties, Varvaressos gave wide publicity to a fresh application to the Ex-Im Bank for a massive loan worth $250 million. Following indications that the Americans felt this was excessive, a more modest request for $25 million was made in September. After lengthy delays, the smaller sum was finally approved in November, but not announced until January 1946.[19]

Following this breakthrough, the stakes were raised as the Greeks sought far larger amounts to finance reconstruction. From the spring of 1946 this campaign was conducted not by the government in Athens, but through the facade of the Greek Reconstruction Claims Committee (GRCC). In a direct address to Truman the GRCC president, Sophocles Venizelos, complained that the former occupying powers had done nothing to make amends for the wartime destruction, and that his country was in no state to finance economic recovery from its own resources. He therefore asked that Greece be suitably rewarded for the sacrifices it had made, and demanded either an American loan to cover its reconstruction costs, to be serviced by the "invaders," or that the Allies themselves foot the bill. He warned that unless either step was taken Greece would "remain in ruins."[20]

Although this emotional appeal was ignored, the offensive was maintained. An attempt by Tsaldaris to press the issue with a visit to Washington was abandoned after the State Department discouraged the trip. Instead, senior Greek officials raised the matter with their American counterparts at the Paris Conference on Reparations in early July. They presented a detailed breakdown of the capital requirements for Greek reconstruction, with the total cost over the following five years assessed at $6.04 billion. Tsaldaris complained to Byrnes that "piecemeal help" alone would not revive the country. Byrnes pointed out the desirability of further negotiations

19. T236/1044, Statement on the Greek Economic Situation and on the Need for Immediate Outside Assistance, K. Varvaressos, April 1945; FRUS, 1945: MacVeagh to the Secretary of State, March 24, 1945, vol. 8, 204–5; Memorandum by Baxter, May 3, 1945, vol. 8, 213; Clayton to Diamantopoulos, May 4, 1945, vol. 8, 213–15; Memorandum by Baxter, May 4, 1945, vol. 8, 215–16; Memorandum by Kohler, July 28, 1945, vol. 8, 232; MacVeagh to the Secretary of State, August 18, 1945, vol. 8, 232–33; Diamantopoulos to Taylor, August 20, 1945, vol. 8, 233–34; Byrnes to MacVeagh, August 25, 1945, vol. 8, 235; Acheson to MacVeagh, September 22, 1945, vol. 8, 236; Memorandum by Unger, September 25, 1945, vol. 8, 237–38. DSR 868.50/11–2845, Byrnes to MacVeagh, Telegram no. 1200, November 28, 1945; DSR 868.50/1–546, Byrnes to MacVeagh, Telegram no. 11, January 5, 1946; Byrnes to MacVeagh, Telegram no. 12, January 5, 1946; DSR 868.50/1–946, Acheson to MacVeagh, Telegram no. 30, January 9, 1946.
20. DSR 868.51/4–1746, Venizelos to Truman, April 17, 1946.

with the Ex-Im Bank, but warned that the requested sums were "not within the realm of possibilities." Such rebuffs did nothing to deter the Athens government. In mid-July, while on a trip to seek British aid, Tsaldaris visited the U.S. embassy in London. He brought up the matter of Ex-Im Bank credits and suggested that a delegation chaired by Venizelos be received in Washington to discuss the country's needs. This last approach met with a cool response in Washington, where it was pointed out that there was little likelihood of any further help given Greece's failure to make any use of the previous $25 million loan. The State Department was prepared to receive the delegation, but only to discuss Greece's general financial and economic problems, particularly those relating to trade. The meeting would take place only if the loan issue was not raised.[21]

Eager for the trip to go ahead, the Greeks gladly consented to the stipulation. When the delegation arrived in Washington at the end of July, its first action was to bring up the prospect of a $500 million loan in interviews given to the press.[22] From its first meeting with American officials, it was clear that the members of the delegation regarded the negotiation of new loans as the "primary purpose" of their visit. The Americans were adamant that no further help would be forthcoming from the Ex-Im Bank, and that Greece would have to wait until the International Bank for Reconstruction and Development (IBRD) commenced operations. Within days, the delegation asked for credits worth $175 million, a sum they described as "modest" and "cut down to a bare minimum." Venizelos stressed that it would be "impossible for him to return" to Athens without securing some assistance. He felt this would create the impression that Greece was being "deserted" by the Allies. The urgency of the plea for aid was reiterated during a direct meeting with Truman.[23]

21. FRUS, 1946. Acheson to Rankin, June 13, 1945, vol. 7, 169–70; Rankin to the Secretary of State, June 18, 1945, vol. 7, 170–71; Acheson to Rankin, June 22, 1945, vol. 7, 171–72; Memorandum by Freeman Matthews, July 5, 1945, vol. 7, 177–79; Harriman to the Secretary of State, July 12, 1946, vol. 7, 180–81; Acheson to Harriman, July 13, 1946, vol. 7, 181–82; FO371/58730 R10375, Copy of Memorandum on Greece's Economic Problem Handed to the Rt. Hon. Ernest Bevin, Secretary of State, and Secretary of State Byrnes by the Greek Premier M. Tsaldaris, Paris, July 3, 1946; DSR 868.51/7–1746, Greek Requests for Economic Assistance, Memorandum by Baxter, July 17, 1946.

22. DSR 868.51/7–1846, Harriman to the Secretary of State, Telegram no. 6808, July 18, 1946; DSR 868.51/7–3146, Memorandum by Baxter, July 31, 1946. Apart from Venizelos, the delegation consisted of Michael Ailianos, deputy minister of coordination, Anastasios Bakalbasis, a former minister of agriculture, and Konstantinos Karamanlis, a member of parliament (later prime minister and president); DSR 868.50/8–546, Memorandum from Baxter to Henderson and Acheson, August 5, 1946.

23. DSR 868.51/8–346, Memorandum from Fetter to Acheson, August 3, 1946; DSR 868.50/8–546, Memorandum by Baxter, August 5, 1946; DSR 8684.50/8–646, Venizelos to Acheson, August 6, 1946; DSR 868.50/8–746, Memorandum from Baxter to Henderson, August 7, 1946.

The pressure was maintained despite the American refusal to offer any further assistance. In early November the foreign exchange fiasco led to a renewed offensive. Desperate to secure financial help, the Athens government not only sought an extension of the Federal Reserve Bank of New York (FRBNY) loan but also the return of its $10 million security together with emergency aid. Within weeks, a personal visit of Tsaldaris to Washington resulted in a further request for credits worth $56 million to finance imports of consumer goods over the following four months. Such appeals continued unabated until the end of January. Thereafter attention was focused on the Porter Mission. Greek officials had welcomed the original decision to dispatch the mission and had urged its speedy departure. Once in Greece, the Porter team was seen as the herald of closer American involvement in the future, and thus went a long way toward both calming fears and raising expectations.[24]

American Misgivings

American advice to the Greeks did not differ substantially from that offered by the British. This reflected a similar understanding of the nature of the crisis, the shortcomings of the government in Athens, and of the measures likely to restore normality to the country. Despite the growing realization that U.S. aid would be necessary, Washington never departed from the stance that internal measures were crucial if Greece was to recover.

This position was made clear in late 1944, in response to the first requests for credits. Washington pointed out that internal monetary reform by the Greek government was a far more appropriate solution to current problems than foreign loans. This stance was maintained throughout the period under review and was reiterated on many occasions. In late 1945, MacVeagh pointed out the need for Greece to make

24. Details of the American refusal are given later in this chapter. For details of the FRBNY loan, see section entitled "Commerical Imports," chap. 5. FRUS, 1946. MacVeagh to the Secretary of State, November 4, 1946, vol. 7, 259–60; The Secretary of State to MacVeagh, January 3, 1947, vol. 7, 286–88; Memorandum by Jernegan, November 18, 1946, vol. 7, 264; DSR 868.5151/11–1246, Memorandum by Rountree, November 12, 1946; DSR 868.5151/11–2546, Memorandum by Jernegan, November 25, 1946; DSR FW-868.51/12–2446, Bank of Greece to FRBNY, December 18, 1946; DSR 868.00/12–2046, Memorandum for the President by Jernegan and Havlik, December 20, 1946; DSR 868.51/12–2446, Burke Knapp to Ness, December 24, 1946; DSR 868.50/12–2046, Memorandum by Baxter, December 20, 1946; DSR 868.51/12–2146, Memorandum by Jernegan, December 21, 1946; FRUS, 1947: Memorandum by Ness, January 22, 1947, vol. 5, 11–12; Porter to Clayton, February 17, 1947, vol. 5, 17–22; DSR 868.50/11–1246, Tsaldaris to Byrnes, Telegram no. 6179, November 12, 1946; DSR 868.50/11–1546, Memorandum from Henderson to Clayton, November 15, 1946; DSR 868.50/8–646, Venizelos to Acheson, November 23, 1946.

a larger contribution to its own recovery by repatriating the large amounts of foreign investments held by Greeks abroad. After the announcement of the $25 million loan, the government in Athens was informed that it would be expected to undertake a series of "rigorous measures" to combat inflation, stabilize the drachma, improve public finance, and foster the recovery of industry and trade. It was clearly suggested that the likelihood of further U.S. economic assistance would depend on the effectiveness of the action taken.[25]

By the summer of 1946, U.S. officials recognized that successive governments had done very little to improve the situation, and frequently expressed dissatisfaction. One major cause of irritation was the inept use of assistance already received. The $25 million loan was not even touched before August, and only $3.4 million was actually disbursed by the end of the year. Moreover, Greek officials had been too lethargic to secure any significant benefit from American credits to purchase surplus property.[26] In such circumstances, the persistent clamor for further loans had little chance of meeting with a sympathetic response. This was even more certain after the breach of promise in sending the Venizelos delegation. The Americans were hardly likely to be impressed by the emissaries' sole focus on the loan issue after the solemn assurance that the matter would not be raised.

The negative impressions were further reinforced by the subsequent contacts with the Venizelos delegation. Its members seemed poorly briefed and appeared to have little understanding of the precise state of their country's economy. The only statistics they produced were either false or had little basis in reality. They were able to offer few suggestions on improving public finances or the balance of payments, or the uses to which foreign assistance would be put. Even worse, they surprised their hosts with their ignorance of how economic problems were being tackled elsewhere, their stance toward wartime profits and controls over trade and capital movements, and their bizarre statements on various issues (particularly the claim that higher taxation would aggravate inflation). The Americans were dismayed, feeling that the delegation was "constitutionally incapable" of grasping the need for progressive taxation, capital levies, and economic controls, and were appalled that a "belief in private enterprise and free trade" should be regarded as a sufficient excuse

25. FRUS, 1944: Stettinius to MacVeagh, November 7, 1944, vol. 5, 224–26; DSR 868.51/10–2645, MacVeagh to the Secretary of State, October 26, 1945; DSR 868.50/11–2845, Byrnes to MacVeagh, Telegram no. 1200, November 28, 1945; DSR 868.50/1–546, Byrnes to MacVeagh, Telegram no. 11, January 5, 1946; Byrnes to MacVeagh, Telegram no. 12, January 5, 1946; DSR 868.50/1–946, Acheson to MacVeagh, Telegram no. 30, January 9, 1946.

26. Patterson, *Financial Experiences of Greece*, 632, 634; DSR 868.51/8–2046, Memorandum from Lincoln and Nortman to Ness and Sumner, August 20, 1946.

for the failure to apply essential measures. A disgusted State Department official suggested that the Greeks should be made to understand that "private enterprise" could not be equated with "private exploitation," and that "private enterprise" was doomed unless it operated for the "people as a whole."[27]

Equally damaging was the confused manner in which U.S. assistance was being sought. As on previous occasions, the request for the original $25 million loan contained little relevant information, and despite the protracted nature of the negotiations, successive applications could still be dismissed as "hurriedly" prepared and carelessly handled. Only with the help of foreign advisers could a suitable document be drafted.[28] The Greeks learned little from this experience. Documentation submitted in July 1946 outlining the capital requirements of Greek reconstruction prompted American criticism that it was riddled with "inconsistencies and errors," while the program presented by the Venizelos delegation in support of its request for $175 million was rejected as "poorly conceived" and "pathetically inadequate." At the Ex-Im Bank, it was felt that the Greek case was "so weak" there was little point in conducting any discussions at that time. By September 1946, American exasperation in Athens led to the decision that no further credits would be made available by the Ex-Im Bank, and that any future approaches should be made to the International Bank of Reconstruction and Development (IBRD) only.[29]

A further source of annoyance in Washington was the way in which the prospect of U.S. aid was being used for political purposes within Greece. In August 1945, MacVeagh simply noted that Varvaressos' references to the $250 million being sought had been mainly for domestic consumption. In the following month the State Department criticized the "unfortunate publicity" generated by the government, which was fueling the impression that the sum had been approved. During

27. DSR 868.51/8–1246, Memorandum by Fetter, August 12, 1946; DSR 868.50/8–2046, Memorandum from McGuire to Henderson, August 20, 1946; DSR 868.51/8–2046, Memorandum from Lincoln and Nortman to Ness and Sumner, August 20, 1946; DSR 868.50/8–2346, Memorandum by Henderson and Baxter, August 23, 1946.

28. FRUS, 1945: MacVeagh to the Secretary of State, October 2, 1945, vol. 8, 243–44; MacVeagh to the Secretary of State, November 29, 1945, vol. 8, 273–74. The tone of the American criticisms is almost identical to British responses to Greek efforts to secure foreign help. In September 1946, Nixon was particularly scathing about a government memorandum submitted to UNRRA, which he dismissed as a "pathetic plea" for "permanent charity"; FO371/58731 R14703, Nixon to Sommerville Smith, September 9, 1946.

29. DSR 868.51/8–946, Memorandum by Fetter, August 9, 1946; DSR 868.51/8–1146, Memorandum by Fetter, August 11, 1946; FRUS, 1946: Memorandum by Unger to the Secretary of State, July 5, 1946, vol. 7, 175–77; Acheson to MacVeagh, August 14, 1946, vol. 7, 190–91; DSR 868.51/9–1946, Memorandum by Jernegan, September 19, 1946; DSR FW-868.51/9–1946, Memorandum from Stenger to Ness, September 20, 1946.

the summer of 1946 they were equally "disturbed" by persistent rumors surrounding a request for $200 million, and deplored the attitude that compliance with the request was virtually taken for granted in Athens despite the lack of any vigorous action by the government. Another similar case occurred in January 1947, when Tsaldaris deliberately suggested that the Americans had committed themselves to further aid. Byrnes dismissed his remarks as regrettable.[30]

The Porter Mission

Despite the many sources of frustration listed previously, the Americans had never denied that some financial assistance would have to be provided to Greece. As already indicated, successive Greek applications for loans had been invariably rejected either because of the lack of clarity as to their purpose, or because of the inflated size. Washington had encouraged the search for credits so long as realistic sums were sought for clearly defined purposes. In late 1944 they indicated a willingness to provide funds to promote industrial recovery, and even during the heated negotiations of 1946 conceded that aid could be made available to finance feasible projects.[31] Once Washington recognized that some increased commitment to Greece was inevitable, it became clear that the agenda needed to be moved away from the somewhat melodramatic approach of Venizelos and Tsaldaris and toward a more hardheaded means of assessment. This required the precise quantification of the country's reconstruction needs and the creation of an efficient mechanism to ensure that these needs could be met. These were to become central aims of the Porter Mission.

Even before Paul Porter, chief of the American Economic Mission to Greece, left for Athens, both questions had received much attention from U.S. officials. In the spring of 1946, Karl Rankin, the American charge d'affaires in Athens, had estimated that Greek reconstruction would require $600 million over the following five years. He assumed that more than half of this amount could be found within Greece itself, with $250 million to come from external sources including reparations. He felt that such a "generous" sum would, if effectively used, restore the country to its

30. FRUS, 1945: MacVeagh to the Secretary of State, August 21, 1945, vol. 8, 234–35; Acheson to MacVeagh, September 22, 1945, vol. 8, 236; FRUS, 1946: Byrnes to Rankin, May 22, 1946, vol. 7, 165; Acheson to Rankin, June 14, 1946, vol. 7, 170; FRUS, 1947: Memorandum by the Secretary of State, January 4, 1947, vol. 5, 1–2.

31. FRUS, 1944: Stettinius to MacVeagh, November 7, 1944, vol. 5, 224–26; DSR 868.51/8–946, Memorandum by Fetter, August 9, 1946; DSR 868.51/8–1146, Memorandum by Fetter, August 11, 1946.

prewar position. However, this could not be taken for granted. Rankin warned of the obstacles likely to arise from the fact that Greece was a "country of free enterprise par excellence." He suspected that if foreign assistance were to be "handled [. . .] on a political basis," not only would far larger sums be required but also the whole process would be delayed interminably. He highlighted the shortcomings of government agencies, which played only a "limited" role in the country's economic life. He also pointed out that officials at various ministries had virtually no idea as to the precise purpose to which U.S. assistance should be put. Rankin therefore suggested that credits would have to be extended on a "project basis," with each individual project to be scrutinized by a competent American firm. Overall, given the shortcomings of the administration, the chaotic fiscal system, and the widespread aversion to income tax and economic controls, U.S. officials had severe doubts whether Greece was "equipped" to handle the sums it had requested.[32]

It was in the light of such perceptions that an investigative mission under Paul Porter was dispatched to Greece to recommend "specific steps" to be taken by the government, and to gauge the "extent of foreign assistance needed." Although the decision to send the mission was a tacit acknowledgment that U.S. resources had to be pumped into Greece, it was also tantamount to a vote of no confidence in the policies of the government in Athens and the estimates of reconstruction costs submitted by Greek officials. The Porter Mission arrived in late January 1947 and conducted a thorough investigation of the economy over the following two and a half months. This involved face-to-face discussions with ministers, officials, industrialists, and academics, and the use of questionnaires to canvass the opinions of interested parties such as commercial and industrial associations. The Porter Mission did not limit its activities to the capital, but devoted several weeks to a tour of the provinces. It also spent a considerable amount of time consulting with members of the BEM and the Currency Committee, and supported them in various dealings with the Greek government.[33]

Porter was not encouraged by what he saw in Greece. His general observations were largely consistent with those made by other American and British officials.

32. DSR 868.50/4–446, Rankin to the Secretary of State, April 4, 1946; DSR 868.50/6–1946, Rankin to the Secretary of State, June 19, 1946; DSR 868.51/8–2046, Memorandum from Lincoln and Nortman to Ness and Sumner, August 20, 1946.

33. DSR 868.50/8–646, Acheson to Venizelos, October 29, 1946; DSR 868.50/1–2347, Porter to the Secretary of State, January 23, 1947; FRUS, 1947: Porter to Clayton, February 17, 1947, vol. 5, 17–22; FO371/67101 R8888, Rapp to FO, June 25, 1947; Amen, American Foreign Policy in Greece, 77, 95–96. For the questionnaires, see A. Angelopoulos, "Απάντηση στο Ερωτηματολόγιο του κ. Πόρτερ" ("A Reply to Mr. Porter's Questionnaire"), 289–96.

He was disappointed that so few active steps had been taken to overcome the crisis. He felt the political system was largely to blame, observing that in the absence of any "western concept of the state," politics was mainly limited to power struggles between individuals for whom economic policy was a low priority. Moreover, he dismissed the civil service as a "depressing farce" and deplored the general "sense of helplessness" within the country. He did not believe that the government would be up to the task of carrying through the necessary reforms and suggested that "guidance by American personnel" would be necessary.[34]

Such perceptions underlay the report of the Porter Mission delivered in April 1947. According to this, the Greek economy was still in a precarious position, and the country had "merely managed to survive" since 1944, despite "substantial foreign aid" worth $700 million and "competent foreign advice." The "time bought" so expensively had been squandered as a result of policies of "drift and expediency." The Porter report recognized that the problems would be insurmountable without fresh injections of external assistance and the adoption by the Athens government of "strong control measures," but stressed that previous mistakes would have to be avoided if U.S. help was to prove effective. It therefore concentrated on three issues: the likely amount to be provided, action to be taken by the government, and means to ensure that American advice was heeded.[35]

In addition to UNRRA, post-UNRRA relief and surplus property imports, it was estimated that a minimum of $300 million would be needed over the following fifteen months. Moreover, a longer-term recovery program was necessary, requiring at least $335 million over the following five years. Most of the sum, particularly in the early period, would have to come from abroad. In addition, it was assumed that military expenditure over the fiscal year 1947–1948 would amount to $180 million, and this would also have to be provided by the United States. Such a level of aid could ensure both a balancing of the budget and an adequate supply of consumer goods, thus minimizing the risk of inflation.[36]

The impossibility of predicting the ultimate costs of the military struggle ruled out any precise assessment of the overall aid requirements. Nevertheless, the Porter report stressed that reconstruction costs would be "substantially reduced" if the government in Athens was prepared to "mobilize the country's own resources" and carry out a series of measures in conjunction with U.S. advisers. Action was

34. FRUS, 1947: Porter to Clayton, February 17, 1947, vol. 5, 17–22.
35. DSR 868.50/4–347, Tentative Report of the American Economic Mission to Greece, April 3, 1947; DSR 868.50/4–3047, American Economic Mission to Greece: Summary and Recommendations of the Report.
36. Ibid.

to be taken in several areas, including public finances, the balance of payments, administration, industry, and agriculture.[37]

Public finances were to be improved by vigorous action to augment revenue and control expenditure. The entire structure of taxation would have to be simplified. Income tax rates needed to be raised by at least 50 percent, and strictly enforced through compulsory registration of all commercial enterprises, which would have to be maintained through prescribed accounts for income tax purposes. Importers were to be prevented from making excessive profits arising from differences between Greek and world prices. All local taxes on the movement of goods would have to be lifted as soon as possible. On the expenditure side, an efficient audit and accounting system had to be created, and the ministry of finance had to be granted tighter control over public spending. All "special funds" had to be abolished, while pension and indigence lists were to be subject to severe scrutiny. Finally, the Porter report advocated an earlier suggestion by Gregory and Patterson, that a wages board be established to adjudicate pay disputes in the state sector.[38]

Several measures were necessary to improve the balance of payments. Policies on the exchange rate and gold sales were to be amended after consultation with the International Monetary Fund (IMF). Strict controls were to be imposed on imports, with utility as the primary criterion for the granting of licenses, and importing luxury goods was to be prohibited. The government would undertake to recover lost markets and secure new markets for exports, promote tourism, and ensure that a greater share of Greek shipping earnings was repatriated. To prevent the illicit flight of capital, the Porter report endorsed another Gregory and Patterson suggestion that all incoming and outgoing mail should be subject to financial censorship.[39]

Other measures included improving the administrative machinery. The civil service was to be pruned and its quality was to be raised via training and selection. It was recognized that a comprehensive system of price controls had little chance of success given public distrust and the lack of suitable means of enforcement. However, existing price, rent, and wage controls needed to be maintained and improved, while an antihoarding campaign should be undertaken, backed up by the threat of confiscations. A wage policy had to be devised and a mechanism for settling labor disputes had to be created. Reconstruction had to proceed according to a master plan, with priorities to be identified by a planning board consisting of economists

37. Ibid.
38. Ibid.
39. Ibid.

and engineers. Foreign capital was to be encouraged for the undertaking of re-construction projects. Industrial recovery was to be promoted via judicious use of credits, favoring imports of raw materials rather than finished goods competing with domestic production, and removing abuses of monopolies and subsidies. The obligation to retain surplus employees had to be abolished. Agricultural produc-tion was to be stepped up by applying intensive methods and better irrigation and drainage. An educational campaign would be employed to disseminate knowledge of best practices. Apart from these long-range measures, farmers should be granted access to credits at low interest rates, and in adequate amounts, through coopera-tives if feasible. Nevertheless, the Porter report looked beyond a mere return to the prewar economic situation. It stressed that Greece needed to become "reasonably self-sufficient" and suggested the drawing up of a development program concen-trating on mining, metallurgy, and agroindustries.[40]

The administration of the U.S. aid to Greece was to be entrusted to an economic mission, which was to include up to fifty high-caliber specialists on various as-pects of the economy. The mission was to have complete control over the use of funds, and was to supervise the planning and execution of reconstruction projects. While the mission was to concern itself with strategic issues, its work was to be complemented by foreign advisers to be placed in key government posts. The latter would concentrate on day-to-day issues. The Currency Committee was to retain its composition, but its powers were to be broadened. To ensure that Greek for-eign trade proceeded along lines consistent with the objectives of the mission, the Porter report advocated adopting yet another idea of Gregory and Patterson. This was the Foreign Trade Administration, to be chaired by a mission member, which was to have the final say on all matters relating to foreign trade and procurement. A final mechanism was needed to ensure consistent compliance with the mission's recommendations: the ultimate power to "curtail or suspend" all aid if its advice was not heeded.[41]

The U.S. Aid Program, 1947–1948

In March 1947, before the Porter report was completed, Truman announced in an address to Congress his determination to extend assistance to Greece. In the speech, which came to be seen as the first articulation of the so-called Truman Doc-trine, the president warned of the dangers threatening Greece and Turkey, and of

40. Ibid.
41. Ibid.

the serious regional and international consequences of allowing those countries to fall into the hands of hostile forces. To counter this threat, he emphasized the need of allocating economic and military aid worth $400 million, of which $300 million would go to Greece. The assistance would enable the government in Athens to restore its authority by overcoming the subversive "armed minority" and to maintain internal order by continuing purchases of vital imports. With the help of U.S. advisers, the aid would be used to ensure Greece's survival as a "free nation" and to create a "stable and self-sustaining economy" conducive to a "healthy democracy." Congress finally approved the request in May 1947.[42] In contrast to the specific and detailed recommendations of the Porter report, the immediate assistance to be given to Greece was articulated in vague and emotive terms with an emphasis on the threat posed by unspecified but clearly communist efforts to subvert the country's independence. Thus the primary aim of the measure was to counter this threat, with economic policies as secondary instruments of the political aim of ensuring internal stability. The political emphasis was reinforced by the reference to democracy, indicating the desire to remove the abuses associated with recent governments in Athens. The following section describes the implementation of the emergency aid package, the problems it encountered and the results it achieved.

The American Mission for Aid to Greece (AMAG)

In the interim period before the dispatch of AMAG, the body created to administer the proposed assistance, more attention was paid to defining its powers than to refining its objectives. After completing his report, Porter had laid special emphasis on the need to ensure that the mission would be equipped to overcome any "refusals by the Greek government to carry out specific measures for recovery." In this spirit, the U.S. aid package was to be made conditional not only upon the granting of sweeping powers to AMAG but also on the undertaking by the government in Athens to carry out vigorous measures of its own. The latter was obliged to endorse a declaration drafted in Washington, outlining the actions it was prepared to take and the degree of authority it would concede to the proposed mission. It promised to marshal the country's resources to the "fullest extent" to achieve the program's aims, and to refrain from enacting any "economic steps" before consulting the mission.[43]

---

42. D. Merrill, ed., *The Truman Doctrine and the Beginning of the Cold War, 1947–1949*, 99–103, 271–74.

43. Amen, *American Foreign Policy in Greece*, 79; FRUS, 1947: The Secretary of State to the Embassy in Greece, May 31, 1947, vol. 5, 182–85. For text of the formal agreement signed on June 20, see Merrill, *Truman Doctrine*, 344–47.

President Truman addressing the Joint Session of Congress, March 12, 1947.
New York Herald Tribune.

When AMAG commenced operations in July, it further strengthened its brief not only by insisting on being consulted on every economic decision but also by declaring that it expected complete adherence to its advice. The mission soon came to resemble a shadow government with a structure closely mirroring that of ministries. Each of its divisions expanded rapidly, and instead of the compact body originally proposed by Porter, it already had a staff of more than 128 by September 1947. It was headed by Dwight Griswold, a former governor of the state of Nebraska, who had been involved in the U.S. military administration in Germany.[44]

Equipped with wide powers and backed up by extensive resources, AMAG set out to realize the ambitious objectives indicated in the Truman address. It rapidly became apparent, as Porter had already understood, that few comprehensive economic controls could be applied in a country with such an inefficient civil service. Thus neither rationing nor controls on prices, production, or distribution seemed feasible, and they were not attempted. The mission concentrated instead on the "major strategic points" of the Greek economy, including public finances, wages, imports, and the external value of the drachma.[45] In each field, AMAG found it

44. Coombs, *Financial Policy in Greece,* 51; Merrill, *Truman Doctrine,* 334, 336, 490.
45. Coombs, *Financial Policy in Greece,* 92–93.

necessary to create new institutional arrangements or to assume an unprecedented degree of control over the actions of the Athens government.

The first such field was public finances. One of the most protracted struggles with the Greek authorities came over the need to solve the perennial problem of budgetary deficits. As on previous occasions, the main difficulty lay in persuading the government to draw up realistic estimates and then to stick to them. A clearly unsatisfactory budget was presented in September. Thereafter, prolonged pressure and substantial input from the Public Finance Division sought to reduce the anticipated deficit by enforcing ruthless expenditure cuts and tapping new sources of revenue. After a lengthy struggle, a detailed budget was finally thrashed out by December. Unlike before, when expenditure estimates were never taken seriously, the extensive powers assumed by AMAG ensured a significant degree of control over public spending. Whereas in the previous period, when the Currency Committee had been invariably presented with a fait accompli, AMAG itself took the initiative by insisting on monthly updates on the state of public finances. These reports were prepared by auditors answering to the mission's budget control adviser. American personnel rigorously screened all requests for additional spending. According to Coombs, AMAG supervision amounted to virtual "day-to-day control over relatively minor items of budgetary expenditure."[46]

A further means of curbing the profligacy of the government was the creation of the Drachma Reconstruction Fund (DRF), a mechanism through which the costs of all reconstruction projects were to be channeled. The DRF, using what were commonly known as counterpart funds, was endowed with the receipts from all consumer goods imports financed by U.S. aid. In contrast with the revenue from UNRRA supplies, which was at the complete disposal of the government, disbursements of the drachma counterpart funds required AMAG approval, and thus could not be diverted for short-term political purposes. Similarly, all receipts from the post-UNRRA program remained under the control of the mission rather than the government in Athens.[47]

Another major concern of AMAG was to formulate an imports program closely geared both to the realities of the Greek balance of payments and the mission's overall objectives. The task of ensuring that actual imports remained consistent with AMAG's assessment of current requirements was entrusted to the Foreign Trade Administration (FTA), created in October 1947. The FTA was charged with overseeing all import license applications, an extension of the temporary powers

46. Ibid., 107–15.
47. Ibid., 90, 137–38.

previously exercised by the Currency Committee. Though formally part of the ministry of national economy, it was headed—but not controlled—by an American official.[48]

An additional issue requiring immediate attention was the gross overvaluation of the drachma, with its damaging effects on Greek exports and invisible earnings. Both AMAG and the government were agreed that a new parity should not be fixed while the crisis continued, as it would soon lose relevance in any case. Moreover, Washington was opposed to any major alteration in the exchange rate without the prior approval of the IMF. The solution was the so-called Exchange Certificate Plan introduced in October 1947. While the official parity was to remain unchanged, all approved foreign currency transactions were to be conducted by the use of "exchange certificates," the value of which would be determined by market forces. This value, effectively a premium on top of the official parity, was to represent the de facto exchange rate of the drachma. The plan's main aim was to reduce the discrepancy between official and black market rates, and to provide an incentive to exporters.[49]

The control exercised by AMAG and the FTA was supplemented by the work of other entities. The execution of reconstruction projects was undertaken directly by American firms. In many cases, the contracts had been placed even before the mission arrived in Athens. The supervision and auditing of reconstruction work was entrusted to the U.S. Army Engineering Corps. Similarly, all purchases of military and bulk foodstuffs were handled directly by U.S. procurement agencies. Use was also made of existing bodies such as the Currency Committee. Originally intended to last until 1947, its existence was prolonged by special legislation. Many of its activities were taken over by various divisions of AMAG, leaving it free to supervise the credit operations of the Bank of Greece. It also assumed additional functions, particularly the regulation of the "Exchange Certificate Plan."[50]

The Fresh Crisis

The extensive powers assumed by AMAG enabled it to achieve a measure of success in persuading the government to adopt a more realistic approach to public

48. Ibid., 54, 154–58; J. C. Warren, Jr., "Origins of the 'Greek Economic Miracle': The Truman Doctrine and Marshall Plan Development and Stabilization Programs," 81.

49. Although the plan failed to create a genuine market for "exchange certificates," it did allow a considerable degree of devaluation (100 percent by January 1948), while maintaining the fiction of an unchanged parity; Coombs, *Financial Policy in Greece,* 94–107.

50. Ibid., 48, 53–54; Amen, *American Foreign Policy in Greece,* 128.

Signing the Agreement on Aid to Greece, June 20, 1947. Ambassador MacVeagh and (to his left) Konstantinos Tsaldaris. Hellenic Photographic News (K. Megalokonomou).

finances. The estimates of September 1947, which had envisaged a deficit of nearly 50 percent, were subjected to a radical revision by the Public Finance Division. The December estimates saw overall spending cut by 23 percent, with the largest economies to be made in military expenditure, which was to be slashed by more than 30 percent. On the revenue side, considerable progress was also anticipated. Diminished returns from the sale of relief supplies were to be almost entirely offset by a rise in yields from taxation. Despite the desirability of taxing income rather than consumption, the Public Finance Division recognized the obvious problems in implementing a proper income tax. Acknowledging that substantial increases could not be achieved immediately, it concentrated on promoting government legislation requiring the proper maintenance of business accounts and records. In the short-term, several new taxes were devised, notably the Special Wartime Contribution, a repackaged version of the Varvaressos levy of 1945, and several retrospective taxes.[51] In combination, it was expected that these would contribute more than half

51. The retrospective measures included taxes on profits from private imports between liberation and March 1947, and on all repayments of bank credits made during the period of high inflation up to January 1946.

of the projected increase in returns from taxation. Indirect taxes were to provide the remainder, although this entailed political difficulties. Neither the government nor the trade unions were keen on measures that would push up prices, a position shared by many members of AMAG itself. In the end, it was agreed to raise customs duties by 150 percent and to stop subsidizing several commodities, particularly bread. Under the new revenue structure, it was anticipated that recurring sources of income would provide almost 60 percent of the total (44 percent and 15 percent from indirect and direct taxes respectively), with 23 percent to come from the sale of relief supplies and 18 percent from extraordinary levies. By such means, it was hoped that the budget deficit could be reduced to a mere 7 percent.[52]

Although AMAG was reasonably successful in overcoming government intransigence on public finances, it proved far more difficult to achieve any significant degree of control over the real economy. Even while the details of the budget were being thrashed out, several dangerous developments threatened to invalidate most of the assumptions on which the new estimates were based. By the end of the year, both public finances and the stability of the drachma were deteriorating rapidly with note circulation, prices, and the sovereign rate all spiraling upwards due to a combination of mistakes by the government and by AMAG itself, as well as circumstances outside the control of both.

The first serious challenge arose from wage concessions. During the summer, civil servants had launched a major campaign in pursuit of pay claims, culminating in the threat of a general strike. Thus instead of pruning the civil service as originally intended, AMAG became immediately involved in heated negotiations over both redundancies and wage demands. Due to the late arrival of the Public Finance Division, advisers from the Civil Government Division, who had little understanding of budgetary matters, conducted negotiations on the AMAG side. Consequently, AMAG gave its approval for a 30 percent pay raise in exchange for the acceptance of an administrative reform package. This opened up a "gaping hole in the budget," with a "flood of new money" pouring into the economy. Unsurprisingly, the agreement soon provoked a response from workers in the private sector, who demanded pay increases not only to take account of the raises given to the civil servants but also to compensate for the subsequent wave of inflation. Although the Labor Division was instrumental in moderating the pay claims, raises averaging 35 to 40 percent were granted in November.[53]

The consequences of the wage concessions soon became apparent. By October the sovereign rate jumped by more than 20 percent. The crisis was compounded

52. Percentages calculated from data in Coombs, *Financial Policy in Greece*, 107–37, 142.
53. Ibid., 79–82.

by fresh AMAG mistakes. The agreement with the civil servants had allowed higher wage increases to compensate for the cancellation of the traditional holiday bonuses. For some unfathomable reason (described by Coombs as an "unexplained failure"), the Public Finance and Labor Divisions failed to coordinate policies when negotiating with the private sector employees in November. As a result, the private sector employees were allowed to retain their bonuses on top of their pay raises. Immediately, indignant civil servants demanded that their own bonuses be restored. Placed in an acutely embarrassing situation, AMAG shied away from the political costs of attempting to cancel the private sector bonus and was obliged to approve the enormous economic costs of acceding to the demands of the civil servants.[54]

Unsurprisingly, the pay raises ushered in a new wave of price increases. At the same time, other developments contributed to an intensification of inflationary pressure. Notable among these was an unavoidable expansion of credit for agriculture. This was partly caused by a severe drought during the summer of 1947 that reduced cereal yields by more than 30 percent. This delayed the repayment of existing loans and necessitated the allocation of far higher sums to avoid a severe curtailment of acreage under cultivation. Moreover, given the continued fighting in the provinces, such credit was deemed opportune to retain the political allegiance of the countryside. Nevertheless, the amounts involved represented an even larger injection of cash into the economy than that resulting from the urban wage increases. Credit to industry from the Bank of Greece was kept under tighter reins by the Currency Committee, but the operations of the private banks, not subject to such restraints, were beginning to reach worrying levels. In late 1947 the Public Finance Division appealed to private bankers to cut their loans, but was met with a lukewarm response.[55]

Further inflationary pressure resulted from the de facto devaluation of the drachma following the introduction of the "Exchange Certificate Plan" and the tax increases. AMAG and the government had naively hoped that the higher costs of both would be absorbed by importers and the business community rather than simply passed on to consumers, but this was little more than wishful thinking. Although the apparent public response was passive acceptance, this seemed unlikely to last for long.[56]

54. Ibid., 169–70.
55. Ibid., 150–54, 159. AMAG's demand that the Bank of Greece be allowed to supervise the private institutions aroused howls of indignation and led to a lengthy stalemate. Eventually, a compromise obliged the banks to accept Currency Committee supervision. A credit squeeze was finally enforced in August 1948 in the face of fierce opposition not only from the banks but also from the cabinet; ibid., 148–51, 213–20.
56. Ibid., 104–5, 134–35.

The dangers of inflation were seriously compounded by a fresh deterioration in the supply position. The blow to domestic food production resulting from the drought and the fighting could be offset only by large increases in imports. However, this failed to materialize. Part of the problem lay in Washington, where it was decided that owing to shortages of aid funds, the value of the post-UNRRA program was to be reduced to $38 million instead of the $50 million originally envisaged. Even more serious was the fact that AMAG's own import program had run into enormous difficulties. It had become painfully obvious that the FTA was undermanned from the start, and its staff was overwhelmed by the immense task of assessing each import application. During the second half of 1947, imports were roughly 50 percent lower than in the corresponding period in 1946. The resulting shortfall in the counterpart funds was overcome only by the help of a temporary loan involving the printing of new drachmae worth $8.3 million, adding further to inflationary pressure. The consequences of the tailing off of imports were complicated by the dislocation of the internal distribution of supplies caused by the fighting and evacuations and the reappearance of extensive hoarding. By the end of November, shortages of several essential commodities became acute.[57]

The economic problems were complicated yet further by the persistence of the political crisis. The failure to bring the civil war to a swift conclusion was proving costly both in financial and human terms. By late summer, the government in Athens was complaining that it had insufficient means to defeat the insurgents, and sought to expand the size of its armed forces. Despite relentless pressure, and the support of MacVeagh, AMAG remained opposed to such a move. Amid general American skepticism as to whether troops were being deployed effectively, Griswold offered suggestions for improving their quality rather than their quantity. However, by September, the progressive deterioration of the security situation persuaded him to modify this stance, and he accepted the need to expand the military establishment. Further increases were sanctioned in December, following a fresh series of guerrilla successes against the Greek army.[58] The increased military costs were to play havoc with the finances of both the government and AMAG.

The fighting created an even greater burden on public finances as a result of the

57. Ibid., 145, 156–58, 163.
58. FRUS, 1947: Memorandum by Witman, July 29, 1947, vol. 5, 265–67; Memorandum by Villard to the Secretary of State, August 7, 1947, vol. 5, 281–84; Memorandum by Villard to the Secretary of State, August 8, 1947, vol. 5, 287–89; Griswold to the Secretary of State, August 11, 1947, vol. 5, 294; MacVeagh to the Secretary of State, August 21, 1947, vol. 5, 303–4; Memorandum by Baxter, August 26, 1947, vol. 5, 314–15; Griswold to the Secretary of State, September 6, 1947, vol. 5, 330; Memorandum of Meeting with State Department Representatives on the Greek Situation, September 17, 1947, vol. 5, 344–46; Lovett to AMAG, December 30, 1947, vol. 5, 478–80.

increasing flood of refugees. At first, people abandoned their homes through fear of guerrilla raids. However, it soon became clear that the numbers of displaced persons were rising rapidly as a result of a decision by the Greek general staff to evacuate remote areas in order to hinder recruitment into the guerrilla forces. Although the civilian divisions of AMAG were fiercely opposed to the policy on economic grounds, the U.S. Army Group Greece (USAGG) overruled them. More than 250,000 people were made homeless by the end of October. By the end of the year the evacuation drive had pushed the number of refugees beyond the half-million mark, necessitating huge emergency relief payments.[59]

In the meantime, fresh agitation for pay raises was creating another potential source of inflationary pressure. Prices rose an average 40 percent between the summer and the end of 1947, making another confrontational round of wage bargaining increasingly probable. The country seemed on the brink of fresh hyperinflation and inevitable economic collapse.[60] With the civil war still unresolved, the likely political price of such a demoralizing outcome galvanized both AMAG and the government into enacting a series of countermeasures.

Dwight Griswold, chief of AMAG, giving a speech at a meeting, October 24, 1947.
M. Katsigeras, *Greece: Twentieth Century, 1946–2000* (Athens, 2001).

59. Coombs, *Financial Policy in Greece,* 167.
60. Ibid., 160–61.

Countermeasures

In early December 1947, relations between AMAG and the government in Athens reached a low point as a result of the mounting crisis. Protesting against what it saw as the inadequacy of the mission's program, the government pressed AMAG for increases in U.S. aid and a substantial diversion of counterpart funds for immediate budgetary purposes. At one point, the whole government threatened to resign unless the mission sanctioned the flooding of the market with consumer goods and unrestricted sales of gold by the Bank of Greece. AMAG found itself in a difficult position. It was fully aware of the problems resulting from the shortfall in imports, but knew that Washington was hardly likely to budge on the second issue. All it could do was to advise the imposition of a wage freeze.[61]

Left with little choice, the government rushed through emergency anti-strike legislation embodying a wage freeze, in response to proposed strike action by banking and public utility employees. For the duration of the civil war the law threatened strikers with draconian punishments, including life imprisonment and death. Although it was not seriously believed that the more severe penalties would actually be enforced, the measure aroused considerable opposition both inside and outside Greece. Nevertheless, it was successful in averting a second wave of strikes and pay raises during subsequent months.[62]

For its part, AMAG made strenuous efforts to address the imports problem. Faced with the cut in the post-UNRRA program and the need to divert resources toward military purposes, the mission appealed to the State Department for an emergency aid package. This was refused as politically inopportune, given the delicate state of negotiations concerning the European Recovery Program (ERP). However, Washington sanctioned the accelerated spending of remaining AMAG funds, hoping that the sums could be replaced from ERP sources as soon as these became available. By such means, and by the diversion of $29 million from reconstruction projects, the mission was able to ensure that imports during the first three months of 1948 were nearly double those of the previous quarter. This allowed a substantial improvement in the supply position, leading to a general downturn in prices by early April.[63]

A further stabilizing factor was the outcome of successive AMAG compromises vis-à-vis the government regarding the latter's traditional safety valve, the sale of

61. Ibid., 119, 174–76.
62. Ibid., 176–77.
63. Ibid., 177–80.

gold. As indicated in the previous chapter, the stampede for gold that almost drained the Bank of Greece's last reserves came to a halt with the revival of confidence after Truman's announcement. Public pressure to buy sovereigns virtually disappeared, with many individuals choosing to resell their gold to the bank. Despite occasional outbursts of panic over the next six months, the situation never approached the critical point it had reached in early March. However, in October 1947 the government sought to reverse increases in the sovereign rate with a new wave of gold sales. At first the mission had been hostile, warning that a "vigorous recovery program" was a far more appropriate way of overcoming the crisis. Washington was equally opposed, pointing out that gold sales did little to control inflation and merely led to the "accumulation of private fortunes," and urged that the proposal be rejected. Nevertheless, AMAG soon felt compelled to agree to a limited volume of sales. Almost forty thousand sovereigns were sold in secret by the end of the month, achieving temporary stability. However, fresh panic ensued within a week. This time the Bank of Greece was permitted to resume sales on condition that the foreign members of the Currency Committee were to supervise operations. Despite this proviso, the advice of Gregory and Patterson was totally ignored and more than one hundred thousand sovereigns were wasted during the following month in a futile attempt to stabilize the sovereign rate at the 135,000 level.[64]

In early December AMAG agreed to further sales only if its Public Finance Division could oversee operations. While the government continued to clamor for a high volume of sales to bring the sovereign rate back down to previous levels, the mission deliberately restricted sales during December and January in an attempt to conserve gold stocks. In such circumstances, with the injection of more drachmae into the economy, the way was open for a speculative rush on gold. With the U.S. Treasury refusing to replace previous losses, and the understandable fear of abandoning the policy at such a time, 60 percent of the Greek gold reserves passed to the speculators within a three-week period. The crisis was temporarily overcome by the conversion of other gold reserves into sovereigns and by announcements that the Bank of Greece would no longer attempt to bring about a substantial reduction in the sovereign rate. The pressure was eased once prices began to stabilize toward the spring. Nevertheless, the pattern continued to be repeated on a smaller scale

64. For regular updates on the gold reserves of the Bank of Greece, see a series of reports contained within FO371/67103, including R3542, March 15, 1947; R3938, March 23, 1947; R4952, April 12, 1947; R6334, May 10, 1947; R7326, May 31, 1947; R9223, July 7, 1947; R9554, July 13, 1947: Coombs, *Financial Policy in Greece*, 189–90; FRUS, 1947: Lovett to AMAG, October 18, 1947, vol. 5, 371–72.

during subsequent months, mainly in response to military and political instability. In total, over a million sovereigns worth $8.7 million were sold between October 1947 and June 1948.[65]

As Table 6.1 indicates, the combined impact of the wage freeze, increased imports, and gold sales had a considerable calming influence on the economy. Prices began to stabilize in March 1948 and even decreased slightly during April and May. The sovereign rate peaked in February and remained largely stable until the summer. The slowdown of prices took place against the background of a continuing increase in the money supply, indicating a substantial reduction in the velocity of circulation. Moreover, a rise in the value of sight deposits as a percentage of the total money supply (from 12.6 percent in December 1947 to 15.75 percent in June 1948) suggested an increased propensity to retain drachmae.

AMAG took advantage of the lull to sponsor further measures to improve public finances. During the spring of 1948, export subsidies were virtually eliminated. In June the cigarette tax was raised by 25 percent, and bread subsidies were finally removed in July. By the end of the fiscal year (1947–1948), public finances were also displaying a degree of improvement. Despite huge military outlays and the enormous cost of maintaining the refugees, the budget deficit amounted to only 6 percent. Moreover, the likelihood of further recourse to the printing press was reduced

TABLE 6.1. Comparative Economic Indicators, 1947-1948

Period	Note Issue	Private Sight Deposits (in billions of drachmae)	Total Money Supply	Sovereign Rate (in thousands of drachmae)	AMAG Price Index (Oct. 1939—1)
June 1947	690	96	786	135	197
July	692	100	792	144	203
August	732	108	840	152	205
September	764	121	885	147	213
October	822	129	951	173	228
November	829	136	965	190	252
December	974	140	1,114	204	273
January 1948	893	146	1,039	207	282
February	866	150	1,016	230	296
March	888	160	1,048	230	299
April	970	161	1,131	230	294
May	956	177	1,133	230	287
June	1,011	189	1,200	230	289

Source: Coombs, *Financial Policy in Greece,* 201.

65. Coombs, *Financial Policy in Greece,* 190–200; Politakis, *Greek Policies of Recovery and Reconstruction,* 243.

by the healthy expansion of the counterpart funds resulting from the increased imports program. Nevertheless, the aggregate figures disguised the continued dependence on foreign aid. Taxation provided only 67.8 percent of total revenue, with the remainder deriving from UNRRA, post-UNRRA, and AMAG aid. There were some grounds for optimism. For the first time, taxation yields exceeded ordinary expenditure by an emphatic 44 percent. The Greek balance of payments had also improved. Thanks mainly to the restraint exercised over licensing, the value of total commodity imports was reduced from $387 million in 1946 to $318 million in 1947–1948. The devaluation of the drachma allowed commodity exports to more than double from $41 million to $95.6 million. Total foreign exchange receipts rose from $102 million to $150.5 million. As with public finances, the balance of payments was heavily dependent on foreign aid worth $177 million, but the overall trend seemed encouraging.[66]

The First Year of U.S. Aid

By the middle of 1948, a modicum of stability had thus been restored to the Greek economy. The improvement in several economic indicators suggested that some progress had been achieved in particularly unfavorable circumstances. This outcome can be interpreted in many ways, depending on the choice of starting point. AMAG had received no detailed blueprint for its activities. As a participant of later American programs in Greece recalled, such a "pioneering" task required "making adjustments as they went along" rather than "well-thought out" plans.[67] American aid must therefore be judged in the general terms suggested by the Truman address rather than by the precise long-term objectives of the Porter report. It fulfilled the most basic expectation, in that Greece obviously had not been conquered by the insurgents. The final outcome was still far from clear, as the insurgents continued to pose a considerable threat. Even so, the temporary economic stability did enable the government to pay much closer attention to the war in the near future, thus increasing the likelihood of an ultimate victory.

As for the other broad aims, the results were equally far from clear. Even if Greece had not fallen into the Soviet orbit, the continued prevalence of fundamental abuses of human rights, particularly the arrests, executions, and deportations,

66. Coombs, *Financial Policy in Greece*, 210–12, 236.
67. James Warren, Jr., Letter to the Author, September 3, 1999.

Statue of President Truman in Athens. Hellenic Photographic News (K. Megalokonomou).

called into question any description of Greece as a "free nation." At first, many of the Americans regarded the Greek Right as little better than the insurgents. Porter was criticized for his belief that "both sides" were "equally unprincipled," and many AMAG members felt that the Greek political elite shared much of the blame for the civil war. While Washington's official stance was to support the elected government, it was indicated that there were limits that should not be crossed. Accordingly, before Griswold left for Athens, he had been warned that while the government might find it necessary to employ "stern and determined measures" to defeat the insurgents, "excesses" were not to be tolerated. With time, the distinctions became somewhat blurred. The Americans seemed generally reluctant to exploit their sweeping powers to soften the government's repressive policies, and their apparent unwillingness to take a stand on the civil liberties issue contrasted with the position adopted by the international press and the British authorities in Athens. This failure to act made Truman's avowed intention to promote a "healthy democracy" seem distinctly hollow.[68]

In economic terms, the results were also decidedly mixed, amounting to little more than maintenance of the existing situation. Truman had offered a vague mixture of short-term expediency (increased imports) and long-term vision (self-sufficiency). Much success was eventually achieved as far as the first aim was concerned. U.S. aid did indeed ensure that necessary imports continued to pour into the country, far in excess of what could have been obtained from Greek export earnings alone. Even this outcome was under threat for a period, as the imports program was almost undermined by the shortcomings of the institutional arrangements imposed by AMAG. Much trouble could have been avoided had the FTA been expanded as rapidly as the mission's own divisions.

The grander goal of the self-sustaining economy was never realistically attainable within a year. As the Coombs figures indicated, Greece's balance of payments and public finances improved over the year, but its dependence on foreign aid was still overwhelming. Truman had offered nothing specific to ensure self-sufficiency, and many of the fundamental problems of the economy remained as intractable as ever. Despite modest successes in several areas, notably the increased efficiency of tax collection, in other areas satisfactory solutions seemed no nearer in 1948 than they had been at any time since liberation. The continuing weakness of the civil service, the regressive nature of the taxation system, the appalling maldistribution of wealth,

68. FO371/67034 R3055, Athens to FO, Telegram no. 559, March 6, 1947; Warren, "Origins of the Greek 'Economic Miracle,' " 76; FRUS, 1947: The Secretary of State to Griswold, July 11, 1947, vol. 5, 219–24; Wittner, *American Intervention in Greece*, chap. 5.

the persistent ability of the rich to shield themselves from the wider problems of the country, and the failure to make any structural adjustments to restore international competitiveness all boded badly for the future and testified to the relative impotence of the mission to effect any sweeping changes.[69]

According to Coombs' later account, AMAG had felt hampered from the start by several erroneous assumptions held by the planners in Washington. The serious underestimation of the tenacity of the insurgents led to unrealistic expectations as to the shares of aid to be allocated for various purposes. The planners had expected that the mission, as the instrument of U.S. aid, would enjoy considerable popular support, and that the "Greek public would enthusiastically rally around" its program. They had also assumed that their efforts to broaden the government in Athens would at last create a source of "decisive leadership" to deal with the country's problems. Besides these miscalculations, they had failed to take account of the strong bargaining power of the trade unions, which rendered the task of maintaining wage stability exceedingly difficult.[70]

AMAG officials had some grounds for complaint. Above all, the military situation had the decisive influence over what could be done in other areas. Porter had anticipated that any escalation of the fighting would necessitate an inevitable squeeze on the funding of nonmilitary objectives, and this was precisely what happened. Even before Griswold departed for Athens, he had been informed that Washington regarded military and economic aims as being of "equal importance." At first, the balance was open to different interpretations. According to Coombs's later account, he initially felt that too much emphasis had been placed on providing economic solutions to essentially political problems. While Griswold reiterated the emphasis on both objectives, by December the U.S. embassy in Athens was stressing that American efforts in Greece could be as easily negated by "economic forces" as by any other. By the beginning of 1948, a senior U.S. official could describe the "Greek problem" as "military [. . .] and political" rather than simply a question of "reconstruction and economic development."[71]

---

69. One particularly glaring example of the continued failure to impose anything heavier than symbolic levels of taxation was the situation with the operators of the Liberty ships sold to Greece in late 1946. Tax rates of little more than 3 to 4 percent were levied on the immense profits earned by these vessels; P. A. Porter, "Wanted: A Miracle in Greece." Efforts to secure higher tax revenue from shipowners met with concerted opposition from the latter and were unsuccessful until 1950; Amen, *American Foreign Policy in Greece,* 116–20.

70. Coombs, *Financial Policy in Greece,* 84–85.

71. Ibid., 84; FRUS, 1947: Marshall to Griswold, July 11, 1947, vol. 5, 219–24; Griswold to the Secretary of State, October 9, 1947, vol. 5, 361–63; Keely to the Secretary of State, December 8,

This gradual shift toward an emphasis on military issues merely helped resolve what had been a consistent dilemma for AMAG. While the overall importance of economic measures was hardly questioned, the choice as to *which* economic measures should take precedence was a long-running source of controversy. As late as October 1947, George McGhee, coordinator of the Greece-Turkey aid program, could inform British officials that alongside the restoration of internal security, both reconstruction and the budget were equally crucial. Certainly, the mission arrived in Greece with little sense of clarity as to immediate priorities, a state of affairs which led to incessant bickering between the heads of various divisions, all of whom were anxious to further their own causes. This proved particularly damaging in the struggle against inflation, where members responsible for civilian projects clashed with those who were anxious to restrict increases in the money supply. The lack of consensus and coordination could prove calamitous, as demonstrated by the course and outcome of the wage negotiations. The Public Finance Division was invariably at loggerheads with the rest of the mission over any action likely to increase the threat of inflation, fighting long battles over the need to restrict reconstruction spending and the issuing of industrial credit. The fundamental rift was succinctly described by Clinton Golden, the head of the Labor Division, who complained scathingly about the actions of the "budget balancers' brigade." According to Coombs, who personified the latter group, the other divisions did not acknowledge the necessity of containing inflation until the advent of the major crisis at the end of 1947.[72]

The steady shift of funds from civilian to military purposes did not mean the abandonment of economic aims per se. After all, a massive $53.5 million was spent on reconstruction and development projects during 1947–1948, easily dwarfing the expenditure of previous years. However, each increase of the military effort involved the temporary sacrifice of planned expenditure on reconstruction, and some longer-term economic goals had to be shelved in order to meet the emergencies of the moment. The first $9 million were diverted in September 1947. Three months later the expansion of the armed forces was achieved at the cost of slashing civilian projects, including $11.2 million from reconstruction, $2.3 million from agricultural rehabilitation, and $0.5 million from the medical program. As already noted, the imports emergency of late 1947 was solved only by diverting yet another $29 million away from reconstruction projects. By June 1948, the sums earmarked for

1947, vol. 5, 438–39; FRUS, 1948: Memorandum by Henderson to the Secretary of State, January 9, 1948, vol. 4, 9–14.

72. FO371/67046 R13868, Wallinger to Norton, October 16, 1947; Coombs, *Financial Policy in Greece*, 56, 143, 150; Wittner, *American Intervention in Greece*, 174.

reconstruction were less than half of what had been envisaged a year before.[73] Thus the growing preoccupation with the twin goals of defeating the insurgency and containing inflation meant unfortunate delays to the reconstruction effort, a tactical abandonment of the most direct path to ultimate self-sufficiency.

Nevertheless, maintaining financial stability could still involve recourse to unwelcome compromises. In December 1947 the political section of the U.S. embassy in Athens had highlighted the urgent need for further economic assistance from Washington. It advised that given the gravity of the situation, the United States should no longer feel bound by "economic theory and sound business principles" when considering the matter. According to Politakis, this was tantamount to a green light for the abandonment of all economic common sense in the single-minded pursuit of a military-political solution, a course that would soon lead to American acquiescence in the resurrection of the detested gold sales policy. The reality was far more complex. There was no soft-pedaling on fiscal orthodoxy, as witnessed by the Public Finance Division's continued vigilance over all budget-related issues. However, AMAG did indeed reverse its initial stance toward gold sales. As one of its senior officials stated, it was "entirely justified" to make exceptions to certain aspects of general economic policy should these conflict with overall political aims. He believed that it was desirable to make use of "palliatives" such as gold sales in order to "buy time" until the military situation improved and the mission's other reforms began to bear fruit. In particular, he felt it was "critically important" to maintain political and economic stability until the forthcoming offensive against the insurgents. Moreover, the endorsement of the gold policy was seen as a source of potential leverage over the government, which was obliged to promise several reform measures. Coombs later argued that the temporary expenditure of gold worth $8.7 million was a small price to pay to save the entire AMAG program.[74]

Thus in essence AMAG found itself adopting a stance eerily reminiscent of that taken by the British two years before. In both cases, longer-term goals were temporarily subordinated to more immediate considerations. If anything, the repetition of the gold scenario merely indicates how little had been achieved on the fundamental problems. Historical accounts of AMAG's role in Greece for the most part emphasize the unprecedented degree of control the U.S. advisers were able to

73. James Warren, Jr., Letters to the author, August 19, 1999, September 3, 1999; FRUS, 1947: Griswold to the Secretary of State, September 15, 1947, vol. 5, 337–40; Lovett to AMAG, December 30, 1947, vol. 5, 478–80; Wittner, *American Intervention in Greece*, 375.

74. FRUS, 1947: Memorandum by the Political Section of the Embassy in Greece, December 6, 1947, vol. 5, 440–49; Howard to the Secretary of State, December 10, 1947, vol. 5, 449–52; Politakis, *Greek Policies of Recovery and Reconstruction*, 234–35; Coombs, *Financial Policy in Greece*, 195, 200.

exercise over the Greeks.[75] However, the fact that the mission felt so compelled to compromise, despite its powers and financial clout, suggests that its control was far from complete. It is worth considering why AMAG was so unable to impose its will on the Greeks on several major issues.

Part of the explanation lies in the general response of the government in Athens. Initially, it seemed that the extensive powers granted to AMAG could be exercised without generating too much friction. Fully aware that the mission was an unavoidable element of the U.S. aid package, the government was happy to agree to stringent conditions. The Greek chargé d'affaires in Washington was under no illusions as to the extent that the arrangements infringed his country's sovereignty, but felt this was a relatively minor issue given the more pressing need to secure U.S. help. The only hostile reaction to Public Law 75, the congressional act approving Truman's proposals for Greece and Turkey, came from the Turkish foreign minister rather than from any Greek official.[76]

This apparent eagerness to cooperate with AMAG, however, did not always translate into a harmonious relationship once the mission was in place. Every controversial measure became a battle of wits between AMAG and the government, creating interminable delays. Thus, the FTA was not set up until October 1947, even though a previous government had approved the measure as far back as February. Despite governmental approval of abandoning bread subsidies, indicated by its acceptance of the December budget, the move was not enacted until the summer of 1948. While Greek politicians deliberately avoided direct confrontation with the mission, they were reticent when it came to publicly supporting its policies. In the meantime, the persistent clamor for increased U.S. aid continued unabated. Coombs felt that the assumption that Greece deserved further help was so taken for granted that any politician who failed to stress the point was risking political suicide. Such attitudes proved unhelpful in the light of AMAG's determination to secure the maximum deployment of Greece's own resources, and with local politicians still reluctant to assume any responsibility for the country's recovery, the mission perceived itself as a "convenient scapegoat" for every unpopular policy.[77] Thus before long, AMAG found itself in a situation far removed from that which had been envisaged, as the public did anything but "rally around" its program.

The difficulties facing AMAG were well illustrated by the obstacles encountered

75. Typical of this approach are the works of Amen, *American Foreign Policy in Greece;* Kofas, *Intervention and Underdevelopment;* Wittner, *American Intervention in Greece;* and T. C. Kariotis, "American Economic Penetration of Greece in the Late Nineteen Forties."

76. Politakis, *Greek Policies of Recovery and Reconstruction,* 213–14.

77. Coombs, *Financial Policy in Greece,* 57–62.

by the administrative reform drive. The September agreement with the civil servants had secured several concessions in exchange for the pay raises. More than fifteen thousand employees, nearly a quarter of the total, were to be laid off, while all
new appointments were to be frozen. A uniform forty-hour week was to be adopted
in all offices and the use of overtime was to be curtailed. According to Hubert Gallagher, who headed the Civil Government Division, these measures proved particularly unpopular, attracting widespread opposition from the government and
the civil service and provoking violent anti-American sentiments from the Athens
press. While delegations of sacked employees protested vociferously, the government obstructed matters by endlessly debating and finally rejecting special legislation to cover the redundancies. Although open strikes were avoided, workplace
disruptions became commonplace as officials resorted to go-slow actions. In the
end, the results of the reform drive were mixed. No more than eighty-five hundred
employees were dismissed, roughly half of the projected total. Even this exaggerated the true picture as most of those laid off were temporary employees, often
wives or daughters of civil servants, while many others were holders of more than
one post. In some cases, vital personnel were deliberately discharged apparently in
an attempt to undermine the entire venture. AMAG claimed greater success with
the other clauses in the agreement, though it was clear that a vast effort would still
be required in the future.[78]

Even more damaging was the general stance of many interest groups within the
country. At first, the Americans were reluctant to judge the wealthy sections of
Greek society too harshly. An official at the U.S. embassy in Athens responded
coolly to complaints about the selfishness of the "Greek business classes" voiced
by Gregory and Patterson, claiming that all private individuals, whether Greek or
otherwise, tended to protect their own interests, and that only government policy could be blamed for the situation. Nevertheless, the same "business classes"
were potentially jeopardizing their interests by failing to cooperate with AMAG. As
Thomadakis points out, they were playing a risky game in antagonizing the mission. They had to regard the Americans as their political allies given that Washington's support was the principal guarantee of a noncommunist Greece. Nevertheless,
they frequently refused to act as economic allies by continuing to pursue their own
self-interest even when this cut across the mission's policies.[79] The persistence of

78. Gallagher, "Administrative Reorganization in the Greek Crisis," 250–58; Colman, "Civil
Service Reform in Greece," 86–93.
79. DSR 868.515/3–2847, Groves to the Secretary of State, March 28, 1947 (Enclosure: Gregory
and Patterson to Maximos, March 10, 1947); S. B. Thomadakis, "The Truman Doctrine: Was
There a Development Agenda?" 47.

gold speculation, capital flight, and resistance to taxation and any form of insti-tutionalized supervision all served to embarrass AMAG throughout its period of activities. The all too frequent inability of both the mission and the government to impose any meaningful restraint on the actions of certain groups allowed such behavior to pass unpunished.

Thus in its dealings with both the government and powerful interest groups, AMAG found itself facing the same relentlessly uphill struggle that had proved so daunting for the BEM. As Fatouros observes, Greek politicians were particularly adept at subverting formal controls to achieve their aims.[80] In such circumstances, the mission's powers could not easily translate into practical results. Like the British before them, the Americans felt obliged to sanction gold sales partly in the hope of staving off immediate disaster, and partly in the belief that such a concession could be used to gain leverage over the Greeks on other issues. Both lines of thinking amounted to a tacit admission of powerlessness.

To a certain extent, AMAG itself was to blame for some of the friction. Its powers were not always used in the most tactful manner. Initially, the overzealous expec-tations of the mission's members, together with their apparent emphasis on "ac-tion almost for the sake of action," their naive assumption that U.S. aid amounted to "pure generosity," and their inflexibility and inclination to "impose American methods" did little to foster smooth relations with the Greeks. Coombs claimed that such difficulties were largely overcome with time. More serious was the consis-tently crude approach of Griswold, who summed up his general stance by claiming that the achievement of "good results" was far more important than worries about accusations of interference. His dealings with Greek politicians were notable for a marked lack of subtlety, particularly during his efforts to broaden the government in the summer of 1947. Moreover, despite clear instructions to exercise great caution of his handling of the press, his concept of public relations left much to be desired.[81]

Not everyone was equally enthusiastic about this approach. Clifford Norton, who had succeeded Leeper as British ambassador in March 1946, claimed he "could never speak to the Greeks" as Griswold did. Even U.S. officials began to feel deep disquiet. Rankin warned that the Greeks were unlikely to warm to such "colonial treatment."[82] More fundamental was the opposition voiced by MacVeagh, leading

80. A. Fatouros, "Building Formal Structures of Penetration: The United States in Greece, 1947–1948," 258.

81. Coombs, *Financial Policy in Greece*, 61–62; FRUS, 1947: Griswold to the Secretary of State, August 5, 1947, vol. 5, 279–80; Wittner, *American Intervention in Greece*, 110–11; J. O. Iatrides, ed., *Ambassador MacVeagh Reports: Greece, 1933–1947*, 726–27.

82. Cited in Wittner, *American Intervention in Greece*, 117.

to a serious rift between the U.S. embassy in Athens and AMAG. When the mission was first proposed, he had specifically requested that it should not be headed by a politician, but his request was ignored. Before long he came to feel deep dismay about the way in which American policy was being conducted. It was MacVeagh who had complained of the apparent one-sidedness of the London Agreement and had likened the powers granted to the British as akin to those once wielded by the German occupiers. Consistent with this stance, he stressed the advisability of "careful non interference in Greek internal affairs" and warned that the mission was in danger of appearing as a "disintegrating factor" thanks to Griswold's meddling in the country's politics. Moreover, he deplored the adverse publicity that some of Griswold's blunter statements were attracting in the international press. However, his opposition failed to sway Washington. The preferred solution to the conflict was not to force Griswold to tone down his approach, but to remove MacVeagh from office. After leaving Athens, the former ambassador warned that the Marshall Plan should take care to avoid the mistakes made in Greece, and predicted dire consequences if the activities of U.S. advisers in Europe were to be subordinated to the "interference and dictation of politically ambitious amateurs."[83]

Conclusions

Between 1944 and early 1947, Washington was subjected to almost continuous pressure from all quarters to become more involved in Greek affairs. While the British sought moral and material support, the Greeks looked to the United States as the only feasible source of large-scale financial assistance and campaigned relentlessly for sizable American credits. In the meantime, officials from both American and international agencies warned of the gravity of events unfolding in the country. Nevertheless, although the full extent of the problems was clearly perceived in Washington, there was little initial interest in taking any direct action. On the contrary, fears of being seen to associate with a British venture deterred the U.S. government from considering anything more than a token commitment. Far from the "Anglo-American struggle for hegemony in Greece" that some accounts portray, the truth was that the Americans were simply not sufficiently interested in Greece to take significant action prior to 1947.[84]

Such apparent indifference rapidly evaporated once Washington started to feel anxious about the potential threat of communism. Whereas the Americans had

83. Iatrides, ed., *Ambassador MacVeagh Reports,* 716–34.
84. Kofas, *Intervention and Underdevelopment,* 31.

A Greek woman and her child in the shadow of the Stars and Stripes, October 29, 1947.
M. Katsigeras, *Greece: Twentieth Century, 1946–2000* (Athens, 2001).

once decried British attempts to exclude any Soviet involvement in Greece, their own conversion to an anti-Moscow line was to culminate in an ideological crusade first suggested by the Truman Doctrine. Whether or not the new American stance was an excuse to launch the Cold War or the response to a British plot to achieve the same end is entirely beyond the scope of this book. What is important is the fact that the United States chose to take over Britain's role in Greece and was thus obliged to face the same problems that had earlier defeated the British. The proposed solutions, subsequent compromises, and ultimate outcome of the American involvement during 1947–1948 are particularly valuable in assessing the earlier activities of the British.

Before the Americans became involved in earnest, they were fully aware that Greek recovery would require immense sums. However, they also understood that little would be achieved if they heeded Greek requests to extend huge credits without any conditions as to how such credits would be used. Given the dismal record of successive governments in Athens, it was clear that any extensive U.S. help would require strict guidelines as to the use to which the aid was put. Fearful of provoking accusations of imperialism from Athens and Washington, the British had always shied away from imposing any effective restraints on Greek government actions. The Americans, anxious both to safeguard their considerable outlays and ensure the country's future as a bulwark against the communist threat, felt no such qualms.

Such perceptions were central to the Porter report, the most detailed summary of American understanding of the Greek crisis and the solutions necessary to restore stability. On the practical side, the Porter recommendations largely tallied with the British approach in that fiscal orthodoxy and currency stability were seen as the only guarantee of a return to economic normality. The Porter report, however, went much further by recommending the deliberate investment of extensive resources to foster economic development.

By and large, British officials gave a favorable reception to the Porter report. It contained "no surprises" for them, as the Porter Mission had consulted extensively with members of the BEM. However, while they accepted that some parts were "full of good sense," they were convinced its entire tone was "over-optimistic." They believed that even if the U.S. program lasted a full five years, its objectives could not be achieved. Moreover, they were critical of the failure to appreciate the difficulties associated with certain measures. They warned that the assumption of a substantial increase in taxation was entirely unrealistic, and the American insistence that firms should maintain detailed business records would be meaningless without the creation of a proper body of auditors. They also clearly saw that Porter's call for even such minor control measures as an antihoarding campaign would necessitate an "onerous" effort. They dismissed his recommendations on industry and agriculture as "well-worn advice" not backed up by any realistic indication as to how it could be enacted.[85]

Apart from such tactical differences, the broad emulation of the British emphasis on fiscal orthodoxy reinforced by selective control measures has attracted considerable criticism from later authors, who reject the anti-inflationary priorities as overly conservative. For Thomadakis, the basic failing of American actions was that they failed to challenge the "existing structure of property relations" and thus the "prerogatives" of the local "bourgeoisie." Elsewhere, he dismisses such institutional arrangements as the FTA as creating not so much a comprehensive "antispeculative program" as a compromise "dual structure," with central supervision imposed on some areas while others were left to "uninhibited private initiative." For Wittner, price controls would have been far more progressive than the measures taken on public finances and wage restraint. According to him, AMAG policies offered nothing more than the "familiar nostrum of free enterprise economics," taken directly from Adam Smith. Kofas goes even further. He castigates the "laissez faire-minded Americans," particularly for agreeing to the raising of import duties while Washington was actively promoting free trade via the General Agreement on Tariffs and Trade (GATT). Moreover, he declares that the excessive emphasis on military expenditure ruled out the chance of a "speedy economic recovery" on the lines of that occurring in Yugoslavia and elsewhere in the Balkans.[86]

Some of these criticisms are confusing, in that AMAG is condemned as being both too laissez-faire and too interventionist. Such views fail to appreciate that economic management as practiced by both the British and the Americans during the war combined state intervention with free enterprise. Although economic controls sought to elevate the broader interests of the state, particularly in the deployment of scarce resources, the private sector was allowed to flourish within certain limits. The failure to implement the full range of potential controls in Greece was due less to an obsession with Adam Smith than to the opposition of powerful interest groups and successive governments in Athens, all of which far exceeded the Americans in their zealous attachment to the laissez-faire approach. For the interest groups this meant continued freedom to exploit the crisis, while for the government it meant doing as little as possible, in the hope that huge injections of foreign aid would provide a

85. FO371/67101 R8888, Comments on Mr. Paul Porter's Report of April 30th 1947, June 24, 1947; Rapp to FO, June 25, 1947.

86. Thomadakis, "Truman Doctrine," 30; S. B. Thomadakis, "Stabilization, Development, and Government Economic Authority in the 1940s," 217; Wittner, *American Intervention in Greece*, 173, 190–91; Kofas, *Intervention and Underdevelopment*, 100, 103–4.

ready-made solution. It is likely that much more could have been achieved had economic abuses been tackled as ruthlessly as the real or imagined political opposition to the right-wing governments after 1946.

More seriously, the criticisms of AMAG imply that it deliberately favored business circles while promoting policies prejudicial to the interests of the working classes. In political terms, there is no doubt that the anticommunist fears of many AMAG officials led to heavy-handed meddling in the affairs of the Greek trade unions.[87] In economic terms, although it is clear that the rich in Greece were consistently able to protect their own interests while the poor were not so fortunate, it is highly debatable whether the Americans should be blamed for such a distasteful outcome. AMAG's failure to enforce a fuller range of controls is less ideologically black-and-white than some authors choose to believe. Porter's conviction that extensive controls would not work in Greece was a reluctant acknowledgment of the weakness of the country's administrative machinery. The suggestion that price controls should have been adopted fails to take account of the enormous effort involved in administering such measures. The main reason why AMAG refrained from insisting on widespread controls, just as the British ceased to press the point, was that a comprehensive system was clearly beyond the pathetically inadequate Greek civil service. The same reality also ruled out meaningful returns from direct taxation, necessitating a reliance on customs duties. The real tragedy of the failure to introduce economic controls was perhaps not so much AMAG's reluctance to take a stand on the issue, but the fact that the government and bureaucracy in Athens had moved no nearer toward accepting the concept despite so many years of outside pressure. While the emphasis on wages may indeed seem morally tainted given the absence of corresponding action on prices, the simple fact was that formal controls on wages were considerably easier to apply. The near disaster of the FTA episode, where highly experienced and zealous officials were overwhelmed by the sheer volume of work, illustrates the enormity of such tasks. How the administration of sophisticated control measures, not to mention the launching of a centrally planned industrialization drive, could have been expected from a state machinery unable even to collect a decent income tax, is left unexplained by the critics of American policy.

The essentially ideological approach taken by much of the subsequent historiography fails to take account of the causes and consequences of inflation. While it is clearly possible to question aspects of American policy toward Greece, particularly its overbearing sense of self-righteousness, its obsession with the communist

87. A. Pollis, "U.S. Intervention in Greek Trade Unions, 1947–1950," 258–74.

threat and its tacit toleration of human rights abuses, its emphasis on fiscal ortho-doxy should not be regarded as a question of moral choices, and should not be portrayed in such terms. The assumption that any solution not based on the im-mediate containment of inflation would have been preferable cannot be sustained. If the outcome was both deeply unsatisfactory and socially inequitable, this was the result not so much of anti-inflationary policies per se, as of the failure to apply the full range of such policies.

Although AMAG was theoretically equipped to overcome the twin restraints that had defeated British efforts in Greece, the relative modesty of the American achievements during 1947–1948 suggests that the real solution to the Greek prob-lem was far more complex. Possessing powers and resources beyond the dreams of the BEM, AMAG was still unable to make meaningful progress in several key areas and was forced into many uncomfortable compromises reminiscent of the earlier British experience. To be fair, the scale of the continuing civil war swallowed up an increasingly large share of the initially handsome resources available, but even so AMAG's record was not especially impressive. Despite the ability to tamper with cabinets and to exercise various forms of leverage over government actions, the mission could not effect any significant economic transformation. This clearly indicates that the degree of effective control wielded by the Americans was more apparent than real. By the middle of 1948, the fundamental problems were still far from resolved and would continue to defy policy makers for a long time to come.

CONCLUSIONS

In October 1944 the returning National Unity Government inherited a colossal economic disaster brought about by the circumstances of the German occupation. While it was inevitable that the task of rescuing a devastated economy and a discredited currency would prove daunting, it seemed reasonable to hope that with a combination of resolute action from the government, material and moral support from the Allies, and popular goodwill, a measure of normality could be restored and made to serve as a basis for future reconstruction. Nevertheless, by the time the British pulled out in early 1947, Greece was no nearer to economic stability. Despite a massive Allied relief effort and sound advice on ways to overcome the crisis, the threat of further rapid inflation hovered constantly in the background.

In the light of theoretical considerations and the previous historical experience of inflation and stabilization, the material addressed in this book suggests three overriding conclusions. First, even if the hyperinflation was caused by the external factor of Axis occupation, the mediocre results of successive attempts to stabilize the economy were almost entirely due to internal factors such as the fiscal ineptitude of the government and its ignorance of and hostility toward any form of economic management. Second, while many authors have chosen to blame foreign intervention for prolonging the crisis, it is clear that the decisions of successive Greek governments were a far more significant factor. Although the British made several mistakes in their dealings with Athens, their advice was invariably orthodox, enshrining the only known solutions to hyperinflation. Such orthodoxy would have involved painful decisions, which Greek governments, determined to hold out for massive foreign aid, successfully managed to avoid. Finally, the book demonstrates how strongly many aspects of post-liberation Greece were rooted in the country's political, economic, and social past.

While economists and economic historians continue to debate the precise combination of measures needed to achieve stabilization, what is most striking in the Greek case was not the relative efficacy of individual policies, but rather the reluctance on the part of Greek authorities to take any decisive action at all. In the absence of a broad attack on inflation, the currency reform of November 1944 achieved little in itself beyond a return to more manageable numbers. The tax

system was never overhauled, and indirect duties continued to provide a significant share of public revenue while corporate profits and most real wealth were left
lightly taxed. This cavalier attitude toward revenue was accompanied by an equally
reckless disregard of the need to keep a check on expenditure. As a result, chronic
budget deficits necessitated continuous recourse to the printing press. Despite the
existence of a nominally independent central bank, issues to the government were
made on a regular basis with little regard for agreed limits. The abandonment of
exchange controls in 1946 had the serious consequence of dissipating a large part
of Greece's foreign currency reserves. No controls over wages were ever seriously
enforced, and price controls were attempted only by Varvaressos, in circumstances
almost guaranteed to ensure failure. Such progress as was achieved was the result of
incessant pressure from the British rather than deliberate policy of any government
in Athens. Some improvements in revenue collection and a degree of discipline in
public spending were pushed through not by officials of the finance ministry but
by accountants from the BEM. Controls over note circulation and foreign exchange
were imposed and administered not by the Bank of Greece but by the Currency
Committee.

While seeking to avoid acting on the advice received from the British (and later
the Americans), Greek governments preferred their own solutions to the crisis—
gold sales, lifting all restrictions on imports, pursuing the maximum amount of
assistance from abroad. All three seemed to offer the advantage of removing the
need to fight inflation with painful and unpopular policies. Nevertheless, not one
of the measures addressed the fundamental problems of an insolvent government
seeking to avoid responsibility for rejuvenating a devastated economy.

Stabilization Measures Enacted in Greece 1944-1947

Measures	Application
Budget Reforms	Government hostility to insistence on balanced budget Unwillingness to reform taxes or curb expenditure Modest improvement thanks to BEM and AMAG pressure
Central Bank	No real control over note issues - role eventually enforced by Currency Committee
Foreign Loans	Persistently sought by Greek side Large sums reluctantly granted by Allies
New Currency	Issued November 1944
Price Controls	Brief episode in 1945 defeated by powerful interest groups Little popular compliance Not accompanied by rationing or state controls over supply and distribution
Wage Controls	Not enforced until after 1947

Greek governments were usually quick to point out the impossibility, irrelevance, or impracticality of policies advocated by the British, and preferred to emphasize the need for substantial economic help from the Allies. By such means, it was possible to blame the foreign advisers for the impasse. Many subsequent authors have chosen to take up this theme, suggesting that foreign interference rather than internal factors compounded the crisis.

It would clearly be naive to accept the assumption that British actions in Greece were simply an act of disinterested benevolence toward a wartime ally. The British were as much guided by political self-interest as any other player in the crisis, and their political stance often did little to help matters. Nevertheless, both theoretical considerations and the historical experience demonstrate that the recommendations they gave to the Greeks were largely correct. The insistence on sound public finances, proper taxation, and supervision of imports, prices, and wages, so strenuously resented by successive governments in Athens, offered the sole reliable basis for recovery. Even if British advisers sometimes found themselves trapped in a cul-de-sac in their haste to tackle inflation—as in their preaching the "gospel of control" in a country demonstrably unable to implement controls, or in their serious lapse of judgment during the imports episode of 1946—their basic advice contained the only feasible long-term solution to the crisis.

Unfortunately for the British, they found themselves with neither carrot nor stick to persuade the Greeks to adopt orthodox fiscal and monetary policies. While the apparent degree of British control was resented by Greek politicians, who complained of interference and affronts to national sovereignty—a concept that has received some acceptance from later historians—the record shows that such control was largely illusory. The advice offered by the British was either consistently ignored or circumvented in a variety of ways, while the imposition of foreign-sponsored institutions achieved little in itself. The work of the BEM and Currency Committee was persistently undermined by withholding information and creating alternative channels to fund additional public spending, while attempts to create such bodies as the GCC to oversee imports came to nothing. The total hollowness of any effective control by the British is demonstrated by the long-running clash on gold sales during 1946–1947. Despite considerable hostility toward the policy, the British were forced to cave in time and time again in the face of Greek intransigence. The real failure of British involvement in Greece was the commitment of so much time, effort, and prestige without the means to guarantee the outcome. However, the later experience of AMAG suggests that even with far more extensive powers and resources, imposing meaningful supervision over Greek governments was far from straightforward.

While the fragile provisional governments of the Center could be partially excused for their reluctance to undertake unpopular measures, the same could hardly be said of the elected governments of the Right after March 1946. Any unwillingness to cooperate with solutions suggested by British advisers would be understandable if Greek governments had possessed their own definite plans to overcome the crisis. However, this was never the case. Only Varvaressos was prepared to implement a coherent program, but his reforms failed to attract any support from the rest of the Greek political establishment. Instead, politicians preferred the easy options of mopping up surplus purchasing power via gold sales and unrestricted imports, while hoping that Greece would be bailed out by massive financial aid from the Allies. It is not impossible that a more generous aid package from the British might have produced a more enthusiastic response from the Greek side, particularly during the euphoric period immediately following liberation, and might have created an atmosphere more conducive to the acceptance of unwelcome advice. However, the reverse seems more compelling—it seems barely credible that large sums would have been simply handed over to governments in Athens given the complete absence of any concrete program. In any case, without appropriate action on the budget, large-scale injections of capital into Greece might have temporarily alleviated some problems, but would have made little difference in the long run.

While bemoaning foreign interference, the refusal of Greek governments to act inevitably prolonged the dependency on foreign capital, and was to prove costly in many ways. Many historians have chosen to blame foreign advisers for foisting socially inequitable policies on Greece, but it is worth remembering that successive governments in Athens chose to ignore persistent British strictures on the need to tax higher incomes and thus helped to create a laissez-faire haven in which the rich and powerful could exploit the crisis on a scale scarcely imaginable anywhere else in postwar Europe. It is possible to follow Varvaressos and castigate the blatant pursuit of self-interest by wealthy Greeks, who compounded many of the country's problems and alienated both British and American observers, but the blame has to lie with the politicians for allowing such excesses to continue unhindered. Greek ministers had once pointed out that the country's universal impoverishment ruled out any increases in taxation, and had argued that anything more than a token income tax amounted to political suicide, but were willing to sanction measures that allowed the rich to protect their wealth via investment in gold and foreign currency. The purchase of more than two million sovereigns and the considerable imports of luxuries testify to the untaxed wealth forsaken by the government in its greatest hour of need. By leaving the fundamental causes of inflation untouched, the crisis was dragged out unnecessarily, prolonging the hardship of the poorer sections of society—those with barely enough drachmae to survive, let alone convert into gold or resaleable commodities. If the militancy of hard-pressed civil servants and industrial workers was customarily defused by frequent wage concessions, this was an empty gesture given that pay raises were inevitably swallowed up by rapid price increases.

Perhaps the events of 1944–1947 should not be seen as too surprising given the general attitudes of Greek politicians over the previous century. Most of the central features—the preoccupation with political squabbling, a reluctance to move beyond laissez-faire, the apparent lack of concern over chronic budget and balance of payments deficits, the consistent pandering to powerful interest groups, and the frequent reliance on foreign capital coupled with a total resentment of any conditions that foreign loans could entail—simply repeated many previous episodes in the country's history. The colossal economic disaster inherited from the Nazis demanded a decisive break with long-established patterns of behavior and a willingness to take heed of the experience of other countries. The technocrat Varvaressos seemed to be virtually alone in grasping this necessity, while the rest, burdened with attitudes so firmly rooted in the past, ensured that Greece was hopelessly ill-equipped to deal with post-liberation realities.

PRINCIPAL CHARACTERS

Acheson, Dean. U.S. Assistant Secretary of State (1941–1945). U.S. Undersecretary of State (1945–1947).

Attlee, Clement. Leader of the British Labour Party and Prime Minister (1945–1951).

Bevin, Ernest. Secretary of State for Foreign Affairs (1945–1951).

Blackburn, T. J. British member of budget committee in the Ministry of Finance.

Board, Sir Vyvyan. Head of industry section (BEM).

Bolton, George. Adviser to the Governor (1941–1948), Bank of England.

Byrnes, James F. U.S. Secretary of State (1945–1947).

Caccia, Harold. Took charge of the British embassy in Athens during Leeper's leave in Britain, 1945.

Churchill, Winston. British Prime Minister (1940–1945).

Clark, Lieutenant General John. Head of BEM in Athens.

Cobbold, Cameron Fromanteel. Executive Director (1938–1945), Deputy Governor (1945–1949), Bank of England.

Coombs, Charles A. The UNRRA statistician in Athens. Head of public finance division (AMAG).

Dalton, Hugh. Chancellor of the Exchequer (1945–1947).

Damaskinos. Archbishop of Athens and All Greece. Prime Minister (October 1945). Regent (1944–1946).

Davidson, Douglas. Senior Treasury official.

Eady, Sir Wilfrid. Senior Treasury official.

Eden, Anthony. Secretary of State for Foreign Affairs (1940–1945).

Ethridge, Mark. U.S. Representative on the UN Commission of Investigation in the Balkans (1947).

Gallagher, Hubert. Head of civil government division (AMAG).

George II. King of the Hellenes (1922–1923, 1935–1941, 1941–1946 in exile, 1946–1947).

Golden, Clinton. Head of labor division (AMAG).

Gregory, Sir Theodore. British member in Currency Committee in Athens, succeeded John Nixon in November 1946.

Griswold, Dwight. Former governor of Nebraska. Chief of AMAG.

Grove, Edward. Head of finance section (BEM).

Helmis, Dimitrios. Minister of Finance in cabinet of Tsaldaris (April–January 1947); and in cabinet of Maximos (January 1947).

Hendrickson, R. F. Director, Food Distribution Administration, War Food Administration; Chairman, U.S. Food Requirements and Allocations Committee. Deputy U.S. member, Combined Food Board (1941–1944). Deputy Director General, Bureau of Supply, UNRRA (January 16, 1944–April 30, 1946).

Hill, Sir Quintin. Financial adviser to British embassy in Athens.

Jackson, R. G. A., C.M.G, O.B.E. (Australia) Director General, Middle East Supply Center (1943–1945). Principal Assistant to the United Kingdom Minister of State in the Middle East (1944). Senior Deputy Director General, UNRRA (February 12, 1945–October 11, 1947).

Kanellopoulos, Panagiotis. Leader of the National Unity Party. Professor of Sociology at the University of Athens. Deputy Prime Minister and Minister of Defense (1942–1943). Minister of Finance and Reconstruction in cabinet of Papandreou (June–September 1944). Minister of the Navy in National Unity Government (September–December 1944). Prime Minister (November 1945). Minister of Public Order and Minister of the Navy in cabinet of Maximos (January 1947).

Kartalis, Georgios. Head of political wing of EKKA (1943–1944). Minister of Press and Information in cabinet of Papandreou and National Unity Government (June–October 1944). Minister without portfolio in National Unity Government (October–December 1944). Minister of Supply in cabinet of Sophoulis (November 1945–March 1946).

Kasimatis, Gregorios. Professor of Law at the University of Athens. Minister of National Economy in first cabinet of Voulgaris (April–June 1945). Minister of Social Welfare in first cabinet of Voulgaris (June–August 1945) and in second cabinet of Voulgaris (August–October 1945). Minister of Finance in cabinet of Kanellopoulos (November 1945).

Keynes, John Maynard. Economic adviser to the Treasury (1940–1946).

Leeper, Sir Reginald. British ambassador to Greece (1943–1946), replaced by Clifford Norton in March 1946.

Leith-Ross, Sir Frederick, G.C.M.G., K.C.B. (United Kingdom), Chief economic adviser to government (1932–1946). Chairman, Inter-Allied Committee on Post-War Requirements (1942–1943). Deputy Director General, Department of Finance and Administration, UNRRA (January 1, 1944–May 1945).

Lehman, Herbert. H. Governor of New York (1932–1942). Director, Office of Foreign Relief and Rehabilitation Operations, U.S. Department of State (1942–1943). Director General of UNRRA (January 1, 1944–March 31, 1946).

Lingeman, E. Economic adviser to British embassy in Athens.

Lithiby, John. Adviser to the Governor (1946–1955), Bank of England.

Lord Catto of Cairncatto. Governor (1944–1949), Bank of England.

McGhee, George. Coordinator of the Greece-Turkey U.S. aid program.

McNeil, Hector. Undersecretary of State for Foreign Affairs (1945–1946).

Maben, Buell. UNRRA chief of mission in Greece (May 17, 1945–September 17, 1947). Regional director, Office of Distribution, War Food Administration (1939–1944).

Macintosh, C. British member of budget committee in the Ministry of Finance.

Mackenzie, C. Board's successor as head of industry section (BEM).

Macmillan, Harold. Minister-Resident, AFHQ, Algiers (1942–1944) and Caserta (1944–1945).

MacVeagh, Lincoln. U.S. ambassador to Greece (1933–1941, 1943–1948).

Mantzavinos, Georgios. Deputy Governor of the Bank of Greece. Minister of Finance in first cabinet of Voulgaris (April–August 1945); and second cabinet of Voulgaris (August–October 1945). Governor of the Bank of Greece (February 1946–February 1955).

Marshall, George. U.S. Secretary of State (1947–1949).

Maximos, Dimitrios. Prime Minister (January–August 1947).

Metaxas, General Ioannis. Seized power by coup d'état on August 4, 1936, and ruled as dictator (1936–1941).

Morgan, General. Supreme Allied Commander in the Mediterranean.

Mylonas, Alexandros. Leader of the Agrarian Democratic Party. Minister of the Navy in cabinet of Papandreou (May–August 1944). Minister of Finance in cabinet of Plastiras (April 1945). Minister of Finance in cabinet of Sophoulis (November 1945–March 1946).

Neubacher, Hermann. German Political and Economic Plenipotentiary for the Balkans.

Niemeyer, Sir Otto Ernst. Executive Director (1938–1949), Bank of England.

Nixon, Sir John. Head of finance section (BEM). British member in Currency Committee in Athens, replaced by Theodore Gregory in November 1946.

Norton, Sir Clifford. British ambassador to Greece, succeeded Reginald Leeper in March 1946.

Papandreou, Georgios. Leader of the Liberal Party. Prime Minister (April 1944–January 1945). Minister of the Interior in cabinet of Maximos (January 1947).

Patterson, Gardner. U.S. member in Currency Committee in Athens.

Pintos, Ieronymos. Professor of Economics at Panteion University. Deputy Minister of Supply (June–September 1945).

Plastiras, General Nikolaos. Prime Minister (January–April 1945).

Porter, Paul. Chief of American Economic Mission to Greece (January–March 1947).

Rankin, Karl. Chargé d'Affaires at the U.S. embassy in Athens.

Rapp, Thomas. British consul general in Thessaloniki (1944–1946). Acted as deputy of BEM from July 1946.

Roosevelt, Franklin D. President of the United States.

Scobie, Lieutenant General Ronald. Commander, British Land Forces, Greece (1944–1946).

Sideris, Georgios. Minister of Finance in cabinet of Plastiras (January–April 1945).

Siepmann, Harry. Adviser to the Governor (1926–1945), Executive Director (1945–1954), Bank of England.

Sophianopoulos, Ioannis. Minister for Foreign Affairs in cabinet of Plastiras (January–April 1945); in first cabinet of Voulgaris (April–July 1945); in cabinet of Sophoulis (November 1945–January 1946).

Sophoulis, Themistocles. Succeeded Eleftherios Venizelos as leader of the Liberal Party (1936). Prime Minister (November 1945–March 1946). Minister of Public Order (February–March 1946). Prime Minister (September 1947–June 1949).

Stephanopoulos, Stephanos. Minister of Coordination in cabinet of Tsaldaris (April 1946–January 1947); and in cabinet of Maximos (January 1947).

Stettinius, Edward R. U.S. Assistant Secretary of State (1943–1944). U.S. Secretary of State (1944–1945).

Svolos, Alexandros. Professor of Constitutional Law at the University of Athens. President of the PEEA (April 1944). Minister of Finance in National Unity Government (September–December 1944).

Truman, Harry S. President of the United States.

Tsaldaris, Konstantinos. Leader of the Populist Party. Prime Minister (1946–1947). Deputy Prime Minister and Minister for Foreign Affairs (1947–1949).

Tsouderos, Emmanuel. Governor of the Bank of Greece (1931–1939). Prime Minister (April 1941–April 1944). Minister of Coordination in cabinet of Sophoulis (November 1945–March 1946).

Varvaressos, Kyriakos. Governor of the Bank of Greece (August 1939–October 1944), (January 1945–September 1945). Minister of Finance in cabinet of Tsouderos (1941–1943). Deputy Prime Minister and Minister of Supply in first cabinet of Voulgaris (June–August 1945); and in second cabinet of Voulgaris (August–September 1945).

Venizelos, Sophocles. Son of Eleftherios Venizelos. Minister of the Navy in cabinet of Tsouderos (1943–1944). Prime Minister (April 1944). Deputy Prime Minister in cabinet of Papandreou (April–August 1944). Deputy Prime Minister in cabinet of Maximos (January 1947).

Voulgaris, Admiral Petros. Prime Minister (April–October 1945).

Waley, Sir David. Senior Treasury official.

Wilson, General Sir Henry Maitland. Supreme Allied Commander in the Mediterranean.

Zafiriou, Rena. Assistant to K. Varvaressos during the war. Head of the "Economic Service of the Vice President" within the Bank of Greece (June–September 1945).

Zolotas, Xenophon. Professor of Economics at the University of Athens. Cogovernor of the Bank of Greece (October 1944–January 1945).

BIBLIOGRAPHY

Unpublished Sources

Archives

Unpublished Sources

Foreign Office (FO) Public Record Office, Kew
FO800/475; FO371/20389, 32206, 43723, 43724, 43725, 43726, 48257, 48261, 48262, 48263, 48264, 48265, 48266, 48267, 48268, 48269, 48272, 48273, 48274, 48275, 48276, 48277, 48278, 48279, 48280, 48282, 48284, 48285, 48286, 48289, 48326, 48327, 48328, 48329, 48330, 48331, 48332, 48333, 48334, 48335, 48336, 48337, 48338, 48347, 48373, 48374, 48375, 48416, 48452, 58667, 58673, 58677, 58678, 58679, 58680, 58681, 58683, 58688, 58697, 58706, 58715, 58720, 58721, 58722, 58723, 58724, 58725, 58726, 58727, 58728, 58729, 58730, 58731, 58732, 58733, 58765, 58766, 58790, 58798, 58803, 58804, 58805, 58806, 58814, 67013, 67014, 67017, 67034, 67039, 67046, 67101, 67102

War Office (WO) Public Record Office, Kew
WO204/3561, 3562, 3564, 8760, 8761, 8765, 8608; 904/8611

Treasury (T) Public Record Office, Kew
T160; T236/139, 149, 1044, 1045, 1046, 1047, 1048, 1049, 1050, 1051, 1052, 1053

Cabinet (CAB) Public Record Office, Kew
CAB65/44, 65/49, 65/53, 128/2, 128/5, 129/4

Bank of England (BE) Bank of England Archive, London
OV80/21, 22, 26, 27, 28

Labour Party National Museum of Labour History, Manchester
International Department, Correspondence on Greece, Boxes 2, 3

United States

Department of State Records (DSR) National Archives and Records Administration, Washington, D.C.
DSR 868.00, 868.50, 868.51, 868.515, 868.516, 868.5151

Greece

Library of the Bank of Greece (LBG) Kyriakos Varvaressos Archive (KVA), Athens
LBG/KVA, (19)9, B(2), B2, B4, B5, B/1, B/2, B/5, Δ3-(B), Δ4-(B), φ11/Δ3(B), φ13/Δ3(B)

Historical Archive of the National Bank of Greece (HANBG) Athens
HANBG, 32(file 38) Occupation-Reconstruction

Personal Communications

Gardner Patterson. Letter to the author, February 24, 1998
Rena Zafiriou. Letters to the author, April 2, 1998, April 21, 1998, May 5, 1998, November 15, 2001
James C. Warren, Jr. Letters to the author, August 19, 1999, September 3, 1999

Published Sources

Official Publications, etc.

Bank of Greece. *The Economic Situation in Greece and the Bank of Greece in 1946: Report for the Years 1941, 1944, 1945 and 1946.* Athens, 1948.
Bank of Greece. *Τα Πρώτα Πενήντα Χρόνια της Τραπέζης της Ελλάδος.* (The First Fifty Years of the Bank of Greece.) Athens, 1978.
Department of State. *Foreign Relations of the United States (FRUS).* Washington, D.C.: U.S. Government Printing Office, vols. 5 (1944), 8 (1945), 7 (1946), 5 (1947).
Food and Agriculture Organization. *Report of the FAO Mission for Greece.* Washington, D.C.: Food and Agriculture Organization, 1947.
League of Nations. *The Course and Control of Inflation: A Review of Monetary Experience in Europe after World War II.* League of Nations, 1946.
Ministry of National Economy and General Statistical Service of Greece. *Bulletin Mensuel du Commerce Special de la Grece avec les Pays Etrangers.* Athens, 1948.

Royal Institute of International Affairs. *South-Eastern Europe: A Political and Economic Survey.* London: Oxford University Press, 1939.

Supreme Reconstruction Council. *Οικονομική Βιβλιογραφία της Ελλάδος* 1945–1948. (Economic Bibliography of Greece 1945–1948.) Athens, 1949.

United Nations Relief and Rehabilitation Administration (UNRRA). *Foreign Trade in Greece.* London: UNRRA (Operational Analysis Papers no. 14), 1946.

Articles in Journals and Collective Volumes

Agapitides, S. "The Inflation of the Cost of Living and Wages in Greece during the German Occupation." *International Labor Review* 52 (1945): 643–51.

Andreopoulos, G. J. "The International Financial Commission and Anglo-Greek Relations (1928–1933)." *Historical Journal* 31 (1988): 341–64.

Angelopoulos, A. "Απάντηση στο Ερωτηματολόγιο του κ. Πόρτερ." ("A Reply to Mr. Porter's Questionnaire.") *Νέα Οικονομία* (Nea Economia) 6 (1947): 289–96.

Cairncross, Sir A. "Reconversion, 1945–51." In *The British Economy since 1945,* edited by N. F. R. Crafts and N. W. C. Woodward (Oxford: Clarendon Press, 1991), 25–51.

Capie, F. H. "Conditions in Which Very Rapid Inflation Has Appeared." In *Major Inflations in History,* edited by F. H. Capie (Aldershot: Elgar, 1991), 3–56.

———, and G. E. Wood. "The Anatomy of a Wartime Inflation: Britain, 1939–1945." In *The Sinews of War: Essays on the Economic History of World War II,* edited by G. T. Mills and H. Rockoff (Ames: Iowa State University Press, 1993), 21–42.

Clive, N. "British Policy Alternatives 1945–1946." In *Studies in the History of the Greek Civil War 1945–1949,* edited by L. Baerentzen, J. O. Iatrides, and O. L. Smith (Copenhagen: Museum Tusculanum Press, 1987), 213–23.

Clogg, R. "The Greek Government-in-Exile." *International History Review* 1 (1979): 376–98.

Colman, W. G. "Civil Service Reform in Greece." *Public Personnel Review* 10 (1949): 86–93.

Creveld, M. Van. "The German Attack on the USSR: The Destruction of a Legend." *European Studies Review* 2 (1972): 69–86.

Delivanis, D. "Greek Attempts at Postwar Monetary Rehabilitation." *Ekonomisk Tidskrift* 52 (1950): 84–97.

Dornbusch, R., and S. Fischer. "Stopping Hyperinflations Past and Present." *Weltwirtschaftliches Archiv* 122 (1986): 1–47.

———, F. Sturzenegger, and H. Wolf. "Extreme Inflation: Dynamics and Stabilization." *Brookings Papers on Economic Activity* 2 (1990): 1–84.

Dritsas, M. "Bank-Industry Relations in Inter-War Greece: The Case of the National Bank of Greece." In *European Industry and Banking between the Wars: A Review of Bank Industry Relations,* edited by P. L. Cottrell, H. Lindgren, and A. Teichova (Leicester: Leicester University Press, 1992), 203–17.

Fatouros, A. A. "Building Formal Structures of Penetration: The United States in Greece, 1947–1948." In *Greece in the 1940s: A Nation in Crisis,* edited by J. O. Iatrides (Hanover, N.H.: University Press of New England, 1981), 239–58.

Gallagher, H. R. "Administrative Reorganization in the Greek Crisis." *Public Administration Review* 8 (1948): 250–58.

Hadziiossif, C. "Economic Stabilization and Political Unrest: Greece 1944–1947." In *Studies in the History of the Greek Civil War 1945–1949,* edited by L. Baerentzen, J. O. Iatrides, and O. L. Smith (Copenhagen: Museum Tusculanum Press, 1987), 25–40.

————. "Η Πολιτική Οικονομία της Μεταπολεμικής Ελλάδας, 1944–1996." ("The Political Economy of Postwar Greece, 1944–1996." In *Εισαγωγή στη Νεοελληνική Οικονομική Ιστορία (18^{ος}–20^{ος} Αιώνας)* (Introduction to Modern Greek Economic History [18th–20th Centuries]), edited by V. Kremmydas, 287–318. Athens, 1999.

Howlett, P. "The Wartime Economy, 1939–1945." In *The Economic History of Britain since 1700,* edited by R. Floud and D. McCloskey (Cambridge: Cambridge University Press, 1994), vol. 3, 1–31.

Kalafatis, T. "Νομισματικές Διαρρυθμίσεις και Κοινωνικές Επιπτώσεις (1944–1946)." ("Monetary Reforms and their Social Impact (1944–1946).") In *Δεκέμβρης του 1944: Νεώτερη Έρευνα Νέες Προσεγγίσεις* (December 1944), edited by G. Farakos, 41–55. Athens, 1996.

Kazamias, G. A. "Turks, Swedes and Famished Greeks: Some Aspects of Famine Relief in Occupied Greece, 1941–44." *Balkan Studies* 33 (1992): 293–307.

Karatzas, G. "The Greek Hyperinflation and Stabilization of 1943–1946: A Comment." *Journal of Economic History* 48 (1988): 138–39.

Kariotis, T. "American Economic Penetration of Greece in the Late Nineteen Forties." *Journal of the Hellenic Diaspora* 6 (1979): 85–94.

Kondonassis, A. J. "The Greek Inflation and the Flight from the Drachma, 1940–1948." *Economy and History* 20 (1977): 41–49.

Laiou-Thomadakis, I. "The Politics of Hunger: Economic Aid to Greece, 1943–1945." *Journal of the Hellenic Diaspora* 7 (1980): 27–42.

Lazaretou, S. "Government Spending, Monetary Policies, and Exchange Rate Regime Switches: The Drachma in the Gold Standard Period." *Explorations in Economic History* 32 (1995): 28–50.

———. "Macroeconomic Policies and Nominal Exchange Rate Regimes: Greece in the Interwar Period." *Journal of European Economic History* 25 (1996): 647–70.

———. "Monetary and Fiscal Policies in Greece: 1833–1914." *Journal of European Economic History* 22 (1993): 285–311.

Makinen, G. E. "The Greek Hyperinflation and Stabilization of 1943–1946." *Journal of Economic History* 46 (1986): 795–805.

———. "The Greek Hyperinflation and Stabilization of 1943–1946: A Reply." *Journal of Economic History* 48 (1988): 140–42.

———. "The Greek Stabilization of 1944–1946." *American Economic Review* 74 (1984): 1067–74.

Mazower, M. "Banking and Economic Development in Interwar Greece." In *The Role of Banks in the Interwar Economy*, edited by H. James, H. Lindgren, and A. Teichova (Cambridge: Cambridge University Press, 1991), 206–31.

———. "The Cold War and the Appropriation of Memory: Greece after Liberation." *East European Politics and Societies* 9 (1995): 272–94.

———. "Policing the Anti-Communist State in Greece, 1922–1974." In *The Policing of Politics in the Twentieth Century*, edited by M. Mazower (Providence, R.I.: Berghahn Books, 1997), 129–50.

Mikesell, R. F. "Financial Problems of the Middle East." *Journal of Political Economy* 53 (1945): 164–76.

———. "Gold Sales as an Anti-Inflationary Device." *Review of Economic Statistics* (May 1946): 105–8.

Mills, G., and H. Rockoff. "Compliance with Price Controls in the United States and the United Kingdom during World War II." *Journal of Economic History* 47 (1987): 197–213.

Papastratis, P. "The Purge of the Greek Civil Service on the Eve of the Civil War." In *Studies in the History of the Greek Civil War 1945–1949*, edited by L. Baerentzen, J. O. Iatrides, and O. L. Smith (Copenhagen: Museum Tusculanum Press, 1987), 41–53.

———. "Purging the University after Liberation." In *After the War Was Over: Reconstructing the Family, Nation, and State in Greece, 1943–1960*, edited by M. Mazower (Princeton, N.J.: Princeton University Press, 2000), 62–72.

Pepelasis, A. A. "The Image of the Past and Economic Backwardness." *Human Organization* 17 (1958–1959): 19–27.

Pepelasis Minoglou, I. "Political Factors Shaping the Role of Foreign Finance: The Case of Greece, 1832–1932." In *The New Institutional Economics and Third World Development*, edited by J. Harriss, J. Hunter, and C. M. Lewis (London: Routledge, 1995), 250–64.

Bibliography

————. "Transplanting Institutions: The Case of the Greek Central Bank." *Greek Economic Review* 19 (1998): 33–64.

Pollis, A. "U.S. Intervention in Greek Trade Unions, 1947–1950." In *Greece in the 1940s: A Nation in Crisis,* edited by J. O. Iatrides (Hanover, N.H.: University Press of New England, 1981), 259–74.

Porter, P. A. "Wanted: A Miracle in Greece." *Collier's* (September 20, 1947).

Psalidopoulos, M. "Μορφές Οικονομικής Σκέψης στην Ελλάδα, 1936–1940." ("Forms of Economic Thought in Greece, 1936–1940.") In *Ελλάδα 1936–1944: Δικτατορία-Κατοχή-Αντίσταση* (Greece 1936–1944), edited by H. Fleischer and N. Svoronos (Athens, 1989), 98–144.

Ritter, H. "German Policy in Occupied Greece and its Economic Impact, 1941–1944." In *Germany and Europe in the Era of the Two World Wars,* edited by F. X. J. Homer and L. D. Wilcox (Charlottesville: University Press of Virginia, 1986), 157–82.

Rockoff, H. "Price and Wage Controls in Four Wartime Periods." *Journal of Economic History* 41 (1981): 381–401.

Sargent, T. J. "The Ends of Four Big Inflations." In *Inflation: Causes and Effects,* edited by R. E. Hall (Chicago: University of Chicago Press, 1982), 41–97.

Sfikas, T. "People at the Top Can Do These Things, Which Others Can't Do: Winston Churchill and the Greeks, 1940–45." *Journal of Contemporary History* 26 (1991): 307–32.

Stathakis, G. "Approaches to the Early Post-War Greek Economy: A Survey." *Journal of Modern Hellenism* 7 (1990): 163–90.

Thomadakis, S. B. "Black Markets, Inflation, and Force in the Economy of Occupied Greece." In *Greece in the 1940s: A Nation in Crisis,* edited by J. O. Iatrides (Hanover, N.H.: University Press of New England, 1981), 61–80.

————. "Stabilization, Development, and Government Economic Authority in the 1940s." In *Greece at the Crossroads: The Civil War and its Legacy,* edited by J. O. Iatrides and L. Wrigley (University Park: Pennsylvania State University Press, 1995), 173–226.

————. "The Truman Doctrine: Was There a Development Agenda?" *Journal of Modern Hellenism* 6 (1989): 23–51.

Valaoras, V. G. "Some Effects of Famine on the Population of Greece." *Milbank Memorial Fund Quarterly* 46 (1946): 215–34.

Varvaressos, K. "Ανοικτή Επιστολή προς τον κ. Αλέξανδρον Διομήδην." ("An Open Letter to Mr. Alexandros Diomidis.") *Νέα Οικονομία* (Nea Economia) 6 (1947): 297–99.

———. "Ἀπολογισμός καὶ Κριτικὴ τῆς Οἰκονομικῆς Πολιτικῆς τῶν Τελευ-
ταίων Ἐτῶν (Ἀπάντησις εἰς τον κ. Ἀλέξανδρον Διομήδην)." ("Review and
Criticism of Recent Economic Policy [A Reply to Mr. Alexandros Diomidis].")
Νέα Οἰκονομία (Nea Economia) 7 (1947): 337–62.

Vergopoulos, K. "The Emergence of the New Bourgeoisie, 1944–1952." In *Greece in
the 1940s: A Nation in Crisis,* edited by J. O. Iatrides (Hanover, N.H.: University
Press of New England, 1981), 298–318.

Warren, J. C. "Origins of the 'Greek Economic Miracle': The Truman Doctrine and
Marshall Plan Development and Stabilization Programs." In *The Truman Doctrine of Aid to Greece: A Fifty-Year Retrospective,* edited by E. T. Rossides (published jointly by the Academy of Political Science [New York] and the American
Hellenic Institute Foundation [Washington, D.C.], 1998), 76–105.

Wilmington, M. W. "The Middle East Supply Center: A Reappraisal." *Middle East
Journal* 6 (1952): 144–66.

Books

Alexander, G. M. *The Prelude to the Truman Doctrine: British Policy in Greece 1944–
1947.* Oxford: Clarendon Press, 1982.

Amen, M. M. *American Foreign Policy in Greece 1944–1949: Economic, Military and
Institutional Aspects.* Frankfurt am Main: Peter Lang, 1978.

Baerentzen, L., J. O. Iatrides, and O. L. Smith. eds. *Studies in the History of the Greek
Civil War 1945–1949.* Copenhagen: Museum Tusculanum Press, 1987.

Brown, A. J. *The Great Inflation 1939–1951.* London: Oxford University Press, 1955.

Butterfield Ryan, H. *The Vision of Anglo-America: The US-UK Alliance and the
Emerging Cold War 1943–1946.* Cambridge: Cambridge University Press, 1987.

Butterworth, J. *The Theory of Price Control and Black Markets.* Aldershot: Averbury,
1994.

Cameron, R. E. *France and the Economic Development of Europe 1800–1914: Conquests of Peace and Seeds of War.* Princeton, N.J.: Princeton University Press,
1961.

Candilis, W. O. *The Economy of Greece, 1944–66: Efforts for Stability and Development.* New York: Praeger, 1968.

Capie, F. H., ed. *Major Inflations in History.* Aldershot: Elgar, 1991.

Cleveland, W., and D. Delivanis. *Greek Monetary Developments 1939–1948: A Case
Study of the Consequences of World War II for the Monetary System of a Small
Nation.* Bloomington: Indiana University Publications, 1949.

Clogg, R. *Anglo-Greek Attitudes: Studies in History.* London: Macmillan, 2000.

———. *A Concise History of Greece.* Cambridge: Cambridge University Press, 1992.

Close, D. H. *The Origins of the Greek Civil War.* London: Longman, 1995.

Cottrell, P. L., H. Lindgren, and A. Teichova, eds. *European Industry and Banking between the Wars: A Review of Bank Industry Relations.* Leicester: Leicester University Press, 1992.

Couloumbis, T. A., J. A. Petropoulos, and H. J. Psomiades. *Foreign Interference in Greek Politics.* New York: Pella, 1976.

Crafts, N. F. R., and N. W. C. Woodward, eds. *The British Economy since 1945.* Oxford: Clarendon Press, 1991.

Dewey, P. *War and Progress: Britain 1914–1945.* London: Longman, 1997.

Eden, A. *The Eden Memoirs: The Reckoning.* London: Cassell, 1965.

Farakos, G. *Δεκέμβρης του 1944: Νεώτερη Έρευνα, Νέες Προσεγγίσεις.* (December of 1944.) Athens, 1996.

Feis, H. *Europe the World's Banker 1870–1914: An Account of European Foreign Investment and the Connection of World Finance with Diplomacy before the War.* Clifton: Augustus M. Kelley, 1974.

Fleischer, H., and N. Svoronos, eds. *Ελλάδα 1936–1944: Δικτατορία-Κατοχή-Αντίσταση.* (Greece 1936–1944.) Athens, 1989.

Floud, R., and D. McCloskey, ed. *The Economic History of Britain since 1700.* Cambridge: Cambridge University Press, 1994.

Foreman-Peck, J. *A History of the World Economy: International Economic Relations since 1850.* New York: Harvester Wheatsheaf, 1995.

Frazier, R. *Anglo-American Relations with Greece: The Coming of the Cold War 1942–1947.* London: Macmillan, 1991.

Freris, A. F. *The Greek Economy in the Twentieth Century.* London: Croom Helm, 1986.

Gregory, T., J. W. Gunter, and D. C. Johns. *Report and Recommendations on Certain Aspects of the Greek Banking System.* Athens, 1950.

Hadziiossif, C. *Η Γηραιά Σελήνη: Η Βιομηχανία στην Ελληνική Οικονομία, 1830–1940.* (Industry in the Greek Economy, 1830–1940.) Athens, 1993.

Hall, R. E., ed. *Inflation: Causes and Effects.* Chicago: University of Chicago Press, 1982.

Harlaftis, G. *A History of Greek-Owned Shipping: The Making of an International Tramp Fleet, 1830 to the Present Day.* London: Routledge, 1996.

Harriss, J., J. Hunter, and C. M. Lewis, eds. *The New Institutional Economics and Third World Development.* London: Routledge, 1995.

Homer, F. X. J., and L. D. Wilcox, eds. *Germany and Europe in the Era of the Two World Wars.* Charlottesville: University Press of Virginia, 1986.

Iatrides, J. O., ed. *Ambassador MacVeagh Reports: Greece, 1933–1947.* Princeton, N.J.: Princeton University Press, 1980.

———, and L. Wrigley, eds. *Greece at the Crossroads: The Civil War and its Legacy.* University Park: Pennsylvania State University Press, 1995.

Jackson, M. R., and J. R. Lampe. *Balkan Economic History, 1550–1950: From Imperial Borderlands to Developing Nations.* Bloomington: Indiana University Press, 1982.

James, H., H. Lindgren, and A. Teichova, eds. *The Role of Banks in the Interwar Economy.* Cambridge: Cambridge University Press, 1991.

Jeffery, J. S. *Ambiguous Commitments and Uncertain Policies: The Truman Doctrine in Greece, 1947–1952.* Lanham, Md.: Lexington Books, 2000.

Jones, H. *"A New Kind of War": America's Global Strategy and the Truman Doctrine in Greece.* New York: Oxford University Press, 1989.

Kasimatis, G. *Το Οικονομικόν Πρόβλημα: Τι Έγινε. Τι Πρέπει να Γίνη.* (The Economic Problem.) Athens, 1945.

Keynes, J. M. *How to Pay for the War: A Radical Plan for the Chancellor of the Exchequer.* London: Macmillan, 1940.

Kingston, P. W. T. *Britain and the Politics of Modernization in the Middle East, 1945–1958.* Cambridge: Cambridge University Press, 1996.

Kofas, J. V. *Authoritarianism in Greece: The Metaxas Regime.* New York: Boulder, 1983.

———. *Financial Relations of Greece and the Great Powers, 1832–1862.* New York: East European Monographs, Boulder, 1981.

———. *Intervention and Underdevelopment: Greece during the Cold War.* University Park: Pennsylvania State University Press, 1989.

Koliopoulos, J. S. *Greece and the British Connection 1935–1941.* Oxford: Clarendon Press, 1977.

Kremmydas, V. *Εισαγωγή στη Νεοελληνική Οικονομική Ιστορία (18os–20os Αιώνας).* (Introduction to Modern Greek Economic History [18th–20th Centuries].) Athens, 1999.

Leeper, Sir R. *When Greek Meets Greek.* London: Chatto and Windus, 1950.

Levandis, J. A. *The Greek Foreign Debt and the Great Powers, 1821–1898.* New York: Columbia University Press, 1944.

Lloyd, E. M. H. *Food and Inflation in the Middle East 1940–45.* Stanford, Calif.: Stanford University Press, 1956.

Margaritis, G. *Ιστορία του Ελληνικού Εμφυλίου Πολέμου 1946–1949.* (History of the Greek Civil War 1946–1949.) Athens, 2000.

Mazower, M. *Greece and the Inter-War Economic Crisis.* Oxford: Clarendon Press, 1991.

———. *Inside Hitler's Greece: The Experience of Occupation, 1941–44.* New Haven, Conn.: Yale University Press, 1993.

———, ed. *After the War Was Over: Reconstructing the Family, Nation, and State in Greece, 1943–1960.* Princeton, N.J.: Princeton University Press, 2000.

———, ed. *The Policing of Politics in the Twentieth Century.* Providence: Berghahn Books, 1997.

Merrill, D., ed. *The Truman Doctrine and the Beginning of the Cold War, 1947–1949.* Vol. 8 of *Documentary History of the Truman Presidency.* University Publications of America, 1996.

Mills, G. T., and H. Rockoff. eds. *The Sinews of War: Essays on the Economic History of World War II.* Ames: Iowa State University Press, 1993.

Milward, A. S. *War, Economy and Society, 1939–1945.* Berkeley: University of California Press, 1977.

———. *The Reconstruction of Western Europe 1945–51.* London: Routledge, 1984.

Mouzelis, N. P. *Modern Greece: Facets of Underdevelopment.* London: Macmillan, 1978.

Orde, A. *British Policy and European Reconstruction after the First World War.* Cambridge: Cambridge University Press, 1990.

Palairet, M. *The Four Ends of the Greek Hyperinflation of 1941–1946.* Copenhagen: Museum Tusculanum Press, 2000.

Papastratis, P. *British Policy towards Greece during the Second World War 1941–1944.* Cambridge: Cambridge University Press, 1984.

Peden, G. C. *British Economic and Social Policy: Lloyd George to Margaret Thatcher.* Oxford: Philip Allan, 1985.

Petrov, V. *Money and Conquest: Allied Occupation Currencies in World War II.* Baltimore: Johns Hopkins Press, 1967.

Pollard, S. *The Development of the British Economy 1914–1990.* London: Edward Arnold, 1992.

Psalidopoulos, M. *Η Κρίση του 1929 και οι Έλληνες Οικονομολόγοι.* (The Crisis of 1929 and the Greek Economists.) Athens, 1989.

Richter, H. *British Intervention in Greece: From Varkiza to Civil War, February 1945 to August 1946.* London: Merlin Press, 1985.

———. *Η Ιταλο-Γερμανική Επίθεση εναντίον της Ελλάδος.* (The Italo-German Attack on Greece.) Athens, 1998.

Robbins, L. *The Economic Problem in Peace and War.* London: Macmillan, 1947.

Rockoff, H. *Drastic Measures: A History of Wage and Price Controls in the United States.* Cambridge: Cambridge University Press, 1984.

Rossides, E. T., ed. *The Truman Doctrine of Aid to Greece: A Fifty-Year Retrospective.* Published jointly by the Academy of Political Science (New York) and the American Hellenic Institute Foundation (Washington, D.C.), 1998.

Sfikas, T. *The British Labour Government and the Greek Civil War 1945–1949: The Imperialism of 'Non-Intervention.'* Keele: Ryburn Publishing, Keele University Press, 1994.

Sheppard, A. W. *Britain in Greece: A Study in International Interference.* London: League for Democracy in Greece, 1947.

Spencer, F. A. *War and Postwar Greece: An Analysis Based on Greek Writings.* Washington, D.C.: Library of Congress, 1952.

Stavrakis, P. J. *Moscow and Greek Communism, 1944–1949.* Ithaca, N.Y.: Cornell University Press, 1989.

Stavrianos, L. S. *The Balkans since 1453.* New York: Holt, Rinehart and Winston, 1958.

Sweet-Escott, B. *Greece: A Political and Economic Survey, 1939–1953.* London: Royal Institute of International Affairs, 1954.

Tsoucalas, C. *The Greek Tragedy.* London: Penguin, 1969.

Venezis, E. *Χρονικόν της Τραπέζης της Ελλάδος.* (Chronicle of the Bank of Greece.) Athens, 1955.

Wittner, L. S. *American Intervention in Greece, 1943–1949.* New York: Columbia University Press, 1982.

Woodbridge, G., et al. *The History of the United Nations Relief and Rehabilitation Administration.* New York: Columbia University Press, 1950.

Xydis, S. *Greece and the Great Powers 1944–1947: Prelude to the "Truman Doctrine."* Thessaloniki: Institute for Balkan Studies, 1963.

Zolotas, X. *Η Πολιτική της Τραπέζης της Ελλάδος: Από 19 Οκτωβρίου 1944 μέχρι 8 Ιανουαρίου 1945.* (The Policy of the Bank of Greece.) Athens, 1945.

Working Papers

Close, D. H. *The Character of the Metaxas Dictatorship: An International Perspective.* London: Kings College London, Center of Contemporary Greek Studies (Occasional Paper no. 3), 1990.

Pepelasis Minoglou, I. *Transplanting Economic Ideas: International Coercion and Native Policy.* London: LSE, Department of Economic History (Working Paper no. 30), 1996.

Dissertations

Coombs, C. A. "Financial Policy in Greece during 1947–48." Ph.D. diss., Harvard University, 1953.

Davies, M. M. "The Role of the American Trade Union Representatives in the Aid to Greece Program, 1947–1948." Ph.D. diss., University of Washington, 1960.

Etmektsoglou-Koehn, G. "Axis Exploitation of Wartime Greece, 1941–1943." Ph.D. diss., Emory University, 1995.

Kondonassis, A. J. "Monetary Policies of the Bank of Greece, 1949–1951: Contributions to Monetary Stability and Economic Development." Ph.D. diss., Indiana University, 1961.

Patterson, G. "The Financial Experiences of Greece from Liberation to the Truman Doctrine (October 1944–March 1947)." Ph.D. diss., Harvard University, 1948.

Politakis, G. "Greek Policies of Recovery and Reconstruction, 1944–1952." Ph.D. diss., Oxford University, 1990.

Ritter, H. "Hermann Neubacher and the German Occupation of the Balkans, 1940–1945." Ph.D. diss., University of Virginia, 1969.

INDEX

Abyssinia, 59–60
Acheson, Dean, 212
Administration: reform of, 102, 222, 243; weakness of, 134, 249. *See also* Bureaucracy; Government
Advisers, 211; British economic, 73–74, 90, 154, 156; Porter Mission as, 221–23. *See also* American Mission for Aid to Greece (AMAG); British Economic Mission (BEM)
Agricultural Bank of Greece, 167
Agriculture, 21, 24, 26, 33, 57, 190; credit for, 167–68, 230; effects of autarky drive on, 28; effects of WWII on, 39, 40; exports of, 30; farmers' resistance to Varvaressos plan, 127, 130; and food distribution, 40–43; imports of, 184; productivity of, 223, 231; recommendations for, 157, 222–23
Aid. *See* Foreign aid; Relief; United Nations Relief and Rehabilitation Administration (UNRRA)
Albania, 85, 212*n16*
Allies: blockade of Greece, 39; currency in Greece for, 84–86; and Greek economy, 83, 98–100, 151; liberation of Greece by, 80; reconstruction aid from, 53–54, 59, 88, 108, 187, 206–7, 214; Varvaressos blaming for failure of plan, 135–36
Alternative government (PEEA), 47–48
American Economic Mission to Greece. *See* Porter Mission
American Mission for Aid to Greece (AMAG), 182, 224–27, 241; conflicts of, 240, 245; criticisms of, 247–50; effectiveness of, 236–42, 250; government relations with, 233–34, 242–44; and Greek military, 231, 239–41; Greek response to, 239, 242; import policy and implementation, 231, 238;

lack of control over government, 241–42; mistakes by, 229–30
Angelopoulos, Angelos, 49
Anglo-Greek Information Service (AGIS), 105
Anticommunism, 19, 48–50, 249; brutality of, 51–52; as goal of British involvement in Greece, 64–65, 68, 77; and Truman Doctrine, 213, 224; of U.S., 77, 207–8, 243, 245–47
Arms manufacturers, 10–11
Asia Minor: Greek military defeat in, 27, 33; refugees from, 17, 24, 36
Askoutsis, Nikolaos, 49
Athens Stock Exchange, 83, 172, 175
Austerity measures, 99, 102. *See also* Stabilization plans; Varvaressos Experiment
Austria, 6, 9
Autarky, drive toward, 25, 28–29, 31
Autonomous Currant Organization (ACO), 23
Axis, 39–40, 57–58. *See also* Nazis

Balance of payments, 159; Britain's, 69–70, 77–78, 155; and import policy, 226–27; improvements in, 31, 222, 236; influences on, 39, 191; weakness of, 29–30, 194
Balkan Wars, 38
Balkans: British involvement in, 60–61, 69, 85; fiscal irresponsibility of, 37–38; partition of, 61–62, 69
Bank of Greece, 38, 85, 121, 230; buying gold, 84, 176, 178; and commercial banks, 28, 192–93, 230*n55;* and Currency Committee, 159, 159*n47*, 227; gold reserves of, 41, 153; gold sales through, 142–43, 149*n20*, 170–72, 175–76, 233–34; and imports, 180, 182; loans to government by, 94, 98; and money supplies, 8, 153–54;

Imports: AMAG policy and implementation, 225, 231, 238; commercial, 180, 185; duties on, 103, 146n16, 163, 185, 229; financing, 143, 197, 202, 216; of food, 39, 43, 231; increasing, 144–45, 152, 183, 233, 236; in stabilization plans, 92, 223; types of, 180, 184, 200–201, 223

Income tax, 32; British pressure for, 10–11, 106; increasing, 103–4, 222; levels of, 162–63

Incomes: rising during war, 10. *See also* Wages

Independence, Greek, 34, 60

India, 178

Industry, 26–27, 30, 33, 114, 134, 157; British, 77–78; controls on, 124, 141n4, 145, 225; credit for, 113, 230, 240; development of Greek, 21, 24–26; imports to stimulate, 144–45, 180, 183; influences on, 28–29, 39; need for stimulation of, 101, 105, 149; opposition to Varvaressos plan, 123, 127–28, 137; recommendations to improve, 222–23; recovery of, 101, 190–94, 223; relief supplies as competition to, 135–36

Inflation, 6–7, 44, 148; British experience with, 10–15; British pressure to control, 100, 141–42, 189–90; causes of, 105, 119, 134, 142, 160–70, 201, 229–30, 230; effects of, 44, 46, 81–82; government response to, 67–68, 145, 217, 251–52; increasing, 81, 90, 124, 141; measures against, 8, 105, 221, 240–41, 248; need to control, 129, 149, 189–90, 250; policies to prevent, 14, 170–90; revenues from, 31, 33; wartime, 40. *See also* Hyperinflation

Inter-Allied Bureau of Post-War Requirements, 54

Interest. *See* Debt, cost of servicing

Interest groups, 203; and AMAG, 243–44; effects on economic policies, 28, 142; exploitation of crisis by, 44–45, 139, 248; resistance to economic remedies, 130, 131

Interest rates, 22, 113, 193

International Bank for Reconstruction and Development (IBRD), 215, 218

International Financial Commission (IFC), 34–39

International Monetary Fund (IMF), 222, 227

Investment, 191, 193; in agriculture, 22–23; foreign, 31, 36; foreign capital not used for, 35, 38; in industry, 24–25; not put into improving productivity, 21–22, 25, 28–29; repatriating, 217

Invisible earnings, 30–31, 77–78

Italy, 34; invasions by, 33, 39, 59–60, 69; in occupation of Greece, 40, 53; war reparations from, 57–58

Jackson, R. G. A., 56, 206

Joint Coordinating Committee (JCC), 101–2

Joint Policy Committee (JPC), 121, 210

Joint Price Fixing Sub-Committee, 101–2

Kannelopoulous, Panayotis, 51, 144, 202

Kartalis, Georgios, 150, 157, 188

Kasimatis, Grigorios, 71, 132, 144, 147–48, 188

KEPES, 23, 28

Keynes, John Maynard, 112–13

KKE. *See* Communist Party of Greece

Kofas, J. V., 248

Labor, 10, 24–25, 106, 157. *See also* Trade unions

Labor relations, 192, 249

Labour, in coalition government, 65

Laissez-faire economics, 110–11, 138–40, 248, 254

Latin America, 6

Latvia, 7

League of Nations, 36, 38

Leeper, Reginald, 56, 62, 66, 70, 74, 106, 146, 175; and aid for Greece, 88, 108; on government role in economy, 134, 141; and Greek politics, 65, 150, 155; and Varvaressos, 131; and Varvaressos, 112–13, 118

Left, the, 65; Far Left, 59, 68; growth of, 46–47, 63–64; and polarization, 52, 61; and Varvaressos plan, 129–30, 138; weakening of, 48–49, 51